D1484169

RED, WHITE, AND BLUE

RED, WHITE, AND BLUE

A Critical Analysis of Constitutional Law

Mark Tushnet

HARVARD UNIVERSITY PRESS
Cambridge, Massachusetts, and London, England
1988

This book is printed on acid-free paper, and its binding
materials have been chosen for strength and durability.

Library of Congress Cataloging-in-Publication Data

Tushnet, Mark V., 1945-
Red, white, and blue : a critical analysis of constitutional law
Mark Tushnet.

p. cm.
Includes index.
ISBN 0-674-75120-5 (alk. paper)
1. Judicial review—United States—History.
2. United States—Constitutional history.
3. United States. Supreme Court—History.
I. Title.
KF4575.T87 1988
342.73′029—dc19   87-20007
[347.30229]   CIP

For Rebecca and Laura

Preface

A GENERATION ago the Supreme Court began to make decisions that altered the way we think about judicial review and democratic government. A number of observers thought that some of the most attractive decisions of the Warren Court, such as the desegregation decisions of 1954, were difficult to reconcile with prevailing theories of judicial review. Until 1970 those who were satisfied with the work of the Warren Court felt little urgency in defending it; from around 1963, after Arthur Goldberg had been appointed to the Court, a liberal majority was in relatively firm control and liberal decisions rolled forth with some regularity. Under those circumstances liberals felt no pressure to develop elaborate justifications for what the Court was doing.

The ease with which liberals could accept the Court's actions changed in 1970 and, more dramatically, in 1972, with the appointment of four conservative Justices. The agenda for liberals who wrote about constitutional law changed accordingly. Now they had to provide justifications for the Warren Court, both to prevent erosions from positions already taken and to encourage extension to new positions, such as attacks on gender-based discrimination and on restrictive abortion laws. The result was an explosion of articles and books on the theory of judicial review, defending the work of the Warren Court and looking nervously at that of the Burger Court. Conservatives such as Attorney General Edwin Meese responded by asserting that *their* preferred theory of judicial review justified some retrenchment on Warren Court decisions.

This book examines the discussions of judicial review over the past generation. Part I takes up theories of judicial review, and Part II discusses the Court's articulated doctrines and implicit views in a number of areas of constitutional law. Unlike the authors of the works and decisions I consider, I am not interested in offering an alternative normative theory of judicial review, nor do I argue that the Court ought to use the reasons I provide as the basis for its decisions in particular cases. Instead I approach these materials in a way that blends the concerns of an intellectual historian with those of a cultural critic. I examine the structure of arguments to expose their sometimes unarticulated presuppositions about the nature of American society and to suggest why commentators and Justices have found those presuppositions congenial, even if they disagree on the implications of those presuppositions in particular cases.

My argument has two basic themes, pursued in various ways in the discussion of different topics. The first theme might be called a *logical* one. Judicial review and, perhaps more fundamentally, theories of judicial review play an integral role in an intellectual program that I call the liberal tradition. Even contemporary conservatives are committed to that program. Yet making judicial review and its theories intellectually coherent requires that the liberal tradition be supplemented by an alternative program from what I call the republican tradition. The difficulty is that, to the extent that we understand that republicanism is essential to the coherence of liberalism, we undermine the need for judicial review. In a sense, the liberal tradition makes judicial review necessary but at the same time makes it impossible.

The second theme of my argument is *sociological*. In general and over the medium to long run, courts are part of a society's governing coalition. Understanding the work of the courts therefore requires that we give it a political analysis. But it is not enough to do what I have already done in referring to the "liberal" Warren Court and the "conservative" Burger Court. We must also examine the political implications of the structural presuppositions shared rather broadly across the American political spectrum.

The Introduction uses a discussion of federalism to describe the liberal and republican traditions. Part I contains five chapters. In Chapter 1 I discuss reliance on history and precedent as theories of judicial review, arguing that the openness with which we may fairly read history and prior cases makes it impossible to consider them as restraints on the power of judges. An appendix to this chapter discusses whether the text alone may ground a theory of judicial review. Chapter 2 examines a powerful theory, offered most recently by John Hart Ely, that requires courts to facilitate the operation of a system of pluralist politics that already works reasonably well. I argue that Ely's theory is flawed by its inability to specify what really facilitates pluralist politics, and by its acceptance of the existing system as a reasonably well functioning one.

Chapter 3 turns to the use of moral philosophy as a ground for judicial review and argues that neither any presently available moral philosophy nor any likely candidate for development can provide sufficient guidance to the courts for it to constitute an acceptable theory of judicial review.

Chapter 4 deals with what I call antiformalist themes in constitutional theory and, in an appendix, with conservative constitutional theory and recent efforts by liberals to appropriate tradition as a basis for a theory of judicial review. Next is Chapter 5, an interlude that examines and rejects the strategy of making judicial review coherent by drawing eclectically from various theories.

The republican alternative to the liberal tradition lies in the background of the discussions in Part I. It moves closer to the foreground in Part II. Each chapter in this part gives an overview of prevailing doctrine and theoretical positions in the area it discusses and offers an alternative interpretation of the law in the area. The chapter titles indicate that my overall topic is the way in which constitutional doctrine constitutes—shapes and defends—important social institutions. Chapter 9, "The Constitution of the Market," deals with commercial speech, campaign financing, and pornography.

The Conclusion cautiously describes what kind of politics—but not what kind of judicial review—might revive the republican tradition. The final paragraphs suggest that identifying such a political program may not constitute the proper conclusion to be drawn from the book's critical inquiry.

THIS BOOK has been gestating for a long time. During the course of its production, portions of it have appeared in various law reviews and have been commented on, both formally and informally, by too many colleagues for me to remember. To avoid omitting any from a list, I have decided to forgo specific mention. But three people must be acknowledged for the various forms of help they have given me. L. Michael Seidman, my sometime collaborator, has regularly commented on my work and in conversations has shaped and deepened my understanding of the issues with which he and I have been concerned. Two former students, Richard Martin and Jennifer Jaff, provided essential encouragement for me to try to work out the ideas in this book more systematically than I had done in class.

As mentioned, some portions of the book have been published as law review articles. But some of the articles have been broken into parts and are published here in separate chapters; all have been updated to take into account developments in the courts and commentary since the time of their original publication, and all have been revised in the light of colleagues' comments and my own further thought on the problems they address. I believe that the product is a book that integrates my prior work in ways that will make the overall argument clearer even to those who have already come across some parts of it.

Contents

RED, WHITE, AND BLUE

Introduction

The Revival of Grand Theory in Constitutional Law

THE past few years have seen a remarkable revival of interest in comprehensive normative theories of constitutional law. These grand theories, as I will call them, attempt to provide justifications for the exercise of the power of judicial review in a democracy, that is, the power that courts whose judges are appointed for life have which allows them to displace decisions made by representatives of the people. Current interest in grand theory is striking for two reasons. First, despite the existence of competing grand theories, each one is in its essentials a revived and purified version of an earlier grand theory.[1] The second characteristic of the current interest in grand theory that invites comment is its timing. An earlier era of grand theorizing occurred a generation ago, when Herbert Wechsler delivered his famous lectures, "Toward Neutral Principles of Constitutional Law,"[2] and when Alexander Bickel brought the best insights of contemporary political analysis to bear on judicial review of *The Least Dangerous Branch*.[3] For a little more than a decade, constitutional theory worked within the confines of the tradition that Wechsler and Bickel had brought to its highest point. Then grand theory became attractive again.

---

1. For example, as Chapter 2 shows, John Hart Ely's theory of "representation-reinforcing review," in which the courts may intervene when they perceive that there are obstacles to the expression and aggregation of preferences in the normal political process, is the contemporary version of a theory articulated in a different context by Chief Justice John Marshall in the early nineteenth century and developed further by Harlan Fiske Stone in the 1930s and the 1940s. Recent use of moral philosophy to justify judicial review, as exemplified in the work of Ronald Dworkin, replicates the prior use of natural law concepts in the early part of this century.

2. Herbert Wechsler, "Toward Neutral Principles of Constitutional Law," in his *Principles, Politics, and Fundamental Law* 3 (1961). See Chapter 1.

3. Alexander Bickel, *The Least Dangerous Branch* (1962).

Interest in grand theory revived partly for political reasons. Ely and others explicitly desire to protect the legacy of the Warren Court at a time when its liberalism has become a beleaguered minority position on the Supreme Court as elsewhere in American society.[4] The idea appears to be that the decisions of the Warren Court can be defended against erosion or overruling by demonstrating that they fit within some grand theory. Yet there is something distinctly odd about that idea. The major grand theories in the field probably provide inadequate defenses for the controversial decisions of the Warren Court.[5] In addition, the grand theorists have not explained how their theorizing activity actually serves their apparent political goals. Theorizing would do so only if the fact that a decision fit into a grand theory implied that it would have greater staying power than one that did not fit into such a theory, but it is difficult to come up with a theory of politics that can plausibly support that argument.

The persistence and recurrent revival of interest in grand theories suggests that there is more to the story of the revival of grand theory than transitory political matters. The most important aspect of that story is the way in which it reflects, indeed is the expression of, the crisis of contemporary liberal political theory. A student of grand theory notices rather quickly that the presentations have a common structure. In "Part I" the theorist offers a critique of all other grand theories, and in "Part II" he presents an assertedly defensible and therefore different grand theory. Yet this structure is obviously flawed. Because we are experiencing a *revival* of grand theory, the critiques are readily available. When Ely gives us

4. See John Hart Ely, *Democracy and Distrust* v (1979) ("For Earl Warren. You don't need many heroes if you choose carefully"); Laurence Tribe, *American Constitutional Law* v (1978) (criticizing early years of Burger Court by comparing it with predecessor).

5. For example, Ely's theory may perhaps justify the reapportionment decisions, but those decisions have suffered at most minor erosion. The Court allows relatively small variations, as compared with those that existed before the Court developed the "one person, one vote" approach, and has indicated its unwillingness to tolerate extreme population disparities. See, e.g., Brown v. Thompson, 462 U.S. 835, 846 (1983) (large variance upheld because of limited scope of challenge presented, but suggesting that result would have been different had litigation strategy differed), 850 (O'Connor, J., concurring) (two Justices of five-person majority expressing "gravest doubts" about the plan as a whole).

Some might think that minor inroads on the reapportionment decisions are more troubling than substantial erosion of the criminal justice decisions, but Ely appears to believe otherwise. See, e.g., Alan Dershowitz and John Hart Ely, "*Harris v. New York*: Some Anxious Observations on the Candor and Logic of the Emerging Nixon Majority," 80 *Yale Law Journal* 1198 (1971). Similarly, Ely's presentation of his theory has little to say about the Warren Court's criminal justice decisions, although they are the ones under most serious pressure. See, e.g., Fred Graham, *The Self-Inflicted Wound* (1970). What has happened is that the liberals have essentially given up on winning anything substantial in the area of criminal procedure, and constitutional theorists have similarly abandoned the effort to defend a position that has been lost anyway.

"representation-reinforcing review," his critics can draw on the literature discussing the inadequacies of Harlan Fiske Stone's version of that theory. Ely in turn can draw on the criticisms of the earlier reliance on natural law that pejoratively characterize that reliance as *Lochnerism*, after the Supreme Court decision holding that a maximum hours law violated a constitutionally protected freedom of contract.[6]

Another effect of the common structure of grand theory appears in its applications. Because the "Part II" of each theory is quite unstable, theorists have to be blind to criticism when they offer specific examples of how their theories work. The applications therefore have a wearying sameness. Once one identifies the grand theory, one knows with a high degree of certainty what its applications will be. If one sees the key words "process values," for example, one knows that we are about to learn that the Constitution requires the implementation of the platform of the 1964 Democratic Party, and if one sees "equal concern and respect," one knows that we are about to learn that the Constitution requires the implementation of the 1972 Democratic platform.

The familiarity of grand theories, and of their critiques, suggests that the enterprise of theory has deep roots. As I will argue in a moment, grand theory's primary function is to explain why the existing system of constitutional law deserves our rational respect. Each grand theory identifies problems around the edges, and offers solutions to them, but grand theory rests on the premise that at the core of the system things are basically all right. Thus, natural law theorists rarely challenge the existing distribution of wealth in a serious way, although they will defend marginal alterations in the distribution of access to particular goods—access to lawyers but not to food, for example. But it is a commonplace of contemporary social thought that Western society is currently experiencing a crisis of legitimacy. "The system" is not delivering the goods, and all the ideological structures designed to explain why the shortfall is defensible, indeed is inevitable, have broken down. Grand theory and its problems are just constitutional law's version of this general crisis of legitimacy.[7]

6. Of course some advances have been made within each grand theory, as progressive refinements and accommodations to criticism occur. For example, there appears to be general agreement that Ely, *Democracy and Distrust*, has substantially clarified the role that the analysis of motivation plays in constitutional adjudication. But these advances may have purified the theories into their highest and best forms. If so, criticism is especially devastating, for if the present versions of the theories are the best that are likely to be devised, and if they succumb to obvious attacks, grand theory may well be pointless.

7. That it truly is a crisis is suggested by the extraordinarily short lifetime of each grand theory. For example, Ely's book was greeted by a symposium of review essays that left his theory in a shambles. Symposium, "Judicial Review versus Democracy," 42 *Ohio State Law Journal* 1 (1981).

The crisis of grand theory is the form that the failure of liberal political theory has taken in constitutional law. The next section examines the role that constitutional theory plays in liberal thought by describing its relation to other institutions of government such as federalism.

Traditions of American Political Theory: The Role of the Constitution

Judicial review is an institution designed to meet some difficulties that arise when one tries to develop political institutions forceful enough to accomplish valued goals and yet not so powerful as to threaten the liberties of the citizenry. By granting substantial power to government, people are able to accomplish more of what they wish, but they find themselves subject to oppression by the government they have created. They may attempt to protect themselves by writing into the Constitution certain restrictions on the power of government, but they still need some mechanism to assure that those restrictions will be honored. Judicial review is one of several mechanisms that the framers designed to enforce constitutional limits. Yet as I will argue, judicial review alone cannot eliminate the possibility of a certain kind of governmental oppression—oppression by the judges themselves. Constitutional theory completes the structure by providing guidance to the judges on when and how they should exercise the power of judicial review and by giving the citizenry widely shared criteria by which to evaluate judicial performance.

An overview of the Constitution's structure will illuminate the role of judicial review and constitutional theory in our society. The Constitution was framed in an era when two general theories about citizenship contended on roughly equal terms.[8] One theory, captured in the liberal tradition,[9] emphasized the individualism of people acting in society and

8. See Forrest McDonald, *Novus Ordo Seclorum: The Intellectual Origins of the Constitution* (1985). Much of the literature, though not McDonald's work, on the framers' worldviews is infected by one major problem: its authors tend to insist that the true view held by the framers was either liberal or republican, although the framers almost certainly had not sorted out the theories in the way that later authors have. Joyce Appleby, "Liberalism and the American Revolution," 49 *New England Quarterly* 3, 7 (1976), suggests that the blending of liberal and republican themes was the product of a "disjuncture in colonial life" that began in the second quarter of the seventeenth century. When read with the caution that both sides of the argument are probably right, useful collections on the framers' views are *How Democratic is the Constitution?* (Robert Goldwin and William Schambra eds. 1980); *The American Founding: Politics, Statesmanship, and the Constitution* (Ralph Rossum and Gary MacDowell eds. 1981).

9. In earlier versions of this work I tended to call this the Lockean tradition, but I have been persuaded by the work of John Dunn and his student James Tully that this designation

examined how social institutions rest on and constrain individual prefer-ences.[10] The other theory, recently labeled the civic republican tradition, emphasized the essential social nature of individual being and examined how individual preferences rest on and constrain social institutions.[11]

By calling these theories traditions I mean to suggest that they pro-vided, and continue to provide, competing general frameworks for ori-enting thought about political life. Few people adopt one or the other framework in its entirety, and systematic thinkers often develop creative syntheses of elements in both traditions.[12] Yet one can arrive at a judg-ment that one or the other tradition has more cultural power at any particular time in the sense that people at that time tend to believe that the then-predominant tradition makes more sense of their daily experience than its competitor does.[13] For example, I will repeatedly suggest that the

---

is inaccurate. See, e.g., John Dunn, "The Politics of Locke in England and America in the Eighteenth Century," in his *Political Obligation in Its Historical Context* 53, 70–77 (1980) (arguing that Locke's works had little direct influence on the framers); James Tully, *A Discourse on Property: John Locke and His Adversaries* (1980) (emphasizing nonindividu-alist dimensions of Locke's thought). By calling this a tradition I intend to avoid locating it in the works of any particular theorist. Most systematic political thinkers have had a more subtle understanding of the problems than those I will describe as inherent in the tradition. Dunn calls the genre in which this kind of tradition is located amateur political theory, which seems exactly right.

10. I draw my analysis of the liberal tradition primarily from Louis Hartz, *The Liberal Tradition in America* (1955); C. B. Macpherson, *The Political Theory of Possessive Individ-ualism* (1962).

11. The historiography of civic republicanism is reviewed in Robert Shalhope, "Toward a Republican Synthesis: The Emergence of an Understanding of Republicanism in American Historiography," 29 *William and Mary Quarterly* 49 (3d ser. 1972); Robert Shalhope, "Republicanism and Early American Historiography," 39 *William and Mary Quarterly* 334 (1982). A recent brief critique, stressing the interplay between ideology and material condi-tions, is Joyce Appleby, *Capitalism and a New Social Order: The Republican Vision of the 1790s* (1984). See also Joyce Appleby, "What Is Still American in the Political Philosophy of Thomas Jefferson?" 39 *William and Mary Quarterly* 287 (1982).

The literature is brought to bear on a specific question of constitutional interpretation in Robert Shalhope, "The Ideological Origins of the Second Amendment," 69 *Journal of American History* 599 (1982); Lawrence Cress, "An Armed Community: The Origin and Meaning of the Right to Bear Arms," 71 *Journal of American History* 22 (1984); "The Second Amendment and the Right to Bear Arms: An Exchange," 71 *Journal of American History* 587 (1984). See also Jennifer Nedelsky, "Book Review," 96 *Harvard Law Review* 340, 343-50 (1982).

12. See, e.g., Gerald Gaus, *The Modern Liberal Theory of Man* (1983), arguing that the modern liberalism of T. H. Green, Bosanquet, Hobhouse, Dewey, and Rawls aims at reconciling individuality and community.

13. Historians rediscovered the republican tradition in their studies of the revolutionary era. See note 11. Their consensus is that the republican tradition gradually became subordi-nated to the liberal tradition as a way of organizing thought about society, and much recent historical work locates the republican tradition in dissenting and subordinate groups. See,

liberal tradition is so dominant today that it has become difficult to appreciate the force of the civic republican tradition.[14]

Traditions are not systematic, well-organized bodies of thought; rather, they help people to understand the world by providing some familiar categories to use. With that caveat we can contrast some of the main elements of the traditions. The liberal tradition stresses the self-interested motivations of individuals and treats the collective good as the aggregation of what individuals choose; the republican tradition has an ill-defined notion that the whole is greater than the sum of its parts.[15] Although it acknowledges the role of public institutions in providing the framework for individual development, the liberal tradition insists that such institutions be neutral toward competing conceptions of the good and tends to emphasize the risks of governmental overreaching. The republican tradition, seeing public institutions as important means by which private character is shaped, is less suspicious of government. The liberal tradition places relatively more emphasis on liberty than on equality,[16] and historically it has been associated with the view that the natural operations of a market economy produce sufficient liberty and equality to necessitate only relatively modest public adjustments. It has tended to be more alert to the threats posed to liberty by government than to those posed by private centers of power. The liberal tradition has given relatively greater weight than has the republican tradition to freeing people of the constraints of tradition, and, in contrast to the more communitarian and therefore exclusionary republican tradition, the liberal tradition has insisted on promoting interests that it views as common to all people. Finally, the liberal tradition has tended to design institutions to separate law from politics, an issue of less concern in the republican tradition.

---

e.g., Sean Wilentz, *Chants Democratic: New York City and the Rise of the American Working Class, 1788–1850* (1984); Steven Hahn, *The Roots of Southern Populism: Yeoman Farmers and the Transformation of the Georgia Upcounty, 1850–1890* (1983); Lawrence Goodwyn, *The Populist Moment: A Short History of the Agrarian Revolt in America* (1978); Alan Brinkley, *Voices of Protest: Huey Long, Father Coughlin, and the Great Depression* (1982).

14. See also William Sullivan, *Reconstructing Public Philosophy* (1982), whose title suggests that reconstruction is needed. This is not to deny the persistence of rhetorical appeals to republican values in our society. See, e.g., Robert Bellah, Richard Madsen, William Sullivan, Ann Swidley, and Steven Tipton, *Habits of the Heart: Individualism and Commitment in American Life* (1985). It is only to suggest that those appeals are unlikely to move beyond rhetoric.

15. See Frank Michelman, "Foreword: Traces of Self-Government," 100 *Harvard Law Review* 4, 28 (1986) (on *telos* in republican tradition).

16. See Michael Kammen, *Spheres of Liberty: Changing Perceptions of Liberty in American Culture* 160–68 (1986).

As this summary suggests, the traditions are distinguished largely by matters of emphasis. Each tradition captures important and valuable aspects of life that no sound understanding of political activity can ignore. Indeed, as the framers considered questions of fundamental institutional design, they discovered that liberalism and civic republicanism converged on some important matters. Each theory suggested that the institutions of government should protect private property, should distribute powers vertically in a federal arrangement and horizontally through the separation of powers, and should provide for judicial review. These institutions, however, reduced the dangers that individualism and community pose to each other only because the framers' society was poised between the stable mercantilist and aristocratic order of the past and the dynamic democratic capitalist society that the Constitution was about to set in motion. After that equilibrium was disturbed, not federalism, separation of powers, or judicial review could adjust individualism and community as the framers believed they could.

We can work our way back to the world of the framers by beginning with the Preamble to the Constitution, where they defined the purposes of their efforts. The new government was designed to "establish Justice, insure domestic Tranquility, . . . promote the general welfare, and secure the Blessings of Liberty." For present purposes I will simplify this by claiming that the Constitution was designed to establish a government of ordered liberty.[17] But ordered liberty can exist only in a society with certain characteristics. For example, the framers had recently experienced Shays's Rebellion, in which irate debtors used armed force to close local courts, thus impeding creditors' efforts to collect the debts they were owed.[18] Generalizing, the framers believed that liberty cannot be promoted unless there is a government with sufficient power to prevent armed marauders from terrorizing the countryside. If "domestic Tranquility" is thus a precondition to ordered liberty, it follows that the institutions of government must be strong. And in general the institutions that the framers designed helped to secure some of the social characteristics that ordered liberty requires. The liberal tradition argued that the institutions secured the social prerequisites of ordered liberty in one way while the republican tradition argued that they did so in a different but complementary way. The triumph of the liberal tradition has destroyed the coherence of the constitutional scheme by eliminating those complementary mechanisms for assuring the preconditions of ordered liberty.

17. The reference is Palko v. Connecticut, 302 U.S. 319, 325 (1937).
18. See John Fiske, *The Critical Period in American History* 179–86 (1888).

The liberal tradition was shaped by its assumptions about how social institutions can best accommodate what it saw as the dominant tendencies in human nature. In the liberal tradition people were considered to be motivated, in large measure, by what C. B. Macpherson has called "possessive individualism."[19] The intellectual history of possessive individualism is fairly familiar by now. It begins with Hobbes, who argued that people want to maximize their material well-being. To do so they will invest their efforts in two activities. First, they may use their physical powers to transform natural materials into human wealth. Second, they may use their physical powers to wrest human wealth from those who have engaged in the first activity. The two activities then create a classic prisoners' dilemma: anyone who foresees the possibility that another person may come along to grab his or her newly created wealth is foolish to create it in the first place.[20] Individual efforts to maximize wealth are individually, and therefore socially, disastrous.[21]

Hobbes and his successors argued that we are better off relinquishing some or all of our individual power to wrest material wealth from others. If we can be assured that the wealth each of us creates will remain ours, we will engage in productive activities without diverting our efforts into unproductive self-defense. We can provide that assurance by banding together and investing a portion of our wealth (necessarily less than we would otherwise devote to self-defense) in an enterprise we can call government. Our investments, now called taxes, will support a police force that we can call upon when we believe that our holdings of wealth are in jeopardy. These are the roots in the liberal tradition of the framers' desire for a strong government.

Property plays a central role in the liberal tradition. As material wealth, property is the aim of human activity, and it is therefore the purpose for which we desire liberty. But property holding also contributes to liberty

19. Macpherson, *Possessive Individualism*, p. 3. See also Martin Carnoy, *The State and Political Theory* 15–19 (1984). For a discussion linking the Hobbesian problem of order to the framers' thought, see Timothy Fuller, "The Hobbesean Problem, the Hobbesean Solution and the American Order" (ms. 1984).

20. For a useful critical discussion, see Gregory Kavka, "Hobbes's War of All against All," 93 *Ethics* 291 (1983).

21. Alternatively, each wealth creator would divert some effort from the primary task of wealth creation into the development of defensive measures, thus reducing the amount of wealth actually created. This is another version of the prisoners' dilemma: if I allocate my investment by giving 90 units to the creation of wealth and 10 units to defense, you can overwhelm my defenses by devoting 40 units to attack and 60 to the creation of wealth. You will end up with the product of 150 units, and I will end up with nothing. I therefore ought to devote more to defense and less to production, thus producing an arms race and ultimate impoverishment.

directly and indirectly. A person holding property cannot be dominated by someone else: the sturdy yeoman farmer owning his own land can never be a peasant under the thumb of a land-"lord." At least the land-owner can sell the land and use the proceeds to finance relocation to a place where no one tries to impose on him or her, perhaps because each resident had fled from similar oppression. In addition, property holding promotes the ordered dimension of liberty. Widespread property holding gives many people a stake in maintaining the order that secures their holdings. Thus, by spreading property holding widely, we help ensure domestic tranquillity. And now another connection between strong government and property appears. Sustained economic growth may be the best way to spread property holding broadly. Government can forestall attacks on existing holdings by developing a police force, to be sure, but it may also do so by ensuring that growth occurs fast enough to provide increasing numbers with a share of an ever-expanding pie.[22] A government must have the power to act decisively when necessary if it is to promote this kind of economic growth.

The liberal tradition understood that a government strong enough to protect property and promote growth might be too strong. After all, those who hold positions in the government can be possessive individualists too. Having disarmed the citizenry to protect each from the other, the government will be in a position to seize whatever it chooses from all citizens. In a major innovation in political theory, the framers believed that they could avoid this result by creating institutions that diffuse governmental power. Federalism diffuses power vertically by granting only specifically enumerated powers to the national government. As Madison put it, the central government's powers are "few and defined," whereas those of the states "extend to all the objects which, in the ordinary course of affairs, concern the lives, liberties, and properties of the people."[23] In addition, federalism allows citizens to avoid localized oppression and secure the services they desire by voting with their feet and moving elsewhere.[24] Thus neither local nor central government can become too powerful. Further, the framers created a federal structure that, as a practical matter, requires the concurrence of many representatives

22. See Henry Hart and Albert Sacks, "The Legal Process" 110–16 (ms. 1958), for an expression in the legal literature. The idea has become part of the political folklore in the expression "A rising tide lifts all boats."

23. The Federalist No. 45 (Madison).

24. See Charles Tiebout, "A Pure Theory of Local Expenditures," 64 *Journal of Political Economy* 416 (1956); Dennis Mueller, *Public Choice* 126–29 (1979); Peter W. Abelson, "Some Benefits of Small Local Government Areas," 11 *Publius* 129 (1981).

with substantial local constituencies before the national government can act.[25]

The framers also diffused power in another way. They insisted that even those powers granted the national government be exercised subject to a number of specifically identified limitations. The courts would review legislation to determine whether it exceeded those limitations and was otherwise within the powers granted to the national government.[26]

These mechanisms for diffusing power created their own problems. The point of the enterprise of institutional design was to create a government strong enough to promote ordered liberty and economic growth. The more that government's power was diffused, though, the less likely it was that the national government could act when action was needed. A government beset by chronic paralysis is no better than no government at all, yet that was what diffusion of power threatened. Judicial review was also an unstable solution to liberalism's problems, because the framers, as liberals, had no reason to think that judges would be any less attached to possessive individualism than were the representatives whom the judges were to restrain. Although the judges' self-interest might be mobilized on different occasions than that of the representatives, it could not be eliminated. Judicial review thus substituted the threat of tyranny by the judges for the threat of tyranny by the legislators. Modern constitutional theory attempts to provide the necessary limits on judges.

The republican tradition, though quite different from liberalism in its origins and intentions, offered solutions to the related problems of potential legislative tyranny, potential paralysis, and potential judicial tyranny. The republican tradition insisted that people are social beings who draw their understandings of themselves and the meaning of their lives from their participation with others in a social world that they actively and jointly create.

Republicans, consistent with their traditionalism, could have been inattentive to questions of institutional design.[27] But in the eighteenth century republicans were deeply concerned about institutions for a number of

25. In this introduction I will not discuss the separation of powers as a horizontal diffusion of power. For some preliminary observations consistent with those made here, see Mark Tushnet, "Critical Legal Studies and Constitutional Law: An Essay in Deconstruction," 36 *Stanford Law Review* 623, 635–46 (1984).

26. The Federalist No. 78 (Hamilton).

27. Saying that people draw the meaning of their lives from social participation has few implications for institutional design. After all, if people are inevitably social beings the institutions that they have define what they are, willy-nilly: a different set of institutions, a different sort of equally social beings. Thus their relative indifference to the details of institutional design tends to make republicans students of the history and traditions of "a people."

mutually reinforcing reasons. As traditionalists, republicans wished that citizens would develop not just any characters—which they inevitably would—but appropriately civic-minded characters. Properly designed institutions can instill civic virtue in citizens. In addition, republicans saw the traditions they revered under assault and naturally looked to institutional design as providing a means to reinvigorate their traditions. Finally, republicans did not romanticize human nature. They understood that people will sometimes heed the call of self-interest rather than that of public interest. They were therefore intensely worried about what they called corruption, the use of public offices for private interest. They believed that corruption explained the assaults on tradition that they witnessed. They argued that alterations in institutional design can constrain corruption directly, by limiting the opportunities in which self-interest can overcome civic-mindedness, and indirectly, by reinforcing the citizenry's dedication to the public interest.

The republican tradition saw diffusion of power as an important element in institutional design. Private property, federalism, and judicial review thus served republican goals as well as liberal ones. Property provides the independent foundation that a citizen needs for proper consideration of the public interest.[28] Those who lack property will be so concerned with securing the material conditions of their lives that they will surely place their immediate private interest before the public interest. In addition, they might be dominated by those on whom they depend; rather than contributing a distinctive voice to the public dialogue, the unpropertied will be reduced to puppets of their superiors.[29] Shielded by private property, then, the republican citizen can enter into public debate without fear.

Federalism fits into republican theory in several ways. First, by ensuring that the most important activities of public life take place in small units of government, federalism makes it easier for citizens to participate. Further, citizens can draw broader lessons from their experience in local government. Small-scale dialogues lead citizens to understand that each of them has to subordinate self-interest to the public business if civic projects are to occur at all. That is, governmental paralysis at the local level will inflict pain on the citizenry, but the cooperative remedies for avoiding pain and

28. See Appleby, *Capitalism and New Social Order*, pp. 94–97.

29. Republicans knew that property holding has a less attractive side. At least above a certain point, the more property one holds, the more likely it is that the desire to retain and increase one's wealth will overwhelm one's attention to the public interest. Other institutions of civic education may be used to offset the impulse to serve self-interest, even though such institutions cannot offset a superior's threats to the material well-being of the unpropertied.

paralysis at that level will be more evident than they would be in larger-scale governments. Thus, participation in local government is itself an especially desirable form of civic education. In addition, citizens can watch one another carefully as they go about the public's business in the locality and can learn which of them has the best character to serve as a delegate to the next larger unit of government. As Madison put it, the people will be "more familiarly and minutely conversant" with their representatives in local governments.[30] This contributes to the final virtue of federalism. The general diffusion of power limits the opportunities for corruption, just as it limits the opportunities for individualistic overreaching in the liberal scheme of things. A republican federalism, however, would not be paralyzed by the diffusion of power. The delegates to the national government would be chosen precisely because they were unlikely to be susceptible to corruption. When the national interest required, they could put aside self-interest—as the delegates in a liberal polity could not—and act without threatening the system of ordered liberty.

In the republican tradition judicial review serves many of the same functions that it does in the liberal tradition. Republicans believed that they could avoid the traps the liberal tradition set for a theory of judicial review. Hamilton emphasized the weakness of the courts, suggesting that the threat posed by judicial corruption is small.[31] More important, the framers emphasized the clarity of the Constitution's proscriptions. Thus, Marshall thought that he clinched his argument in *Marbury v. Madison* by listing three provisions and implying that it would be absurd to hold that judges could not invalidate "a duty on the export of cotton" or "such a bill" of attainder or a statute declaring that "*one* witness [would be] sufficient for conviction" of treason.[32] Modern readers are often puzzled by Marshall's assurance on this point, for it seems to us that he finessed the central issue: Conceding that courts need not enforce a bill of attainder, they may wonder why the courts' determination that a piece of legislation is "such a bill" should prevail over Congress' judgment that it is not. In the eyes of those in the republican tradition, the limits the Constitution places on the government are stated in terms whose meaning is readily understood within the relevant communities.[33] Legislatures

30. The Federalist No. 46 (Madison). See Gordon Wood, "Democracy and the Constitution," in *How Democratic Is the Constitution?* pp. 12–14. Cf. Abelson, "Small Governments," p. 130 ("coordination costs" lower in smaller units).

31. The Federalist No. 78 (Hamilton).

32. 5 U.S. (1 Cranch) 137, 179 (1803).

33. For a discussion of the framers' theory of interpretation, see H. Jefferson Powell, "The Original Understanding of Original Intent," 98 *Harvard Law Review* 885 (1985). See also Chapter 1.

might become corrupt and disregard the plain meaning of the Constitution, but the independence given the judges makes it unlikely that they too will be corrupted.[34] The judges will therefore enforce the terms of a readily understood Constitution. The republican tradition had available a theory of constitutional interpretation; the liberal tradition did not.

This description of the role of institutions in the republican tradition suggests that its account of institutions is more complete than that offered in the liberal tradition. Possessive individualism will systematically affect institutions designed in the liberal tradition, and ordered liberty can be purchased only by risking a governmental paralysis that itself can threaten order and liberty. In contrast, corruption is an inevitable but essentially random characteristic of those who staff republican institutions. Yet the republican tradition has become remote from our present experience because of the commitment to private property it shared with liberalism as a means of diffusing power.

That the republican tradition has become remote seems incontestable,[35] and exploring some aspects of that remoteness illuminates its most important causes. The republican tradition assumed that leaders will arise from local constituencies whose members will become familiar with their capacities by experiencing their leadership in local government. Representatives will remain familiar with their constituencies, drawing insights and knowledge about social problems and their solutions from those contacts. Much of what we know about contemporary politics belies these arguments. Mobility among the citizenry, a virtue in the theory of federalism, has so increased that fewer and fewer of us have roots in any particular

---

34. In this regard giving judges life tenure (itself a term derived from property law) is like giving them property interests to assure their independence.

35. I take this to be the descriptive thesis of Bellah et al., *Habits of the Heart*. For a historian's account of the creation of "a new reality" because of commercial expansion, see Appleby, *Capitalism and New Social Order*, pp. 37–38; Joyce Appleby, "Commercial Farming and the 'Agrarian Myth' in the Early Republic," 68 *Journal of American History* 833 (1982). For discussions of the resulting confusion in the constitutional law of federalism, see Gordon Clark, *Judges and the Cities: Interpreting Local Autonomy* (1985); M. David Gelfand, "The Burger Court and the New Federalism: Preliminary Reflections on the Roles of Local Government Actors in the Political Dramas of the 1980's," 21 *Boston College Law Review* 763 (1980).

It is important to emphasize that the argument of this book is concerned with the liberal tradition, that is, liberalism as lived and experienced in the culture rather than the systematic thought of particular thinkers. It could be that some specific liberal intellectual worked all the problems out. If any did, however, those solutions have not been, and are not likely to be, deeply assimilated into the culture. What are assimilated if at all are some broad concepts—for example, that the rule of law is a solution to some of the problems that Hobbes discussed or that the welfare state is not inconsistent with the premises of liberal individualism.

community. Even when we do the scale of local government has grown to the point where only the most avid followers of politics have contact with their local governments. Further, political experience on the local level is no longer the most obvious route to national political office. People can become widely known as radio broadcasters, military heroes, or star athletes—or can create celebrity by spending their money freely—and can use their fame as the basis for political careers.[36] As the scale of the national government increases, direct contact between representatives and citizens diminishes.[37] Legislators become the heads of staff bureaucracies and direct their ghostwriters to say what the legislators mean. Interest groups rather than constituents become the major source of information about social problems. Judicial power has increased to the point that many citizens believe that judges are their primary oppressors. These facts make it difficult to remain confident that republican institutions operate as smoothly as republican theory suggests.

Indeed, the republican tradition as it stood in the late eighteenth century understood that the risk of corruption has to be contained by noninstitutional means. It stressed the importance of civic education so that the citizenry will be alert to corruption and active in fighting it. Yet the tradition understood that some people will believe that their lives will be better if the social order is turned upside down. Civic education may not be enough to overcome this sort of self-interest. It has to be coupled with deference toward social leaders. The republican tradition did not envision nearly universal suffrage. The nation's population was divided into citizens and others. The others were not expected to participate in politics and so would not require the guarantees of independence that property holding provides. The republican tradition therefore did not postulate *widespread* property holding as a condition for ordered liberty. But as did the liberal tradition, the republican tradition somehow had to ensure order. "Noncitizens" do not have the kind of stake in republican institutions that citizens do, or that everyone does in liberal institutions. Civic education in the republican tradition would instead cultivate a culture of deference. Within the citizenry, deference to other citizens dampens self-interest and reduces the risk of corruption. Outside the citizenry, deference to superiors dampens disorderly urges. Republican theory did not rely on institutions alone to promote ordered liberty.

By the time of the framing forces were in motion that rapidly weakened the noninstitutional supports republican theory needed. That theory's

36. Here is a bipartisan list of Senators described in the text: Jesse Helms, John McCain, John Glenn, Bill Bradley, Frank Lautenberg.

37. See Abelson, "Small Governments," pp. 138–39 (contacts between households and representatives greater in smaller units of government).

commitment to a hierarchical traditionalism was under sustained intellectual attack. The relatively less propertied had gained sufficient political power to make it impossible to restrict the franchise over the long term. Once suffrage was more widely available the republican tradition had to rest on widespread property holding as its guarantor of order. Thus the liberal and republican traditions converged in supporting the institution of private property and, not incidentally, in the policy of sustained economic growth to assure that property holdings would be widely distributed.

The political system that this convergence produced provided the framework for a dynamic economy whose long-term growth transformed society in the United States and abroad. The transformation also produced the mobility and the growth and bureaucratization that have made it difficult to accept the program of the republican tradition.[38] All this has left the liberal tradition without substantial challenge in our present public life. Yet, as I have argued, that tradition provides an unstable solution to the problem of securing ordered liberty: it leads either to paralysis and disorder without liberty or to unrestrained liberty and a different kind of disorder.

The framers tried to solve these problems by drawing on the republican tradition. The liberal tradition understood that self-regarding behavior is pervasive. Liberal economic theory turned vice into virtue: the invisible hand of the market uses self-regarding behavior to produce the benefits of a dynamic economy. Liberal political theory tried to accomplish the same results in politics by establishing institutions that operate not to transform private vice into private virtue but to *use* private vice to produce public virtue. With respect to the courts, the framers had to explain why judges would not be purely self-regarding—out to maximize their personal power—or indirectly self-regarding—out to promote the interests of narrow groups with which they were affiliated. Their answers were that judges, like others in the national government, would "discern the true interest of their country"[39] because they were selected from a nationwide pool and were given guarantees of tenure that assured that they would interpret the Constitution responsibly. The framers' commitment to private property eventually invalidated these answers. Judicial appointments have become politically sensitive matters, and the idea that the Constitution has a "plain meaning" is now implausible. Grand theorizing in constitutional law can be understood as an effort to fill the gap

---

38. See generally Richard Stewart, "Federalism and Rights," 19 *Georgia Law Review* 917 (1985).

39. The Federalist No. 10 (Madison).

created by the decline of the republican tradition in the framers' approach to institutional design.

In the absence of republicanism even grand theory is bound to fail. Here a metaphor from economics, the paradigmatic science of the invisible hand, may be useful. Economists have attempted to analyze the ways in which groups of people can arrive at collective decisions. One famous result in the field of public choice is Arrow's theorem, which states that if we make certain apparently uncontroversial assumptions about rationality and individual preferences, we cannot design a mechanism for social choice that will satisfy all the assumptions. Because I use Arrow's theorem metaphorically, I do not intend to discuss it in detail.[40] For my purposes only one of its assumptions is interesting: the rule of nondictatorship.[41]

Arrow's theorem as a metaphor helps us understand the problems of constitutional theory in more conventional terms. Our society has a very complicated mechanism for arriving at public policy. For present purposes, though, its complexities can be simplified to this. In general the choice made by a majority is to be respected, but on some issues and in some contexts majoritarian decisions may be overridden. Through exercise of the power of judicial review, the courts say when and how that can properly occur. Unhappily, we are left with a choice of dictatorships: sometimes the majority will be the dictator, and sometimes the judges will. Judicial review is often defended as the only way to escape the potential tyranny of the majority, but it simultaneously creates the potential for the tyranny of the judges. The general function of constitutional

40. For introductions, see Mueller, *Public Choice*, pp. 184–88; Alfred Mackay, *Arrow's Theorem: The Paradox of Social Choice* (1980). See also Chapter 2. A skeptical view of the relevance of Arrow's theorem is given in Gordon Tullock, *Toward a Mathematics of Politics* 37–49 (1967). See also Brian Barry and Russell Hardin, "Epilogue," in *Rational Man and Irrational Society?* 375–78 (Brian Barry and Russell Hardin eds. 1982).

41. A second assumption is that of "unrestricted domain": there are no limitations on the preferences of the individuals in relevant society. One can try to escape the powerful result of Arrow's theorem in several ways. By rejecting the assumption of unrestricted domain, we could bar some preferences from figuring in the process of social choice. This is the route taken by Ronald Dworkin, who does not allow what he calls "external" preferences—those reflecting a simple desire to hurt someone else—to be counted. Ronald Dworkin, *Taking Rights Seriously* 240–58 (1978). See Ely, *Democracy and Distrust*, p. 67n. At least in the context of the metaphor, this exclusion runs up against the nondictatorship assumption, for who is to decide what kinds of preferences are, as a normative matter, to be ruled out? Alternatively, one might make the empirical claim that in contemporary American society the domain of preference is in fact restricted enough to allow us to have a coherent mechanism of social choice. It is hard to test the truth of that claim. But even if it is true, new questions arise. For example, how is it that in a liberal society that prides itself on tolerating diverse preferences, the domain of preferences is actually restricted? See Chapter 9.

theory has been to specify how judicial review can exist without becoming judicial tyranny. The Arrow theorem metaphor suggests that constitutional theory must fail in that task.

If the problems I have discussed arise because of inadequacies within the liberal tradition, an obvious alternative is to look to the republican tradition for solutions. Republicanism does indeed provide the backdrop against which much of the argument of this book is played out. Nonetheless, I doubt that revitalizing the republican tradition can solve the present difficulties of constitutional law. Republicanism made sense only in a specific social setting, with a restricted franchise and substantial equality of wealth among the citizenry. It is both unrealistic and irresponsible to suggest that the franchise be restricted once again. Yet reconstituting the other social condition to republicanism—that is, assuring substantial equality of wealth among a fully enfranchised population—is no small thing. In addition, as I suggested earlier, republicanism has no strong implications for institutional design. In particular, in a vital republican society judges might well exercise the power of judicial review entirely unselfconsciously, seeing it, as Marshall did, simply as one among many republican institutions of government. Normative conclusions about the present-day institution of judicial review cannot be drawn from the republican tradition.

The remainder of this book therefore concentrates on grand theory in the liberal tradition. Part I surveys a number of prominent grand theories of constitutional law. Each chapter attempts to provide the best arguments for the theory it discusses and then considers what the defects in that theory are. This gives the part a certain single-mindedness, in that the discussion does not consider whether it would be desirable or possible to combine the best elements from a variety of theories into an eclectic approach to constitutional law. Chapter 5 explains why two kinds of eclectic strategies fail to solve the problems of constitutional theory.

I

THE CRITIQUE OF GRAND THEORY

I

The Jurisprudence
of History

IN 1985 PUBLIC controversy erupted over apparently esoteric questions of constitutional theory. Attorney General Edwin Meese III gave a widely publicized speech criticizing the Supreme Court and arguing that the Court should return to a "jurisprudence of original intention," in which it would construe the Constitution precisely in line with the intentions of the framers. Three months later Justice William Brennan delivered an equally well publicized speech, generally taken to be a response to Meese, that rejected such a jurisprudence as impossible.[1] Meanwhile a less widely noted controversy over following precedent has been simmering. Liberals who formerly admired courts for rejecting restrictive precedents began to see the wisdom of adhering to the beleaguered rulings of the Warren Court, whereas conservatives began to say that it was all right to turn the clock back (and overrule recent decisions) if the clock was telling the wrong time.[2] Two Supreme Court decisions enforced older precedents that, it was conceded, had little to commend them, but following the precedents was almost reason enough.[3]

These two controversies reflect continuing concern about the vitality and propriety of the two least controversial grand theories, neutral principles and originalism (sometimes called interpretivism). According to the neutral principles theory, "the main constituent of the judicial process is

1. Edwin Meese, "The Attorney General's View of the Supreme Court: Toward a Jurisprudence of Original Intention," 45 *Public Administration Review* 701 (1985); Symposium, "Construing the Constitution," 19 *University of California Davis Law Review* 1–30 (1985) (reprinting addresses by Brennan, Justice John Paul Stevens, and Meese).

2. The "turning the clock back" metaphor was used in a television interview by Grover Rees III, at the time the assistant to Attorney General Meese responsible for selection of nominees for the federal courts. He attributed the metaphor to C. S. Lewis.

3. Miller v. Fenton, 474 U.S. 104 (1985) (O'Conner, J.); Vasquez v. Hillery, 474 U.S. 254 (1986) (Marshall, J.). See also Wallace v. Jaffree, 472 U.S. 38, 48 (1985) (chastising district judge for rejecting applicable precedents).

precisely that it must be genuinely principled, resting with respect to every step that is involved in reaching judgment on analysis and reasons quite transcending the immediate result that is achieved ... [resting] on grounds of adequate neutrality and generality, tested not only by the instant application but by others that the principles imply."[4] According to the originalism theory, judges "should confine themselves to enforcing norms that are stated or clearly implied in the written Constitution."[5] Such norms are found by interpreting the text with recourse when necessary to the original intent of the framers. These are of course only initial formulations, but they state the theories in general terms. Roughly, they tell judges to do what the Constitution says and to do that in good faith, committing themselves to the logical implications of what they decide.

Many theorists believe that originalism and neutral principles provide the necessary framework for their activity. For example, Michael Perry has said that any constitutional theory must be principled in the required sense, and John Hart Ely, in his more expansive moments, treats his theory as "the ultimate interpretivism."[6] These theories are responsive to the liberal tradition's need to control people's attempts to secure the most they can for themselves, without regard for others. We will see that these two theories are plausible only on the basis of assumptions that themselves challenge important aspects of the liberal tradition.

Originalism attempts to implement the rule of law by assuming that the meanings of words and rules used in the past can be retrieved without distortion in the present; neutral principles does the same by assuming that we all know, because we all participate in the same culture, what the words and rules used by judges mean. The only coherent basis for the requisite continuities of history and meaning is found in the communitarian assumptions of the republican tradition; indeed, only these assumptions can provide the foundations upon which both originalism and neutral principles ultimately depend. The republican tradition places society prior to individuals by developing the implications of the idea that we can understand what we think and do only with reference to the social matrix within which we find ourselves. The liberal account of the social world is inevitably incomplete, for it proves unable to provide a constitutional theory of the sort that it demands without depending on communitarian assumptions that contradict its fundamental individualism.

---

4. Wechsler, *Principles, Politics, and Fundamental Law*, p. 21.
5. Ely, *Democracy and Distrust*, p. 1.
6. Michael Perry, "Why the Supreme Court Was Plainly Wrong in the Hyde Amendment Case: A Brief Comment on Harris v. McRae," 32 *Stanford Law Review* 1113, 1114 (1980); Ely, *Democracy and Distrust*, p. 88.

Originalism and neutral principles are two powerful theories, but they cannot stand on liberal premises. Because the republican tradition rejects the premises that make theory necessary, it need not develop an alternative theory. The most it must do is elaborate the ways in which we are dependent on one another not just for peace or material well-being but for meaning itself. Yet just as the republican tradition correctly emphasizes our mutual dependence, the liberal tradition correctly emphasizes our individuality and the threats we pose to one another. It may be that we live in a world of tension, in which no unified social theory but only a dialogue between the traditions is possible. Constitutional theory is then either impossible or unnecessary.

Originalism and Historical Knowledge

Attorney General Meese supports the jurisprudence of original intent for two basic reasons.[7] First, that jurisprudence treats the Constitution like a contract. When the framers created our government by writing the Constitution, they limited the government's powers in the same document. Courts can enforce their agreement by figuring out what limits the framers intended to place on the government that they created. But, according to Meese, if courts depart from the intent of the framers, they are assuming a power to restrict government that they were never given. Second, the jurisprudence of original intent is the safest way to avoid judicial tyranny. By confining the judges to the words of the Constitution as understood by the framers, we ensure that they will not go too far; we bar them from making decisions that in a democratic society are properly made by a political majority.[8]

Treating the Constitution like a contract seems sensible, yet doing so is difficult to defend cogently.[9] First, the argument faces an embarrassment:

7. There is a large literature on originalism. Useful summaries of the arguments, coming to different conclusions, are Pierre Schlag, "Framers Intent: The Illegitimate Uses of History," 8 *University of Puget Sound Law Review* 283 (1985), and Earl Maltz, "Some New Thoughts on an Old Problem—The Role of the Intent of the Framers in Constitutional Theory," 63 *Boston University Law Review* 811 (1983). See also David Richards, "Constitutional Interpretation, History, and the Death Penalty: A Book Review," 71 *California Law Review* 1372 (1983).

8. These two arguments are identified and criticized along some of the lines developed here in Michael Perry, "The Authority of Text, Tradition, and Reason: A Theory of Constitutional 'Interpretation,' " 58 *Southern California Law Review* 551, 572–87 (1985). They are exhaustively discussed in Larry Simon, "The Authority of the Framers of the Constitution: Can Originalist Interpretation Be Justified?" 73 *California Law Review* 1482 (1985) (using slightly different categories).

9. Marbury v. Madison, the Supreme Court's first assertion of the power of judicial review, can be read as adopting a version of the contract argument. 5 U.S. (1 Cranch) 137

the framers themselves do not appear to have held an originalist theory of constitutional interpretation.[10] Influenced by the republican tradition, they believed that the meaning of the Constitution's terms was so clear to a fair-minded reader that the Constitution did not need to be interpreted in any subtle or sophisticated way.[11] An originalist approach to constitutional interpretation was not part of the contract the framers entered, and courts that adopt such an approach cannot justify it merely by invoking the framers' intent.[12] They must go beyond the contract to find the principle that the contract should be interpreted according to the framers' intent. If they can go beyond it for that, why not go beyond it for other things as well?[13]

Further, few people today believe that phrases like *due process of law* or *the freedom of speech* have the kind of plain meaning that the framers believed they had. This may be the result of greater sophistication about language and law, or the outcome of a long process by which a self-interested elite has hoodwinked the public, or the product of cultural decline. Whatever its source, our skepticism would surely be triggered by judges who said that they were simply enforcing the plain meaning of the Constitution.[14]

(1803). Chief Justice John Marshall justified the exercise of the power of judicial review by a number of arguments, prominent among which was his appeal to the idea of a written constitution. According to Marshall, the Constitution is law, albeit supreme law, and so is to be treated just as other legal documents are. Thus, when the Court is asked to determine what the Constitution means it is to do what it does when faced with other legal instruments. This enterprise is characteristically "originalist": judges must look both to the words of the document and, because the words of the Constitution (such as "equal protection" and "due process of law") are too opaque, to the intent of those who wrote the document. For a discussion of text-based theories that ignore the intent of the framers, see the appendix to this chapter. See also Warren Lehman, "How to Interpret a Difficult Statute," 1979 *Wisconsin Law Review* 489 (arguing that proper mode of interpreting opaque document does not require recourse to drafters' intent).

10. See Powell, "Original Understanding."

11. For a discussion of how corruption might lead legislators to disregard the plain meaning of the Constitution, see the Introduction.

12. The problem of "interpretive intent" is discussed in Ronald Dworkin, "The Forum of Principle," 56 *New York University Law Review* 469, 493–97 (1981).

13. The answer is the argument from avoiding judicial tyranny, discussed in the remainder of this section.

14. Justice Hugo Black did say that, but—confirming the observation in the text—nobody believed him. Some conservatives reiterate this position today, see, e.g., Lino Graglia, "How the Constitution Disappeared," 81:2 *Commentary* 19 (1986), but in their hands it is simply a lie. Despite Graglia's claim, the words *due process of law* do not have a meaning immediately apparent to any reader; one must merely listen to citizens addressing their city council meetings to know that for most people "denying due process of law" means "treating someone unfairly."

A second problem with the contract argument is that none of us entered the contract. The framers did, and it might be fair treatment of James Madison to enforce the contract against him. But he died a long time ago, and it is not obvious that it makes sense to think that people alive today are somehow parties to a contract in a way that would make it unfair to us to interpret the Constitution without regard to the framers' intentions.[15] Bruce Ackerman has tried to explain why an originalist theory is attractive for contractlike reasons.[16] He distinguishes between two forms of politics. Ordinary politics is dominated by private interests, bargaining, compromise, and the like. Constitutional politics, in contrast, occurs during periods of heightened democratic consciousness, when the public is alert to and seeks to advance the public interest in a relatively principled way.[17] For Ackerman, the fact that the Constitution's most important provisions were adopted during these special periods explains the fact that the Constitution prevails over ordinary legislation adopted during times of ordinary politics.[18]

Ackerman's argument rests on the proposition that they—the citizenry during constitutional periods—were better than we—the citizenry during times of ordinary politics. This seriously overestimates the differences between them and us. Democratic consciousness and ordinary horse trading always coexist, and their proportions do not shift as dramatically as Ackerman suggests. Ackerman calls his use of history "egregiously selective,"[19] but it is more than that. Actually, he selects aspects of the past of which he approves and ignores those of which he disapproves. For example, he identifies "two peaks" of heightened democratic consciousness,

15. We might be tempted to stretch the contract metaphor to say that we are the third-party beneficiaries of the contract that the framers wrote, or that we, or at least some of us, are in some sense the successors in interest to the framers and so should be bound by their contract. As third-party beneficiaries we could decide whether we prefer originalist interpretation or not; that theory is not forced on us by the contract metaphor. And most of us today—women, blacks, children and grandchildren of immigrants—are not successors in interest to the framers in any sense that makes the contract analogy compelling.

16. Bruce Ackerman, "The Storrs Lectures: Discovering the Constitution," 93 *Yale Law Journal* 1013 (1984).

17. Id., p. 1039. L. Michael Seidman has criticized Ackerman's argument from a different direction: To the extent that we want the Constitution to protect some sort of private sphere from public regulation, we should be worried about rules adopted at a time when, as Ackerman defines it, the rule-making body was relatively inattentive to private-regarding concerns. L. Michael Seidman, "Public Principle and Private Choice: The Uneasy Case for a Boundary Maintenance Theory of Constitutional Law," 96 *Yale Law Journal* 1006 (1987).

18. Ackerman argues in addition that some periods, such as the New Deal, saw widespread exercises in constitutional politics even though they yielded only legislation, not significant constitutional amendments. Ackerman, "Storrs Lectures," pp. 1051–57.

19. Id., p. 1052.

the initial framing of the Constitution and the adoption of the Reconstruction amendments. The distinction between normal politics and constitutional politics cannot easily be sustained even as to these peaks.

Consider James Madison. During the debates in Virginia over the adoption of the Statute for Religious Freedom, a predecessor of the establishment and free exercise clauses, Patrick Henry was Madison's main adversary. Madison's friend Thomas Jefferson wrote to Madison from France that people on Madison's side might well pray for Henry's death. Adopting a less drastic course, Madison deployed his skill at ordinary politics to ensure Henry's election as Governor, thus removing him from participation in the legislative debates.[20] As the states were debating the ratification of the Constitution, Madison maneuvered its presentation so well that the antifederalist opponents of ratification charged, probably wrongly but certainly credibly, that Madison had interfered with the mails to delay debates over ratification in North Carolina until momentum had been built by ratification in New York.[21]

The Reconstruction amendments were forced through by a Congress that effectively deprived many white southerners of the possibility of democratic choice in the matter, by insisting that the states ratify the fourteenth amendment as a condition for the withdrawal of military government.[22] Finally, one might be skeptical about the claim that ordinary politics today displays a lack of democratic awareness; the debates over such central issues as abortion and desegregation are probably about as informed by democratic awareness as were those at the time of the framing. Ackerman's attempt to explain why we should be bound by what the framers did by invoking their relatively greater democratic awareness is unpersuasive.

This leaves us with the argument that originalism is the best available way to prevent judicial tyranny. For about thirty years, roughly from 1940 to 1970, the argument from judicial tyranny was unpersuasive as well. Originalism had a bad reputation, largely because, allied as it was to

20. See Lance Banning, "James Madison, the Statute for Religious Freedom, and the Crisis of Republican Convictions," paper prepared for the Virginia Statute for Religious Freedom: A Bicentennial Symposium, Sept. 19–21, 1985.

21. See Robert Rutland, *The Ordeal of the Constitution: The Anti-Federalists and the Ratification Struggle of 1787–1788*, 281–82 (1966). This book describes in detail Madison's brilliant political maneuvers during the ratification process.

22. See J. G. Randall and David Donald, *The Civil War and Reconstruction* 633–37 (2d ed. 1961). One might fairly find that Ackerman's criteria for "amendments" by extensive legislation encompass the restrictive Jim Crow laws adopted in the South after 1890. See, e.g., C. Vann Woodward, *The Strange Career of Jim Crow* (2d ed. 1966); C. Vann Woodward, *The Rise of the New South, 1877–1913* (1951).

politically conservative positions,[23] it seemed too vulnerable to the criticism that a strict adherence to originalism imposes "the dead hand of the past" on us. It seems to require that we find legislation valid unless it violates values that are both old-fashioned and seriously outmoded.

Originalists deflect this criticism by invoking the specter of judicial tyranny.[24] Sometimes they argue that only originalism is consistent with democracy. But within the liberal tradition democracy means majority rule tempered by some sort of judicial review; originalists cannot persuade by stipulating a particular definition of democracy when what is at stake is precisely what sort of judicial review is consistent with a liberal idea of democracy.[25]

Another defense of originalism is more powerful. Of course, the argument goes, originalism does mean that we will be subject to the risk that the legislature will develop novel forms of tyranny. Empirically, however, novelty in tyranny is relatively rare, and because the framers were rather smart, they managed to preclude most of the really troublesome forms of tyranny in the Constitution that they wrote. Some risk of novel forms of tyranny remains, but that risk is significantly smaller than the risk of judicial tyranny that would arise were we to allow the judges to cut free from interpreting the text. In this sense, according to the originalist, we are indeed better off bound by the dead hand of the past than subjected to the whims of willful judges trying to make the Constitution live.

This pragmatic argument is fairly powerful. Of course it can be challenged on pragmatic grounds. For example, Michael Perry has argued that the record of the Supreme Court in modern times provides substantial support for the view that the Court's use of nonoriginalist modes of interpretation has been, on the whole, beneficial to our society.[26] This approach has the advantage of putting the applicable political judgments out in the open, but it has some obvious disadvantages. Many people disagree with Perry's assessments of recent decisions, and changes in the composition of the courts make it difficult to sustain Perry's confidence that nonoriginalism will be used only in behalf of the interests he favors.

There are other reasons to question the pragmatic justification for originalism. It rests in part on an empirical claim about novelty that is suspect in light of social change. The possibilities of innovative legislative tyranny are in fact great because the social and material world in which

23. See, e.g., United States v. Butler, 297 U.S. 1 (1936).
24. See, e.g., Raoul Berger, *Government by Judiciary: The Transformation of the Fourteenth Amendment* (1977); Lino Graglia, *Disaster by Decree: The Supreme Court Decisions on Race and the Schools* (1976).
25. See Perry, "Authority of Text," pp. 575–76.
26. Id., pp. 578–79. See Chapter 3.

we live has changed drastically since 1789. Wiretapping provides a standard example of innovation that originalism can accommodate only with great difficulty.[27] The drafters of the fourth amendment obviously could not have contemplated wiretapping when they thought about searches. Yet if originalism means that we cannot respond to that kind of innovation, it fails to guard against legislative tyranny. Wiretapping is thus a prime illustration for the claim that, because of the broader scope of legislative action, the domain of innovation in legislative tyranny is more extensive than that in judicial tyranny.[28] This raises questions about the pragmatic dimension of the argument that originalism averts judicial tyranny.

Moreover, originalists often contend that if we look to the historical record we will discover that the framers had a fairly limited conception of what legislative tyranny is. For example, Leonard Levy, the most careful recent student of first amendment history, concluded in a controversial work that the framers did not intend the amendment to prohibit sedition laws, that they meant it to prohibit only prior restraints on publication and not subsequent punishment, and that they did not intend it to insulate speech from regulation simply because the speech is political.[29] Similarly,

27. See, e.g., Michael Perry, "Interpretivism, Freedom of Expression, and Equal Protection," 42 *Ohio State Law Journal* 261, 281 (1981); Robert Bork, "Introduction," in Gary McDowell, *The Constitution and Contemporary Constitutional Theory* x (1985). Henry Monaghan calls Perry's description of originalism "splendid," Monaghan, "Our Perfect Constitution," 56 *New York University Law Review* 353, 360 n. 54 (1981), and I take it as the best available, although Perry is not himself an originalist.

28. One would be hard pressed to defend the claim that in contemporary society more tyranny is exercised by willful judges than by willful legislators. If the current complaints of self-styled conservatives are taken as a measure of judicial tyranny, the instances that they identify, with one exception, pale in comparison. The elimination of prayer in schools and the limited use of pupil transportation remedies in desegregation cases, though important to some, do not have the broad impact of instances of possible legislative oppression, such as an out-of-control budget or inadequate spending for defense (from a conservative point of view). The issue of abortion is more problematic, but the extent to which the increase in abortions is attributable solely to judicial action is open to question. The women's movement was achieving some legislative victories before Roe v. Wade, 410 U.S. 113 (1973), and might well have continued to succeed in the legislatures. It bears emphasizing that, even after the first Hyde Amendment terminated federal financing of abortions, Departments of Labor and Health, Education, and Welfare Appropriation Act, 1977, P. L. 94–439, §209, 90 Stat. 1418, 1434 (1976), legislatures and state courts responsible to the electorate continued to provide such assistance in the states in which 85 percent of the nation's Medicaid abortions were performed before the cutoff. See Willard Cates, "The Hyde Amendment in Action," 246 *Journal of the American Medical Association* 1109, 1110 (1981); Jesse Choper, "Consequences of Supreme Court Decisions Upholding Individual Rights," 83 *Michigan Law Review* 1, 189 (1984).

29. Leonard Levy, *Freedom of Speech and Press in Early American History: Legacy of Suppression* ix (Torchbook ed. 1963). These conclusions are qualified, though not in ways

the Bill of Rights provided protection, such as it was, against encroachment only by the national government, not by the states.[30] Because a
genuine originalism would thus protect only against limited varieties of
legislative tyranny, it fails to achieve its objective. When the real risks of
legislative tyranny are recognized, they appear more serious than the
prospects of judicial tyranny.

At this point the pragmatic defense of originalism begins to seem weak.
Originalism seems to constrain judges only at the cost of leaving legislatures too little constrained. One might expect critics to abandon originalism, but they sometimes attempt to salvage it. Revisionist critics such as
John Hart Ely and Douglas Laycock accuse originalists of being half-
hearted in their commitment to their theory. These critics contend that if
we examine the Constitution closely we will discover clauses concerning
which the framers intended the courts to have a free, nonoriginalist hand.
Ely relies on the portion of the fourteenth amendment that bars the states
from making "any law which shall abridge the privileges and immunities
of citizens of the United States."[31] Laycock relies on the ninth amendment:
"The enumeration in the Constitution, of certain rights, shall not be
construed to deny or disparage others retained by the people."[32] In other
words, an originalist approach to the Constitution reveals provisions that
license nonoriginalist theories.

Originalists reject these revisions for two reasons. First, to the extent
that the revisionists are trying to play the game of theory on the originalists' terms, they can be attacked on historical grounds. When the revisionists invoke the privileges and immunities clause or the ninth amendment,
they are met by a barrage of evidence from originalists that these suppos-

---

that affect my argument, in Leonard Levy, *Emergence of a Free Press* (1985). See also
William Mayton, "Seditious Libel and the Lost Guarantee of a Freedom of Expression," 84
Columbia Law Review 91 (1984) (arguing that framers held view Levy attributed to them
but solely because they also believed that Congress had not been granted affirmative power
to regulate expression).

30. Barron v. Mayor of Baltimore, 32 U.S. (7 Pet.) 243 (1833). After the fourteenth
amendment was adopted, the Court "selectively incorporated" the Bill of Rights into the
due process clause and thereby significantly expanded the safeguards against at least some
forms of legislative tyranny. See Louis Henkin, " 'Selective Incorporation' in the Fourteenth
Amendment," 73 *Yale Law Journal* 74 (1963). Whether this development is consistent with
the intent behind the amendment is quite controversial. Compare Berger, *Government by
Judiciary*, pp. 134–56, with Michael Curtis, *No State Shall Deny: The Fourteenth Amendment and the Bill of Rights* (1986).

31. Ely, *Democracy and Distrust*, at 22–30.

32. Douglas Laycock, "Taking Constitutions Seriously: A Theory of Judicial Power," 59
Texas Law Review 343, 349–53 (1981).

edly broad clauses actually had narrow and well-defined meanings.[33] The ninth amendment, for example, is said to mean that the Constitution itself does not authorize courts to deny other rights and to have no implications for legislative authority to deny those rights.

The second response is more interesting. The originalist concedes the possibility that some provisions of the Constitution license nonoriginalist theories. But, the originalist contends, we can at least rule out some results under those theories on originalist grounds. Suppose that the framers, while they were drafting one of the nonoriginalist provisions, were aware of a specific practice. Suppose further that, as far as the record shows, they agreed overwhelmingly that the provision would not make the practice unconstitutional. Surely, the originalist claims, given these assumptions we could not rely on the nonoriginalist provision to invalidate the practice even if the provision otherwise authorized invalidation.[34] That claim seems hard to dispute. Unhappily for the revisionists, though, this second originalist response states in general terms the relevant history of the fourteenth amendment with respect to school segregation. As Michael Perry puts it: "Segregated public schooling was present to the minds of the Framers; they did not intend that the [equal protection] clause prohibit it; and no historical evidence suggests that they meant to leave open the question whether the clause should be deemed to prohibit the practice."[35] If nonoriginalist constitutional interpretation must have an originalist warrant, *Brown v. Board of Education* seems unjustifiable.

Originalism is attractive enough that, even at this point, revisionists need not throw up their hands, and they usually do not. Instead they can rely on Ronald Dworkin's distinction between generic "concepts," such as equality, and specific "conceptions," such as ideas of what equality meant in particular circumstances.[36] Dworkin argues that the fourteenth amendment enacts the concept of equality, not specific conceptions. The framers had a conception of equality that regarded segregated schools as equal, but they enacted something more general, something that they knew would develop in ways they knew not. Constitutional provisions that embody concepts license nonoriginalist approaches.

33. See, e.g., Berger, *Government by Judiciary*, pp. 20–36 (privileges and immunities clause); Raoul Berger, "The Ninth Amendment," 66 *Cornell Law Review* 1 (1980); Perry, "Interpretivism," pp. 272–73 (ninth amendment).

34. Perry, "Interpretivism," pp. 299–300.

35. Id., p. 300.

36. Dworkin, *Taking Rights Seriously* 134–36. For a critique, see Stephen Munzer and James Nickel, "Does the Constitution Mean What It Always Meant?" 77 *Columbia Law Review* 1029, 1037–41 (1977).

Here again the originalist has two reasons not to accept the revisionists' position. First, like Ely and Laycock, Dworkin might be called upon to live up to the originalists' historiographic standards if he wants to play their game. He therefore might be required to produce evidence of an originalist sort that the framers knew that they were enacting provisions that embodied a moral content richer than their own moral conceptions. And, simply put, there is no evidence at all that they did.[37] The distinction relies on modern theories of law that were quite foreign, indeed probably would have been incomprehensible, to the framers of the Bill of Rights and the fourteenth amendment. Their theories of law were at the same time more positivistic and more allied to theological versions of natural law theories than is the secularized vision of moral philosophy from which Dworkin draws his distinction.[38]

The second objection rests on a frontal attack on the proposed distinction between concepts and conceptions, a distinction that reflects a general problem in constitutional theory. Frequently an analysis turns completely on the level of generality at which some feature of the issue being analyzed is described.[39] But the choice of that level must be made on some basis external to the theory. For example, why describe the concept of equality on a level of generality so high that it obliterates the specific intention to permit segregation? After all, the concept is at least in part built up from particular experiences of what is seen as equal treatment; it is to that extent derived from the conceptions of equality.

37. Perry, "Interpretivism," pp. 297–98.

38. See Robert Cover, *Justice Accused: Antislavery and the Judicial Process* 8–30 (1975); William Nelson, "The Impact of the Antislavery Movement upon Styles of Judicial Reasoning in Nineteenth Century America," 87 *Harvard Law Review* 513 (1974). Chapter 3 discusses Dworkin's nonoriginalist defense of his position, that judges' choices are constrained by a shared and evolving grasp of the political theory of their society. This approach makes originalism, which appears to be a theory of meaning, depend upon a political theory and is in that way located in the republican tradition.

39. See, e.g., Tribe *American Constitutional Law*, p. 946 (in determining whether homosexual preferences deserve constitutional protection, "it is crucial, in asking whether an alleged right forms part of a traditional liberty, to define the liberty at a high enough level of generality to permit unconventional variants to claim protection along with mainstream versions of protected conduct"). Terrance Sandalow, "Constitutional Interpretation," 79 *Michigan Law Review* 1033, 1035–36, 1045–46 (1981), discusses the "level of generality" problem and concludes, "By wrenching the framers' 'larger purposes' from the particular judgments that revealed them, we incur a loss of perspective . . . that might better enable us to see that the particular judgments they made were . . . a particular accommodation of competing purposes. In freeing ourselves from those judgments, we are . . . making room for the introduction of contemporary values." See also Bork, "Introduction," p. x ("The question is always the level of generality the judge chooses when he states the idea or object of the Framers"; accepts application of fourth amendment to wiretapping, but rejects "a still higher level of generality").

The critiques developed so far do not demolish the pragmatic defense of originalism as a method of avoiding judicial tyranny. The responses to those critiques, however, weaken the theory seriously. The most coherent version of originalism protects us against only those few specific forms of legislative tyranny that the framers had in mind. Had they been more visionary, originalism would be quite protective. But that is not how things were. Still, originalists can argue with some force that originalism is better than the alternatives. It gives us a Constitution with many opportunities for legislative tyranny, some (though few) limits on legislatures, stringent limits on judges, and few opportunities for judicial tyranny. The alternatives provide many opportunities for judicial tyranny, few limits on judges, and an unknown mixture of opportunities for and limits on legislative tyranny. As is true of all pragmatic discussions, this one cannot come to a firm conclusion without an explicit consideration of the political consequences of following one or the other theory.

There are deeper problems with originalism, however. The first step toward an understanding of those problems is an argument that an intellectually credible originalism must rest on an account of historical knowledge more subtle than the view that past attitudes and intentions are directly accessible to present understanding. The second step identifies the most plausible such account, the view—sometimes called hermeneutics—that historical understanding requires an imaginative transposition of former worldviews into the categories of our own. The third step is an argument that such a transposition can take many forms, none of which is more correct than the others. This indeterminacy means that originalism cannot constrain judges as the liberal tradition requires.

We can approach the problems of historical knowledge by using one of the examples currently favored by conservatives. Attorney General Meese and other conservatives have pointed to the Supreme Court's decisions on religion to show that a jurisprudence of original intent would restrain the judges.[40] Justice Rehnquist's dissent in *Wallace v. Jaffree* presents the current conservative view of original intent.[41] The majority in *Wallace* held unconstitutional an Alabama statute authorizing schools to open their classes each day with a moment of silence or prayer. It emphasized the legislature's intent to promote religion in amending a previous "moment of silence" statute to include the words "or prayer." Justice Rehnquist offered what Justice White, who agreed with the dissent, called a

40. See, e.g., Meese, "Attorney General's View," pp. 703–4.

41. 472 U.S. 38 (1985). See also Robert Cord, *Separation of Church and State: Historical Fact and Current Fiction* (1982).

"basic reconsideration" of the Court's general approach to establishment clause problems.[42]

The prevailing view of the intent of the framers regarding the establishment of religion is that they adopted the position urged by Jefferson and Madison in the course of their long struggle to enact the Virginia Statute for Religious Freedom of 1786.[43] Madison's eloquent and widely distributed *Memorial and Remonstrance against Religious Assessments* argued against a bill that would have imposed a tax to support Christian ministers. Madison argued that the bill contradicted the premise that society has no authority over religious conscience, as was illustrated by the bill's preference for Christianity over other religions: "Who does not see that the same authority which can establish Christianity, in the exclusion of all other religions, may establish with the same ease any particular sect of Christians in exclusion of all other sects? That the same authority which can force a citizen to contribute threepence only of his property for the support of any one establishment may force him to conform to any other establishment in all cases whatsoever?"[44] Madison set the specific argument against the tax into a general philosophical framework that denies social authority over conscience. Equality requires that we grant "an equal freedom to those whose minds have not yet yielded to the evidence which has convinced us." The prevailing view is that Madison's approach was the basis on which the establishment clause of the first amendment was adopted in 1789.

Justice Rehnquist challenged this view. He noted that the debate on the establishment clause "does not seem particularly illuminating." To Justice Rehnquist, in 1789 Madison was "an advocate of sensible legislative compromise, not . . . an advocate of incorporating the Virginia Statute . . . into the . . . Constitution." Others who spoke saw the "evil to be aimed at" as "the establishment of a national church, and perhaps the preference of one religious sect over another, but it was definitely not concerned about whether the Government might aid all religions evenhandedly." Justice Rehnquist concluded that the clause "should be read no more broadly than to prevent . . . the governmental preference of one religious sect over another." This conclusion is supported by actions of the first Congress, which enacted the Northwest Ordinance providing that "religion . . . being necessary to good government, . . . schools . . . shall forever be encouraged" and urged President Washington to issue a Thanksgiving

42. 472 U.S., at 91.

43. On the Virginia background, see Thomas Buckley, *Church and State in Revolutionary Virginia, 1776–1787* (1977).

44. Quotations from the *Memorial and Remonstrance* are taken from Cord, *Separation*, pp. 244–49.

Proclamation referring to "almighty God." Later Jefferson negotiated a treaty with the Kaskaskia Indians in which the United States provided cash support for the tribe's Roman Catholic priest.[45]

This appears to make a powerful case for the originalist interpretation that the establishment clause bars penalizing people for being irreligious, a concern addressed as well by the free exercise clause, and prohibits granting aid to some religions but not others. But there are three classes of difficulties with Justice Rehnquist's arguments: historical ambiguity, inference from limited evidence, and social change. As we will see these problems afflict all originalist arguments.

The problems of historical ambiguity are simple. Justice Rehnquist noted the thinness of the debates on the establishment clause. Leonard Levy has published a detailed examination of the clause's original meaning. A careful historian, Levy finds the historical record murky. For example, he says that those who urged that a Bill of Rights be added to the Constitution did not clearly identify what they meant by an establishment of religion, although no one favored the establishment of a national religion and many expressed concern about preferential aid. Levy shows that the establishment clause went through several versions, some of which were narrow prohibitions of preferential aid. But "Congress very carefully considered and rejected the wording that seems to imply the narrow interpretation." Examining the colonial experience, Levy argues that the framers were familiar with multiple establishment of several churches, a fact which, as he says, weakens the argument that the evil they had in mind was mere preference for *one* church over all others.[46]

An additional problem for any originalist approach is that the framers' thought about religion was located within their entire worldview, their—to us—confusing blend of the liberal and republican traditions. Focusing only on what they thought about tax support for churches or treaties with Native American nations overlooks how their conception of those things fit together in, and was in some ways derived from, a universe of concepts that made sense to them. For example, the republican strand in the framers' thought supports the idea that religion is important in contributing to the moral education of the good citizen.[47] But precisely because our

---

45. 472 U.S., at 95, 98, 100–103.

46. Leonard Levy, *The Establishment Clause: Religion and the First Amendment* 83, 60–61, 65–77 (1986). See also Thomas Curry, *The First Freedoms: Church and State in America to the Passage of the First Amendment* (1986).

47. See David Little, "The Virginia Statute of Religious Freedom, 1786–1886: The Spread of Mr. Jefferson's Ideas," paper presented at the annual meeting of the Organization of American Historians, Apr. 5, 1985; Michael McConnell, "Accommodation of Religion," 1985 *Supreme Court Review* 1.

conceptual universe is different from theirs, we cannot simply lift what they thought about one particular matter and insert it into a body of law that makes sense in our terms. As Robert Gordon has put it, "The old text will be rendered almost wholly archaic if it can be shown to embody a set of conceptions—about human nature, property, virtue, freedom, representation, necessity, causation, and so forth—that was a unique configuration for its time and in some ways strikingly unlike what we believe to be our own."[48]

The problems of inference from limited evidence are related to those of historical ambiguity. Justice Rehnquist drew from his historical survey the rule of nonpreference among religions. The evidence he relied on would equally well support a rule of nonpreference among Christian denominations.[49] The treaty with the Kaskaskia might show that even preferential aid is permitted. Or, in light of the insecure military position of the early Republic and its vulnerability to attack by Native American nations, the treaty might show that the government can support religion only when the most urgent needs of national security compellingly require that such support be provided.

Finally, the problem of social change is that institutions, such as the Thanksgiving Proclamation, meant one thing in the framers' society but another in ours. To Washington and his contemporaries, the proclamation reflected a deeply felt belief that God had chosen to look after the United States in a religiously meaningful way. Today we celebrate Thanksgiving with turkeys and football games; even if the presidents who issue Thanksgiving Proclamations are themselves sincere in their expressions of religious belief, the general population does not take the proclamations to be anything more than mere ritual. In broader terms once the society contains religious denominations that have religious grounds for rejecting governmental aid, the concept of nonpreferential aid to religions becomes incoherent.

This examination of a recent originalist approach to the establishment clause shows that originalism is not a satisfactory answer to people concerned about judicial tyranny. In resolving historical ambiguity, drawing

48. Robert Gordon, "Historicism in Legal Scholarship," 90 *Yale Law Journal* 1017, 1021 (1981). For additional discussion, see the text accompanying notes 68–69.

49. Joseph Story, who articulated a version of the "no preference" position, did include "the Armenian, the Jew, and the Infidel" on his list of denominations protected against the establishment of a national church. See Cord, *Separation*, at 15. But he also wrote that "the real object of the amendment was . . . to exclude all rivalry among Christian sects." Quoted in Wallace v. Jaffree, 472 U.S., at 104 (Rehnquist, J., dissenting).

The occasional incompleteness or distortion of the documentary record also deserves note. See James Hutson, "The Creation of the Constitution: The Integrity of the Documentary Record," 65 *Texas Law Review* 1 (1986).

inferences from limited evidence, and taking account of social change, originalist judges have as much room to maneuver as nonoriginalist ones.[50]

The difficulty goes deeper than this, however. Originalist history requires definite answers (because it is part of a system in which judgment is awarded to one side or the other) and clear ones (because it seeks to constrain judges). The universal experience of historians belies the originalist effort. Where the originalist seeks certainty and clarity, the historian finds ambiguity.[51] We have already seen one originalist view of the history of the first amendment. Yet if we were able to sit down for a talk with Thomas Jefferson about civil liberties, a good historian will tell us, we would hear an apparently confused blend of assertions: libertarian theory, opposition to the enactment of sedition laws, the use of sedition laws once in office, and so on. Jefferson's "intent" on the issue of free speech is nothing more than this jumbled set of responses.[52]

Because evidentiary materials are frequently incomplete and fail to yield answers of sufficient clarity, originalists must rely on supplementary evidentiary rules. Raoul Berger, for example, proposes a burden of proof: One who claims that the framers intended to alter substantially the relations that existed in 1871 between state and national government must provide more persuasive evidence than one who claims that they did not intend to alter those relations.[53] Similarly, he invokes lawyers' rules about legislative debate: statements made on the floor of the Senate are to be given more weight than statements made in private letters.[54]

50. All three problems are embraced in the standard criticism of "law office" history. Originalism calls for a historical inquiry into the intent of the framers. That inquiry is conducted by lawyers imbued with the adversary ethic. The standard criticism is that lawyers are bad historians because they overemphasize fragmentary evidence and minimize significant bodies of conflicting or contradictory evidence in the service of their partisan goals. See Alfred Kelly, "Clio and the Court: An Illicit Love Affair," 1965 *Supreme Court Review* 122, 155–58.

51. For a historian's discussion of her professional discomfort about providing expert testimony at a trial, see Alice Kessler-Harris, "Equal Employment Opportunity Commission v. Sears, Roebuck and Company: A Personal Account," 35 *Radical History Review* 57 (1986).

52. Leonard Levy, the source of the narrow originalist view of the first amendment, gave one of his books on the subject the title *Jefferson and Civil Liberties: The Darker Side* (1963), suggesting that there was a brighter side as well. See also Norman Rosenberg, *Protecting the Best Men: An Interpretive History of the Law of Libel* (1986) (emphasizing the role of free speech theory in competing political visions); David Rabban, "The Ahistorical Historian: Leonard Levy on Freedom of Expression in Early American History," 37 *Stanford Law Review* 795 (1985) (same).

53. Berger, *Government by Judiciary*, pp. 17, 153–55.

54. Id., pp. 6–7. Other examples of Berger's use of supplementary evidentiary rules can be found in id., pp. 49–50, 74, 75–76, 116, 124, 136–37, 157, 160, 194–95, 207, 223.

These supplementary evidentiary rules are simultaneously helpful and misleading. The rules may have two functions. They may be crystallized expressions of what more detailed inquiries have shown to have been usually true. Berger's federalism burden-of-proof rule, for example, is partly justified by the fact that when we examine the range of uncontroversial situations where national-state relations were altered, we discover a lot more evidence about the relevant intent in the situations where those relations were altered substantially than in the situations where they were altered less substantially. In addition, the rules may embody policy judgments that are independent of their role in promoting accurate reconstructions of the past. The intent rule, for example, may be justified on the ground that the originalist should look for a "special" kind of intent—the kind exhibited on relatively formal occasions and expressed in relatively formal terms—rather than the "private intent" of letters and the like. To restrict the focus of the inquiry to such a "special" kind of intent is to make a policy judgment that expressions of opinion on relatively formal occasions ought to be given special weight. The federalism rule can also serve as an example: it is partly justified by a policy preference for maintaining the existing distribution of authority between state and nation.

These independent policy bases of the supplementary rules distort the historical inquiry. In particular, they deflect attention from the political and intellectual contexts in which the Constitution was developed, precisely because considering those contexts would introduce all the ambiguities that lawyers must ignore.[55] To the extent that the supplementary

---

55. For additional discussion of the role of supplementary rules ("canons of interpretation"), see Philip Soper, "Legal Theory and the Obligation of a Judge: The Hart/Dworkin Dispute," 75 *Michigan Law Review* 473, 489–98 (1977). A dramatic illustration of the difference between the history done by originalists and that done by historians is the contrast between the sources of evidence used by Berger, *Government by Judiciary,* and Harold Hyman, *A More Perfect Union: The Impact of the Civil War and Reconstruction on the Constitution* (1973). Berger concentrates on the congressional debates over the pro-. posed fourteenth amendment, with occasional allusions to secondary accounts of the history of Reconstruction. Hyman augments his attention to the debates with detailed and illuminating analyses of the political and social history of Reconstruction. For an even broader view, see Morton Keller, *Affairs of State: Public Life in Late Nineteenth Century America* (1977).

It is almost painful to read Berger's work after reading a far more subtle study by a serious historian, J. R. Pole, *The Pursuit of Equality in American History* (1978). I find it instructive that Berger only occasionally cites works by these historians, who have given us our best recent studies of the Reconstruction period; when he does it is only for points that are marginal to their arguments. See also Michael Curtis, "The Fourteenth Amendment and the Bill of Rights," 14 *Connecticut Law Review* 237 (1982); Eric Schnapper, "Affirmative Action and the Legislative History of the Fourteenth Amendment," 71 *Virginia Law Review*

rules are based on policy grounds, the liberal project is defeated: they demonstrate that originalism rests on a particular political or social vision.

The originalist project requires the discovery and use of unambiguous historical facts; the only way that originalists can find such facts is to embrace what are fundamentally flawed historiographic methods. Underlying the originalists' reliance on these methods is the view that individuals are the primary units of human experience and history and that larger social wholes are best understood as aggregates of such individuals. From this view it follows that an individual's beliefs, intentions, and desires have their character independent of, or prior to, the larger social and conceptual context in which they occur, a context that the liberal tradition sees as a product of all antecedent individual perspectives. The project of the liberal historian thus is to study the historical record for evidence of what the intentions and beliefs of historical actors actually were.

On this account intentions must be real, determinate entities; the originalist must be able to identify and understand specific intentions of the framers with respect to one part of the Constitution or another. Leo Marx's *Machine in the Garden,* an important work on American history, shows how the problems of ambiguity and social change undermine this approach to historical knowledge.[56] The book discusses the ways in which Americans thought about technological change. One of Marx's central items of evidence, used to great effect, is a painting of a pastoral scene through which a railroad train is peacefully passing. Marx's point is that historians cannot reconstruct a world in which railroads did not exist but everything else remained the same. The existence of railroads affected how people thought about their relation to the natural world, and those conceptions in turn affected the desire to invest and the value placed on growth. Because railroads had the cultural value that Americans gave them, they encouraged Americans to invest in risky enterprises that exploited novel technologies. If they had had a different cultural value—for example, if they had been understood as "Satanic" as William Blake might have understood them—Americans might have responded by investing in family firms that took no risks on modern technology.[57]

---

753 (1985); Earl Maltz, "The Fourteenth Amendment as Political Compromise—Section One in the Joint Committee on Reconstruction," 45 *Ohio State Law Journal* 933 (1984). These articles are also infected with the lawyer's urge to find "the answer," but taken together they demonstrate the complexity and ambiguity of the history of the framing of the fourteenth amendment, which most originalists are forced to overlook.

56. Leo Marx, *The Machine in the Garden* (1964).

57. See also Alan Trachtenberg, *The Incorporation of America: Culture and Society in the Gilded Age* (1982).

As Marx's work shows, perspectives, beliefs, and intentions are thoroughly interwoven with the concrete social and economic realities of their day. Marx's insight is that the contents or meanings of beliefs and intentions are shaped by the entire societal context in which those beliefs and intentions arise and which they in turn alter. When originalists presume that they can detach the meanings that the framers gave to the words they used from the entire complex of meanings that the framers gave to their political vocabulary as a whole and from the larger political, economic, and intellectual world in which they lived, they slip into the error of thinking that they can grasp historical parts without embracing the historical whole.

These problems raise doubts about an easy acceptance of an originalism whose theory of historical knowledge presumes that past beliefs and intentions are determinate and identifiable. Those doubts can be deepened by comparing this theory of historical knowledge with its main rival, the hermeneutic tradition. In that tradition historical knowledge is "the interpretive understanding of [the] meanings" that actors gave their actions.[58] The historian must enter the minds of his or her subjects, see the

---

58. Russell Keat, *The Politics of Social Theory: Habermas, Freud and the Critique of Positivism* 3 (1981). (The text's discussion of the hermeneutic approach does not distinguish among a variety of more sharply defined schools within this approach, such as structuralism and phenomenology.) R. G. Collingwood, *The Idea of History* (1956), is the best presentation of this view for those accustomed to Anglo-American styles of philosophical writing. See also Arthur Danto, *Analytical Philosophy of History* (1968). Collingwood goes far along the way to the conclusions that I draw here but does not quite state them openly. He is criticized for that by Paul Ricoeur, *The Reality of the Historical Past* 5–14 (1984).

The long background of the hermeneutic tradition is described in Donald Kelley, "Hermes, Clio, Themis: Historical Interpretation and Legal Hermeneutics," 55 *Journal of Modern History* 644 (1983). From very different perspectives Jurgen Habermas and Hans-Georg Gadamer have explored aspects of the hermeneutic tradition using a different style of philosophical writing. (Grouping Habermas and Gadamer is like saying that Justices Brennan and Rehnquist are similar in that they are both judges.) For summaries, see Keat, *Politics of Social Theory*, pp. 202–3; Anthony Giddens, *Central Problems in Social Theory: Action, Structure and Contradiction in Social Analysis* 175–77 (1979); Thomas McCarthy, *The Critical Theory of Jurgen Habermas* 162–239 (1978); Anthony Giddens, *New Rules of Sociological Method: A Positive Critique of Interpretive Sociologies* 54–65 (1976); Anthony Giddens, *Profiles and Critiques in Social Theory* 1–17 (1982). For lawyers' perspectives, see Kenneth Abraham, "Statutory Interpretation and Literary Theory: Some Common Concerns of an Unlikely Pair," 32 *Rutgers Law Review* 676 (1979); Kenneth Abraham, "Three Fallacies of Interpretation: A Comment on Precedent and Judicial Decision," 23 *Arizona Law Review* 771 (1981); Symposium, "Law as Literature," 60 *Texas Law Review* 373 (1982); Walter Probert, "Interpretation: Its Relevance in Courts, Criticism and Jurisprudence," 25 *Washburn Law Journal* 1 (1985); Comment, "Philosophical Hermeneutics: Toward an Alternative View of Adjudication," 1984 *Brigham Young University Law Review* 323; Allan Hutchinson, "Part of an Essay on Power and Interpretation (with

world as they saw it, and understand it in their own terms.[59] Justice Brandeis' eloquent opinion in *Whitney v. California*, which recreates one version of the worldview of the framers, is the best example in the case law of a hermeneutic effort to understand the past. This reconstruction, though partial and largely unsupported by specific references to what any framer actually said, does in the end bring us into the framers' world. Brandeis wrote:

> Those who won our independence believed that the final end of the State was to make men free to develop their faculties; and that in its government the deliberative forces should prevail over the arbitrary. They valued liberty both as an end and as a means. They believed liberty to be the secret of happiness and courage to be the secret of liberty. They believed that freedom to think as you will and to speak as you think are means indispensable to the discovery and spread of political truth; that without free speech and assembly discussion would be futile; that with them, discussion affords ordinarily adequate protection against the dissemination of noxious doctrine; that the greatest menace to freedom is an inert people; that public discussion is a political duty; and that this should be a fundamental principle of the American government. They recognized the risks to which all human institutions are subject. But they knew that order cannot be secured merely through fear of punishment for its infraction; that it is hazardous to discourage thought, hope, and imagination; that fear breeds hate; that hate menaces stable government; that the path of safety lies in the opportunity to discuss freely supposed grievances and proposed remedies; and that the fitting remedy for evil counsels is good ones. Believing in the power of reason as applied through public discussion, they eschewed silence coerced by law—the argument of force in its worst form. Recognizing the occasional tyrannies of governing majorities, they amended the Constitution so that free speech and assembly should be guaranteed.[60]

By echoing Pericles' famous oration, Brandeis recalls to us the framers' belief in a republic dominated by civic virtue. It matters not very much that their views on specific aspects of governmental design may have

Suggestions on How to Make Bouillabaisse)," 60 *New York University Law Review* 850 (1985).

Although I do not believe that fashions in historical scholarship necessarily move in the direction of truth, I think it worth noting that originalists who rely on the positivist tradition are out of step with the dominant tendency in contemporary historical scholarship, which finds in the hermeneutic tradition a better understanding of the enterprise. See also Philip Kurland, "Curia Regis: Some Comments on the Divine Right of Kings and Courts 'To Say What the Law Is,' " 23 *Arizona Law Review* 581 (1981).

59. Although not cast in these terms, Dworkin's concern that the concept of intention be adequately developed, Dworkin, "Forum of Principle," pp. 477–78, is one that is repeatedly raised within the hermeneutic tradition.

60. 274 U.S. 357, 375–76 (1927).

differed in detail from Brandeis' reconstruction; what matters is that they designed a government that comported with their sense of a world in which civic virtue reigned. The significance and the ramifications of this sense are what Brandeis strove to capture, and they are what originalism too must recognize to be central. The ways in which people understand the world give meaning to the words that they use, and only by recreating such global understandings can we interpret the document the framers wrote.

The dilemma of originalism is that if it is to rely on a real grasp of the framers' intentions—and only this premise gives originalism its intuitive appeal—its method must be hermeneutic, but if it adopts a hermeneutic approach it is foreclosed from achieving the determinacy about the framers' meanings necessary to serve its underlying goals. The originalists' premise of determinate intentions is essential to their project of developing constraints on judges. The hermeneutic approach to historical understanding requires that we abandon this premise. In imaginatively entering the world of the past, we not only reconstruct it but—more important for present purposes—we also creatively construct it.[61] Such creativity is the only way to bridge the gaps between that world and ours. The past, particularly the aspects that the originalists care about, is in its essence indeterminate; the originalist project cannot be carried to its conclusion.

Consider an example. We have already seen that originalism's most plausible version leads one to conclude that school segregation is not unconstitutional. In *Brown v. Board of Education*, however, the Court said, "In approaching this problem, we cannot turn the clock back to 1868 when the [Fourteenth] Amendment was adopted . . . We must consider public education in the light of its full development and its present place in American life throughout the Nation."[62] Chief Justice Warren need not be taken as rejecting the use of historical inquiries in constitutional law; he can instead be read to be approaching the task of discovering the past in a hermeneutic way.

Suppose that we did turn the clock back so that we could talk to the framers of the fourteenth amendment. If we asked them whether the amendment outlawed segregation in public schools, perhaps enough of them would answer no. We could pursue our conversation by asking

---

61. One interesting version of the imaginative reconstruction of history is that offered by some writers in the law-and-economics tradition, who claim that, as a matter of observed fact, courts in the past developed common law rules that were consistent with the requirements of economic efficiency. See Chapter 6. This reconstruction allows them to argue that their efforts to develop a set of rules guided solely by efficiency concerns is simply a continuation of what courts have been doing for years.

62. 347 U.S. 483, 492–93 (1954).

them what they had in mind when they thought about public education. We would find out that they had in mind a relatively new and peripheral social institution designed (say) to civilize the lower classes.[63] In contrast, they thought that freedom of contract was extremely important because it was the foundation of individual achievement, and they certainly wanted to outlaw racial discrimination with respect to that freedom. Returning to 1954 and the question for the Court in *Brown*, we might conclude that the hermeneutic enterprise demonstrated that public education as it exists today—a central institution for the achievement of individual goals—is in fact the functional equivalent not of public education in 1868 but of freedom of contract in 1868.[64] Thus, *Brown* was correctly decided in light of a hermeneutic originalism.[65]

The need to identify equivalents over time necessarily imports significant indeterminacy—and therefore discretion—into the originalist account; alternative hermeneutic accounts of *Brown* are also possible. Consider, for example, the implications of Herbert Wechsler's argument

63. See Paul Peterson, *The Politics of School Reform, 1870–1940*, 10–11 (1985) (public schools "tenuously established" shortly after Civil War).

64. This situation is but one of many in which substantial historic change obstructs attempts to equate the institutions known by the framers with modern versions that go by the same name. A similar difficulty attends Robert Nagel's effort, "Federalism as a Fundamental Value: *National League of Cities* in Perspective," 1981 *Supreme Court Review* 81, 97–109, to defend contemporary enforcement of the rights of states, see, e.g., National League of Cities v. Usery, 426 U.S. 833 (1976), overruled, Garcia v. San Antonio Metropolitan Transit Auth., 469 U.S. 528 (1985), by reciting the admittedly important values that the framers thought that federalism served. See also Andrzej Rapaczynski, "From Sovereignty to Process: The Jurisprudence of Federalism after Garcia," 1985 *Supreme Court Review* 341 (drawing also on process-oriented theories to identify the relevant values). In a world in which the so-called community school boards in New York City would have represented populations in 1967 only slighly smaller than the population of the entire state of New York in 1790, compare Charles Morris, *The Cost of Good Intentions* 114 (1980) (average population of thirty-community school district in New York City in 1967 would have been 275,000), with U.S. Bureau of the Census, *Historical Statistics of the United States, pt. I*, at 32 (1975) (1790 population of New York State was 340,000), the "states" that were protected by *National League of Cities* are not the same as the entities the framers had in mind, even though the geographic borders of some of them have not changed since 1789.

65. For another example, consider how originalists deal with a problem noted earlier—that of innovations in tyranny, such as wiretapping. The prototypical defense of originalism is that the framers had in mind a prohibition on governmental intrusions on privacy that they then described by the word *searches*. If wiretapping is "different in no significant respect" from what the framers thought of as searches, it is unconstitutional. Perry, "Interpretivism," p. 281. Again, defending the theory by relying on functional equivalences between contemporary and past practices weakens the theory to the point of collapse: The originalist is unable to give a content to the idea of functional equivalence sufficiently determinate to enable us to know which contemporary practices are enough like past ones to fall under the framers' ban.

that *Brown* is problematic because it failed to consider the impact of desegregation on the interest of white parents and students in associating only with those of whom they approved.[66] A hermeneutic defense of that criticism might argue that education today is an important part of American civil religion[67] and that it is therefore the secular functional equivalent of true religion in 1868. The framers would certainly have regarded forced association in churches as improper; thus Wechsler's point is established. Originalists claim that their approach is able to limit judges, but by allowing judges to look hermeneutically for functional equivalents, they reintroduce the discretion that they want to eliminate.

The difficulty, however, runs deeper than the indeterminacy of identifications of functional equivalents. The hermeneutic tradition tells us that we quite literally cannot understand the acts of those in the past without entering into their mental world. Because we live in our world, the only way to begin the hermeneutic enterprise is by thinking about what in our world initially seems like what people in the past talked and thought about. Usually we begin with a few areas in which we and they use the same rather abstract words to talk about apparently similar things. Thus, we and the framers share a concern for democracy, human rights, and limited government. But as we read what they said about democracy and limited government, we notice discontinuities: they described their polity as a democratic one, for example, when we would think it obviously nondemocratic. As we examine this evidence, we adjust our understanding to take account of these "peculiarities." With a great deal of imaginative effort, at the end of the process we can indeed understand their world, because we have become immersed in it.[68] Yet the understanding we achieve is not the unique, correct image of the framers' world. On the contrary, our imaginative immersion is only one of a great many possible reconstructions of that segment of the past, a reconstruction shaped not only by the character of the past but also by our own interests, concerns, and preconceptions. The imagination that we have used to adjust and readjust our understanding makes it impossible to claim that any one reconstruction is uniquely correct. The past shapes the materials on which we use our imaginations; our interests, concerns, and preconceptions shape our imaginations themselves.

Still, the intellectual world of the framers is one that bears some resemblance, which is more than merely genetic, to our own. A hermeneutic

66. Wechsler, *Principles, Politics, and Fundamental Law,* pp. 46–47.

67. See, e.g., Robert Bellah, *The Broken Covenant: American Civil Religion in Time of Trial* x-xi, 76–83 (1975).

68. This approach is congenial with that of Michel Foucault, *The Archaeology of Knowledge* (1972).

originalism would force us to think about the social contexts of the resemblances and dissimilarities. It would lead us not to despair over the gulf that separates the framers' world from ours but rather to the crafting of creative links between their ideals and our own. In recognizing the magnitude of the creative component, we would inevitably lose faith in the ability of originalism to provide the constraints on judges that the liberal tradition demands.[69]

Nevertheless, the hermeneutic tradition does identify something that constitutional theory should take seriously. A fanatic adherent of the hermeneutic method might deny that we can ever understand the past, because the world of the past is not the world within which we have developed ways of understanding how others act.[70] That, however, goes too far. We can gain an interpretive understanding of the past by working from commonalities in the use of large abstractions to reach the unfamiliar particulars of what those abstractions really meant in the past. The commonalities are what make the past *our* past; they are the links between two segments of a single community which extends over time.[71] The commonalities are both immanent in our history and constructed by us as we reflect on what our history is. Originalism goes wrong in thinking that the commonalities are greater than they really are, but hermeneutics would go wrong if it denied that they existed. The task is to think through the implications of our continued dedication to the large abstractions when the particulars of the world have changed so drastically. That process will lead us to face questions about what kind of community we have and want.

It seems appropriate to conclude this discussion by examining an exemplary case in which the Court adopted an originalist approach. Chief Justice Taney's opinion in *Dred Scott v. Sandford* was originalist to the

69. The diehard originalist might acknowledge how different our world is from the framers' and concede that hermeneutic history reveals the indeterminacy of constitutional limitations on power but still contend that the constitutional grants of power remain sufficiently clear and determinate to provide meaningful constraints. See, e.g., Graglia, "How the Constitution Disappeared," p. 23 (semble). Cf. Perry, "Interpretivism," pp. 282–84 (suggesting differential treatment of power-granting and power-limiting provisions). That cannot be so. The framers thought of the government that they were creating as an integrated system of grants and limitations, set in a society animated by civic virtue. The Congress that exists when the limits are conceded to be indeterminate, or when civic virtue has been lost, is not the Congress that the framers created, even though it has the prescribed two houses and the like. See Sandalow, "Constitutional Interpretation," pp. 1048–49.

70. See, e.g., Peter Winch, *The Idea of a Social Science and Its Relation to Philosophy* 86–91 (1958).

71. I must, however, note the obvious ethnocentricity of this statement. Clearly, the history of kingship in West Africa (see Jan Vansina, *Kingdoms of the Savannah* [1968]) is as much part of our past as is the history of the Constitution. See also Chapter 4 (appendix).

core.[72] To Taney the issue was whether, at the time of the framing, blacks could have been "citizens of different States" for purposes of establishing their entitlement to invoke the power of the federal courts. He devoted ten pages of his opinion to a historical survey of colonial legislation, the circumstances of the Declaration of Independence, and legislation in non-slaveholding states. In it he emphasized that phrases like *all men are created equal* could be reconciled with the continuing acceptance of slavery only if people in the framers' era did not regard blacks as men.[73] He summarized his interpretation of history:

> It is difficult . . . to realize the state of public opinion in relation to that unfortunate race, which prevailed . . . when the Constitution of the United States was framed and adopted . . .
> They had for more than a century before been regarded as beings of an inferior order, and altogether unfit to associate with the white race, either in social or political relations; and so far inferior, that they had no rights which the white man was bound to respect; and that the negro might justly and lawfully be reduced to slavery for his benefit . . . This opinion was at that time fixed and universal in the civilized portion of the white race. It was regarded as an axiom in morals as well as in politics, which no one thought of disputing, or supposed to be open to dispute; and men in every grade and position in society daily and habitually acted upon it in their private pursuits, as well as in matters of public concern, without doubting for a moment the correctness of this opinion.[74]

Obviously more could have been said that would have blurred the originalist clarity of the decision. For example, the framers in 1789 had more conflicts over slavery, and a fortiori over the status of free blacks, than Taney admitted. But when all the evidence is assembled, what we make of it will depend on the past that we choose to identify. In the 1960s Taney might have been simultaneously condemned and admired for facing up to the implications of the nation's racist heritage, whereas today he may be simply derided as a racist because we are deep in the process of convincing ourselves that we have decisively repudiated that heritage. Originalism attributes our choices to people in the past and so displaces our responsibility for constructing our society on the basis of the continuities we choose to make with our past.

72. 60 U.S. (19 How.) 393 (1857). The best modern scholarship, Don Fehrenbacher, *The Dred Scott Case: Its Significance in American Law and Politics* (1978), concludes that Taney wrote an opinion in which a majority of the Court concurred.
73. 60 U.S. (19 How.), p. 410.
74. Id., p. 407.

Neutral Principles, Rules, and Institutions

The hermeneutic tradition suggests that historical discontinuities are so substantial that originalism must make incoherent claims because it can achieve the necessary determinacy about past intentions only by smuggling in an implausible claim about the ability to retrieve meaning across time. The theory of neutral principles fails for similar reasons. It requires that we develop an account of consistency of meaning—the meaning of rules and principles—within the liberal tradition. Yet the premises of that tradition tend to treat each of us as an autonomous individual whose choices and values are independent of those made and held by others. These premises make it exceedingly difficult to develop such an account of consistent meaning. The autonomous producer of choice and value is also an autonomous producer of meaning.

The rule of law, according to the liberal conception, is meant to protect us against the exercise of arbitrary power. The theory of neutral principles asserts that a requirement of consistency, the core of the ideal of the rule of law, places sufficient bounds on judges to reduce the risk of arbitrariness to an acceptable level. The question is whether the concepts of neutrality and consistency can be developed in ways that are adequate for the task. This section examines two candidates for a definition of neutrality.[75] It argues that each fails to provide the kinds of constraints on judges that the liberal tradition requires: The limits they place on judges are either empty or dependent on a sociology of law that undermines the liberal tradition's assumptions about society.[76]

If neutrality is to serve as a meaningful guide, it must be understood not as a standard for the content of principles[77] but rather as a constraint on the process by which principles are selected, justified, and applied. Thus, the possible explications of neutrality focus on the judicial process and the need for "neutral application." This focus transfers our attention from the principles themselves to the judges who purport to use them.

One preliminary difficulty should be noted. The demand for neutral application ultimately rests on the claim that without neutrality a decision "wholly lack[s] . . . legitimacy."[78] In this context legitimacy is a normative

75. Other possible definitions are discussed in Mark Tushnet, "Following the Rules Laid Down: A Critique of Interpretivism and Neutral Principles," 96 *Harvard Law Review* 781, 805–6 (1983).

76. A comprehensive survey of the argument that law cannot be made certain is Anthony D'Amato, "Legal Uncertainty," 71 *California Law Review* 1 (1983).

77. Principles cannot be neutral in content because they necessarily specify, in general terms, who will prevail in a dispute.

78. Perry, "Why the Supreme Court Was Wrong," p. 1127.

concept.[79] Wechsler claimed that neutral principles are an essential component of the practice of judging in our society. Such an appeal to the essence of a social practice draws on a vision of how ideal courts act, a vision stimulated by reflection on the proper place of the courts in our social fabric. Legitimacy is a matter of concordance with the demands of this ideal. These demands, however, ultimately prove empty, for rather than constrain the proper role of courts the concept of neutrality presupposes a shared understanding and acceptance of any constraints.

What, then, are methodologically neutral principles? The best explication looks to the past. It would impose as a necessary condition for justification that a decision be consistent with the relevant precedents.[80] Michael Perry's discussion of the abortion funding cases exemplifies this approach. Perry, in the best recent application of the theory of neutral principles, attempts to identify the operative principle in *Roe v. Wade*, a highly abstract principle concerning the relation between governmental powers and constitutional protections, and to criticize the Court's later ruling in *Harris v. McRae* for inconsistency with that principle.

In 1973 the Supreme Court held in *Roe v. Wade* that state criminal statutes restricting the availability of abortions were unconstitutional.[81]

79. *Legitimacy* has another possible meaning, common in the sociological literature on government: legitimate actions are those that are accepted by the relevant public. For a brief discussion, see Mark Tushnet, "Perspectives on the Development of American Law," 1977 *Wisconsin Law Review* 81, 100–102. See also Alan Hyde, "The Concept of Legitimation in the Sociology of Law," 1983 *Wisconsin Law Review* 379. Decisions that lack legitimacy in this empirical sense are undesirable, because a court's main resource in effectuating its decisions is public acceptance, and illegitimate decisions deplete its limited capital. (This is the thesis of Jesse Choper, *Judicial Review and the National Political Process: A Functional Reconsideration of the Role of the Supreme Court* [1980].) It is implausible, however, that neutral application of principles is an important source of public acceptance of judicial decisions. The general public is unlikely to care very much about a court's reasoning process, which is the focus of neutral principles theory; its concern is with results. Of course, to the extent that influential publicists—columnists for the *New York Times*, for example—accept the theory, they may invoke it to criticize the Court. The criticisms might then affect elite readers, from whom the effect might, so to speak, trickle down to the public. See Henry Monaghan, "Book Review," 94 *Harvard Law Review* 296, 310–11 (1980). The extent to which such criticisms affect the public and the Court's legitimacy is an empirical question, the investigation of which would require us to distinguish between the trickle-down effect of views about reasoning and the effects of views about the merits of decisions. Skepticism seems warranted by the few studies that point to the areas of interest. (The evidence is summarized in Austin Sarat, "Studying American Legal Culture: An Assessment of Survey Evidence," 11 *Law and Society Review* 427, 438–41, 466–69 [1977].) Hyde argues that there is no reason to think that legitimation is a significant dimension of law's social effect.

80. This links the theory to general theories of precedent-based adjudication in nonconstitutional areas.

81. 410 U.S. 113 (1973).

Seven years later the Court upheld legislation that denied public funds for abortion to those otherwise qualified for public assistance in paying for medical care.[82] Perry contends that the abortion funding decision is "plainly wrong" because it "is inconsistent with the narrowest possible coherent reading of *Roe*." Perry extracts that reading as follows. The Court struck down the statutes in *Roe* because the pregnant woman's interest in terminating the pregnancy is greater than the government's interest in preventing the taking of the life of the fetus. According to Perry, this entails the conclusion that "*no* governmental action can be predicated on the view that ... abortion is per se morally objectionable."[83] Perry's premise is that government is permitted to use a factor as a predicate for restrictive legislation only if that factor is entitled to no constitutional protection.

Perry rejects as "deeply flawed" and "fundamentally confused" the position taken by the Court in the funding cases and repeated by Peter Westen.[84] This position is that *Roe* barred the government from criminalizing abortions only because criminal sanctions place an undue burden on the woman's interest in terminating the pregnancy; refusing to fund abortions does not similarly burden that interest. Perry claims that *Roe* is coherent only if it precludes the government from taking *any* action predicated on the view that abortion is wrong. To allow the government to take such action would force us to the "rather strange" position that the Constitution permits the government "to establish a legal principle" and simultaneously "protect[s] a person's interest in disregarding that principle once established."[85]

There is nothing strange, however, about the supposed paradox; whether we think the position is strange depends on how we define principles and interest. The applicable general principle might be that government can take all actions predicated on the moral view except insofar as they unduly burden some individual interest.[86] Alternatively, we

82. Harris v. McRae, 448 U.S. 297 (1980).

83. Perry, "Why the Supreme Court Was Wrong," pp. 1114, 1120, 1115–16.

84. Id., p. 1117; Peter Westen, "Correspondence," 33 *Stanford Law Review* 1187, 1188 (1981).

85. Perry, "Why the Supreme Court Was Wrong," pp. 1116–17.

86. Perry presumably thinks that such a principle is inconsistent with other areas of constitutional law, for it recognizes a kind of acceptance of civil disobedience that is not recognized elsewhere in constitutional law. Westen gives the example of Coker v. Georgia, in which the Court held that, although Georgia could make unaggravated rape—if such there be—a crime because it is morally wrong, it was not constitutional to make it a capital offense. Coker v. Georgia, 433 U.S. 584 (1977); Westen, "Correspondence," p. 1188. Perry rejects the "counterexample" of Brandenburg v. Ohio, 395 U.S. 444 (1969), in which the Court protected certain kinds of advocacy from criminal prosecution even though it could

might identify an *independent* moral principle for objecting to tax-funded abortions—for example, that governments may be responsive to the views of taxpayers who object, on moral grounds, to the use of their money to pay for abortions. The government would not be taking the view that abortion is wrong, and its actions would therefore not be inconsistent with what Perry describes as the minimum principle of *Roe*.

The argument just made can be generalized. At the moment a decision is announced we cannot identify the principle that it embodies. Each decision can be justified by many principles, and we learn what principle justified Case 1 only when a court in Case 2 tells us.[87] Behind the court's statement about Case 1 lies all the creativity to which the hermeneutic theory of historical understanding directed our attention. When *Roe* was decided we might have thought that it rested on Perry's principle, but the funding cases show us that we were "wrong" and that *Roe* "in fact" rested on one of the alternatives just spelled out. The theory of neutral principles thus loses almost all of its constraining force. We have only to compare Case 2, which is now decided, with Case 1 to see if a principle from Case 1 has been neutrally applied in Case 2. If the demand is merely that the opinion in Case 2 deploy some reading of the earlier case from which the holding in Case 2 follows, the openness of the precedents means that the demand can always be satisfied. And if the demand is rather that the holding be derived from the principles actually articulated in the relevant precedents, differences between Case 2 and the precedents will inevitably demand a degree of reinterpretation of the old principles. New cases always present issues different from those settled by prior cases.[88] Thus, to decide a new case a judge must take some liberties with

---

"take [other] action predicated on the view that such advocacy is morally objectionable." He argues that the advocacy in *Brandenburg* is protected to avoid a chilling effect on truly protected speech. Thus *Brandenburg*'s real protection is given to "interests *distinct from*" the interest in advocating unlawful activity. Perry, "Why the Supreme Court Was Wrong," pp. 1118, 1119.

The same argument can be developed in the abortion context, however. Consider the narrow principle that government may not take action predicated on the view that abortions are immoral in cases in which the woman has not consented to the sexual contact that caused the pregnancy. *Roe v. Wade* might then be defended on the ground that governmental inquiries into whether consent had been given, particularly in light of the obvious controversy over what consent might mean, would intrude on the independent interest in informational privacy. Because refusal to fund abortions does not intrude on that interest, it is permissible according to this interpretation of *Roe*.

87. Sandalow, "Constitutional Interpretation," pp. 1064–65.

88. Indeed, if it did not so depart we ought to wonder why the later case was litigated at all. Compare George Priest, "The Common Law Process and the Selection of Efficient Rules," 6 *Journal of Legal Studies* 65 (1977), with George Priest, "Selective Characteristics of Litigation," 9 *Journal of Legal Studies* 399 (1980).

the old principles if they are to be applied at all. There is, however, no principled way to determine how many liberties can be taken; hence this reading of the theory likewise provides no meaningful constraints.

The central problem here is that, given the difficulty of isolating a single principle for which a particular precedent stands, we lack any criteria for distinguishing between cases that depart from and those that conform to the principles of their precedents. In fact, any case can compellingly be placed in either category. Such a universal claim cannot be validated by example. But two examples of cases that simultaneously depart from and conform to their precedents can at least make the claim plausible.

The first is *Griswold v. Connecticut,* in which the Court held that a state could not constitutionally prohibit the dissemination of contraceptive information or devices to married people.[89] *Griswold* relied in part on *Pierce v. Society of Sisters*[90] and *Meyer v. Nebraska.*[91] *Pierce* held unconstitutional a requirement that children attend public rather than private schools; *Meyer* held that a state could not prohibit the teaching of foreign languages to young children. In *Griswold* the Court said that these cases relied on a constitutionally protected interest, conveniently labeled "privacy," that was identical to the interest in the contraceptive case.

In one view *Griswold* tortures these precedents. Both were old-fashioned substantive due process cases, which emphasized interference "with the calling of modern language teachers . . . and with the power of parents to control the education of their own." In this view the most one can fairly find in *Meyer* and *Pierce* is a principle about freedom of inquiry, rather narrower than a principle of privacy. Yet one can say with equal force that *Griswold* identifies for us the true privacy principle of *Meyer* and *Pierce*, in the way that the abortion funding cases identify the true principle of *Roe v. Wade*. Just as hermeneutic originalism emphasizes the creativity that is involved when judges impute to the framers a set of intentions, so the retrospective approach to neutral principles must recognize the extensive creativity exercised by a judge when he or she imputes to a precedent "the" principle that justifies both the precedent and the judge's present holding.

A second example is *Brandenburg v. Ohio.*[92] The state of Ohio had prosecuted a leader of the Ku Klux Klan for violating its criminal syndicalism statute, which prohibited advocating the propriety of violence as a means of political reform. The Court held that the conviction violated the first amendment, which, according to the decision, permits punishment of

89. 381 U.S. 479 (1965).
90. 268 U.S. 510 (1925).
91. 262 U.S. 390 (1923).
92. 395 U.S. 444 (1969).

advocacy of illegal conduct only when "such advocacy is directed to inciting or producing imminent lawless action and is likely to incite or produce such action." Remarkably, the Court derived this test from *Dennis v. United States*, in which the Court upheld the convictions of leaders of the Communist Party for violating a federal sedition law.[93] This reading is, to say the least, an innovative interpretation of *Dennis*, which explicitly stated a different test—"the gravity of the 'evil,' discounted by its probability"—that left the decision largely to the jury.[94] A dispassionate observer would find it hard to reconcile the results in *Dennis* and *Brandenburg* without invoking the extralegal point that Cold War hysteria obviously affected the 1951 decision in *Dennis*. Again the requirement of retrospective neutrality may be satisfied if we interpret *Brandenburg's* use of *Dennis* as the creative reworking of precedents within authorized bounds.

The examples illustrate a general point. In a legal system with a relatively extensive body of precedent and well-developed techniques of legal reasoning, it will always be possible to show how today's decision is consistent with the relevant past ones, but, conversely, it will also always be possible to show how today's decision is inconsistent with the precedents. This symmetry, of course, drains "consistency" of any normative content.

The difficulties with neutral principles theory are on a par with the problems in understanding originalism that were noted earlier. Understanding the intentions of the framers requires a special kind of creative re-creation of the past; the creativity involved in such a re-creation dashes any hopes that originalism can effectively constrain judicial decisions, because many alternative re-creations of the framers' intentions on any given issue are always possible. In the same way, the result of the inquiry into neutral principles theory indicates that, although it is possible to discuss a given decision's consistency with previous precedents, requiring consistency of this kind similarly fails to constrain judges sufficiently and thereby fails to advance the underlying liberal project.

This critique points the way to a more refined version—what I will term the craft interpretation—of the neutral principles theorists' calls for con-

---

93. 341 U.S. 494 (1951).

94. *Brandenburg* applied a categorical test that looks to the character of the words uttered—they must be an "incitement" and nothing else—and to the immediate circumstances in which they are uttered. *Dennis* used an approach that is explicitly more variable: Speech that very likely would lead to a less serious evil might be punished, as might speech that had a small probability of leading to an extremely serious evil. Of course, if categories proliferated, the *Brandenburg* approach would blend into the *Dennis* one. See Chapter 9.

sistency. The failings of this alternative bring out the underlying reasons why the demand for consistency cannot do the job expected of it.

Every decision reworks its precedents. A decision picks up some threads that received little emphasis before and stresses them. It deprecates what seemed important before by emphasizing the factual setting of the precedents. The techniques are well-known; indeed, learning them is at the core of legal education. But they are techniques. This recognition suggests that we attempt to define consistency as a matter of craft. When push comes to shove, adherents of neutral principles simply offer us lyrical descriptions of the sense of professionalism in lieu of sharper characterizations of the constraints on judges. For example, Charles Black attempts to resolve the question whether law can rely on neutral principles by depicting "the art of law" living between the two poles of subjective preference and objective validation in much the same way that "the art of music has its life somewhere between traffic noise and a tuning fork—more disciplined by far than the one, with an unfathomably complex inner discipline of its own, far richer than the other, with inexhaustible variety of resource."[95] The difficulty then is to specify the limits to craft. One limit may be that a judge cannot lie about the precedents, for example by grossly mischaracterizing the facts.[96] Black adds that "decision [must] be taken in knowledge of and with consideration of certainly known facts of public life."[97] Clearly these limits are not terribly restrictive.

If we cannot specify limits to craft, perhaps we could identify some decisions that are within and some that are outside the limits, in order to provide the basis for an inductive and intuitive generalization. The limits of craft, however, are so broad that in any interesting case any reasonably skilled lawyer can reach whatever result he or she wants.[98] The craft interpretation thus fails to constrain the results that a reasonably skilled judge can reach and leaves the judge free to enforce his or her personal values, as long as the opinions supporting those values are well written. Such an outcome is inconsistent with the requirements of the liberal tradition in that, once again, the demand for neutral principles fails in any appreciable way to limit the possibility of judicial tyranny.

95. Charles Black, *Decision according to Law* 81 (1981). See also id., pp. 21–24; Sandalow, "Constitutional Interpretation."

96. See, e.g., Dershowitz and Ely, *"Harris v. New York"*; Tushnet, "Critical Legal Studies and Constitutional Law," pp. 631–33.

97. Black, *Decision according to Law*, p. 82.

98. Much turns here on the definition of *interesting*. Cases decided by the Supreme Court would fit any reasonable definition. See Frederick Schauer, "Easy Cases," 58 *Southern California Law Review* 399, 408–10 (1985). See also the appendix to this chapter.

The best example of this problem is *Roe v. Wade*. It seems to be generally agreed that, as a matter of simple craft, Justice Blackmun's opinion for the Court was dreadful.[99] The central issue before the Court was whether a pregnant woman has a constitutionally protected interest in terminating her pregnancy. When his opinion reached that issue, Justice Blackmun simply listed a number of cases in which "a right of personal privacy, or a guarantee of certain areas or zones of privacy," had been recognized. Then he said, "This right of privacy, whether it be founded in the 14th Amendment's concept of personal liberty . . . or . . . in the Ninth Amendment's reservation of rights to the people, is broad enough to encompass the woman's decision whether or not to terminate her pregnancy."[100] This may well fail to satisfy the current requirements of the craft.

The conclusion that we are to draw, however, is either uninteresting or irrelevant to constitutional theory. Insofar as *Roe* gives us evidence, we can conclude that Justice Blackmun is a terrible judge. The point of constitutional theory, though, would seem to be to keep judges in line. If the result in *Roe* can be defended by judges more skilled than Justice Blackmun, the requirements of craft would mean only that skillful judges can do things, and can survive professional criticism, that less skillful ones cannot. For example, John Hart Ely argues that although *Roe* is beyond acceptable limits, *Griswold* is within them (perhaps near the edge).[101] Justice Douglas' opinion for the Court in *Griswold* identified a number of constitutional provisions that in his view explicitly protect one or another aspect of personal privacy. The opinion then noted that the Court had in the past protected interests closely related to those expressly protected. By arguing that those "penumbral" interests overlap in the area of marital use of contraceptives, Justice Douglas could hold the statute unconstitutional.

If *Griswold* is acceptable we need only repeat its method in *Roe*. Indeed, Justice Douglas followed just that course in a brilliant concurring opinion. Even if *Griswold* is rejected as well, skilled lawyers could rewrite *Roe* to defend its outcome.[102] There is in fact a cottage industry of constitutional law scholars who write revised opinions for controversial deci-

99. See, e.g., John Hart Ely, "The Wages of Crying Wolf: A Comment on *Roe v. Wade*," 82 *Yale Law Journal* 920 (1973); Richard Epstein, "Substantive Due Process by Any Other Name: The Abortion Cases," 1973 *Supreme Court Review* 159; Laurence Tribe, "Toward a Model of Roles in the Due Process of Life and Law," 87 *Harvard Law Review* 1, 2–5 (1973).

100. 410 U.S. 113, 153 (1973).

101. Ely, "Wages," pp. 929–30.

102. See, e.g., Donald Regan, "Rewriting *Roe v. Wade*," 77 *Michigan Law Review* 1569 (1979).

sions.[103] Thus, even the craft version of neutrality in application collapses. Neutral principles, like other theories, are supposed to guarantee that judges do not do whatever they want. The craft version means that untalented judges will not be able to get away with whatever they want, but talented judges will be able to use the tools of the craft to do what they want. It is not easy to see what this theory has to recommend it, beyond its self-interested defense of elitist academic lawyers.

The other difficulty with the craft interpretation runs deeper. Craft limitations make sense only if we agree on what the craft is. But consider the craft of "writing novels." Its practice includes Trollope writing *The Eustace Diamonds,* Joyce writing *Finnegan's Wake,* and Mailer writing *The Executioner's Song.*[104] We might think of Justice Blackmun's opinion in *Roe* as an innovation akin to Joyce's or Mailer's. It is the totally unreasoned judicial opinion. To say that it does not look like Justice Powell's decision in some other case is like saying that a Cubist "portrait" does not portray its subject in the manner that a member of the academy would paint it. The observation is true but irrelevant to the enterprise in which the artist or judge was engaged and to our ultimate assessment of his or her product.

We can now survey our progress in the attempt to define "neutral principles." The proposed definitions left us with judges who can enforce their personal values unconstrained by the neutrality requirement. The craft interpretation may seem plausible because it appeals to an intuitive sense that the institution of judging involves people who are guided by and committed to general rules applied consistently. But the very notions of generality and consistency can be specified only by reference to an established institutional setting. We can know what we mean by "acting consistently" only if we understand the institution of judging in our society. Thus, if the theory of neutral principles proves unable to satisfy its demand for rule-guided judicial decision making in a way that can constrain or define the judicial institution, in the final analysis it is the institution—or our conception of it—that constrains the concept of rule guidedness.

103. See, e.g., Louis Henkin, "Shelley v. Kraemer: Notes for a Revised Opinion," 110 *University of Pennsylvania Law Review* 473 (1962); Louis Pollak, "Racial Discrimination and Judicial Integrity," 108 *University of Pennsylvania Law Review* 1 (1959).

104. Dworkin observes that a person asked to add one chapter "in the best possible way" to a collaborative novel-in-progress faces limits similar to those that precedents place on judges. Ronald Dworkin, " 'Natural' Law Revisited," 34 *University of Florida Law Review* 165, 167 (1982). He fails to appreciate that, by disrupting our expectations about what fits best, the creative author may force us both to reinterpret all that has gone before and to expand our understanding of what a "novel" is. For additional discussion, see Chapter 3.

Consider the following multiple choice question: "Which pair of numbers comes next in the series 1, 3, 5, 7 . . . ? (a) 9, 11; (b) 11, 13; (c) 25, 18."[105] It is easy to show that any of the answers is correct. The first is correct if the rule generating the series is "List the odd numbers"; the second is correct if the rule is "List the odd prime numbers"; and the third is correct if a more complex rule generates the series.[106] Thus, if asked to follow the underlying rule—the "principle" of the series—we can justify a tremendous range of divergent answers by constructing the rule so that it generates the answer we want. As the Legal Realists showed, the result obtains for legal as well as mathematical rules.[107]

105. This example is suggested by Winch, *Idea of Social Science*, at 29–32, who draws on Ludwig Wittgenstein, *Philosophical Investigations* (G.E.M. Anscombe trans. 3d ed. 1958). See also "Spiro" (pseud.), "Elastic Aptitude Test," 8:4 *Games Magazine* 22–23 (Apr. 1984) (including the question "What are the next three terms in the following series? 1, 3, 5, 7, . . . , . . . , . . . " and defending the answer "8, 9, 10" by explaining that it is the series of positive numbers with the letter *e*).

106. One possible rule is $f(1) = 1$; for n greater than 1, if n is divisible by 5, then $f(n) = n^2$; if $(n - 1)$ is divisible by 5, then $f(n) = f(n - 1) - f(n - 2)$; if neither n nor $(n - 1)$ is divisible by 5, $f(n) = 2n - 1$.

Schauer, "Easy Cases," p. 427, responds to this example by "adding a number of other choices," including "(d) 9, 11, 13; . . . (i) Reggie Jackson, Babe Ruth; (j) Cleveland, Newark," and claiming that these answers are "clearly incorrect, at least in this world." This misunderstands the structure of the example. The issue confronting the test taker is not "Are these answers within the range of possible ones?" but is rather "Given that these answers are listed among the possible answers, how could a rational test giver think that they are in the ballpark so as to make it sensible to include them on the list of answers?"

A test taker could sensibly resolve that issue as to every one of the answers that Schauer thinks is obviously wrong. For example, given that "Cleveland, Newark" appears on the list, the test taker could reasonably think that the inclusion of these answers demonstrates that the test giver is a numerologist and would then convert the suggested answers to the corresponding number and develop an appropriate mathematical rule. As to "9, 11, 13," the test giver might be following a rule whereby *pair* means "three numbers," a possibility familiar in the philosophical literature from Nelson Goodman, *Fact, Fiction, and Forecast* 74–81 (2d ed. 1965), where it appears as *grue*, meaning "green until now, and blue hereafter." Or—the alternative I prefer—the test giver likes to play with words, notices that *pair* sounds like *pear*, and thinks that, as the numbers appear on a page, "9, 11, 13" looks like a pear.

The hypothetical in the text demonstrates that we cannot resolve the ambiguities by recourse to the meaning of the words *pair of numbers*; we must also know something about the social practice of giving tests. The hypothetical explanations of strange answers are cousins to, though not expressly derived from, the social practice of administering literacy tests to southern blacks in the 1950s. See also Sanford Levinson, "What Do Lawyers Know (And What Do They Do with Their Knowledge): Comments on Schauer and Moore," 58 *Southern California Law Review* 441, 449 n. 38 (1985).

107. This is a standard point in post-Wittgensteinian philosophy. See, e.g., *Wittgenstein: To Follow a Rule* (Steven Holtzman and Christopher Leich eds. 1981); Saul Kripke, *Wittgenstein on Rules and Private Language* (1982).

Yet there is something askew in this conclusion. After all, we know that no test maker would accept (*c*) as an answer, and indeed we can be fairly confident that test makers would not include both (*a*) and (*b*) as possible answers, because the underlying rules that generate them are so obvious as to make the question fatally ambiguous.[108] Another example may sharpen the point. The examination for people seeking driver's licenses in the District of Columbia once included this question: "What is responsible for most automobile accidents? (*a*) The car; (*b*) the driver; (*c*) road conditions." Anyone who does not know immediately that the answer is (*b*) does not understand what the testing enterprise is all about.[109]

In these examples we know something about the rule to follow only because we are familiar with the social practices of intelligence testing and drivers' education. That is, the answer does not follow from a rule that can be uniquely identified without specifying something about the substantive practices. Similarly, although we can use standard techniques of legal argument to draw the conclusion from the decided cases that the Constitution requires substantial equality in the distribution of wealth (see Chapter 3), we know that no judge will in the near future draw that conclusion. The failure to reach that result is not ensured because the practice of "following rules" or neutral application of the principles inherent in the decided cases precludes a judge from doing so. Rather it is ensured because judges in contemporary America are selected in a way that keeps them from thinking that such arguments make sense. This branch of the argument thus makes a sociological point about neutral principles. Neither the principles nor any reconstructed version of a theory that takes following rules as its focus can be neutral in the sense required by the liberal tradition, because taken by itself, an injunction to follow the rules tells us nothing of substance. If such a theory constrains judges, it does so only because they have implicitly accepted some version of what the rules in controverted cases ought to be before they apply those rules in the case at hand.[110]

108. But see Winch, *Idea of Social Science*, pp. 30–31 (assuming that the problem has no ambiguity). One can also imagine a fiendish test maker regarding (*c*) as the correct answer precisely because the ambiguity precludes the test taker from deciding between (*a*) or (*b*).

109. Coaching the Scholastic Aptitude Test is geared to this way of understanding multiple choice tests. See David Owen, *None of the Above: Beyond the Myth of Scholastic Aptitude* 121–40 (1985) (describing method of analyzing choices by considering how "Joe Bloggs" would assess them). See also Charles Taylor, *Philosophy and the Human Sciences* 29–30 (1985) (survey research into goals and values must consider "how did we design our questionnaire," which relied on implicit understanding of those goals and values in its formulation of questions to ask).

110. Recent work in literary theory emphasizes the role that interpretive communities play in determining the authoritative meaning of texts, and some of that work questions the

The theory of neutral principles is attractive because it affirms the openness of the courts to all reasonable arguments drawn from the decided cases. But if the courts are indeed open to such arguments, the theory allows judges to do whatever they want. If it is only a consequence of the pressures exerted by a highly developed, deeply entrenched, homeostatic social structure that judges seem to eschew conclusions grossly at odds with the values of liberal capitalism, sociological analysis ought to destroy the attraction of the theory. Principles are "neutral" only in the sense that they are, as a matter of contingent fact, unchallenged, and the contingencies have obvious historical limits.[111]

Conclusion: The Republican Tradition

The critiques of originalism and neutral principles have led to the same point. To be coherent each theory requires that our understandings of social institutions be stable. Originalism requires that judges be able to trace historical continuities between the institutions that the framers knew and those that contemporary judges know. The theory of neutral principles requires that judges be able to rely on a shared conception of the proper role of judicial reasoning. The critiques have argued that there are no determinate continuities derivable from history or legal principle. Judges must choose which conceptions to rely on. Their choice is constrained, but explaining the constraints demands a sociological understanding of the ways the system within which they operate is deeply entrenched and resistant to change.[112] If this sociological understanding is to have not merely descriptive validity but normative force as well, we find ourselves drawn into the domain of the republican tradition, in which variable individual conceptions are seen to be derivative from— and subsidiary to—an underlying societal perspective.

---

basis on which an interpretive community gains its authority. For introductions, see Stanley Fish, *Is There a Text in This Class?: The Authority of Interpretive Communities* (1980); *The Politics of Interpretation* (William Mitchell ed. 1983); Christopher Butler, *Interpretation, Deconstruction, and Ideology: An Introduction to Some Current Issues in Literary Theory* (1984). A helpful discussion of some of the ambiguities in Fish's arguments is David Luban, "Fish v. Fish or, Some Realism about Idealism," 7 *Cardozo Law Review* 693 (1986).

111. On the contingency of neutral categories, see Steven Collins, "Categories, Concepts, or Predicaments? Remarks on Mauss's Use of Philosophical Terminology," in *The Category of the Person* 46 (Michael Carrithers, Steven Collins, and Steven Lukes eds. 1985); Louis Dumont, "A Modified View of Our Origins: The Christian Beginnings of Modern Individualism," id., p. 93; John Comaroff and Simon Roberts, *Rules and Processes* (1981) (stressing the construction of disputes by rules).

112. See Paul Brest, "Interpretation and Interest," 34 *Stanford Law Review* 765, 770–71 (1982) (offering brief sociology of coercive creation of interpretive communities).

The problem faced by both judge and constitutional theorist is how to find or construct the requisite shared conceptions. This problem is analogous to the interpretive difficulties that confront us in many aspects of our social experience. Consider an ordinary conversation between two people. Alice hears Arthur use the word *arbogast*. She thinks she knows what he means, but as the conversation continues Alice realizes that Arthur is using the word in a way that comes to seem a little strange. She interrupts, so that Arthur can explain what he means. Instead things get worse. His explanation shows that his entire vocabulary rests on the way that he has lived until that moment. Because Arthur's life is by definition different from Alice's, she finds herself left with only an illusory understanding of what Arthur says.[113] Her task is then to identify the point at which she can "think her way into" Arthur's life, so that she can understand what he means by understanding how he developed.[114] In this story "understanding what Arthur means when he says *arbogast*" plays the role of "following the rule in *Roe v. Wade*."

The question is how to overcome these gaps in understanding. Of course we go along each day with some taken-for-granted understandings of the world. But anyone can disrupt what is taken for granted simply by placing it in question. Usually such challenges have a limited scope, so that the challengers can be viewed by the rest of us as deviant in that limited way but as otherwise part of the community of understanding. Sometimes, however, the challenges are total, producing a sense that our world has come apart at the seams (see the appendix to this chapter). Courts are institutions in which challenges to the taken-for-granted may be made as a matter of course. If society is to be stable, those challenges must be rebuffed in ways that preserve the shared societal understandings.

Here the parable of the conversation is central. As experience has taught us, Alice and Arthur need not give up in despair; if they keep talking they can build bridges between their two idiosyncratic dialects. Just as the historian can understand the past through hermeneutic efforts, we can understand each other by creating a community of understanding. The parable also reminds us that we cannot assume that people who talk to each other are part of such a community merely because they seem to be speaking the same language.[115] Similarly, communities of understand-

113. See generally Winch, *Idea of Social Science*. For a collection discussing the issues Winch raises, see *Rationality* (Bryan Wilson ed. 1970).

114. See Taylor, *Philosophy and Human Sciences*, pp. 125–26, for a description of this process, and Kammen, *Spheres of Liberty*, for a case study.

115. Bruce Ackerman's argument, *Social Justice and the Liberal State* (1980), is flawed by the assumption that one can think of a dialogue without having a prior understanding of

ing are not defined by geographic boundaries. They are painstakingly created by people who enter into certain kinds of relations and share certain kinds of experiences.[116]

The republican tradition argued that such relations demand substantial equality of power and of access to material resources; others identify the experiences as confrontations with scarcity or similar natural kinds of experiences.[117] For our purposes we need not identify exactly what the prerequisites for a community of understanding are. It is enough to recognize that we must develop a shared system of meanings to make either originalism or neutral principles coherent. But in developing such a system we will destroy the need for constitutional theory: the shared system, not the artificial design of our governing institutions, will constrain lawmakers. In the end we may decide to retrieve the liberal tradition in

---

the language in which the dialogue is conducted and therefore of the society in which the dialogue occurs. Ackerman notices the difficulty, id., pp. 71–74, but assumes erroneously that he need not discuss it.

Schauer, "Easy Cases," p. 418, commits a similar error. He asks us to imagine a person fluent in English "who knows nothing of the history, politics, law, or culture of the United States. If we were to show this person a copy of the Constitution, . . . that person [would] glean from that collection of marks on a piece of paper alone at least some rudimentary idea of how this government works and what types of relationships exist between the central government and the states, between the different branches of government, and between individuals and government." See also Sotirios Barber, *On What the Constitution Means* 15–16 (1984).

With respect to federalism, the separation of powers, and the relation between individuals and state governments, however, Schauer is probably simply wrong. Much about federalism and the separation of powers cannot be found in the Constitution; the role of political parties, the structure of the administrative bureaucracy, the relationships that the President and Congress have worked out, all are central features of "how this government works" that cannot be found in, or even readily inferred from, the Constitution. Nor is it easy to see from the text of the Constitution that most of the guarantees of the Bill of Rights protect citizens against their states; the due process clause of the fourteenth amendment is the textual source of those protections, and it is not apparent from the terms of that clause that it has anything to do with things like freedom of expression. See note 30. See also Sandalow, "Constitutional Interpretation," pp. 1039–43, for a more complete discussion.

For further discussion of dialogic approaches to constitutional law, see Chapter 4.

116. For theoretical discussions of the processes by which individuals constitute social groups, see *Advances in Sociological Theory and Methodology: Toward an Integration of Micro- and Macro-Sociologies* (Klaus Knorr-Cetina and Aaron Cicourel eds. 1981).

117. Jurgen Habermas, "Toward a Theory of Communicative Competence," in *Recent Sociology No. 2*, 138 (Hans Peter Drietzel ed. 1970), discussed in Giddens, *Central Problems*, pp. 65–69; Keat, *Politics of Social Theory*, pp. 180–90; McCarthy, *Critical Theory*, pp.272–357; Jean-Paul Sartre, *Critique of Dialectical Reason* (1976); George Lakoff and Mark Johnson, *Metaphors We Live By* 56–60 (1980). See also Michael McPherson, "Mill's Moral Theory and the Problem of Preference Change," 92 *Ethics* 252, 264–65 (1982).

order to affirm its insistence on the otherness of other people, but we can do so only after we have thought through the implications of our dependence on one another.

Appendix: Textualism in Constitutional Theory

This chapter has challenged the view that recourse to the meaning of the Constitution as revealed by the framers' intent is an adequate constitutional theory. This appendix addresses the contention that some provisions of the Constitution need not be interpreted but need only be applied, because they are entirely clear, because the meaning of the text itself is directly available to courts without interpreting it, or because the text itself excludes enough possible interpretations to reduce the dangers thought to lurk in unrestrained approaches to constitutional adjudication. I will call this contention textualism. Unsophisticated textualism offers little of substance, but Robert Nagel and Douglas Laycock have recently offered sophisticated versions that raise interesting questions.[118] Ultimately, however, textualism suffers from the same flaws that the attacks on originalism have exposed.

Unsophisticated textualism contends that some provisions of the Constitution are so unambiguous that, were Congress to violate them, judges could almost instantaneously and without analysis identify the violation. Typical examples involve what might be called the "mathematical" provisions: that the President's term is four years,[119] that the President must be at least thirty-five years old,[120] and the like. If Congress voted for and the President signed a statute extending the term to six years or for the duration of a national emergency, or if the President of the Senate directed that votes cast in the electoral college for a sixteen-year-old guru be

118. Robert Nagel, "Interpretation and Importance in Constitutional Law: A Re-assessment of Judicial Restraint," 25 *Nomos: Liberal Democracy* 181 (J. Roland Pennock and John Chapman eds. 1983); Laycock, "Taking Constitutions Seriously." See also Frank Easterbrook, "Statutes' Domains," 50 *University of Chicago Law Review* 533 (1983). Stephen Carter, "Constitutional Adjudication and the Indeterminate Text: A Preliminary Defense of an Imperfect Muddle," 94 *Yale Law Journal* 821 (1985), offers a similar argument focusing on the structural provisions creating the separation of powers. But his argument is so heavily qualified, and concedes so much to the antitextualist arguments, that it is unconvincing on its face. Significantly, Carter writes near the conclusion of his article, "Some portion of the Constitution *must* provide . . . a structure within which the intermittent judicial policymaking can occur and yet be confined." Id., p. 864 (emphasis added). There is a lot of political theory and faith bound up in that *must*. A less qualified version is Peter Shane, "Conventionalism in Constitutional Interpretation and the Place of Administrative Agencies," 36 *American University Law Review* 573 (1987).

119. U.S. Constitution, art. II, §1, cl. 1.

120. Id., cl. 5.

counted,[121] "everybody" would know that the Constitution had been violated. A theory that authorizes judges to invalidate *these* actions could not possibly allow judges willfully to invalidate actions with which they simply disagree. It is said that textualism is just such a theory.

In such an unsophisticated form, textualism is obviously vulnerable in several respects.[122] First, Frank Easterbrook has noted that the mathematical provisions, like all the others, have "reasons, goals, values, and the like" behind them. The age limit might have been imposed "as a percentage of average life expectancy"—to guarantee, for example, that the President had both abundant practical experience before election and relatively few chances to interfere in national politics after leaving office—or "as a minimum number of years after puberty"—to guarantee, for example, a sufficient level of maturity in the President without substantially narrowing the pool of eligible candidates.[123] In this view the words "thirty-five Years" in the Constitution are simply the shorthand the framers used to express their more complex policies, and we could replace them by "fifty years" or "thirty years"[124] without impairing the integrity of the constitutional structure.[125]

Second, the assertedly clear provisions are located in a document that contains a number of other provisions. A court could readily take its task to be interpreting the Constitution as a whole to see its bearing on the statute under review.[126] Here we must imagine the circumstances in which the actions said to violate the clear provisions might occur.[127] Suppose that the guru's supporters sincerely claim that their religion includes among its tenets a belief in reincarnation. They argue that even by the

121. Id., amend. XII.

122. I simply note in addition that justiciability doctrines might keep the courts from acting. Who would have standing to challenge the extension of the President's term, or the counting of the votes? Compare Valley Forge Christian College v. Americans United, 454 U.S. 464 (1982), with Youngstown Sheet & Tube Co. v. Sawyer, 343 U.S. 579 (1952). Even if someone has standing these contentions may raise political questions. See Gilligan v. Morgan, 413 U.S. 1 (1973). Cf. United States v. Richardson, 418 U.S. 166 (1974). This is not to say that one cannot imagine a justiciable lawsuit challenging the hypothesized actions, only that adjudication of challenges on the merits is not assured.

123. Easterbrook, "Statutes' Domains," p. 536.

124. I rely on Easterbrook's calculations for these figures.

125. Easterbrook does not endorse this argument, for reasons to be discussed and criticized shortly.

126. Schauer, "Easy Cases," p. 433, argues that "almost all free speech claims are outside the range of claims allowed by the fourth amendment." Surely, though, it is easy to construct arguments that what we now cast as free speech violations "actually" are searches (of the mind, a part of the "person") within the fourth amendment.

127. The importance of the fact that we must *imagine* these circumstances will be discussed shortly.

narrowest definition of "age," their guru is well over thirty-five years old although the guru emerged from the most recent mother's womb only sixteen years ago. Further, if the President of the Senate had rejected their definition of "age," she would have established a particular religious view about the definition of age and violated their rights under the free exercise clause, as well as their right grounded in democratic theory to choose those who will govern them.[128] The same would be true if the courts overturned the decision made by the political branches.[129]

Thus, the reason that the provisions at issue seem to be clear is the unlikelihood under present circumstances that the political branches would find it necessary to violate them. With that reason in mind, we can understand that what is at stake is the nature of our community, within which the meanings of some words are taken to be uncontroversial and the meanings of others are the subjects of deep, if not essential, contestation. The hypothetical situations just described are designed to bring into view circumstances in which linguistic contestation might be extended into presently uncontroversial areas. The fragmentation of the linguistic community by political discord is central to those circumstances.[130]

Unsophisticated textualism rests on implicit claims about the nature of our political community. It is thus related to the conservatism of most contemporary right-wing publicists and, in another way, to the republican tradition. Its role in contemporary conservatism is to preserve a conservative commitment to constitutionalism in a political context that makes conservatives want to defend majoritarianism. In the recent past constitutional law has been used to advance the goals of contemporary liberalism. This has forced conservatives into the awkward position of being somewhat inconstant defenders of populism (see Chapter 4, appen-

---

128. See Powell v. McCormack, 395 U.S. 486, 547 (1969).

129. Schauer, "Easy Cases," pp. 420–23, thinks that he addresses these cases by discussing the "argument from weird cases." See also Kenney Hegland, "Goodbye to Deconstruction," 58 *Southern California Law Review* 1203, 1208–10 (1985). Schauer conceives of the weirdness as residing in their mathematical improbability or their political pointlessness. My arguments and Easterbrook's provide the political context in which the asserted weirdness disappears. When that occurs, the linguistic constraints on which Schauer pins so much disappear as well. Or, to put it another way, the cases are weird up to the moment at which someone finds it worthwhile to pursue them. Then we see that what we thought were constraints built into the language were only constraints built into our accepted ways of doing things. It is emphatically not that the weird cases test the fringes of concepts that have a settled core of meaning, as distinct from concepts that exist within a contingently stabilized context. Hegland, pp. 1208–9 n. 19, confines to a footnote his recognition of the fact that the concepts are contingently stabilized by "shared intuitions" without acknowledging the importance of the sociology that must justify those intuitions.

130. This is the real content of the definition of those "particularly extreme situation[s]" which, to Schauer, exemplify the weird cases. Schauer, "Easy Cases," p. 424.

dix), claiming in broad terms that it is impermissible in a democratic republic for courts to displace judgments made by representative legislators. Their populism in turn requires conservatives to develop some theory that preserves their commitment to limited government. Unsophisticated textualism serves that end perfectly: it allows conservatives to agree that there are constitutional limits on legislative power that courts can enforce, thus remaining within the liberal tradition, while vociferously denouncing the courts for doing anything at all, because in our society the only enforceable limits unsophisticated textualism acknowledges are not about to be violated.

Yet conservatives cannot readily explain why violations are unlikely to occur. Easterbrook comes close to recognizing this but understandably pulls back. He acknowledges that "if the meaning of language depends on a community of understanding among readers, none is 'right.' " He then immediately concludes by invoking necessity in an explicitly conservative form: "Unless the community . . . is to engage in ceaseless (and thus pointless) babble—and unless, moreover, the community is willing to extend almost boundless discretion to judges," something more is needed.[131] There are two related difficulties with this position. First, the critique of unsophisticated textualism claims that radical indeterminacy of meaning is, within a liberal community, inevitable. That critique is not squarely met by saying that indeterminacy gives boundless discretion to judges. That judges have boundless discretion demonstrates the incoherence of the liberal tradition; it does not vitiate the critique.

Second, the "babble" that Easterbrook fears need be neither ceaseless nor pointless. He assumes that the community of readers is well-defined. Those who offer alternative resolutions of indeterminacy of meaning—the guru's followers—either are claiming that they are not part of the community of readers in which their interpretations are rejected or, what amounts to the same thing, are attempting to reconstitute the community quite literally on their terms.[132] Easterbrook thus falls into the trap that

131. Easterbrook, "Statutes' Domains," p. 536.
132. Earlier Easterbrook also relies on the assumption that a community of readers exists. Id., pp. 533–34 n. 2. He writes that "meaning lies in shared reactions to text. If readers have a common understanding of structure they may decipher meaning accurately." The guru's followers try to use "our" understanding of structure, as it derives from texts other than the thirty-five-year-old clause, to create a new but still shared reaction to that particular text. There is nothing bizarre about that effort. In the same note Easterbrook again sounds the theme of conservative despair: "If statutes' words do not convey meaning and bind judges, why should judges' words bind or even interest us?" I make no claims about why the judges should bind us, but surely their words should interest us for many reasons, not the least of which is that folks with guns often stand ready to back up the judges' words.

awaits all conservatives since the emergence of bourgeois society: he must assume that a single community of readers exists, although critics of the liberal tradition claim that that community is continually being created by acts of will and can be reconstituted by (only!) choosing differently. The "babble" would cease if the community were reconstituted, and that is its point.[133]

Robert Nagel draws on the republican tradition for a more powerful defense of sophisticated textualism. He begins by noticing that as an empirical fact large parts of the Constitution "draw [their] meaning from practice rather than from interpretation." When this happens the meaning "is not fully formalized, articulated, or closed. It is a recognition based on everyday experience." The practice continues "partly because of habit, familiarity, and a sense of normalcy.[134] This is the language of the republican tradition. The text constrains all of us, including judges, because we find ourselves, as a matter of contingent but unavoidable fact, located in a specific community with its own history from which we cannot completely escape. To Nagel, the "uninterpreted Constitution" is durable because it expresses the nature of that historical community.

The flaws in Nagel's position appear when he tries to pin down why so much of the Constitution is uninterpreted. The only reason that the uninterpreted Constitution is durable is that no social group has arisen to challenge those parts of our community whose nature the uninterpreted Constitution expresses. Spinning out hypothetical scenarios in which challenges of that sort could occur is important because the scenarios demonstrate that durability rests on contingent social facts that are indeed avoidable.

Nagel's three reasons for the durability of the uninterpreted Constitution are informality, generality, and caution.[135] Informality promotes durability by diffusing potential conflicts. A person who justifies his or her action today by invoking an informal norm may act somewhat differently tomorrow and will never have to face the charge of acting inconsistently. In the ill-defined space marked out by informal norms, people may cooperate often enough so that stable practices develop. In contrast, formal norms reduced to words and doctrines create winners and losers, who develop stakes in their "positions." Generality, like informality, promotes stability by giving people who might disagree some common ground.

---

133. See also Owen Fiss, "Objectivity and Interpretation," 34 *Stanford Law Review* 739, 746–47 (1982).

134. Nagel, "Interpretation," pp. 187–88. See also Carter, "Constitutional Adjudication"; Stephen Carter, "The Right Questions in the Creation of Constitutional Meaning," 66 *Boston University Law Review* 71 (1986).

135. Nagel, "Interpretation," pp. 193–98.

"Because the meaning inherent in the practice settles so little, many can abide it."[136] Again in contrast, interpretation requires that meaning be pinned down; it cuts away much of the common ground by specifying with some precision what some constitutional provision means. Finally, caution promotes durability by removing some potentially destabilizing conflicts from the arena of legal disputes.

Nagel's invocation of caution as a reason for durability indicates that his position ultimately requires "agreement that certain issues ought not to be contested." The existence of such agreement is a prerequisite to his conclusion that interpretation, by rejecting generality, "leads to the illusion . . . that nearly everything is subject to challenge."[137] Nagel is of course correct in observing that such agreement has in fact existed concerning the uninterpreted Constitution. That agreement makes it essential for him to explain why no agreement has existed concerning the rest of the Constitution. Probably the main reason for the durability of the uninterpreted Constitution is that subcommunities in "our" society have not found it worth their while to challenge its provisions. The interpreted Constitution consists in all those provisions that have become the objects of political contention. They are therefore interesting to those who see the Constitution as the liberal tradition's effort to resolve political contention. The difficulty with Nagel's argument is that provisions can be transferred from the uninterpreted Constitution to the interpreted one at will—not, as he seems to think, at the will of the judges but at the will of those groups in the society who find it politically useful to get the courts involved in political strife.[138]

Although most contemporary political liberals are comfortable with nontextualist theories of the Constitution, Douglas Laycock has offered a politically liberal textualism which reflects his understanding that the prevalent complacency about nontextualist approaches is unwarranted and which embodies his effort to retrieve the text of the Constitution from the center-right. Unfortunately, his theory will not work.

Laycock's textualism requires that every part of the Constitution be given meaning and be enforceable by the courts. In particular, the ninth amendment, which states that "the enumeration in the Constitution, of certain rights, shall not be construed to deny or disparage others retained by the people," must have meaning. Similarly the clause in the fourteenth amendment barring states from enforcing laws that "abridge the privileges and immunities of citizens of the United States" must mean something. To have specific meanings, both provisions must refer

136. Id., p. 196.
137. Id., pp. 196–97.
138. See id., p. 198, for Nagel's recognition of this point.

to unenumerated rights—and, because enumerated rights are enforceable by the federal courts, it would "disparage" the unenumerated ones to deny judicial enforcement.[139] Laycock argues that the unenumerated rights can be identified by looking to other provisions of the Constitution, including, in the case of the "privileges and immunities" clause, the ninth amendment. Each of the other provisions regulates a more or less narrow sphere of governmental activity, but each is also justified by a set of broader values. For example, one clause requires freedom of navigation by prohibiting Congress from requiring ships bound for one state to enter or pay duties to another. According to Laycock, this narrow clause identifies a broader value of national unity. The courts cannot interpret this clause alone as a guarantee of national unity, but the broader value can inform judicial interpretation of the ninth and fourteenth amendments so as to authorize the courts to enforce a general right to travel.[140]

Laycock develops his textualism with elegance and care.[141] The difficulty with his textualism is that it allows us to proliferate underlying values essentially at will and then provides no constraints on the courts in choosing how to accommodate this plurality of values in any particular case.

Laycock himself suggests the flaw in his approach. He identifies a set of "good" values in the Constitution: national unity, individualism, personal autonomy, and private association. He mentions that there are countervailing "bad" values, such as state sovereignty. Private property and the social control thereof could be added to the list.[142] And then, alas, the game is over, for every exercise of governmental power will intrude on at least one of these values.

Laycock's discussion of state sovereignty illustrates this difficulty. The ninth and fourteenth amendments are to be construed by referring to specific provisions of the Constitution. Laycock argues that the value of state sovereignty operates differently. It is a "countervailing value . . . of constitutional dimension, and courts must give effect to *specific constitutional provisions* that state or imply limitations on the protec-

139. Laycock, "Taking Constitutions Seriously," pp. 349–50.

140. Id., pp. 363–64.

141. For example, he anticipates and explains why he rejects the objection that each clause serves only its own purposes: That objection has force insofar as the courts enforce the clauses themselves but is irrelevant when the courts utilize the clauses to construe the ninth and fourteenth amendments. Id., pp. 365, 370.

142. The state action requirement provides the textual basis for direct judicial control over private property, because private property exists in the manner that it does only as a result of the protections the state gives it. See generally Tribe, *American Constitutional Law*, pp. 1147–74.

tion given a constitutional valùe."[143] State sovereignty, because it does not deal with the "rights of the people" referred to in the ninth amendment, cannot be used "to protect the liberties or immunities of governmental entities.[144] It is instead just a limitation of the rights enforced through the ninth amendment. This way of looking at state sovereignty is not compelling. The generalized protection of state sovereignty in the Constitution rests on values related to individual rights to the same extent that the generalized protections of individualism, autonomy, and private property do. As we saw in the Introduction, state sovereignty enhances—or ought to enhance—the citizenry's control over important decisions that affect their lives and serves—or ought to serve—the end of connecting individuals to the public life of their communities. In this view, which is at least as compatible with the text as is Laycock's, state sovereignty is not a specific limitation on unenumerated rights but is rather a value that must inform the construction of the ninth and fourteenth amendments themselves.

Laycock adopts his view of state sovereignty for obvious reasons. Where there are countervailing values of constitutional dimension, the courts must resolve the tension by balancing the constitutional values.[145] Laycock could not get very far with his liberalism if all he could establish was that the courts have to balance the good values of individualism and autonomy against the bad one of state sovereignty. Thus, he criticizes the Court for "crippl[ing] enforcement of the fourteenth amendment in the name of" state sovereignty,[146] yet the pejorative characterization would be plainly unwarranted if state sovereignty simply had to be balanced against the enforcement of unenumerated rights. His discussion of the "extraordinarily difficult" abortion cases, which are hard because constitutional values must be balanced, is notably more restrained.[147]

There is another difficulty with Laycock's textualism: it would provide a basis on which the interventionist legislation of the welfare state could be held unconstitutional. One unenumerated right is the protection of private property. Statutes setting minimum wages interfere with private property, and national minimum wage laws interfere with state sovereignty.[148] The same can be said of statutes that prohibit discrimina-

143. Laycock, "Taking Constitutions Seriously," p. 364 (emphasis added).
144. Id., p. 366.
145. Id., pp. 364, 376.
146. Id., p. 365.
147. Id., p. 376.
148. See Lochner v. New York, 198 U.S. 45 (1905); Hammer v. Dagenhart, 247 U.S. 251 (1918). Laycock argues that these cases are wrong because "the Constitution explicitly

tion based on race and gender by private employers and places of business. Although he does not address this difficulty directly, Laycock's analysis suggests that he would have to rely on a right to autonomy and individualism, so that the courts would have a countervailing constitutional value to balance. Notice, however, how curious the right to autonomy and individualism must be to do the necessary work: it must amount to a right to have governments enact minimum wage and antidiscrimination laws. That is a nice idea, and many people might endorse such a right, but Laycock would have to stretch the text a great deal to find it there.[149]

Even if Laycock could find a textual basis for such rights to autonomy and antidiscrimination laws, there is a final and fatal difficulty: his endorsement of balancing as a judicial technique. He recognizes that when balancing occurs "it would be idle to pretend that the Constitution uniquely dictate[s] the Court's solution, or that the Court's views of sound policy [do] not influence its discretion."[150] Balancing might be acceptable to contemporary liberals so long as the courts must balance—perhaps juggle would be a better metaphor—good values like individualism and autonomy. But once the balls of state sovereignty, private property, and its social control are in the air, liberals are bound to worry that the courts will drop one of the values they like. By incorporating balancing as a central element in judicial technique, Laycock's textualism fails to satisfy the demands that the liberal tradition places on constitutional theory.[151]

Textualism in all its forms suffers from a fatal defect. It gives us a Constitution with the politics left out. At some level that is its point. But if the Constitution is just another form of politics, the problem of social order recurs. I close with some textualism of my own. The Constitution provides that the Senate "shall be composed of two Senators from each

---

authorizes the regulation of commerce." Laycock, "Taking Constitutions Seriously," p. 374. But it authorizes only national regulation of commerce; thus, it remains open to a libertarian to find in the Constitution a generalized protection of commercial transactions from state regulation. In addition, because even national regulation of commerce, though authorized by the Constitution, necessarily intrudes on state sovereignty, Laycock's approach would require that the courts balance the importance of the national interest being promoted against the degree of intrusion on state sovereignty. This is not promising.

149. I pass over as too obvious to need more than this note the difficulty at the other end of the spectrum, that Laycock's textualism licenses judicial imposition of socialism through application of the values of individualism, autonomy, and social control of private property.

150. Laycock, "Taking Constitutions Seriously," p. 376.

151. See Mark Tushnet, "Anti-Formalism in Recent Constitutional Theory," 83 *Michigan Law Review* 1502, 1509–16 (1985).

State."[152] For at least seven years, at least nine states had no Senators.[153] How that came to be, and how the text of the Constitution came to accommodate that situation, tells us a great deal about textualism.

152. U.S. Constitution, art. I, §3, cl. 1. Article V provides in addition that "no State, without its Consent, shall be deprived [by an amendment to the Constitution] of its equal suffrage in the Senate."

153. From 1861 to 1868 Alabama, Arkansas, Florida, Georgia, Louisiana, and North Carolina were not represented in the Senate. The Senators from South Carolina resigned in 1860 when the election of Lincoln was certain; new Senators from that state sat in 1868. Mississippi and Texas were unrepresented from 1861 to 1870. In addition, Virginia was unrepresented from 1864 to 1869. One of Tennessee's Senators resigned in 1861, the other (Andrew Johnson) in 1862 to assume the military governorship of the state; new Senators were installed in 1865. If it makes a difference, the Senators from Arkansas, North Carolina, Texas, and one from Virginia were expelled from the Senate. See U.S. Senate, *Rules and Manual* 715–75 (1971).

Arguably one state today has four Senators. See James Randall, *Constitutional Problems under Lincoln* 433–76 (rev. ed. 1951).

2

The Jurisprudence
of Democracy

THE liberal tradition insists that, in the making of public policy, no one's view of the good take priority over anyone else's view.[1] If public policy is to be made it must result from the aggregation of individual preferences. That aspect of the liberal tradition generates an approach to constitutional law that John Hart Ely calls "representation reinforcing review." If policy is to be based on the aggregation of preferences, there is a strong prima facie case that policy should be made through voting. The voting process asks people to express their preferences; policies based on those revealed preferences emerge from that process. Just as the market for goods aggregates consumer choice through the mechanism of demand and supply, the market for public policy aggregates citizen choice through voting.[2]

The economic market can fail to respond properly to real demand. For example, limited budgets restrict what consumers can purchase, monopolies artificially restrict supply, and the costs of acquiring information about some goods may restrict the consumer's choice. Contemporary analyses of the economic market justify government intervention when these or other failures occur. Analogously, there may be failures in the political market that prevent the proper aggregation of citizen choice.

1. See, e.g., Ronald Dworkin, "Liberalism," in *Public and Private Morality* 113, 127 (Stuart Hampshire ed. 1978); Ackerman, *Social Justice*. On a lower level, see Terry Eastland, "Radicals in the Law Schools," *Wall Street Journal*, Jan. 10, 1986, p. 16 ("The reason we need the rule of law . . . is precisely because we do not all agree on what constitutes justice.") When he published this comment Eastland was director of public affairs at the Department of Justice.

2. On this level of generality I am not concerned with majority rule or any other specific rule that determines how many votes are needed before a policy is adopted. Making relatively uncontroversial assumptions, public choice theorists have shown that majority rule actually provides the "best" outcomes overall. See, e.g., Mueller, *Public Choice*, pp. 207–10.

Representation-reinforcing review justifies judicial intervention either to eliminate the failures of the political market so that it would work properly in the future or, more controversially, to mimic the results that would have occurred had the political market been operating properly. Failures in the political market take two basic forms. First, some preferences may not be revealed, either because some people are not allowed to vote or because everyone is kept from voting for some specific policy. Representation-reinforcing review intervenes to rectify these failures and, it is said, justifies one strand of the law under the equal protection clause of the fourteenth amendment and some aspects of the law of free expression. Second, some preferences may be revealed but will not be taken into account when preferences are aggregated. Representation-reinforcing review is said to justify certain prohibitions on discrimination that result from this kind of failure in the political market.

Ely argues that this theory provides the only justification for judicial review. It appears to be a perfect reconciliation of judicial review with the majoritarian aspects of democracy.[3] As many critics have pointed out, however, the theory provides such a reconciliation at the cost of adopting a severely constricted conception of democracy.[4] Democracy in this view consists entirely of the rule by a true majority; it has no room for "basic" or "fundamental" rights unrelated to the political process.[5] Such a view of democracy has seemed inadequate to most political theorists, who argue that democracy, properly conceived, requires the protection of some fundamental but nonpolitical rights.[6]

The theory of representation reinforcement need not, however, find its sole justification in a narrow conception of democracy. It might be justified by the judgment that it is the best theory available to limit legislators enough without licensing judges to do too much. We saw in Chapter 1 that the affirmative arguments for originalism are quite weak but that the

3. See Bruce Ackerman, "Beyond *Carolene Products*," 98 *Harvard Law Review* 713, 715 (1985).

4. The most widely cited criticism along these lines is Laurence Tribe, "The Puzzling Persistence of Process-Based Constitutional Theories," 89 *Yale Law Journal* 1063 (1980).

5. One could incorporate such rights as privacy or property into this view of democracy by demonstrating that they were empirically necessary prerequisites to participation in politics. See, e.g., San Antonio Independent Sch. Dist. v. Rodriguez, 411 U.S. 1, 113–17 (1973) (Marshall, J., dissenting) (arguing that relative equality in education is necessary for sufficiently equal participation in politics); Frank Michelman, "Process and Property in Constitutional Theory," 30 *Cleveland State Law Review* 577 (1982) (same as to property). But these arguments tend to seem strained, perhaps because they derive more from the republican tradition's concern for establishing the conditions for civic virtue.

6. This seems to be common ground between John Rawls, *A Theory of Justice* (1971), and Robert Nozick, *Anarchy, State, and Utopia* (1974), although they of course differ on what the protected rights should be.

arguments from avoiding judicial tyranny are more substantial. The situation with representation-reinforcing review is similar: the affirmative arguments for it rest on a narrow and probably indefensible conception of democracy, but it might be a decent theory if it constrains both legislators and judges enough for us to be satisfied that the remaining opportunities for tyranny are small and does so better than any alternatives. The main argument of this chapter is that the theory does not provide those constraints.[7]

Introduction: Representation Reinforcement and Federalism

Although the theory has been given the name *representation-reinforcing review* only recently, its historical antecedents go back to Chief Justice John Marshall, who sketched the theory in a number of important federalism cases. The theory was further developed by Harlan Fiske Stone in the 1930s and 1940s, so that, in the context of federalism, it was reasonably well developed prior to its transfer to more controversial contexts. Further, and more important for our purposes, the critique of the theory in federalism cases can be transferred as well.

Two relatively uncontroversial cases clarify the application and defects of the theory in other, more interesting and controversial cases. The first example involves "states' rights." Can the courts ever properly overturn national legislation on the ground that it infringes on the constitutionally recognized interests of states? Here the theory, at least as presented by most of its adherents, says no. Because the interests of the states are expressed in a completely open and unobstructed way in the national political process, the courts cannot overturn on states' rights grounds legislation that emerges from that process. The second example involves commerce between the states. Under what circumstances may the courts prevent states or localities from regulating commercial activity that has its origin or impact in other states? Here the theory appears to support a fair degree of judicial intervention, because the outsiders who are affected are said to have no role in the local legislature.

The defect in the theory, in federalism cases as elsewhere, is that representation-reinforcing review must consider whether formal or informal obstacles in the political process are to be removed. If the theory focuses on formal obstacles alone, it is subject to serious criticism, for removing

7. I have developed the theory in what I regard as its most defensible form. Most of its adherents appear to resist some of the conclusions I draw, by relaxing some of the premises in an ad hoc manner, for what seem to me to be straightforward political reasons: without the ad hoc adaptations the theory yields results that those adherents find politically unacceptable.

the formal obstacles would do little to alleviate the risk of tyranny. Yet if the theory takes informal obstacles into account, judges will be called upon to make controversial assessments of political reality and the theory loses its constraining force. Thus the theory, designed to prevent both legislative and judicial tyranny, can prevent one only by creating the risk of the other.

The Supreme Court discussed this theory in the important early case of *Gibbons v. Ogden*. The New York legislature had granted Robert Fulton a monopoly to operate steamboats between New York and New Jersey. Relying on the grant a New York court ordered a competitor to refrain from similar operations. The competitor argued that a federal statute authorized its operation and overrode the New York statute. Chief Justice Marshall agreed with the competitor. Congress, he said, had the power to regulate this sort of commerce. To those concerned about states' rights, Marshall responded, "The wisdom and the discretion of Congress, their identity with the people, and the influence which their constituents possess at elections are, in this, as in many other instances, as that, for example, of declaring war, the sole restraints on which they have relied, to secure them from its abuse. They are the restraints on which the people must often rely solely, in all representative governments."[8]

Jesse Choper has exhaustively elaborated this representation-reinforcing analysis of congressional power and states' rights.[9] Choper identifies the formal and the informal—functional or political—ways in which the interests of states are represented in the national political process. The formal mechanisms include the overrepresentation of small states in the Senate and, in the past, the role of state legislators in selecting Senators. Similarly, state legislators influence the composition of the House of Representatives by their power to draw and redraw district lines when reapportionment occurs. The President too must respond to state concerns, because votes in the electoral college are apportioned not entirely on the basis of population but include a uniform two-vote bonus that exaggerates the importance of small states and influences the campaign strategy of presidential candidates.

Everyone who has written on these matters in the past few years has been quite properly uncomfortable with justifying restricted judicial review of states' rights issues by invoking only these formal mechanisms of state representation. As one observer noted, "Scholars rely on . . . [the argument's] conclusions while they question—in their footnotes—the ob-

8. 22 U.S. (9 Wheat.) 1, 197 (1824).
9. Choper, *Judicial Review*, pp. 176–93. This work updates arguments made earlier by James Madison, in The Federalist Nos. 45 and 46, and by Herbert Wechsler, "The Political Safeguards of Federalism," in *Principles, Politics, and Fundamental Law*, p. 49.

servations leading ... to those conclusions."[10] The seventeenth amendment eliminated legislative participation in the selection of Senators. The Supreme Court's decisions on reapportionment have restricted, though not eliminated, the states' power to influence the composition of the House. The electoral college has been reduced to a purely ceremonial function. More important than all of these, the development of a national two-party system seriously diminished the importance of local governments as structural constraints on the exercise of national power.

Choper and others who rely on representation-reinforcing theories understand and are uncomfortable with the apparent conclusion of their argument to this point. If representation-reinforcing review is justified only where formal mechanisms of representation are absent, review of states' rights claims will be unjustified despite the patent weakness of the current formal mechanisms of representation. One can easily cite congressional statutes in which the feeble formal mechanisms had no effect at all; an example might be the Education for All Handicapped Children Act of 1975, which imposed substantial financial and organizational costs on local schools without providing any money to cover those costs. Formal representation thus provides too few opportunities for judicial review in the face of real possibilities that Congress will tyrannize over the states.

Proponents of representation-reinforcing review therefore attempt to salvage the theory by explaining that the formal mechanisms are augmented by informal mechanisms of representation, which they identify by examining how the national political process actually works. When informal constraints are taken into account, they argue, the criticisms lose force. For example, Choper mentions bipartisan caucuses of House delegations from each state, the political positions such as Governor held by members of Congress before their election to Congress, the deep personal ties members have to their localities, and the importance of "state political chieftains" in generating support for those who would seek the presidency.

There are serious difficulties in relying on this kind of evidence. Most of Choper's citations are to research on how politics really works that was done between 1950 and the early 1970s. For each item on which he relies one can find another that substantially weakens the point. As to the prior political positions of Senators, for example, one can say that, although several former Governors still serve, the trend is sharply against prior political experience on the state and local levels. The increased cost of campaigning has opened the Senate to rich outsiders and to those who

---

10. Stewart Baker, "Federalism and the Eleventh Amendment," 48 *University of Colorado Law Review* 139, 183 n. 203 (1977).

have access to media attention even if they are not officeholders. Similarly, reforms in the nominating process have, as Choper notes, weakened the grasp of state and local politicians on the gate to the presidency. If the party system is what overrides the ability of the formal mechanisms to check Congress, so geographic mobility overrides many of the informal political constraints on Congress.[11]

The items that Choper and others have presented about contemporary politics are obviously significant. The difficulty is that those who live by empirical research die by empirical research as well. Choper offers one interpretation of contemporary politics that is supported by some empirical findings. But there are other empirical findings that cut against his analysis. Political scientists can readily say that reality is very messy, the political system is very complicated, and the like. But constitutional theorists need something relatively solid to serve as the constraint on judges. If the Justices argue over which set of empirical findings more accurately reflects "what really happens," they will inevitably resolve the dispute by consulting their intuition and prior inclinations. A states' rights judge will emphasize mobility, a nationalist judge will emphasize the lobbying forces of governmental organizations, and in the end the constraining force of representation-reinforcing review will disappear.

This example of the theory in action illustrates its general problems. If representation consists in formal mechanisms, the theory appears to be inadequate to guard against tyranny by a congressional majority; but if representation occurs through informal mechanisms as well, the theory loses its force as a guard against tyranny by the judiciary. This dialectical exchange between formal and informal mechanisms of representation and between legislative and judicial tyranny, occurs whenever one attempts to use representation-reinforcing review.

11. The majority opinion and Justice Powell's dissenting opinion in Garcia v. San Antonio Metropolitan Transit Auth., 469 U.S. 528 (1985), disagreed over precisely these questions. Of course, impressive evidence can be amassed to show that recent Congresses have in general been quite responsive to state interests. Congress has enacted large-scale programs, such as revenue sharing and block grants, in which state and local governments receive federal funds with relatively few strings attached, and it has recognized state interests in a large number of smaller-scale programs. For example, when Congress authorized the Attorney General to sue to rectify unconstitutional conditions in state prisons and mental institutions, it allowed such suits to be brought only after the Attorney General engages in a complex set of notifications and negotiations with state officials. 42 U.S.C. §1997. The question, however, is not whether the contemporary array of political power means that state and local governments will frequently come out ahead. Rather the question is whether recent outcomes result from the happenstance of a specific set of political forces or from forces that, though not built directly into the Constitution as are the formal constraints, are nonetheless enduring enough to be a barrier against tyranny.

Our second example of the theory's operation is also drawn from federalism, here the question of the courts' power to declare state legislation unconstitutional on the ground that the legislation interferes with interstate commerce. Once again the theory appears stable when only formal matters are considered, but it seems inevitable that informal matters will be injected into the discussion; the theory then collapses. As the second stage in the analysis, this example will have more detail than the first.

John Marshall again showed the way. *McCulloch v. Maryland* involved a tax that Maryland imposed on the activities of banks that were not chartered by the state legislature.[12] One such bank was the Second Bank of the United States, whose creation and actions were the subject of high political controversy. Marshall's opinion is a classic because of the force with which it defends Congress' power to create the bank. In addition to attacking Congress' assertion of power, however, Maryland insisted that barring states from imposing such taxes would in effect deprive them of one essential attribute of sovereignty. Its argument rested on an asserted equality between state and national governments. As Maryland's lawyers put it, the power of taxation is "concurrent": whatever the national government can tax, the states can tax too. "Every argument which would sustain the right of the general government to tax banks chartered by the States, will equally sustain the right of the states to tax banks chartered by the general government."

Marshall denied that the arguments were symmetrical:

> The people of all the States have created the general government, and have conferred upon it the general power of taxation. The people of all the States, and the States themselves, are represented in Congress, and by their representatives, exercise this power. When they tax the chartered institutions of the States, they tax their constituents . . . But, when a State taxes the operations of the government of the United States, it acts upon institutions created, not by their own constituents, but by people over whom they claim no control . . . The difference is that which always exists, and always must exist, between the action of the whole on a part, and the action of a part on the whole.[13]

The idea is straightforward. State banks are represented by—are the constituents of—members of Congress, but a national bank is not represented by anyone in the Maryland legislature.

All would be well if the argument could be pursued on the purely formal level. But, as Ely points out, it cannot be pursued on that level

12. 17 U.S. (4 Wheat.) 316 (1819).
13. Id., pp. 435–36.

alone.[14] Maryland treated out-of-state banks differently from the way it treated in-state banks, but banks do not vote anyway. We therefore have to consider the way in which "persons whose interests are tied up with" banks' interests will protect their own, and therefore the banks' interests. Surely there were some citizens of Maryland—rich creditors, investors in the national bank—whose interests were tied up with the bank's. But the most we can say is that these citizens were outnumbered, and indeed were bound to be outnumbered, among the population of Maryland. If we are to save the theory we must now introduce informal mechanisms of representation.

We can further the inquiry by considering a slight variation of a recent case.[15] North Carolina apple growers are politically well organized and powerful. The growers discover that local consumers prefer to purchase apples grown in Washington State, which the consumers can identify by a stamp "Washington Grade A" placed on the cartons in which apples are shipped. North Carolina's apple growers therefore persuade the legislature to enact a rule prohibiting the sale of apples from cartons that display anything other than the applicable U.S. grade, which North Carolina growers already use. Justice Stone described why this statute ought to be unconstitutional: "When the regulation is of such a character that its burden falls principally upon those without the state, legislative action is not likely to be subjected to those political restraints which are normally exerted on legislation where it affects adversely some interests within the state."[16] Yet, as will soon be evident, Washington apple growers have formal access to a legislature with authority to override North Carolina's decision. That legislature is Congress. The courts could justify their invalidation of North Carolina's statute only by invoking informal characteristics of access to Congress. But then the inevitably controversial nature of the choice of which informal mechanisms to invoke will undermine the theory.

Since *McCulloch* and *Gibbons* it has been clear that Congress has power to regulate apple labeling in whatever way it wants. It could prohibit all labeling, it could develop a set of "U.S. grades" that would differentiate some apples by quality standards, or, most important here, it could explicitly permit each state to develop its own grading system and simultaneously prohibit state regulation of the systems developed in other states. Washington's apple growers have complete access to Congress, and if they do not succeed in securing protection at the national level it is

---

14. Ely, *Democracy and Distrust*, pp. 85–86.
15. Hunt v. Washington State Apple Advertising Comm'n., 432 U.S. 333 (1977).
16. South Carolina Highway Dept. v. Barnwell Bros., 303 U.S. 177, 184 n. 2 (1938).

not because they face a political process that is stacked against them there, as they do when they try to influence the North Carolina legislature.

If this point can be sustained, it narrows the scope of representation-reinforcing review substantially. In the United States legislatures are arranged in a hierarchy: a superior legislature may override decisions made at a lower level. According to the version of the theory being considered here, courts must ignore an obstacle to representation in a subordinate legislature if representation in a superior legislature is unobstructed. In our system that means that representation-reinforcing review is appropriate only with respect to obstacles to representation in Congress, for, as we will see, Congress is the superior legislature not just with respect to regulation of commerce but with respect to the entire range of civil rights and civil liberties.[17]

When scholars write about the commerce clause they routinely invoke the framers' fear of economic balkanization, of parochial regulation that would fracture a unified nation into a congeries of self-contained, warring states.[18] Some national perspective on economic regulation seems essential to avoid this outcome. If the argument from the legislative hierarchy is correct, we are left with a situation in which only Congress can provide that perspective. We can be reasonably confident that Congress will rarely do so. How likely is it, after all, that a Congress absorbed with massive revisions in taxing and spending programs can devote attention to the regulation of apple sales in a single state? As Justice Jackson said,

> These restraints are individually too petty, too diversified, and too local to get the attention of a Congress hard pressed with more urgent matters . . . The sluggishness of government, the multitude of matters that clamor for attention, and the relative ease with which men are persuaded to postpone troublesome decisions, all make inertia one of the most decisive powers in determining the course of our affairs and frequently gives to the established order of things a longevity and vitality much beyond its merits.[19]

17. This conclusion challenges general understandings about the structure of constitutional law. The standard quotation is from Justice Holmes: "I do not think the United States would come to an end if we lost our power to declare an Act of Congress void. I do think the Union would be imperiled if we could not make that declaration as to the laws of the several States. For one in my place sees how often a local policy prevails with those who are not trained to national views and how often action is taken that embodies what the Commerce Clause was meant to end." Holmes, "Law and the Court," in his *Collected Legal Papers* 295–96 (1920). See also Black, *Decision according to Law*, pp. 35–42.

18. See H. P. Hood & Sons v. DuMond, 336 U.S. 525, 539 (1949).

19. Duckworth v. Arkansas, 314 U.S. 390, 400 (1941) (Jackson, J., concurring). See also Commonwealth Edison Co. v. Montana, 453 U.S. 609, 637–38 (1981) (White, J., concurring).

Jackson's observation is, in one interpretation, a critique of a purely formal theory. Invoking what we all know about the realities of the legislative process, Jackson explained that a formal theory will leave in place local regulations that lack merit. The observation also points the way to a reconstructed theory. By talking about political reality we can avoid relying on intervention by the hierarchically superior legislature, which we know will rarely occur. But the reconstruction fails for two reasons: although judicial intervention appears at first blush to be representation reinforcing, on analysis it can seem representation denying, and the injection of political reality to counter the formalism of the "hierarchy" argument makes it impossible to treat out-of-state interests as unrepresented in local legislatures.

The first line of attack on the reconstructed theory begins by asking what it is about political reality that gives force to Jackson's observation. The answer surely is that Washington's apple growers are simply not going to be able to bring sufficient political force to bear on a busy Congress. That answer is seriously misleading. One can easily imagine ways in which they could bring that force to bear. They could refuse to support, or could campaign against, any Representative who failed to endorse their legislative program. Washington's Senators might learn that their political survival depends on securing what the apple growers want, and they might be persuaded to make that program a central element in the ordinary process of legislative bargaining. The Senators could withhold support of deregulation of natural gas unless those seeking deregulation agreed to the apple growers' program. Nor are the apple growers confined to influence on Washington's delegation to Congress. They can give campaign contributions to candidates throughout the country. As the delegation can, the apple growers can bargain. They can inform the Teamsters, for example, that they will use their influence on the Washington delegation to oppose deregulation of trucking if the Teamsters will influence *their* friends to support the apple growers' program.

It is not, therefore, that the apple growers lack sufficient political power. Rather they have chosen not to exert the power they have. But that is *their* choice, not one forced on them by the political system. If North Carolina's apple regulations bother them enough, the Washingtonians can do something about it. If the courts stand ready to intervene, the apple growers can use the inexpensive judicial method of overriding local decisions instead of the more costly congressional method. Again, the example illustrates a more general point. Political influence depends on both numbers and the willingness to act in the political arena. People who care deeply about an issue regularly have a larger influence in the legislative process than their numbers alone would suggest. Intense minorities—rifle owners, supporters of restrictions on abortions—can be found with no difficulty.

How representation-reinforcing review deals with the issue of intensity is clearly a central difficulty. When one observes an outcome of the political process, how can one be sure that it results from obstacles to representation rather than from lack of sufficiently intense concern on the part of those affected? Even more, the issue of intensity is symmetrical in the following way. Suppose the courts do overturn North Carolina's regulation. Now North Carolina's apple growers can object that, as beneficiaries of the preintervention status quo, they had no reason to seek congressional approval of their regulation, and they are therefore being treated unfairly. They will claim that they cared enough about the regulation that, had they known of its necessity, they would have secured approval from Congress. Of course, the Washington apple growers can respond that the North Carolinians should now go ahead and lobby with Congress—just as the North Carolinians would have said to the Washingtonians if the courts had remained above the dispute.

To generalize slightly, the issue is one of allocating the associated burdens of inertia and lack of intensity. Ideas about representation alone cannot specify the starting point or status quo allocation of those burdens. That, after all, is why the commerce clause cases routinely invoke the fear of balkanization, a normative criterion unrelated to representation, to justify what appears to be judicial displacement of local choices but what is actually a judicial determination of the group upon whom the burdens of inertia and lack of intensity will rest. Thus, the courts necessarily weaken the representation of one group in the course of reinforcing the representation of their opponents.[20]

The analysis of inertia and intensity shows that Jackson's reconstructed theory, which relies on informal obstacles to representation, must invoke premises other than that of representation-reinforcing review. A second critique notes that out-of-state interests are not really unrepresented and that in-state interests are not really unaffected; it is just that out-of-state interests are "principally" burdened by regulation. In-state interests, pri-

20. Judicial review in commerce clause cases is special, though, because Congress can always return the substantive situation to that which existed before the courts acted. If the courts invalidate North Carolina's regulation of apple selling, Congress can always authorize it. See Geoffrey Stone, L. Michael Seidman, Cass Sunstein, and Mark Tushnet, *Constitutional Law* 253–56 (1986). The losers in the judicial forum are procedurally disadvantaged by the burdens of inertia and lack of intensity, but they are not absolutely barred from securing what they want. As we will see, when the courts invalidate exclusions from the local franchise instead of exclusions from the local market, they do irremediably displace the choices that the losers want made. That result cannot be defended on representation-reinforcing grounds.

marily those of consumers, are also burdened. But once we are concerned only with disproportionate adverse effects, the courts will be forced to make controversial judgments about political reality, which in turn removes the constraint that the theory is supposed to provide.

The difficulty arises at the heart of the Stone-Jackson theory of the commerce clause. Everyone agrees that overtly discriminatory rules, those that shield local producers from foreign competition, should almost always be unconstitutional.[21] And it seems that representation-reinforcing review would yield that result. After all, the out-of-state competitors have no formal representation in the local legislature, whereas the in-state producers receiving protection do. *Buck v. Kuykendall* is a crude but effective example.[22] The state required interstate carriers to secure a certificate of convenience and necessity before operating in the state. One reason offered for denying the certificate in *Buck* was that the area was already adequately served by existing carriers. This, the Court said, amounted to excluding foreign competition just because it is competition.

Initially *Buck* looks like a simple case. Carriers already in the market had their market shares shielded from reduction by competition with a new carrier. Yet because competition had been effectively reduced, prices for shipping and ultimately for the goods that had been shipped were higher than they otherwise would have been. Thus, the burden of the discriminatory law did not fall only on the shipper kept out of the market. It fell on local consumers as well. Further, if the rule regarding "adequate service" was applied with an even hand, potential local entrants into the market were barred. Although a foreign shipper cannot vote for state legislation, local consumers and potential competitors can. The Stone-Jackson theory must explain why political restraints inadequately protect the interests of consumers, which happen to coincide with those of foreign carriers.

Since that theory was developed a standard answer has been devised. The general consumer interest, it is said, is at a systematic disadvantage in legislative combat against organized groups.[23] Consumers are dispersed

---

21. See, e.g., Cities Service Gas Co. v. Peerless Oil & Gas Co., 340 U.S. 179, 186–87 (1950) (among "the only requirements consistently recognized . . . [is] that the regulation not discriminate against or place an embargo on interstate commerce"). But see Maine v. Taylor, 106 S. Ct. 2440 (1986).

22. 267 U.S. 307 (1925).

23. See generally Mancur Olson, *The Logic of Collective Action* (1965). For summaries with applications to questions of regulatory law, see Roger Noll, "Government Regulatory Behavior: A Multidisciplinary Survey and Synthesis," in *Regulatory Policy and the Social Sciences* 9 (Roger Noll ed. 1985); Harold Bruff, "Legislative Formality, Administrative Rationality," 63 *Texas Law Review* 207, 214–18 (1984).

throughout the community. If a consumer-oriented lobbying effort gets started, each consumer may become a free rider. That is, each consumer will correctly see that the reduction in prices that will occur if more carriers are allowed into the market will be quite small, certainly less than the cost of supporting the lobbying effort. Consumers will therefore hold back, hoping to benefit from the lobbying effort without having to contribute to it. The general consumer interest therefore cannot mobilize political resources commensurate with its numbers. In contrast, narrower interest groups can see that the benefits of reducing competition will be substantial to each one of them. Members of such groups, like the local truckers in *Buck*, will be willing to invest in lobbying, letter-writing campaigns, and focused political contributions, because they expect the returns from the legislation they procure to exceed their initial investments.

This argument too is plausible. Recent experience has shown, however, that it rests on too narrow a view of what people care about. It treats consumers as economic actors, who are concerned only with financial returns. The consumer and environmental movements of recent years demonstrate that consumers have other motivations as well. They may be altruists, in effect giving away their own money to consumer lobbying groups so that others will benefit. An economist might say that altruists receive a nonmonetary return on their investments, which, when added to the tiny financial returns, gives them a positive net return. The apparent precision of the free rider analysis thereupon dissolves. Further, entrepreneurs—in the literature called moral entrepreneurs—may discover that there are enough altruists out there to give them a secure financial and nonfinancial income so long as they produce what the altruists want.[24] In a world populated by economic calculators, altruists, and moral entrepreneurs, it will be difficult indeed to identify systematic disadvantages placed on consumer representation.

The fundamental difficulty with a theory that allows the courts to consider political reality is that suitable plausible guesses about intensity, moral entrepreneurs, and free riders would allow the courts to invalidate or uphold any regulation. The theory then loses its constraining force on judges. Yet if we do not allow the courts to take political reality into

24. For a study of one group of moral entrepreneurs, see Andrew McFarland, *Common Cause: Lobbying in the Public Interest* (1984). The rise of deregulation poses a serious challenge to the public choice analysis of regulation. For a critique emphasizing the role of ideas and economists, see Martha Derthick and Paul Quirk, *The Politics of Deregulation* (1985), concluding that the public choice analysis of Congress is "quite misleading" as "a general or comprehensive account." Id., p. 142.

account, we are driven to a purely formal theory, which fails to constrain legislatures.

Representation Reinforcement, Disfranchisement, and Free Speech

The critical analysis of the two preceding examples developed arguments about the hierarchy of jurisdictions and the unfortunate but necessary role played by considerations of political reality that can be deployed against the theory of representation-reinforcing review in areas of greater contemporary controversy. These areas cover exclusions from the franchise, the law of antigovernment speech, and the law of race and gender discrimination. There are three reasons to discuss these areas in detail. First, the franchise and speech areas involve the process of representation itself. If representation-reinforcing review fails as a theory there, its intuitive appeal will be significantly reduced. Second, in presenting the theory in its most attractive form, Ely devotes most of his arguments to the speech and discrimination areas. Finally, Harlan Fiske Stone developed the theory in the famous "footnote 4" of *United States v. Carolene Products Co.*[25] The footnote suggests that the theory would invalidate "legislation which restricts those political processes which can ordinarily be expected to bring about repeal of undesirable legislation"—that is, disfranchisements and restrictions on speech—or statutes resting on "prejudice against discrete and insular minorities . . . which tends seriously to curtail the operation of those political processes ordinarily to be relied upon to protect minorities"—that is, discriminatory statutes of a particular sort. If the theory is flawed at what its supporters describe as its core, we can conclude that the theory is almost certainly flawed in all its applications.

Kramer v. Union Free School District No. 15 illustrates the problems that the existence of a hierarchy of jurisdictions poses for representation-reinforcing review.[26] Kramer, a thirty-year-old stockbroker, lived with his parents in Atlantic Beach, New York. State law provided that voting in school district elections would be restricted in certain districts, including Atlantic Beach, to parents of school-age children, taxpayers, and renters. The Supreme Court held that this statute was unconstitutional because it disfranchised many people who in fact were interested in school district elections but allowed others to vote who had "at least, a remote and indistinct interest in school affairs." This decision appears to fit the

25. 304 U.S. 144, 152–53 n. 4 (1938).
26. 395 U.S. 621 (1969).

theory of representation-reinforcing review: The Court removed an obstacle to participation in the political process because that obstacle was not precisely designed to advance state purposes unrelated to participation.

But the problem of legislative hierarchy poses a serious difficulty. Justice Stewart's dissent pointed out that although Kramer could not vote in school district elections, he could vote for state legislators who support the repeal of the local disfranchisement. If we consider only formal obstacles to representation, the theory would not justify judicial review so long as the disfranchised person can vote in elections for a legislature that can repeal voter disqualification rules that it or subordinate legislatures have imposed.[27]

Of course we are often skeptical about the ability of the locally disfranchised actually to get the attention of the superior legislature, just as we were skeptical about the ability of Washington's apple growers to get the attention of Congress. However, although relatively few people might be in Kramer's position, numbers alone do not matter. Owners, renters, and parents cared enough to insert the exclusion in the statute book, presumably over the objection or inertia of people like Kramer. Of course there are more owners and parents than there are people like Kramer. But there are always losers in the political process. Kramer's loss does not disable him from rectifying the injury he suffers. Again we must face the problem of intensity. Kramer has lost in the New York legislature because he cares less about disfranchisement than, for example, the gun lobby cares about registration of handguns. He has not organized, made alliances, or threatened legislators

---

27. More recently the Court has edged toward adopting Justice Stewart's position. Ball v. James, 451 U.S. 355 (1981), involved an Arizona statute regulating elections to the board of a large public water reclamation district. Only landowners could vote for directors, and their votes were proportional to the number of acres they owned. In addition to regulating water storage and delivery, the district provided electricity to most of the people in the area, which included a large part of Phoenix and its suburbs. Indeed, 98 percent of the district's operating income came from the sale of electricity.

The Court observed that the Arizona legislature had recently amended the electoral system: Owners of less than one acre were permitted to cast fractional votes, and four members, elected at large on a "one landowner, one vote" basis, were added to the board. In addition, its penultimate footnote reads, "The [challengers], of course, are qualified voters in Arizona and so remain equal participants in the election of the state legislators who created and have the power to change the District." Justice Powell amplified this footnote in a concurring opinion by observing, "The District is large enough, and the resources it manages are basic enough, that the people will act through their elected legislature when further changes in the governance of the District are warranted"—or, more precisely, are desired. See generally Melvyn Durschlag, "*Salyer, Ball,* and *Holt*: Reappraising the Right to Vote in Terms of Political 'Interest' and Vote Dilution," 33 *Case Western Reserve Law Review* 1 (1982).

with single-issue voting. It is true that, when we try to evaluate Kramer's prospects in the New York legislation, we will probably conclude that they are rather slim. No one else is likely to care much about the issue, although this indifference suggests that Kramer would not face fierce opposition if he did appeal to the state legislature. Now, however, we are deep into the details of political reality, which, as we have seen and will see again, eliminates the theory's constraining force.

Kramer illustrates a related difficulty with representation-reinforcing review. The statute Kramer challenged was not of statewide uniformity. Thus, New York offered him a range of municipalities with different services. Some provided bad schools, good sewers, and no voting for the school board; others provided good schools, bad sewers, and voting. New York offered Kramer a choice: Live with your parents and have no vote, or live elsewhere and have a vote. As noted at the beginning of this chapter, representation-reinforcing review is a political version of market economics, and there is a market theory of local government. According to that theory, each local government provides a distinctive bundle of services, and people vote with their feet by moving to the place that gives them their preferred combination of services at a price they are willing to pay.[28] If the conditions of the theory are met, it is hard to see why we should not hold Kramer to his choice, or, more obviously, why we should allow the courts to override the choices of those who chose to live in Atlantic Beach precisely because of its mix of services and disfranchisements.

The conditions of the market theory of local governments are in fact quite stringent, and it is unlikely that New York satisfied them. Still, under those circumstances we must decide whose preferences, among those forced to choose from a limited range of possibilities, should be respected. That decision cannot be made on the basis of representation-reinforcing premises alone. The Jackson reconstruction, as applied in *Kramer*, systematically allocates the burden of lack of intensity to those who benefit from disfranchisements, but it does not, because it cannot, explain why that allocation is appropriate.[29] The very neutrality of the theory between one preference and another, its exclusive concern that

28. Tiebout, "Pure Theory of Public Expenditures."

29. Ira Lupu, "Choosing Heroes Carefully," 15 *Harvard Civil Rights–Civil Liberties Law Review* 781, 797 n. 62 (1980), argues that the allocation is justified by a substantive preference for an enlarged electorate; exclusions may distort the outcomes of local elections before the state legislature can act. But the concept of distortion itself requires a prior specification that the preferences of people like Kramer ought to be taken into account. That is precisely what is at stake, and although the judgment that those interests should be taken into account is certainly defensible, it cannot be made on the grounds of representation alone.

preferences, whatever they are, be taken into account, bars it from making any allocation at all.

Jackson's reconstruction dealt with the commerce clause. Once we reached Congress there was nothing more to say, because what Congress does is acceptable within the bounds of the theory. In the voting context the theory may still have some force. The argument about *Kramer* establishes that, when we are concerned with formal questions, the theory prohibits only exclusions from the franchise for elections to hierarchically superior legislatures. So long as the complainant has access to such a legislature, his or her exclusion from the vote for local bodies is unassailable within the theory. Now suppose Kramer is for some reason barred by New York statute from voting for New York legislators. Does that validate the result in *Kramer*? The answer returns us to the issue of federalism, for the question can be rephrased, Is Congress a hierarchically superior body over state legislatures with respect to disfranchisements?

Both precedent and the theory say that Congress is indeed superior. The Voting Rights Act of 1965 provided that people who achieved Spanish-language literacy in Puerto Rican schools could not be denied the vote in any election because they lack English-language literacy. *Katzenbach v. Morgan* held that Congress acted constitutionally in overriding New York's English literacy requirement.[30] Its rationale was that Congress could reasonably have concluded that those excluded might receive discriminatory treatment in the provision of governmental services. This rationale has been criticized,[31] and the Court has backed away from the broadest implications of *Katzenbach*.[32] But the theory itself justifies the result. The only objection to congressional authority in this setting is based on federalism. When Congress overrides New York's exclusion it significantly affects the way in which New York has chosen to arrange its affairs. We have already seen, however, that proponents of the theory such as Choper conclude that no congressional actions should be subject to constitutional attack on federalism grounds.

Within the theory then, challengers ought to be able to attack only exclusions from the national franchise. And now the theory appears to have almost no content at all, because there are today no controversial exclusions from the national franchise. At the outset the theory appeared to constrain the majority in decisions to deny people the vote, but in fact the constraint is purely theoretical. True, if Congress ever enacted an

30. 384 U.S. 641 (1966).

31. See, e.g., Robert Burt, "*Miranda* and Title II: A Morganatic Marriage," 1969 *Supreme Court Review* 81.

32. Compare Oregon v. Mitchell, 400 U.S. 112 (1970), with City of Rome v. United States, 446 U.S. 156 (1980).

exclusion the theory would justify its invalidation. But the critique is that that protection, albeit not trivial, is hardly enough; the forms of majority tyranny are more various than exclusions from the national franchise.

We have been considering what might be characterized as geographic difficulties with the theory. The difficulties multiply when we consider exactly why the geographic ones arise. Representation-reinforcing review begins with the perception that if public policy is to result from the aggregation of preferences, we must be sure that all preferences are revealed. Yet the theory says nothing about *whose* preferences must be revealed. The geographic difficulty arises because as the argument proceeds we move back and forth between regarding the relevant community as Atlantic Beach (or New York) and regarding it as New York (or the United States). The theory does not tell us on what level of generality to proceed.

The question of determining whose preferences are to count has been faced before. The original Constitution apportioned representation in the House of Representatives according to the states' populations, calculated "by adding to the whole Number of free Persons, . . . three fifths of all other Persons."[33] In effect, the three-fifths clause defined slaves and, as the Court held in the *Dred Scott* case,[34] blacks generally, as not being members of the relevant community. Their preferences could therefore be disregarded. At the federal level the same was true of women until the adoption of the nineteenth amendment in 1920. These observations are designed to indicate that we cannot take as unproblematic the definition of the relevant community.[35] Providing that definition undermines representation-reinforcing review. Originalists would note that the Constitution was designed for "the People of the United States," as the Preamble

33. U.S. Constitution, art. I, §2, para. 3.

34. 60 U.S. (19 How.) 393 (1857).

35. One solution would be to allow the legislature to define the community: if legislation allows blacks to vote their votes must be counted. This is obviously unsatisfactory. For one thing, if the failure to count the votes is authorized by state law, then to that extent state legislation does not allow blacks to vote. More important, the solution would preclude the use of the theory against decisions not to enfranchise.

An alternative solution is to invoke one version of the judgment of history, that the relevant community includes all people, defined in a commonsense way. Yet serious difficulties attend this solution too. One is geographic again. Why should only the preferences of citizens of the United States count? The lesson of the commerce clause cases is that people whose interests are adversely affected by local decisions should have some forum in which they can express their preferences. Yet the citizens of El Salvador and Namibia are affected by American policy just as Washington apple growers were affected by North Carolina's policy. For a discussion of the extraterritorial application of the Constitution, see Stephen Legomsky, "Immigration Law and the Principle of Plenary Congressional Power," 1984 *Supreme Court Review* 255, 275–77.

says, that the equal protection clause says that no state shall deny to any person "within its jurisdiction the equal protection of the laws," and that the due process clauses, although they say "no person" and lack the jurisdictional language, must be read against that background.[36] But grand theories must be pure; representation-reinforcing review cannot survive if, at convenient places, it requires an infusion of originalism. (See Chapter 5.)

An alternative approach would treat the United States, by reason of its history, as something like a natural entity. The sense of naturalness here is not obvious, though; why is the United States a natural entity and, for example, the white community or the male community is not?[37] And to the extent that long-standing ties of mutual exchange create communities, consider the relations between (some of the citizens of) the United States and (some of the citizens of) Mexico.[38] The point here is not that the theory requires that those interests be taken into account. Rather it is that these are hard issues that cannot be resolved by invoking only concepts of representation.

A third approach relies on notions of "virtual representation."[39] That is, those actually represented in a legislature can sometimes be counted on to present the views of those not actually represented, to the same degree and with the same intensity that the unrepresented have. Still, sometimes virtual representation is unlikely to work well. If the preferences of the represented are complex or not uniformly shared, we will be unable to evaluate the performance of the virtual representatives. In the absence of other information we might as well assume that the distribution of preferences among the virtually represented is the same as that among the actually represented.[40] Usually we have other information, though, and that information frequently demonstrates a conflict of preferences be-

36. U.S. Constitution, preamble, amends. V, XIV.

37. For a superb discussion, see John Dunn, *Western Political Theory in the Face of the Future* 55–79 (1979). See also Michael Walzer, "The Distribution of Membership," in *Boundaries: National Autonomy and Its Limits* 1 (Peter Brown and Henry Shue eds. 1981).

38. See Gerald Lopez, "Undocumented Mexican Migration: In Search of a Just Immigration Law and Policy," 28 *UCLA Law Review* 615 (1981); Timothy King, "Immigration from Developing Countries: Some Philosophical Issues," 93 *Ethics* 525 (1983). For further discussion of community in constitutional theory, see Chapter 4 (appendix).

39. See Ely, *Democracy and Distrust*, pp. 82–87.

40. For example, some of the rhetoric of discussions of abortion raises interesting questions about the existence of a conflict of interest. Those who prefer to restrict the availability of abortions often raise these questions by asking, How would you feel if your mother had had an abortion? This suggests a conflict of interest between living legislators and not-yet-born people. Yet philosophers find such questions exceedingly hard to address, worrying, for example, about whether it is coherent to talk about the fetus' interest in being born. The leading work on this subject is Derek Parfit, *Reasons and Persons* (1984).

tween the actually and the virtually represented. We must allow the courts to intervene when that occurs if the preferences of the virtually represented are to be taken into account. Unfortunately, conflicts of interest between the actually represented and the virtually represented are pervasive.[41] The theory thus appears to justify quite far-reaching judicial intervention. Representation-reinforcing review can be made coherent only if we specify the community whose members must be represented, for we cannot tell whether government is failing to take some preferences into account until we know whose preferences have to be counted.[42] Nothing in the theory tells us that.

We turn now to an analysis of some free speech issues. The analysis of disfranchisements introduced a kind of recursive process in its emphasis on the role of legislative hierarchies: an objection at one level was met by a move to another level. A similar recursive process aids in analyzing restrictions on speech and leads to the conclusion that the theory may justify invalidation of national sedition statutes, and nothing else. The theory then is inadequate to guard against legislative tyranny because such tyranny expresses itself in laws other than sedition statutes.

The theory requires that policy result from the aggregation of revealed preferences. Disfranchisements prevent some people from using the vote to reveal their preferences whatever they are. Limitations on speech prevent people from revealing *particular* preferences, those for the policy about which speech is limited. For example, if a statute makes it unlawful to advocate racial segregation, those who prefer segregation will be unable to reveal that desire. The conclusion that only national laws can be attacked under the theory follows easily from the analysis of disfranchisements. Local restrictions on speech can be remedied by state or national legislation that prevents local legislatures from enacting such restrictions. For example, in *Pennsylvania v. Nelson* the defendant had been convicted of "sedition against the United States," in violation of Pennsylvania law.[43] The Court held that in enacting the national sedition laws Congress had

---

41. Again, philosophers have faced these questions in connection with issues relating to the interests of the dead, and respecting those interests by means of validating living wills, and the interests of animals, who can be said to have an unambiguous preference to avoid unnecessary pain. See generally Peter Singer, *Animal Liberation* (1975); Jerrold Tannenbaum and Andrew Rowan, "Rethinking the Morality of Animal Research," 15:5 *Hastings Center Reports* 32 (1985). For an inadequate dismissal of this problem, see Ackerman, *Social Justice*, pp. 101–2.

42. This is a notable problem in discussions of the abortion issue, which can be phrased as a dispute over whether fetuses count as people for purposes of constitutional analysis. It is also central to the analysis of political gerrymandering. See Davis v. Bandemer, 106 S. Ct. 2797 (1986).

43. 350 U.S. 497 (1956).

intended to preempt all state regulation of the subject. *Katzenbach v. Morgan* and its supporting principle show that *Nelson* states a general proposition about congressional power to displace state regulations of speech.[44] For example, if Congress thought that communication about sexual matters was particularly important, it could exercise its power to enforce the first amendment and provide that no state shall enforce obscenity laws.

What sort of national legislation is prohibited by the theory of representation-reinforcing review? The electorate chooses public policies from among those offered by politicians competing for votes. May politicians be barred from offering some public policies to the electorate? Representation reinforcement suggests that policies inconsistent with the process of representation may (but need not) be excluded.

An example will show how the argument develops. Today's policy, adopted by some electorate's representatives in the past, is No discrimination on the basis of gender is permitted. Suppose Sam Spade wants to discriminate on the basis of gender. What can he do? As a first step he can use the processes of representation—such as lobbying, publicity, and voting—to seek repeal of the antidiscrimination policy. Now suppose that today's policy also is No advocacy of repeal of antidiscrimination laws is permitted. Spade can attempt to secure the repeal of the antiadvocacy law, and then repeal of the antidiscrimination law. Thus, the antiadvocacy law poses no formal obstacle to the alteration of present policies. Nothing so far is inconsistent with the process of representation.

We have now set up the recursive process referred to earlier. It can terminate in three ways. The Constitution might be seen to take some policies as beyond change, even through the use of the processes of representation; such policies would have to be determined by some other theory. Advocacy of repeal of antidiscrimination laws might be defined as an act of discrimination; the antidiscrimination law would in a sense be self-referential.[45] Finally, the Constitution might be seen to allow Congress to prohibit advocacy of changes in the fundamental processes of representation; that would be a sedition law.

We began with Spade's effort to repeal the antidiscrimination law. Suppose that instead of lobbying for its repeal Spade simply violated the law.[46] His action is inconsistent with the process of representation and may be prohibited; indeed, it is hard to see what the law could mean if its

44. This shows why we cannot limit *Nelson* by noting that the state statute by its own terms regulated a matter of national interest.

45. Self-referential statutes are very briefly analyzed in note 50.

46. The argument that follows draws from Robert Bork, "Neutral Principles and Some First Amendment Problems," 47 *Indiana Law Journal* 1 (1971).

violation could not be prohibited.[47] The same point applies to advocacy of lawbreaking. The advocate urges people to reject the outcome of the process of representation. A wise legislature might want to tolerate such advocacy as a useful part of the system of informal representation. But the theory does not allow us to distinguish between lawbreaking and its advocacy as a constitutional matter.[48]

The next step occurs when Spade says, "Any system that produces laws like this ought to be changed. Let's vote for a monarchy with me as King." Can his advocacy of overall constitutional change by constitutional means be prohibited? In one sense it is not inconsistent with the process of representation, because Spade proposes to invoke that process itself. Yet the substance of what he plans to put to a vote is inconsistent with the process, because Spade plans to substitute a nonrepresentational process for the existing one. The general criterion that representation-reinforcing review yields is that we may prohibit only speech that is inconsistent with the process of representation. Spade's advocacy of constitutional change is both consistent and inconsistent with the process. Ely ends his presentation by edging up to, and then fleeing from, this problem. He anticipates an objection to an exclusive concern with participation: a theory limited in that way prevents judicial invalidation of Nazi legislation. Not surprisingly, he rejects that objection by invoking the equal protection aspects of the theory: "A regime this horrible is imaginable in a democracy only because it so quintessentially involved the victimization of a discrete and insular minority."[49] Unfortunately this is not responsive to the real problem. The theory may be able to deal with Nazi legislation but not with the elections effectively abolishing the Weimar constitution.[50]

47. The situation does not change if Spade defends his action by calling it civil disobedience and by arguing that one method of persuading majorities to change the law is to show that it generates widespread disobedience. A legislature might be wise to allow a defense of civil disobedience in appropriate circumstances, but the idea of representation compels it neither to adopt nor to reject such a defense. If lawbreaking is defined as part of the representational process, any action could be similarly defined, and the theory would then mean that no action can be prohibited. Surely that conclusion is unacceptable.

48. It might do so if we insisted that there be a constitutional constraint responsive to concerns that juries might improperly find a causal connection between advocacy of law-breaking and actual lawbreaking. See text accompanying notes 51–52.

49. Ely, *Democracy and Distrust*, pp. 181–82.

50. This seems to me a version of one of the classical paradoxes of self-reference. Ordinarily such paradoxes are resolved by placing them in some transcendent framework. Representation-reinforcing review does not allow recourse to such a framework. Instead all questions must be resolved by talking about representation. Questions such as those raised by a self-referential statute could be answered by recourse to the higher language of the Constitution, yielding the relatively minor result that states may not enact statutes the advocacy of whose repeal itself violates the statutes.

Finally, there is the true sedition law, which prohibits the advocacy of overall constitutional change by nonconstitutional means. If such advocacy can be identified precisely the sedition law is indistinguishable from a ban on advocacy of lawbreaking.[51]

A chart will help clarify the point we have reached:

Advocacy of:

1	2	3
Lawbreaking	Overall constitutional change by constitutional means (Weimar election)	Overall constitutional change by nonconstitutional means (sedition)

Can it be prohibited?

Yes	Perhaps not	Yes

A few additional conclusions can be forced from the theory if we stipulate that it protects advocacy of overall constitutional change by constitutional means. If Category 2 is protected obviously we need a way to distinguish between speech that falls in protected Category 2 and prohibitable Categories 1 and 3. Standard first amendment theory approaches this problem by identifying two different categories which completely overlap the categories in the chart. In some situations, notably but not exclusively the classic sedition laws, the legislature has specified that a certain type of speech—advocacy of criminal anarchy or overthrow of the government by force and violence, for example—*is* advocacy of overall constitutional change by nonconstitutional means. In other situations the legislature has specified only a prohibited goal, such as obstruction of the draft, and a prosecutor seeks to show that a defendant's speech is causally connected to the accomplishment of the prohibited end. To convict when a defendant is charged with the first type of crime, the prosecutor must persuade a jury only that the defendant made the speech at issue and that the words constituted advocacy of the proscribed doctrine. To convict in the second situation, the prosecutor must persuade a jury not only that the defendant made the speech but also that the words used were sufficiently likely to lead to the proscribed behavior. The theory may tell us to analyze these situations differently.

It is easier to get something out of the "proscribed goal" category. We know that prosecutions for obstructing the draft will usually occur in

51. Incitement is a subcategory of advocacy of lawbreaking: an inciting statement causes listeners to break the law, thus bypassing the process of representation.

times of high excitement and substantial public support for the activities of the government. We also know that political dissidents frequently use words that either are ambiguous or have esoteric meanings within the dissident group and whose general meaning may seem more threatening. The Communist Party's advocacy of "the dictatorship of proletariat" will serve as an example. Given these facts we might be concerned that juries would improperly classify protected advocacy of change by constitutional means as proscribed advocacy of change by nonconstitutional means or might improperly infer a causal connection between speech and law violation on the basis of insufficient evidence. To guard against that kind of mistake, it might be helpful to provide what has been called a "breathing space" for protected speech. That is, we can identify a buffer zone around protected speech.[52] Words in that zone might formally constitute unprotected advocacy, but the risk of error about protected advocacy is so high that we allow some people who utter unprotected words to go unpunished so that the troubling kind of error is unlikely to occur.[53]

To summarize the analysis of free speech under the theory of representation-reinforcing review: The theory clearly prohibits statutes that make it illegal to advocate their own repeal. We can stipulate that it prohibits statutes that make it illegal to advocate overall constitutional change by constitutional means. By assuming that judges are rather stalwart, we can

52. For a fuller discussion, see Lillian BeVier, "The First Amendment and Political Speech: An Inquiry into the Substance and Limits of Principle," 30 *Stanford Law Review* 299 (1978). Ely, *Democracy and Distrust*, pp. 111–15, develops the idea that core first amendment rights require additional protection by means of giving a "breathing space" in which speech not truly protected by the first amendment nonetheless must remain free from state penalty. The point is an old one, as Gerald Gunther's analysis of a dispute between Learned Hand and Oliver Wendell Holmes over prosecutions during World War I has established. See Gerald Gunther, "Learned Hand and the Origins of Modern First Amendment Doctrine," 27 *Stanford Law Review* 719 (1975).

53. In this type of case the underlying problem is essentially one of evidence. The courts have general rules to control jury decisions based on insufficient evidence. See Schenck v. United States, 249 U.S. 47 (1919). Why are those methods inadequate in this setting? Ely suggests that judges, as do jurors, suffer from the passions of the times. Ely, *Democracy and Distrust*, pp. 107–8. But the breathing space is defined by precisely those judges who are thought to be unable to control juries through ordinary means. Instead of applying ordinary evidentiary tests with a speech-suppressive hand, judges instructed by the theory may just as easily contract the breathing space.

Sometimes we regard the jury as itself a short-term representative of the community. See Taylor v. Louisiana, 419 U.S. 522 (1975); Herbert Storing, *What the Anti-Federalists Were For* 18–19 (1981). To the extent that we do, structuring the law to restrict the jury's ability to decide certain questions amounts to overriding the decision of that representative body and so cannot be defended as reinforcing the process of representation. See also Frederick Schauer, "The Role of the People in First Amendment Theory," 74 *California Law Review* 761 (1986).

generate the need for some breathing space in "proscribed goals" cases. These results are not insignificant, although the more powerful of them occur only because of stipulations and assumptions that come from outside the theory itself. But just as with the analysis of disfranchisements, the results here are obviously vulnerable to even a fairly restrained challenge that they do not protect very much.

Representation Reinforcement, Equal Protection, and Due Process

So far we have refused to look beyond the formalities of the representational process. Once we let informal obstacles into the theory of course we will discover more significant results. But we will also lose the constraining force of the theory. This section argues that identifying informal obstacles requires that judges make controversial assessments of political reality. It begins with a critique from the right and concludes by sketching a critique from the left: a different set of assessments of political reality would show that informal obstacles to representation are far more pervasive than the theory's adherents seem willing to admit. Taken together these critiques demonstrate that a theory that considers informal obstacles to representation cannot constrain judges. Its adherents find it attractive because it falsely appears to them as a defense of the main lines of contemporary American liberal thought.

This argument can be developed by considering the third context in which the theory has been applied—the law of discrimination under the equal protection clause. The third paragraph of the *Carolene Products* footnote refers to "discrete and insular minorities." How does that fit into the theory? According to the theory, public policy must be based upon revealed preferences. The law of disfranchisement and free speech deals with how preferences are revealed. The law of equal protection deals with how policy is based on revealed preferences. Discrete and insular minorities are groups who are allowed to participate in the representative process but whose voices will not be listened to. The basic issue in this branch of the theory is then to distinguish between "discrete and insular minorities" and other minorities. People litigate constitutional claims when they seek to alter the result of the representational process in which they were losers. That is, such claims are made only by those who were in the minority on the issue when it was before the legislature. The theory must therefore distinguish between discrete and insular minorities, whose preferences are not taken into account, and other minorities, who are simple losers. Yet if we regard the political process as pluralist, even fairly weakly pluralist, as Ely does,[54] we run up against rather serious difficulties as we try to draw the required lines.

The difficulties take several forms, although they all occur when we regard the political process as one in which identifiable groups bargain with each other, deal and trade, and the like. The first form of the pluralist difficulty is one version of the problem of intensity that we have already seen. It occurs because groups have complex political agendas with many items. For example, suppose that women are interested in maintaining or increasing the level of public assistance to families with single parents. They are also interested in repealing portions of the Social Security laws that disadvantage working wives with dependent husbands. If enacted the public assistance item will help some women, and it will also help some blacks and Chicanos, some social workers, and others. The campaign for public assistance can then consist of an alliance of the affected groups. We can assume that the possibilities of alliance in regard to the Social Security reforms are smaller. It would then not be surprising to discover, when all was said and done, that public assistance had been maintained but Social Security not reformed. If we treated women as a discrete and insular minority, the courts might be authorized to invalidate the discriminatory Social Security provisions. But for all we know women were ordinary losers in their Social Security campaign. They may have cared enough about public assistance to build an alliance in which they did not extract a reciprocal commitment to reform Social Security. If the courts intervene even on the facially discriminatory statute, they may be displacing political judgments that resulted from a process in which all preferences were in fact taken into account. This outcome may occur whenever a group is not equally concerned about all the items on its agenda.

The standard move to counter an invocation of intensity as an explanation of political losses is to say that we cannot be concerned about single losses in the political process but must instead ask whether the group is a systematic loser in that process. When do we know that a group is a systematic loser? One possibility is that whenever a statute mentions the group it imposes a disadvantage on the group. The idea here is that a group is a systematic loser if whenever groupness becomes politically relevant the group loses. But this must be rejected for reasons already given. It ignores all items on the group's agenda that are won by statutes that do not classify at all. It fails to recognize the possibility that the group-disadvantaging statutes form part of a larger system of public policies in which, on balance and as a result of political bargaining, the

54. See Richard Parker, "The Past of Constitutional Theory—and Its Future," 42 *Ohio State Law Journal* 223 (1981).

group is better off than it would have been without the bargains. In a sense this definition of "systematic disadvantage" assumes that women are concerned only about "women's issues" narrowly conceived; that assumption is surely controversial.

An alternative is to define systematic losers as those who lose with respect to every item on their agendas.[55] So defined, the category is likely to be empty. In a minimally pluralist society every group has votes that will interest some other group attempting to put together a coalition.[56] Of course, one can imagine a group so marginalized or so small that it is simply disregarded as a potential coalition partner. But consider a tiny 1 percent group, ignored by everyone else, discovered by those who have struggled their way to assemble a 49.5 percent coalition. The incentive to satisfy some of the tiny group's interests will be quite high.[57]

The second form of the pluralist difficulty arises in Ely's presentation of the theory. Equal protection arguments have a fundamental structure. We are given a statute that treats one group of people in a manner different from the way in which another group is treated. We must decide whether that difference in treatment is justified. Ordinarily we will examine the statute to see what its purposes are and will find the difference justified if the groups differ in some characteristic relevant to the goal.[58]

---

55. That is, they lose across the entire range of interests they have. But suppose that some people are indifferent to all issues but one (or have the same distribution of preferences as the rest of the population does, except for one issue), and that is the issue on which they lose. Should they be regarded as systematic losers? The problem is posed by Tribe's criticism of Ely on the ground that Ely's theory cannot distinguish between respectable systematic losers and losers like exhibitionists. Tribe, "Puzzling Persistence," p. 1076. The example is particularly effective because it seems plausible that the issue on which exhibitionists lose is precisely the issue that goes to the heart of their self-definitions.

56. There is one situation where the pluralist process breaks down. This is the case of "backlash," where a coalition's effort to form an alliance with another group produces a net loss of support, as more people leave the coalition than are attracted to it from the new group. See Ackerman, "Beyond *Carolene Products*," pp. 732–33 (discussing "pariah groups" and suggesting that they are rare). A case can be made that this characterized the situation of blacks until roughly the 1930s, but even Ely concedes that the case is hard to make for the recent past. See Ely, *Democracy and Distrust*, pp. 151–52; Ackerman, "Beyond *Carolene Products*," pp. 744–45.

57. Ackerman argues that discreteness and insularity reduce the problems of organizing a group. Ackerman, "Beyond *Carolene Products*," pp. 724–28. Discreteness and insularity may give smaller groups a relative advantage in organization over larger ones. But the formalization of the point in Olson, *Logic of Collective Action*, pp. 22–33, is directed at groups much smaller than the ones with which Ackerman is concerned, which almost certainly have crossed the threshold beyond which size provides no relative disadvantages.

58. The classic exposition is Joseph Tussman and Jacobus ten Broek, "The Equal Protection of the Laws," 37 *California Law Review* 341 (1948). For a discussion of one approach to determining legislative purposes, see Chapter 6.

Ely argues that we can identify discrete and insular minorities by think-ing about the implications of this fundamental structure.[59] Observers can note the generic characteristics of legislators. Those characteristics—they are, in the main, white, male, and relatively well-to-do, for example—define the "we" who in practice enact legislation. "They" will tend to be relatively less understood than "we" are. For example, male legislators will tend to think of women as homemakers despite the fact that women participate in the formal labor force at rates approaching those of men. The legislators may therefore pass laws whose justification is ultimately that women tend to be homemakers. For example, Congress enacted a statute regulating dependency allowances for members of the armed forces.[60] The wives of servicemen were presumed to be dependent; the husbands of servicewomen could receive dependency allowances only if they showed that they contributed less than half of the family income. The government tried to defend the statute by saying that most wives were in fact homemakers whereas most husbands were in the formal labor force. The Court held the statute unconstitutional because this factual assump-tion was unsupported.[61]

Again pluralism intervenes. The we's have a political interest in re-sponding to the interests of the they's. Most Democratic legislators are white and relatively well-to-do, yet that has not prevented blacks and labor unions from becoming important parts of the Democratic coalition. More generally, the interests of the we's considered as members of one group (men, for example) are frequently not congruent with, although

59. Ely, *Democracy and Distrust*, pp. 145–70.

60. Frontiero v. Richardson, 411 U.S. 677 (1973).

61. There is one additional problem. Sometimes statutes are predicated on what might be called "true stereotypes," that is, statistical generalizations about a population that are largely accurate. For example, Craig v. Boren, 429 U.S. 190 (1976), involved an Oklahoma statute permitting women but not men between the ages of eighteen and twenty to buy 3.2 percent beer. The state presented empirical studies demonstrating that a much higher proportion of men than women in that age group was arrested for drunk driving. The difficulty is that the empirically based generalization on which the statute rested is most likely the product of cultural factors—the "macho" image held by young men, for exam-ple—that are themselves the products of legislative and social classifications of men and women.

It is not obvious why the "true stereotype" ought to be accepted as the basis for legislation, yet Ely's presentation of the theory of representation reinforcement suggests that it would have to be. See also Catharine MacKinnon. "Pornography as Sex Discrimination," 4 *Law and Inequality* 38, 39 (1986) ("Women are coerced to perform for pornography . . . [which] then is forced on women who are forced to act it out, to correspond to the way pornography uses and presents the women in it. It then becomes possible to point to the world pornography has created and say that it truthfully expresses women's nature, because it corresponds to their reality").

they may overlap, the interests of the we's considered as members of another group (whites). When white men want to enact legislation disfavoring women, they may find it helpful to bargain with black men. They therefore have an incentive to be accurate in their attribution of characteristics of blacks. Again, in general all they's are potential allies on some issues, which probably cannot be identified in advance. The we's have a political incentive to learn about the they's so that alliances can be built in the future.[62]

There is a further difficulty when the possibility of misattributing characteristics is invoked. The we-they analysis seems likely to work fairly well in cases involving statutes that impose disadvantages on nonmarital children. Most legislators are not bastards and are likely to think of nonmarital children as the products of unstable relationships quite foreign to the legislators' normal experience. The risk of stereotypical misattribution of characteristics seems reasonably high. But consider a case like *Trimble v. Gordon*, where the Court held unconstitutional an Illinois statute that allowed marital children to inherit from both parents in situations where there was no will but allowed nonmarital children to inherit only from their mothers in similar situations.[63] This looks like a classification based on legitimacy and gender. Yet it need not be so treated. The classification affected only children of fathers who died without leaving wills. Few male legitimate legislators are likely to think that they will die without wills. Instead of a we-they statute, then, we have a they$_1$-they$_2$ statute: The statute regulates two groups to neither of which the legislators belong. And it is hard to see why legislators would attach stereotypes to one group but not another.[64]

Of course there is something unnatural about the technique of collapsing purposes into classifications. *Trimble v. Gordon* involved a classification that, in large part, distinguished illegitimate children from legitimate children, and such classifications ought to be related to char-

---

62. See Ackerman, "Beyond *Carolene Products*," p. 734 n. 39.

63. 430 U.S. 762 (1977). This analysis is drawn from Note, "Legislative Purpose, Rationality, and Equal Protection," 82 *Yale Law Journal* 123 (1972).

64. If any stereotype is at work it is one that has something to do with irresponsibility, but images of irresponsibility in fathering a nonmarital child and irresponsibility in failing to leave a will might easily be involved in a complex mixture.

The Court has used the trick of redefining the classification to eliminate the sense of discreteness and insularity. In Parham v. Hughes, 441 U.S. 347 (1979), the Court upheld a Georgia law that allowed a mother but not a father to sue for the wrongful death of a nonmarital child. Observing that a father who had formally acknowledged that the child was his, prior to the child's death could sue, Justice Stewart wrote, the "classification does not discriminate against fathers as a class but instead distinguishes between fathers who have legitimated their children and those who have not."

acteristics that distinguish those groups not some other imaginable groups. The we-they theory has going for it an unarticulated sense that there are natural categories like race and gender. Yet statutes rarely use those categories in their pure form. The lines are drawn within specific contexts, like intestacy, wrongful death, and the like. The we-they theory gives no reason for selecting the broad generic category over the narrower contextualized category as the basis for the we-they analysis. Further, even if we can tolerate "natural" categories, how do we know where to stop? With race, or old age, or youth, or mental retardation, or size, or . . . ? Deciding what is a natural category is an act of judgment not determined by the premises of the theory. As the term suggests, the idea of natural categories probably flows from a natural law sense of things. But allowing natural law to intrude at this point destroys the purity of the theory and opens up the question If natural law is allowed here why is it not allowed everywhere?

The argument so far is this: (a) when the theory is confined to formal obstacles to representation, it yields so few constraints on legislative behavior that criticisms are convincing; (b) when the theory is adjusted to take account of informal obstacles, we can develop a powerful criticism from the right that what some might identify as informal obstacles are from another viewpoint just normal aspects of the operation of a pluralist system; (c) the theory cannot tell us which point of view the judges should take; (d) it therefore leaves the judges unconstrained and fails to eliminate the risk of judicial tyranny; and (e) it is open to the equally powerful criticism that even as modified the theory does too little to reduce the risks of legislative tyranny.[65]

A Realistic Politics of Process?

Informal obstacles can be invoked to invalidate social and economic legislation that most of the theory's proponents want to preserve. "Social and economic legislation" includes the limited benefits to the poor that the American welfare state has seen fit to provide; thus informal obstacles exist that would justify judicial imposition of much more extensive programs of wealth redistribution.

Railway Express Agency v. New York upheld a traffic regulation that generally prohibited the placement of advertising on the sides of trucks but allowed businesses to advertise their own activities on the sides of

65. Ely, Democracy and Distrust, is the most elaborate recent treatment of this theory. He concludes that the theory treats the following groups as minorities: blacks (with some labor on Ely's part), gays, and perhaps women with respect to statutes enacted prior to around 1950. On the whole the theory does not appear to be very powerful in this setting.

their own trucks.[66] This appears to be a simple they$_1$-they$_2$ classification. Looking at the generic groups involved we cannot say that many members of the New York City Council were owner-operators of trucks with advertising. But recall that our consideration of informal obstacles to representation allows us to look at political reality. Council members respond to more than the interests of generic groups to which they belong; they also respond to those who assist in their elections. As a group locally based owner-operators are likely to have more influence in local elections than Railway Express. Standing alone that fact shows only that Railway Express is an ordinary loser in politics. We can, however, find an inaccurate stereotype at work. Imagine what happens when the lobbyist for the owner-operators comes to the city council and proposes the regulation. One council member asks why it should be adopted. A hard-nosed but probably ineffectual lobbyist might say, "Because we want it, and we have the money and the votes." Indeed, there is a hard-nosed version of the theory which imagines that politics works that way.[67] Being hard-nosed is not being realistic, though, and that version underestimates the importance legislators attach to (purportedly) rational arguments in support of legislation.[68] If only to build a paper record, legislators want to hear reasons. So the better lobbyist will say something like, "Well, you know how greedy these big operators like Railway Express are." That is, the lobbyist will appeal to a generally shared stereotype that is probably less accurate than legislators and the public think it is.

In this example even if big operators are greedier than owner-operators, a proposition that is by no means obviously true, it is hard to see how greed translates into allowing more distracting advertising on their trucks. When the Court considered the case it too endorsed the stereotype without explaining why it was accurate enough. Justice Douglas' opinion, for example, said in a conclusory way that "those who advertise their own wares on their trucks [might] not present the same traffic problem in view of the nature or extent of the advertising which they use." Justice Jackson's more elaborate concurring opinion worked its way up to this: "There is a real difference between doing in self-interest and doing for hire, so that it is one thing to tolerate action from those who act on their

---

66. 336 U.S. 106 (1949).

67. See, e.g., Hans Linde, "Due Process of Lawmaking," 55 *Nebraska Law Review* 197 (1976).

68. Normative arguments against hard-nosed theories are presented in Lisa Newton, "Representation: The Duties of a Peculiar Station," in *Ethical Issues in Government* 41 (Norman Bowie ed. 1981).

own and it is another thing to permit the same action to be performed for a price." But what the real difference is, he failed to say.[69]

Similar informal obstacles to representation appear to occur in what are traditionally classified as substantive due process cases. In the *Slaughterhouse Cases* the Louisiana legislature required that all butchers in New Orleans use the facilities of the Crescent City Slaughter-House Company.[70] The burden of this monopoly fell in the first instance on the butchers excluded from their jobs, and between Crescent City and the butchers it is hard to find practical obstacles to political representation. The discussion of the commerce clause showed that producer-protective legislation such as the slaughterhouse monopoly imposes burdens on the consuming public. That discussion demonstrated that practical political obstacles exist to the full representation of the consumer interest. The organizers of the monopoly were able to extract money from potential beneficiaries, which they then distributed to legislators. They could do so because each potential beneficiary could see how the future returns would exceed the investment in bribery. In contrast, the benefits that competition yields to consumers are, for each consumer, small enough to make it hard to justify an offsetting "antibribery" bribe.[71]

One can go through the substantive due process cases to show producer protection at work.[72] For example, *Muller v. Oregon* upheld a maximum

69. 336 U.S., at 110, 116.

70. 83 U.S. (16 Wall.) 36 (1873). For the background, see Charles Fairman, 6 *History of the Supreme Court: Reconstruction and Reunion, 1864–88, Part One* 1321–24 (1971); Frances Olsen, "From False Paternalism to False Equality: Judicial Assaults on Feminist Community, Illinois 1869–1895," 84 *Michigan Law Review* 1518, 1527–28 n. 42 (1986).

71. More elaborately: Representatives are interested in election and reelection. Campaigning is costly, and candidates need to raise money for the campaigns. Narrow interest groups can collect money from their members, promising a net positive return to be based on regulations that will be adopted and that will raise prices to consumers by enough to cover the investment in the election and still yield a profit. They contribute this money to politicians in exchange for promises of, and as rewards for, supporting the regulations the interest groups desire.

The consumer interest in lower prices is at a disadvantage, because although consumers as a class benefit from deregulation, no individual consumer will gain enough to justify his or her own investment in political influence. Further, lower prices are a "public good" in the sense that their benefits are indivisible: Lower prices will be paid by every consumer and not just by those who invested in political influence. Even if some consumers resist the temptation to take a free ride on the activities of others, there will be underinvestment in political activity. Representatives will receive a distorted message about the relative desires of consumers and narrow interest groups, and overregulation will result.

72. See Neil Komesar, "Taking Institutions Seriously: Introduction to a Strategy for Constitutional Analysis," 51 *University of Chicago Law Review* 366, 414–25 (1984); Bernard Siegan, *Economic Liberties and the Constitution* 113–25 (1980); Sidney Tarrow, "Lochner versus New York: A Political Analysis," 5 *Labor History* 277 (1964).

hours law for women working in factories and laundries.[73] In practical terms that statute involved a deal struck between laundry operators and their male employees that imposed burdens on women laundry workers and consumers.[74] According to the informal branch of the theory, the Court should carefully examine the justifications offered for such statutes.

The argument so far is perfectly compatible with the way in which proponents of representation-reinforcing review identify and then rely on informal obstacles to representation. Perhaps because its conclusions are incompatible with the political inclinations of its proponents, its defects seem clear. Like all systematic theories about social processes, this version of the theory produces its insights by drastically simplifying its vision of the political process. For example, "economic regulation" is not the undifferentiated mass of legislation that the prior discussion suggests. Political scientists have identified four types of legislation, varying according to whether the costs are diffused broadly across all consumers and whether the benefits are concentrated on narrow interest groups.[75] But much contemporary regulation, sometimes called social regulation, involves situations in which costs are concentrated on the regulated entities while benefits are diffused.

We might try to deal with these situations in two ways. First, we could distinguish among the corporations in an industry subject to social regulation like antidiscrimination or consumer product safety laws. Larger and better-organized corporations will find it easier to adapt their operations to these laws, by hiring affirmative action specialists and safety engineers, than will their smaller competitors, who will have to increase the burdens on their generalist employees. The larger corporations will thus gain a competitive advantage as a result of social regulation and can be expected to provide sufficient lobbying support for it.

---

73. 208 U.S. 412 (1908).

74. Again to elaborate: The male workers found that competition for their jobs had increased. The pool of potential new workers was large enough to affect the wages of those working in laundries. A lower wage allows—and under competition requires—employers to reduce the prices they charge for laundry services. But again the difference between the prices is small from the consumer's point of view relative to the cost of influencing the legislature. The male laundry workers, though, were each likely to suffer a severe decline in total income as a result of the lower wage. By pooling their resources the male workers could contribute an amount up to the difference between their present wages and the threatened lower ones. They used this money to secure legislation excluding their potential competitors from the job market. Note, however, that Louis Brandeis' brief in support of the law argued that men and women did not in fact compete in the same labor market. Olsen, "False Paternalism," p. 1541.

75. See James Wilson, *The Politics of Regulation* (1980).

Second, legislators are interested in reelection. They will be concerned only with securing the votes of those who will be alive at the next election, and they will be indifferent to the interests of future generations, except insofar as the present electorate cares about those interests. But the present electorate tends to suffer from one form of the "fiscal illusion." Regulatory costs to be borne in the future are more severely discounted than the rate of interest justifies. As voters, consumers who are subject to the fiscal illusion will compare present benefits and excessively discounted costs and will vote for policies that are not in their self-interest, because they will contribute to an inflation that the voters, as consumers and parents, will come to regret.[76]

Both of these suggestions are plausible enough that no judge could be condemned for failing to respect the requirements of the theory were he or she to adopt them as the basis for invalidating social regulation. It should also be clear that something has gone seriously awry with the theory at this point. To the extent that the theory is augmented to take into account the complexity of the real world of politics, it loses its attractiveness as a ground for a constitutional theory. For example, in the real world of politics, the statute in *Muller* was the product of a complex alliance among labor unions, social workers, ideologues, and the like.[77] If an augmented theory allowed this sort of alliance to qualify as a systematic distortion of the political process, it is hard to see what would not count. Constitutional theory must resist that conclusion.

A similar expansion of one's vision of political reality leads, finally, to the critique of representation-reinforcing review from the left. The theory translates the political scientists' analysis of the American polity as pluralist into the domain of constitutional theory.[78] That analysis, which flourished in the 1950s and 1960s, has been seriously challenged. Participation in politics is so low as to raise questions about the representativeness of the process as a whole. Poor people take a strikingly small part in pluralist politics, and they do so because poverty and political weakness reinforce each other.

Political theorists have developed a twofold argument that describes the structural bases for the political advantages held by business and for the political weakness of workers in the United States. According to

---

76. E. Donald Elliott, "Constitutional Conventions and the Deficit," 1985 *Duke Law Journal* 1077, 1091–95, explains the persistence of budget deficits along these lines, although he assumes that voters are purely self-interested and do not care about the welfare of their children and ignores the effects of the fiscal illusion. Elliott proposes constitutional revisions that would alter politicians' incentives. Alternatively, we could invoke the theory of representation reinforcement to explain why courts should remedy the budget problem.

77. See Olsen, "False Paternalism," pp. 1539–40.

78. As before, this argument draws on Parker, "Past of Constitutional Theory."

Charles Lindblom, business has a strategic position in the political process.[79] In a decentralized capitalist economy, business carries out functions that affect employment, prices, and the like. Because their continuation in office depends on favorable economic conditions, politicians must provide the climate within which business can perform those functions. Doing so involves providing appropriate incentives to investment, which in turn limits the range of policies that can be chosen if politicians are to retain office. For example, business approval is needed so that the tax revenues produced by a climate hospitable to business can be sustained. Thus, items are kept off the political agenda not primarily by statutory exclusion but by what Lindblom calls a process of "molding" the population's sense of what sorts of items ought to be taken seriously.[80] People rationally have preferences that stabilize the existing order, although they might prefer different things if the political structure provided different incentives for rational choice.

Appropriately organized, people might challenge the free enterprise system itself; if they did the structural advantages of business would disappear. But the structure of politics impedes anti–free enterprise activities. Claus Offe has argued, for example, that although business can measure its interests solely by considering profits, labor must be concerned with a range of interests, from wages to working conditions to time available for leisure. As a result, he argues, labor must organize itself internally along two lines: a bureaucratic structure concerned with rationally maximizing the goals it is given and a democratic structure designed to communicate to the bureaucracy what the members want. Further, labor can accomplish its goals only by collective activity, which means that some sort of solidarity must be developed to replace an entirely individualist orientation. This is a difficult enough task, but in addition its accomplishment may be self-limiting. Offe argues that unions must be large if they are to be strong enough to carry out successful industrial action. But as they grow so does their internal bureaucracy, thus weakening the forces of internal democracy and reducing their members' attachment to the union. This limits their ability to carry out successful collective action.[81]

79. Charles Lindblom, *Politics and Markets* (1977); Charles Lindblom, "The Market as Prison," 44 *Journal of Politics* 324 (1982). See also Amartya Sen, "The Moral Standing of the Market," 2:2 *Social Philosophy and Policy* 1 (1985).

80. See, e.g., Peter Bachrach and Morton Baratz, *Power and Poverty: Theory and Practice* (1972). A useful summary of Lindblom's argument is Book Review, "Liberalism, Separation and Speech," 1985 *Wisconsin Law Review* 79, 95–97.

81. See generally Claus Offe, *Disorganized Capitalism: Contemporary Transformations of Work and Politics*, chs. 6, 7 (1985).

Along similar lines but more concerned with the particular structure of American politics, Joshua Cohen and Joel Rogers argue that workers rationally choose short-term gains through collective action rather than seek larger potential gains through broader political action.[82] The structure of American government makes it difficult to coordinate challenges to the free enterprise system: the separation of powers on the national level and the dispersal of significant governmental authority to the states place substantial barriers in the way of coordinated anti–free enterprise political action. Consider, for example, how difficult it would be to develop an effective program to limit the ability of long-established companies to relocate their plants if economic circumstances, as determined by the companies' managers, warranted. The problems are most likely to be experienced by one locality at a time, but localized regulations might be held to violate the commerce clause by impeding the free flow of capital and in any event are likely to be ineffective in light of the ability of managers to mobilize and relocate financial assets rather than plants. Securing legislation from Congress would be difficult, too, because of such characteristics of the separation of powers as the fact that only one-third of the Senate is elected every two years. These difficulties place workers at a structural disadvantage in political contention.[83]

Given *this* analysis of American politics we can turn the theory against its proponents. Legislation that disadvantages the poor is likely to result from a process that fails to take the interests, though not the rational existing preferences, of the poor fully into account. The courts should therefore insist that legislation be supported by reasons other than a

82. Joshua Cohen and Joel Rogers, *On Democracy: Toward a Transformation of American Society* (1983). For additional discussion of the ways in which institutional arrangements shape preferences that are then rationally aggregated in the political process, see Chapter 9.

83. It is important to emphasize that the arguments of these political scientists do not invoke controversial notions of "false consciousness," to which Ely and Ackerman have directed attention. See Ely, *Democracy and Distrust*, pp. 164–66; Ackerman, "Beyond Carolene Products," pp. 736–37. For a discussion of how choices can be "tainted" by "distorted attitudes," see Paul Gewirtz, "Choice in the Transition: School Segregation and the Corrective Ideal," 86 *Columbia Law Review* 728, 745–48 (1986). They are describing rational responses to existing political structures.

These responses combine in an interesting way with the public choice analysis of the role of organized interest groups such as unions. Critics like Offe and Cohen and Rogers argue that labor is at a systematic disadvantage vis-à-vis capital; public choice theorists argue that consumers are at a systematic disadvantage vis-à-vis organized labor. The interaction of these processes may be particularly damaging to labor, whose gains from their advantage over consumers are limited by the power of capital and are confined to labor unions and their members. This may lead consumers to see organized labor as a primary source of their problems and further weaken, or at least stabilize the weakness of, labor.

desire to disadvantage the poor.[84] Thus, the theory of representation reinforcement would allow judges to impose either a strict regime of laissez-faire or a socialist economy, all in the name of rectifying defects in the process of representation. The basic difficulty is that the political process is enormously complex.[85] If the theory directs judges to develop a realistic view of that process, their decisions will be determined by which among numerous empirically defensible views they choose to adopt. It will therefore fail to constrain the judges. Yet if the theory discards its realism about politics, it leaves us with a purely formal analysis that fails to constrain legislators.

The complexity of modern American politics makes the theory unsatisfactory as an approach to judicial review. That complexity also suggests some reasons for the weakness of the republican tradition. The dynamics of economic growth reduced the effectiveness of localized cooperative activities; with such activities seeming less important citizens turned their attention to the more centralized institutions of government. But localized institutions allowed people to develop moral attitudes of mutual respect and responsibility; they approach the more remote institutions of the national government seeking primarily to get something for themselves. As Joseph Schumpeter and others have argued, once that happens the moral support for both capitalism and democracy erodes.[86]

This suggests, finally, that we might conclude our consideration of representation reinforcement by directing attention to the process values served by federalism. Drawing on the theory of public choice, Andrzej Rapaczynski has evoked the republican tradition in explaining that federalism helps in "protecting individual rights against a tyrannical government," which is something valuable that we all desire but would prefer that someone else pay for—a public good.[87] As we have seen, smaller

---

84. Ely says that "what typically disadvantage the poor are various failures on the part of the government (or anybody else) to alleviate their poverty by providing one or another good or service" and that such failures result from a "constitutionally innocent" "reluctance to raise the taxes needed to support such expenditures." Ely, *Democracy and Distrust*, p. 162. This maneuver is coherent only because Ely characterizes "reluctance to raise taxes" as "innocent"; he can get away with doing this only so long as we do not direct a challenge to the private property system itself. When that challenge is made, "we don't want to raise taxes" means "we like what we get out of the private property system and don't care if you don't like, and indeed are seriously disadvantaged by, it."

85. For a discussion framed in public choice terms, see Gordon Bergsten, "Toward a New Normative (Economic) Theory of Politics," 39 *Review of Social Economy* 67 (1981).

86. See Michael Taylor, "On 'Normative' Rational-Choice Theories of Politics," in *Politics as Rational Action: Essays in Public Choice and Policy Analysis* 25 (Leif Lewin and Evert Vedung eds,. 1980); *Dilemmas of Liberal Democracies: Studies in Fred Hirsch's Social Limits to Growth* (Adrian Ellis and Krishnan Kumar eds. 1983).

87. Rapaczynski, "Sovereignty to Process," p. 376.

groups are easier to organize than larger ones, and groups concentrated in one location are likely to develop ties of friendship and cooperation that further ease the burdens of organizing in opposition to outside efforts at control.[88] In addition, the republican tradition emphasized the value of political participation as a method of civic education, which could be best achieved in small units of government.[89] In these ways federalism is as much a process of representation as voting is. Of course state and local governments are still too large and in any event have been themselves weakened by economic growth and the accretion of power in the national government.[90]

We would have a quite attractive democratic representative process if we could perfect it. But the courts certainly cannot, and the citizenry might find the task overwhelming.

88. See Ackerman, "Beyond *Carolene Products*," pp. 725–26; Rapaczynski, "Sovereignty to Process," pp. 386–88.

89. See Chapter 1; Rapaczynski, "Sovereignty to Process," pp. 401–3.

90. For a discussion of impediments to direct democracy on the state level, see Richard Briffault, "Distrust of Democracy," 63 *Texas Law Review* 1347 (1985). The impediments, which include size and the effects of the existing distribution of wealth, seem to be the same as those that affect representative democracy.

3

The Jurisprudence
of Philosophy

ONE day, as Justice Oliver Wendell Holmes was leaving to go to the Supreme Court, a friend said to him, "Well, off to do justice again!" Holmes is said to have replied, "Sonny, I don't do justice; I just make sure that people play by the rules." The preceding chapters have shown that judges in the liberal tradition cannot merely ensure that people play by the rules. Holmes's quip suggests that there is nothing else that they can do, and thus, if the preceding chapters are correct, that they cannot do even that. But the Justice's friend appealed to a deeply rooted sense that judges can do something else—they can provide justice. For our purposes doing justice means making sure that the legal process produces morally acceptable outcomes.[1] In this view judges should uphold statutes that are morally permissible and strike down those that are morally impermissible.[2]

What could be wrong with having judges make their decisions with reference to moral imperatives? This chapter examines several types of theory that rely on moral philosophy.[3] It argues that each type must

1. A stronger version of this approach would demand that the legal process produce the outcomes that morality requires rather than merely those that morality permits. The conclusions in this chapter, which derive from an analysis of the weaker version, would hold were the stronger version adopted.

2. This approach has a rather long lineage in constitutional law. Dicta in Justice Chase's opinion in Calder v. Bull, 3 U.S. (3 Dall.) 386 (1798), and an alternative ground for decision in Fletcher v. Peck, 10 U.S. (6 Cranch) 87 (1810), indicate that members of the Court at those times believed that it could invalidate legislation on the ground that it violated principles of natural justice.

3. Brian Barry, "The Strange Death of Political Philosophy," 15 Government and Opposition 276 (1980), and William Ruddick, "Philosophy and Public Affairs," 47 Social Research 734 (1980), provide intellectual histories of the revival of interest in substantive political theory in the late 1960s. Both mention the influence of the Vietnam War experience and the publication of Rawls, Theory of Justice. In constitutional law the experience of the Warren Court was also important in attracting people to moral philosophy as a basis for constitutional decisions, in part because the alternative constitutional theories did not seem

resolve some important conceptual questions, which may be impossible, and that in any event there is little reason to believe that judges in our society—today, not twenty years ago or twenty years from now—can really do justice.

The Positive Case for Philosophy

We have seen that there are few persuasive arguments supporting originalism or representation-reinforcing review as affirmatively desirable theories of judicial review; the best arguments were that they were good enough, and better than alternative theories. Initially the case for relying on moral philosophy seems different. It almost has to be true that it is a good thing to have judges assess a statute's constitutionality by considering moral requirements. The *almost* is important, though, because there are several grounds for challenging the positive case for relying on philosophy.

First, it might be that there simply are no discoverable moral truths against which statutes can be measured. Philosophers call this position metaethical skepticism,[4] and these days they have tended to reject it.[5] Metaethical skepticism does play a continuing role in our culture, perhaps because it is one way to make sense of the liberal tradition's insistence that in ordering our public institutions we may not give one person's view of the good more weight than another person's. Metaethical skepticism seems to explain why that is so, but it is not the only explanation for the political theory of the liberal tradition. It therefore is appropriate simply to note that if today's philosophers are wrong and metaethical skepticism is right, the project of the theory of relying on moral philosophy would be defeated at the outset.[6]

---

to justify decisions—such as Shapiro v. Thompson, 394 U.S. 618 (1969) (holding unconstitutional a one-year residency requirement for receipt of public assistance)—that alleviated some of the burdens placed on poor people.

4. See, e.g., Gilbert Harman, "What Is Moral Relativism?" in *Values and Morals: Essays in Honor of William Frankena, Charles Stevenson, and Richard Brandt* 146–48 (Alvin Goldman and Jaegwon Kim eds. 1978); Richard Brandt, "Ethical Relativism," in 3 *Encyclopedia of Philosophy* 75 (Paul Edwards ed. 1967).

5. See, e.g., Richard Rorty, *Consequences of Pragmatism* 166–67 (1982); Tom Beauchamp, *Philosophical Ethics: An Introduction to Moral Philosophy* 33–52 (1982). But see Bernard Williams, *Ethics and the Limits of Philosophy* (1985) (defending a form of skepticism).

6. The project, at least within a liberal society, would also be defeated if it turned out that the proper moral philosophy were a theological one. That is, suppose that the basic justification for moral commands is that they are the word of God. A justified judicial decision relying on morality will then necessarily invoke a theological conception of morality, which will be inconsistent with the secular commitments of liberal society. An elaborate

Second, perhaps it is a bad thing to have *judges* decide that some statutes are morally impermissible. One strong version of this argument is that majorities just cannot make moral mistakes. In this view morality consists in aggregating what people want and seeing how the calculation comes out. This is, however, a particularly unattractive form of utilitarianism. It assumes that what people want now is all that morality cares about. The best modern utilitarians argue, in contrast, that a person's present preferences might be distorted in a host of ways—for example, by lack of information or by experiences that make her or him unable to assess properly the degree to which some action will produce what she or he actually wants—and that these distortions can be corrected by a sort of "cognitive therapy." Judicial review might sensibly be seen as one element in the therapeutic endeavor.[8]

Even if majorities can make moral mistakes it might be better overall to allow a majority to decide some questions in a morally incorrect way than to override those decisions. For example, we might then get a system of moral education that would produce better results in the long run. The majority might learn from its moral mistakes and rectify them itself. If forced to forgo what it now wishes to do, the majority may resent the courts for overriding its present desires and may not grow in its understanding of what the good is.

Nearly everyone seems to accept the force of this argument as to some issues. Some versions of moral philosophy are particularly greedy, tending to divide human conduct into the two domains of the morally prohibited and the morally required.[9] If courts were to enforce the judgments of those versions of moral philosophy, they would make all the society's decisions. But because judges can make moral mistakes too, we might end up with less good in the long run than if we let people learn from their mistakes. If we could figure out the issues on which learning from experience should be preferred to the immediate imposition of morally correct solutions, things would be all right.

---

examination of the relation between liberalism and religion is Kent Greenawalt, *Religious Convictions and Political Choice* (1987).

7. See, e.g., Richard Brandt, *A Theory of the Good and the Right* (1979). For a survey of recent utilitarianism, see James Griffin, "Modern Utilitarianism," 36 *Review of International Philosophy* 331 (1982).

8. Representation-reinforcing review, discussed in Chapter 2, which corrects some (arguably cognitive) errors, is a version of this endeavor. But the errors it corrects are too limited to make it an acceptable utilitarian theory.

9. Philosophers regard utilitarianism as a greedy theory in this way. See, e.g., Peter Singer, "Famine, Affluence, and Morality," 1 *Philosophy and Public Affairs* 229 (1972). It is criticized not only for its extensive scope but for its failure to include a concept of supererogatory acts.

Other moral philosophies add a third category of acts to the prohibited and the required. These are morally permissible acts, about which moral theory is neutral. These philosophies must identify the boundaries between the categories. That task resembles the need to identify issues on which moral learning is preferable.

The line drawing and issue identification tasks have produced consensus on the formulation of the solution. We have to distinguish between fundamental, basic, or human rights on the one hand and nonfundamental, less basic rights on the other. On matters involving fundamental rights we reject the solution of learning from our experience in making moral mistakes; or, on such matters there are no morally neutral actions. Then, according to the present theory, courts can enforce the judgments of moral philosophy. First they must decide whether a fundamental right is implicated by the statute in question. If it is courts must then decide whether the statute has reached a morally impermissible result.[10]

The positive case for relying on moral philosophy thus turns on the ability of judges to distinguish between fundamental and other rights and then to decide what moral philosophy requires, all within the framework of the liberal tradition's concern that judges be appropriately constrained. The case against relying on moral philosophy is that judges cannot—and perhaps should not—do what the positive case requires of them.

Systematic Moral Philosophy

It is convenient to distinguish between two types of moral philosophy. This section and the next deal with systematic moral philosophy: the application of the tools of reason and analysis to a set of relatively abstract principles, which are themselves defended in relatively abstract ways, from which conclusions are drawn about the moral status of particular laws or conduct. Then the chapter considers a variety of ways that constitutional theory might rest on the morality implicit in a community's way of life.

We have seen that metaethical skepticism is one challenge to systematic moral philosophy. Another challenge would examine the high-level principles of whatever systematic philosophies people offer, to see if they

10. There are slight differences between the two approaches: In a two-category system finding that no fundamental right is implicated means that we might have a morally impermissible result but prefer under these circumstances to learn from experience. In a three-category system finding that no fundamental right is implicated means that the statute is morally neutral.

make moral sense; that is a task for philosophers.[11] This section offers two
other challenges. The first suggests that the abstract analysis of systematic
moral philosophy is the wrong way to engage in moral thought. This
challenge holds that even if there are moral truths they cannot be discovered by the characteristic methods of systematic moral philosophy. The
second challenge considered here is that, no matter what might be said
about moral reasoning in the abstract, the judges who will actually be
called upon to make the decisions are not different enough from legislators to justify relying on them rather than on legislators for moral
wisdom.

The challenge to abstract analysis must be set in the general framework
for all constitutional theory: the requirement that theory provide constraints on judges. As we have seen, it follows from this requirement that
theories must provide rules that both guide and constrain judicial discretion. Judges would not be constrained if they were told simply to assimi-
late all the information relevant to a decision and then issue a judgment
without explaining how the information led them to that decision.[12] In the
present context the liberal tradition's insistence that judges be constrained
commits it to a rule-oriented moral philosophy, in which relatively general rules are stated and applied to individual cases.[13]

The challenge to rule-oriented moral philosophy can take a wholesale
or a retail form. The wholesale challenge is that rule-oriented moral
philosophies are not good ones no matter what the rules are.[14] Such
philosophies focus on the rational manipulation of relatively abstract

11. From the perspective of a consumer of the philosophers' discussions of such important issues as abortion and distributive justice, the discussions have one striking characteristic. They appear to be controversies not over premises but over what one would have
thought were deductions. In the discussions of abortion, for example, everyone agrees that
Kantian ideals of respect for persons ought to control the results. See, e.g., *The Rights and
Wrongs of Abortion* (Marshall Cohen, Thomas Nagel, and Thomas Scanlon eds. 1974).
Disagreement rages over what the characteristics of a person are so as to bring the Kantian
ideal into play, over what entities have the agreed-upon characteristics, and over what
constitutes the required respect for those entities. Similarly, concerning distributive justice,
both John Rawls and Robert Nozick begin with the premise that the just society is in some
way the product of decisions by self-directed and autonomous individuals. In that sense they
too are both Kantians. Yet their descriptions of the just society differ about as much as can
be imagined. See also Rorty, *Consequences of Pragmatism*, pp. 167–68.

12. Max Weber called this form of the administration of justice "khadi" justice, describing the activities of a Moslem judge dispensing justice while sitting under a tree. See Max
Weber, *Law in Economy and Society* 213 (Max Rheinstein ed. 1954).

13. In describing adjudication in the liberal tradition as relatively rule oriented, I do not
mean to suggest that it is a deductive process.

14. Note that this challenge does not require one to take a position on what the morally
correct rules are. See note 11.

principles. There is a competing tradition in moral philosophy that insists that moral judgments can be made only in a holistic, completely contextualized way. That tradition captures much more of our sense of how we evaluate, or ought to evaluate, actions by ourselves or others. Consider for example a woman's decision to have an abortion or complete her pregnancy. It seems clear that this decision is frequently a difficult one, even for people who believe in principle that every woman has a right to make that decision unaffected by coercive governmental regulation.[15] Before deciding whether the woman's decision to have the abortion or bear the child is the right thing to do,[16] most of us would want to know a lot about her individual circumstances: her age, her relation to the father, the conditions under which the pregnancy occurred, her notions of her own potential, her aspirations, her religious convictions, and on almost indefinitely. Of course the consideration of context must end at some point, for she must make a decision one way or the other. But moral rules are likely to play a small part in the process or in our evaluation of her decision.[17]

The example of the decision to abort or not suggests that individual moral deliberation about particular acts is substantially more context oriented than rule oriented. Does this imply anything about the way that social institutions such as courts should consider the morality of general laws? The wholesale argument against rule-oriented morality is that the only sound method of moral decision making is holistic and contextualized.[18] This has two implications. One is a general presumption in favor of

15. See Kathleen McDonnell, *Not an Easy Choice: A Feminist Re-examines Abortion* (1984); Linda Franke, *The Ambivalence of Abortion* (1978).

16. This evaluation can take place outside the context of adjudication; we might be thinking about the woman's choice for purposes of our moral evaluation of the woman or for purposes of our own moral growth.

17. See Williams, *Limits of Philosophy*, p. 180 ("as often in moral philosophy, if one puts in the detail the example may begin to dissolve"); George Eliot, *The Mill on the Floss* 469 (Everyman's Library ed. 1908) ("All people of broad, strong sense have an instinctive repugnance to the men of maxims; because such people early discern that the mysterious complexity of our life is not to be embraced by maxims, and that to lace ourselves up in formulas of that sort is to repress all the divine promptings and inspirations that spring from growing insight and sympathy. And the man of maxims is the popular representative of the minds that are guided in their moral judgment solely by general rules, thinking that these will lead them to justice by a ready-made patent method, without the trouble of exerting patience, discrimination, impartiality, without any care to assure themselves whether they have the insight that comes from a hardly-earned estimate of temptation, or from a life vivid and intense enough to have created a wide fellow-feeling with all that is human").

18. This is one reading of some versions of feminist theory. See, e.g., Carol Gilligan, *In a Different Voice: Psychological Theory and Women's Development* (1982); Jean Grimshaw, *Philosophy and Feminist Thinking* (1986); Kenneth Karst, "Woman's Constitution," 1984 *Duke Law Journal* 447; Suzanna Sherry, "Civic Virtue and the Feminine Voice in Constitu-

a fairly anarchistic system of social order, precisely because anarchism denies the moral propriety of regulating life according to rules.[19] The other implication, more directly relevant here, is that judicial review in the liberal tradition cannot be based on a sound method of moral deliberation, precisely because the tradition requires that judicial review be rule oriented.

Perhaps, though, context-dependent judgments actually rely on a limited, albeit complex, assessment of context. If so we could examine a number of such judgments to extract the evaluative criteria actually being used and from those criteria develop the moral rules we might be looking for. Or perhaps moral deliberation on the social level properly uses methods that differ from those used on the individual level. The wholesale argument might then fail. There is, however, a powerful "retail" argument against the use of systematic moral philosophy as a theory of judicial review. The retail argument is that, whenever we look at claims that some set of moral truths implies that certain social arrangements are morally required, permissible, or prohibited, we find that the connections between the general truths and the particular results are incredibly ad hoc.[20] This produces a well-grounded skeptical belief that people are just

---

tional Adjudication," 72 *Virginia Law Review* 543 (1986); Paul Spiegelman, "Court-Ordered Hiring Quotas after Stotts: A Narrative on the Role of the Moralities of the Web and the Ladder in Employment Discrimination Doctrine," 20 *Harvard Civil Rights–Civil Liberties Law Review* 339 (1985); Ann Scales, "The Emergence of Feminist Jurisprudence: An Essay," 95 *Yale Law Journal* 1373 (1986). Cf. Christina Whitman, "Individual and Community: An Appreciation of Mr. Justice Powell," 68 *Virginia Law Review* 303 (1982) (similar perspective offered by female law professor, without expressly describing it as feminist). Gilligan's work is assessed in "On *In a Different Voice:* An Interdisciplinary Forum," 11 *Signs* 304 (1986).

19. An anarchist system of social order might have rules of thumb, defeasible presumptions, or general rules that always provide exceptions when they are appropriate, without any particularization of what *appropriate* means. It should be emphasized that anarchism does not deny that there will be some mechanisms of developing social order, such as socialization, shared holistic judgments, and the like. See generally Michael Taylor, *Community, Anarchy, and Liberty* (1982). For a useful speculative examination of the social order of anarchy, see Ursula Le Guin, *The Dispossessed* (1974), discussed in Philip Smith, "Unbuilding Walls: Human Nature and the Nature of Evolutionary and Political Theory in *The Dispossessed*," in *Ursula K. Le Guin* 77 (Joseph Olander and Martin Greenberg eds. 1979); John Brennan and Michael Downs, "Anarchism and Utopian Tradition in *The Dispossessed*," id., p. 116.

20. One false issue should be put aside. One might assume that the truths of moral philosophy are complex and that judges, removed from the pressures of political life, are better able to develop appropriately complex resolutions of moral problems. But moral truths need not be complex. A complex process of reasoning may lay behind a philosopher's conclusion that abortion is murder, but the conclusion is simplicity itself.

dressing up their personal preferences and presenting them as the products of abstract moral reasoning.

The retail argument cannot be made comprehensively, because it is an argument about how people argue about free speech, abortion, equality, and so on down the line, and because it is an argument about the likelihood—not the abstract possibility—of connecting general moral truths to particular results, given the apparent failure of each effort to do so. A comprehensive retail argument would have to enumerate every area of law and every available moral argument, which would be tedious at best and impossible at worst. The alternative way to support the retail argument is to examine one or two areas, exposing the form of retail arguments and suggesting in conclusion that an inductive generalization seems appropriate: Someone who claims that systematic moral philosophy yields real conclusions about actual statutes would have the burden of producing a solid example that is invulnerable to retail challenges. In short, it is not enough to say that judges should do justice; we have to see that they actually can do it.

Consider, then, a problem in the general area of the constitutional law of family life. David A. J. Richards, one of the scholars most seriously dedicated to developing a theory of nonabstract constitutional rights, has examined this area of law on the premise that "we must philosophically conceive and explicate the conflicting rights of children, parents, and society, as a matter of general moral and constitutional principle." The principles he seeks must be "systematic," must avoid "balancing . . . principles . . . in an intuitionistic way," and must "organize . . . and explain [our intuitions] as the consequences of deeper premises." Richards finds in the Constitution a theory of human rights involving "the belief that every person has a capacity for autonomy, and . . . the principle that every person has the right to equal concern and respect in pursuit of his autonomy." After presenting his theory in a general way, he applies it to problems of family life. According to Richards, under the Constitution children are beneficiaries of rights to equal opportunity and of liberal paternalism; parents "as such, have rights over their children derived from liberal paternalism."[21]

Equal opportunity requires that children have access to resources for socialization and education sufficient to give them a fair chance in life. This requires in turn that they have a stable relationship with a psychological parent. What is most striking about Richards' presentation is his assumption that biological parents in nuclear families are the "natural"

---

21. David Richards, "The Individual, the Family, and the Constitution: A Jurisprudential Perspective," 55 *New York University Law Review* 1, 5–6, 20 (1980).

providers of the required material and psychological resources. To Richards it is "a startling failure of imagination to conclude that . . . communal rearing [is] required," because "although some forms of communal rearing undoubtedly may provide the individualized care that is morally due children, others do not," and "extreme forms . . . violate the rights of children more than any but the most abusive parents might." In contrast, "the nuclear family accommodates the end of individualized care naturally." Richards writes that parents have a "right . . . to raise *their* children," derived in part from "the presumption that parents have the ability and the willingness that best fulfills each child's right to individualized care" and in part from the fact that "one's children are the test of one's life and aspirations." Richards assumes that biological parents are "most suited to custody and control" because "they often have the strongest motives to provide the . . . environment that is the child's right."[22]

Surely here Richards himself suffers from a failure of imagination. The values he attributes to biological parenthood are actually characteristics of *social* arrangements to which we have become accustomed.[23] A useful example is *Lehr v. Robertson*, which involved a biological father who had not married his daughter's mother.[24] The mother married another man and the couple made plans to adopt the child. The biological father had continuously attempted to locate his daughter and even hired a detective agency to find her. Once he found his daughter her mother refused to permit him to see her. The Supreme Court rejected his claim that he had

22. Id., pp. 21, 28 (emphasis added), 36.

23. A fanatic who misunderstands the teaching of sociobiology might claim that, despite the general pervasive influence of social arrangements, there remains a residue of purely genetic concern for the preservation of the genetic material each parent has provided. See Edward O. Wilson, *On Human Nature* (1978). Yet the emphasis on "reciprocal altruism" in sociobiological thought demonstrates that nothing turns on the existence of such a residue. Suppose, for example, that infants were separated from their mothers at birth, were placed in hospital nurseries, and were brought out at random to mothers who wanted to see "their" children. Clearly in such a system no one would have any greater sociobiological interest in advancing the cause of the child he or she brought home from the hospital than in advancing the cause of any other child. A fanatic might claim that the procedures by which nurses bring infants out from the nursery to mothers is genetically influenced. The variability in child-rearing practices of that sort is so great as to make that claim implausible.

The few suggestions that sociobiology should be used in legal analysis are not terribly persuasive—see, e.g., Jon Beckstrom, *Sociobiology and the Law: The Biology of Altruism in the Courtroom of the Future* (1985); David Maleski, "Sociobiology and the California Public Trust Doctrine: The New Synthesis Applied," 25 *Natural Resources Journal* 429 (1985); Joseph Shepher and Judith Reisman, "Pornography: A Sociobiological Attempt at Understanding," 6 *Ethology and Sociobiology* 103 (1985)—primarily because they systematically underestimate the influence of social arrangements, which are contingent facts even within the sociobiological paradigm, on legal ones.

24. 463 U.S. 248 (1983).

an absolute right to notice of the pending adoption. It distinguished between "a developed parent-child relationship," in which the parents' "emotional attachments . . . derive from the intimacy of daily association," and what it termed an "inchoate relationship." *Lehr v. Robertson* established as a matter of contemporary constitutional law that the relevant parent-child relationship is affectional and emotional, not biological. Thus, this relationship is largely dependent on social arrangements independent of the law, such as the mother's ability to conceal the location of her child. If "the family" is defined by ties of affection rather than blood, it is hard to see a distinction between rights pertaining to "the family" and those pertaining to "the family of man," that is to people generally. The exercise attempted to specify some subset of human rights derived from notions of autonomy and equal concern. Given the role that social institutions play in defining what counts as a family, though, the derived subset is the same as the original one.

Richards of course might respond by claiming that *Lehr v. Robertson* was wrongly decided. But the broader point, the contingency of the relationship between biological parenthood and the values from which Richards attempts to derive parental rights, can be seen in another way by imagining a society only slightly different from our own. We can think of our system of family law as assigning to older people responsibility for the care of younger ones. It is a system of usually implicit licensing, which becomes explicit only when evidence of abuse or neglect raises questions of parental fitness. Imagine instead a system in which the initial assignment of younger people to older people is routinely reconsidered after two years.[25] The older people who receive the initial assignment will probably not find in the younger ones "the test of [their] li[ves] and aspirations."[26] In the alternative, imagine a society in which everyone is conscious that family law includes a licensing system. There, perhaps, people will begin to think about putting the assignments up for grabs at birth or before. Some older people will be licensed as physically and mentally fit to "produce" children, others as fit to rear them. But one license would not need to accompany the other.[27] In that society biologi-

25. Again there may be some psychological objections raised here, on the ground that infants develop attachments to psychological parents and that it alters their development in a troubling direction to sunder those attachments by reassignments. I wonder whether those attachments would develop to the same extent in a society in which the norm was reassignment rather than retention in the original family and whether sundering the attachments in such a society necessarily would alter development in a troubling rather than an encouraging direction.

26. See Richards, "Individual, Family, and Constitution," p. 28.

27. See Hugh Lafollette, "Licensing Parents," 9 *Philosophy and Public Affairs* 182 (1980).

cal parenthood would not give rise to rights at all. Yet no feature of that society appears to violate the principles of autonomy and equal concern with which Richards began. In addition, although this is less clear the concept of "parenthood" in that society would be so different from ours that its members might not think of "parents" as having rights at all.

One example cannot establish that retail arguments will always demonstrate the impossibility of drawing conclusions about particular problems from the high-level abstractions of systematic moral philosophy.[28] Nonetheless, the example seems typical. The abstractions of systematic moral philosophy have to be connected somehow to actual social institutions like the family as it is today. The point of imagining somewhat different societies is to emphasize that the connections are deeply dependent on the state of the institutions; conjuring up imaginary situations actually emphasizes the real social contexts in which moral reasoning necessarily takes place. Retail arguments repeatedly point out that the connections between abstractions and institutions can be made only by invoking descriptions, themselves pervaded by implicit moral judgments, of those very institutions.[29] To speak of certain young people as "my" children is already to be committed to a rather comprehensive moral theory. Retail arguments thus undermine the arguments of systematic moral philosophy by injecting considerations of history and context into the abstract systems.[30] When they are effective retail arguments provide support for the more general view that moral judgments must be tightly bound to particular contexts, that is for the wholesale argument.

It should be emphasized that the wholesale argument is not a defense of metaethical skepticism, although it is sometimes taken to be. For example, Charles Fried writes, "The corrosive skepticism which doubts the possibility of such stable conceptions [of the relation of the individual to the state] must also doubt the possibility of understanding and applying moral conceptions such as cruelty or courage and in the end deny the historical and geographical unity of the human race."[31] It is significant that Fried invokes the abstract evil of cruelty and the abstract virtue of courage. The difficulty with systematic moral philosophy lies in its inability to explain why a particular instance of real behavior should be classi-

---

28. Another example, involving the right to reproductive choice, is developed in Mark Tushnet, "An Essay on Rights," 62 *Texas Law Review* 1363 (1984), and Mark Tushnet and L. Michael Seidman, "A Comment on Tooley's Abortion and Infanticide," 96 *Ethics* 350 (1986).

29. See Taylor, *Philosophy and Human Sciences*, pp. 294–96.

30. See generally Sandel, *Liberalism and Limits of Justice*.

31. Neither Fried nor I can recall where he made that statement, but he has ratified it. Letter from Charles Fried to Mark Tushnet, Aug. 19, 1986.

fied as cruel or courageous. Arthur Leff, the most skeptical of recent legal scholars, concluded his critique of moral philosophy this way:

> As things now stand, everything is up for grabs.
>> Nevertheless:
>> Napalming babies is bad.
>> Starving the poor is wicked.
>> Buying and selling each other is depraved.
>> Those who stood up to and died resisting Hitler, Stalin, Amin, and Pol Pot—and General Custer too—have earned salvation.
>> Those who acquiesced deserve to be damned.
>> There is in the world such a thing as evil.
>> [All together now:] Sez who?
>> God help us.[32]

Put aside the last line for a moment. "Napalming babies is bad." Presumably that is intended to evoke memories of the Vietnam War. Consistent with Leff's skepticism the systematic moral philosophers will tell us that the act of napalming babies can be described as the act of using appropriate weapons to fight a war, that by the principle of double effect "napalming babies" is then not bad if the war is not bad, and that we have to worry not about napalming babies—a discrete, particular act—but about the complexities of the "just war" doctrine.[33]

Whichever way we approach the question of deciding what moral truth is in a real setting, we get lost. If we start with a general truth we cannot identify the particular truth that the general one is supposed to encompass. If we start with a judgment about truth in a particular setting—a situation ethics—we are met immediately with plausible redescriptions of the setting that shake our confidence in our initial judgment. Why does this happen to people who are not skeptics? Here Leff's invocation of God can be set against Fried's reference to "the historical and geographical unity of the human race." One strand of religious thought—call it Christian—does indeed deny those unities. God's intervention at a particular time and place, his intervention in history, allows us to know the Truth. The Christian insight is precisely that Truth must be historicized, that we cannot know the particular Truth until our lives have been transformed.

At this point one is frequently met with cries of "relativist." But the historicist is not a relativist. He or she does not deny that there are transcendent Truths but claims that the human capacity to apprehend those Truths is limited by historic circumstances. A republican histori-

---

32. Arthur Leff, "Unspeakable Ethics, Unnatural Law," 1979 *Duke Law Journal* 1229, 1249.

33. Phillipa Foot, "The Problem of Abortion and the Doctrine of Double Effect," 5 *Oxford Review* 5 (1967).

cism, for example, can contend that the circumstances of contemporary society limit our capacity to apprehend particular Truths. In this view the appeal to systematic moral philosophy fails as a theory of constitutional law precisely because it requires us to make particularized judgments that are now beyond our capacity. We have, as a result of long struggle, a glimpse of Truth: we see the abstraction and generality of respect for persons. More particularized Truths, however, lie ahead of us, beyond another transformative struggle. In the end then the wholesale argument indeed puts everything up for grabs.

Suppose, however, that sometimes retail arguments are not effective, so that the inductive support for the wholesale argument is weakened. In those situations it is possible in theory to work down from the abstract principles of systematic moral philosophy to judgments about particular statutes. The theory of judicial review based on moral philosophy might still be challenged. Judicial review means that courts can sometimes displace judgments made by legislators. The theory being considered here would fail if judges were not better than legislators at working down from abstract principles to particular judgments. There are several reasons, though, to be skeptical about claims that judges are indeed systematically better than legislators.

Judges are not that different from legislators in terms of gross demographic characteristics. To some extent those characteristics implicitly describe certain types of socialization into ways of thinking about moral issues, and to that extent we will not find judges doing moral reasoning in particularly distinctive ways.[34] Those who write about constitutional law tend to ignore or discount the moral rhetoric that pervades politicians' discourse, but there seems to be little reason to be any more skeptical about politicians' sincerity in using that language than about judges'. In addition, judicial appointments are ordinarily matters of rather ordinary patronage politics.[35] We should not expect that the typical judge will be much different from the typical patronage appointee.[36]

Judges are indeed different from legislators in that judges do not have to run for reelection at regular and fairly short intervals.[37] Defenders of judicial review say that this insulates judges from "political" pressure;

34. Although many legislators are lawyers all appellate judges are, which may affect the way they assess moral issues. But that is not an obvious advantage.

35. See David O'Brien, *Storm Center: The Supreme Court in American Politics* 52 (1986).

36. There is a level on which one wants simply to point to the present federal bench and ask whether anyone seriously believes that, in terms of moral insight, in the aggregate these men and women have any advantage over legislators in the aggregate.

37. Even so, we should not exaggerate the differences between legislators and judges. At the congressional level reelection is quite frequent, so that members of the House of Repre-

judges need not be sensitive to the demands made by so-called special interests.[38] Yet the same phenomenon can be described more generously. Because legislators must seek reelection, they are more likely than judges to be sensitive to the ways in which laws—or the absence of laws when judges find some statutes unconstitutional—actually affect the lives of real people.[39] Once again, if context matters in moral judgment legislators may be better than judges in arriving at sound moral decisions.

Finally, we could compare the records of the courts and legislatures in making moral judgments. Much will certainly turn on what moral answers we think are the right ones. But it seems fair to say that on the big issues—racial and sexual equality, the distribution of wealth, and the like—and over the entire course of U.S. history courts and legislators have not been very different. Those who decry legislative support for segregation can be countered by pointing to the political antislavery movement; *Brown v. Board of Education* has to be set against *Dred Scott*; for moments like the Warren Court in its heyday there are moments like Populism in its heyday; for every Earl Warren, a Hubert Humphrey, for every Felix Frankfurter, a Paul Douglas. On many issues today it would be hard to choose between the Supreme Court and the House of Representatives, and on some issues—most notably national security—the choice pretty clearly goes against the Court.[40] Some may believe that the level of moral discourse in our public life is not very high, but it is difficult to conclude that it has been systematically higher in the courts than in legislatures.

The wholesale, retail, and institutional arguments against judicial review based on systematic moral philosophy can be augmented by two additional arguments. Perhaps there are moral right answers that judges can derive, in the appropriate way, from the abstractions of systematic

sentatives in effect have tenure during good behavior. See Morris Fiorina, *Congress: Keystone of the Washington Establishment* 5 (1977).

38. See, e.g., Michael Perry, *The Courts, the Constitution, and Human Rights* 100–101 (1982).

39. Judges themselves know that that is morally relevant information. Many judges object to statutes that limit their discretion in imposing sentences on convicted criminals precisely because when it comes time to impose sentences, they have much more morally relevant information about the crime, the victim, and the criminal than legislators do when they are writing the sentencing statutes.

This may illustrate a more general phenomenon, that legislatures, as a result of political pressures, the need to make many decisions quickly, and other factors, may offer simple solutions to complex problems. But as suggested in note 20, sometimes simple solutions are morally appropriate. It is not obvious how subjects can be apportioned between those requiring complex solutions and those requiring simple ones.

40. See, e.g., Haig v. Agee, 453 U.S. 280 (1981) (court upholds administrative action depriving anti-CIA activist of passport).

moral philosophy without making entirely contextual, non-rule-bound decisions. But first, even if the best law there could be would replicate the teachings of some systematic moral philosophy, we might not want to invoke that philosophy today. If our society deviates in many ways from the best society there can be, eliminating one deviation might not get us closer to that society. For example, John Rawls develops a theory of justice that assumes a society in which the conditions of justice are almost secure.[41] In such a society a court could rectify the occasional deviations from justice by directly imposing what it requires. Where the deviations from justice are substantial and widespread, such actions might not be sensible.[42]

The economic theory of second best provides a useful metaphor. Economists have specified the conditions under which a society's resources would be allocated efficiently. Their theory of second best shows that where there are many deviations from those conditions there is no reason, in general, to think that alleviating one deviation will yield more efficient outcomes; changes can be justified only by a detailed examination of the precise setting in which the occasion for decision arises.[43] The analogy to political action is appealing, for some actions that alleviate an immediate problem may, by reducing political pressure, delay the rectification of other, perhaps greater, injustices.[44]

41. Rawls, *Theory of Justice*, p. 351.

42. Strikingly, both Rawls and Robert Nozick suggest rather strongly that the contemporary United States contains numerous substantial deviations from the requirements of justice. See, e.g., id., pp. 274–84; Nozick, *Anarchy, State, and Utopia*, pp. 152–53, 231.

43. See R. G. Lipsey and Kelvin Lancaster, "The General Theory of Second Best," 24 *Review of Economic Studies* 11 (1956–57). Norman Daniels, *Just Health Care* 223–29 (1985), makes the same point, without invoking the economic version, for moral philosophy.

44. For example, it can be argued that Goldberg v. Kelly, 397 U.S. 254 (1970), which required that public agencies go through at least the forms of fairness before they terminate public assistance, diminished the political forces favoring redistribution of wealth by deflecting them into a fruitless struggle against a bureaucracy that proved able to absorb the judicially prescribed requirements without materially altering its behavior. See Chapter 7. Contra Edward Sparer, "Fundamental Human Rights, Legal Entitlements, and the Social Struggle: A Friendly Critique of the Critical Legal Studies Movement," 36 *Stanford Law Review* 509, 561–63 (1984) (providing hearings an important weapon in aiding organizing efforts, because it restricts the ability of welfare agencies to retaliate against activists).

It is not easy to tell a judge to worry about the problem of second best. Sometimes a judge might decide to perpetuate an existing injustice that hurts real people present before her or him so that an indefinite but it is hoped larger number of people will be hurt less in the more or less distant future. (This dilemma is not resolved by adopting the view, now apparently the prevailing one among philosophers of professional ethics, that the fact that the judge occupies a particular social position confers on her or him no immunity from ordinary moral requirements that would be applied to people in other social roles. See, e.g., David

The defense of judicial review requires one last step: that it is morally appropriate for one social institution, the judiciary, to impose the right answer on a lot of people who have come to a different answer. Certainly people who know the answers ought to try to convince others, but perhaps they should not coerce them. (See Chapter 4.)

The preceding arguments are not conclusive against the theory being considered here. Perhaps abstract rules are better than contextual judgments; perhaps judges can get to particular results from general theories; perhaps judges are better than legislators at all this; perhaps it is all right to coerce people to virtue, or at least to justice. But the counter-arguments are enough to make one skeptical—not metaethically skeptical, just skeptical—about the theory.

The Pragmatic Defense of the Theory

Yet there is a lingering sense that, all things considered, it is good to have judges thinking that they should do the right thing. *Lingering* is the operative word here. It is a residue of the nation's experience with the Warren Court. Kenney Hegland has artfully explained why it "would be a bad thing" for people, especially judges, to stop thinking that they should protect fundamental rights. He describes his experience in the summer of 1965, working in Albany, Georgia, with a prominent black attorney and using the courts to protect civil rights demonstrators. "I recall sitting in a Federal District Court with C. B. King and listening to the judge tell a rural sheriff, 'The law requires you to protect the demonstrators. If you don't, I have no choice but to hold you in contempt.' Be this illusion, I would not blithely dispel it."[45]

Luban, *The Good Lawyer: Lawyers' Roles and Lawyers' Ethics* (1983). The issue here is not whether there is a special role morality to which the judge is peculiarly subject but is instead what are the general requirements of morality, applicable to everyone.)

Political philosophers have discussed this problem under the heading "dirty hands." See, e.g., Michael Walzer, "Political Action: The Problem of Dirty Hands," 2 *Philosophy and Public Affairs* 160 (1973). The best society might be nonviolent, yet it is not obvious that the route from contemporary society to the best one involves only nonviolent political action. (Of course powerful arguments can be made that the best way to transform society is to live today as one wants to live in the best society; that is what the tradition of nonviolent resistance to evil is about. But the point is that arguments must be made. It does not follow simply from the identification of a moral truth that we ought immediately to make it our policy.)

45. Hegland, "Goodbye to Deconstruction," p. 1219. See also Sparer, "Fundamental Human Rights"; Elizabeth Schneider, "The Dialectic of Rights and Politics: Perspectives from the Women's Movement," 61 *New York University Law Review* 589 (1986); John Denvir, "Justice Brennan, Justice Rehnquist, and Free Speech," 80 *Northwestern University Law Review* 285 (1985).

This is an essentially pragmatic defense of the theory: whatever the theory's analytic merits or defects, it works in society to protect valued interests.[46] Like all pragmatic arguments, this one must be examined in light of the actual operation of today's courts.

In the last four years of the Burger Court, the Supreme Court upheld a few more than a dozen free speech claims and rejected about twice as many. A pragmatic assessment of the Court's record requires the specification of the goal one is trying to reach. Consider, then, the record from the point of view of a relatively liberal Democrat concerned solely with the degree to which the Supreme Court's decisions advance her or his political agenda and unconcerned with questions about the propriety of judicial review in the abstract. (A relatively conservative Republican would simply reverse the evaluations of the Democrat and so need not be considered separately.) The cases are a rather mixed lot. Many involve issues with the most remote connection to political programs. Liberals (and conservatives) are likely to find it an extremely close question whether the net effect of the Court's recent decisions favors their cause; moderates are likely to find the decisions a matter of nearly complete indifference.

The cases fall into three main groups.[47] The first involves political speech and campaigning. The Court struck down a $1,000 limitation that

46. One difficulty with this position, to the extent that it truly does concede the validity of the challenges to the theory, is that it assumes that political opponents will not figure out that something is going wrong in the constitutional theory that is being used to harm them. At the least one would think that some clever political opponents would figure it out and hire themselves out to those who do not understand the problem but who want to fight the people who are using the theory to hurt them politically.

Actually Hegland may not have given us a good example of the pragmatic defense of the theory. First, judges rarely "have to" hold people in contempt; they have many devices short of that one to induce compliance with their orders. This suggests that the judge was overstating "the law" to intimidate the sheriff. Second, the sheriff had to comply with the threat because it was credible, and the threat was credible in large part because there was real political force in the national government willing to back it up. In Hegland's terms, "the law" had not changed between 1957, when President Eisenhower equivocated on his support for *Brown v. Board of Education*, and 1966, but the judge's threat in 1966 was credible in a way that a similar threat in 1957 would not have been.

47. There are some minor, unclassifiable cases: Brockett v. Spokane Arcades, 472 U.S. 491 (1985) (invalidating statute's reliance on "lust" but upholding statute as a whole); City of Los Angeles v. Preferred Communications, Inc., 106 S. Ct. 2034 (1986) (holding first amendment considerations applicable to cable television but remanding for fact findings before first amendment ruling would be made); Regan v. Time, Inc., 468 U.S. 641 (1984) (invalidating statute that allowed photographic reproduction of U.S. currency "for philatelic, numismatic, educational, historical, or other newsworthy purposes" while banning all other photographic reproduction of currency; upholding limitation on color and size of permissible photographic reproductions).

Congress had placed on expenditures by political action committees[48] and defined the procedures unions must use in refunding the portion of union dues used for political purposes to people who object to those uses.[49] It invalidated a prohibition on editorializing by public broadcasters who receive federal funds,[50] held unconstitutional an Ohio statute that restricted the ability of third-party presidential candidates to get on the ballot,[51] and barred Ohio from requiring that the Socialist Workers' Party disclose the names of contributors to its campaign fund.[52] It also invalidated a statute prohibiting political demonstrations on the sidewalks around the Supreme Court.[53] It limited the states' ability to keep fund-raisers from charging more than 25 percent of the contributions they generate as expenses, because sometimes high expenses are associated with the costs of spreading information and of advocacy.[54] Finally, the Court held that political advocacy groups could not be excluded from official charity drives simply because the government disagrees with the groups' political positions.[55]

The second group of cases upheld the rights of the press, increasing their access to pretrial proceedings[56] and defining the procedural aspects of libel trials to make it harder for plaintiffs to prevail.[57] The final group involves the free speech rights of commercial enterprises. The Court held that a state could not impose a tax on the paper used for newspapers even though the newspapers were exempt from the state sales tax.[58] It also held that advertisements for contraceptives could not be kept out of the mails.[59] It barred states from disciplining attorneys for using nondeceptive visual aids in their advertisements.[60] Finally, the Court invalidated Califor-

---

48. Federal Election Comm'n. v. National Conservative Political Action Committee [NCPAC], 472 U.S. 480 (1985).

49. Chicago Teachers' Union v. Hudson, 475 U.S. 292 (1986).

50. Federal Communications Comm'n. v. League of Women Voters of California, 468 U.S. 364 (1984).

51. Anderson v. Celebrezze, 460 U.S. 780 (1983).

52. Brown v. Socialist Workers '74 Campaign Committee, 459 U.S. 87 (1982).

53. United States v. Grace, 461 U.S. 171 (1983).

54. Secretary of State of Maryland v. Munson, 467 U.S. 947 (1984).

55. Cornelius v. NAACP Legal Defense and Educational Fund, 473 U.S. 788 (1985).

56. Press-Enterprise Co. v. Superior Court, 464 U.S. 501 (1984) (voir dire); Press-Enterprise Co. v. Superior Court, 106 S. Ct. 2735 (1986) (preliminary hearing).

57. Bose Corp. v. Consumers Union of United States, 466 U.S. 485 (1984); Philadelphia Newspapers, Inc. v. Hepps, 475 U.S. 767 (1986); Anderson v. Liberty Lobby, Inc., 106 S. Ct. 2505 (1986).

58. Minneapolis Star & Tribune Co. v. Minnesota Commissioner of Revenue, 460 U.S. 575 (1983).

59. Bolger v. Youngs Drug Products Corp., 463 U.S. 60 (1983).

60. Zauderer v. Supreme Court of Ohio, 471 U.S. 626 (1985).

nia's attempt to require utilities in the state to include in their billing enve-
lopes statements prepared by the utilities' public interest adversaries.[61]

What does this record add up to? Not much from any point of view.
Liberals might be pleased by some of the political cases, although it is
difficult to believe that, for example, editorializing by public broadcasters
is likely to do a lot for the liberal cause. They should be troubled by the
campaign finance case, though.[62] The commercial speech cases might be
troubling too, insofar as they limit the ability of the public to control large
capitalist enterprises, but because they involved such trivial efforts to
control capital, liberals probably would not care much either way. The
libel cases are harder to assess. Making it more difficult for plaintiffs to
win libel judgments tends to protect large media conglomerates, who,
more than the underground or dissenting press, have the resources to
utilize every advantage the legal system gives them.[63] There are some side
benefits to less established news organs, though, and the adversary culture of the press sometimes places it in opposition to some segments of
"the establishment," which means that many plaintiffs in libel cases will
be relatively conservative figures.[64]

Liberals thus have gotten some things from recent first amendment
cases, but they have lost some things as well. Of course that means that
conservatives are in the same situation. For both groups the pragmatic
balance seems close enough that neither could possibly feel that it had lost
something that had been of great value to it recently if the Court went out
of the first amendment business entirely.[65] We could, however, put the
question of net gain or loss aside, because the statutes involved in these
cases are, in the larger political universe, really rather trivial.[66]

61. Pacific Gas & Electric Co. v. Public Utilities Comm'n., 475 U.S. 1 (1986).

62. For a more complete discussion, see Chapter 9.

63. See Renata Adler, *Reckless Disregard* (1986); Rodney Smolla, *Suing the Press*
(1986).

64. This describes only a tendency, which will vary a great deal in different locations. For
example, one would expect greater adversariness in large cities than in small ones.

65. In a pragmatic assessment one is barred from saying that the law is correct in
principle, and one cannot claim that the Court made some mistakes and should have
invalidated more statutes (and not invalidated some others).

66. Perhaps *NCPAC* and *Pacific Gas & Electric* are not trivial decisions. But it is worth
emphasizing that they are both conservative invalidations and that the pragmatic defense of
the theory tends to be made by liberals. These cases involved legislative efforts to control
private power, and political liberals might be suspicious of judicial review generally because
it can only come into play after a legislature has acted. In principle judicial review can be
action forcing. In our society, however, the chances that it will be are rather slim, so a
pragmatic liberal might be suspicious of judicial review. The relatively recent experience of
the Warren Court, and the relatively limited incursions on that experience made by the

The triviality of the cases in which the Court has recently upheld first amendment claims might be misleading, though. The cases that reach the Court are, almost by definition, at the margins of what society believes can permissibly be regulated. If the political process does not produce statutes that raise central questions about free speech, the Court will inevitably decide only trivial matters. If the political process works the way it does because only the possibility of judicial review imposes some discipline on legislators, we would be foolish indeed to abandon judicial review. Finally, we might owe a great deal to judicial review if the Court had established a general framework for legislation affecting speech, which itself supported and restrained the political process that produces only modest threats to free speech values. None of these propositions is obviously correct.

We can begin by assuming that the urge to repress is deeply ingrained[67] and that it would be desirable to eliminate it. The structure of constitutional litigation may ensure quite the opposite, that the urge to repress will be sustained.[68] Every case that gets to the Supreme Court, and thereby focuses public attention on free speech issues, arises at the margins of contemporary politics. Put another way, every free speech case that actually reaches the Court involves a claim that most people will see as extreme.

Take the two recent cases in which the Court was most uncontroversially correct.[69] Why do protesters feel compelled to demonstrate on the Supreme Court grounds rather than across the street? They cannot imagine that they will have more influence on the Justices if they are fifty feet closer to the Court building, nor is it obvious that they will have any greater impact on the public once it becomes clear that their demonstration is protected by law. Or why do political advocacy groups need to take part in official charity drives when they can raise money in so many other ways? It certainly looks as if they are trying to take advantage of donors' unconsidered belief that United Way drives benefit crippled children and the like. The Court may frequently or rarely sustain free speech claims, but whenever it does it will fuel resentment by upholding a claim that seems extreme to a fair number of people. That resentment is at least one source of the urge to repress.

Burger Court, have overwhelmed liberals' judgment on this issue, so I confine my observations to this footnote.

67. See Lee Bollinger, *The Tolerant Society: Free Speech and Extremist Speech in America* (1986).

68. The argument that follows is developed from Robert Nagel, "How Useful Is Judicial Review in Free Speech Cases?" 69 *Cornell Law Review* 302 (1984).

69. Both *Grace* and *Cornelius* were unanimous on the points discussed here.

Consider what might happen if the Court announced that five years from now it would no longer entertain free speech claims. We would be driven back upon ourselves, forced to confront our desire to repress. Perhaps for a while we might yield to the temptation. But if, as many theorists of the first amendment have told us, repression of speech is bad for society and for each of us, we might come to understand what we lose when we give in to this desire. As suggested we might learn from our mistakes and gradually take control of our lives. The scenario sketched here depicts a society that takes a risk. That risk may be offset by the reality that judicial review entrenches the repressive urges that it then must attempt to control.

What makes the scenario troubling to some is their sense that legislators would go hog-wild once the threat of judicial review was removed. Right now they just try to repress at the margins, knowing that if they do more the courts will step in, but unleashed they would go to the core, imposing criminal penalties on innocuous dissenters, closing down traditional methods of public protest, and the like. The scenario includes a five-year delay to provide a period for civic education and thoughtful consideration of fundamental questions. If we knew that we had to rely on our legislators, we might become more careful in choosing them.[70] But we might not.

Further, the rosy image of contemporary law can be darkened by considering that today's legislators might be made irresponsible precisely because they know that the courts will bail them out if they go too far. If that is so legislators will always be probing at the margins of the constitutionally permissible. They will ask themselves Can we get away with it? rather than Is it a good idea? And, unfortunately but inevitably, sometimes they will get away with it. Not every statute is challenged, sometimes challengers are unlucky and draw an unsympathetic judge, sometimes a challenge is brought too soon or too late in light of changing political conditions. Obviously we ought to be worried about removing judicial review when we have legislators who tend always to probe the margins, because without judicial review there would be no margins at all. But again we might have different legislators if we did not have judicial review.

Judicial review in first amendment cases is thus a mixed blessing. Surely, though, it seems to have been a blessing, giving us a basic structure of first amendment protections that guards against the worst kinds of

---

70. See James Thayer, *John Marshall* 85–86 (1901) (judicial review "comes from the outside, and the people thus lose the political experience, and the moral education and stimulus that come from fighting the question out in the ordinary way, and correcting their own errors"); text accompanying notes 8–9.

excesses, which we have known in the past and which are common elsewhere in the world. Yet even that structure may not be as solid as it initially seems.

Again, recall that the desire to suppress speech is deeply ingrained. In uncontentious times public officials may refrain from acting on that desire because they have more pressing things to do; as discussed in Chapter 2, we need a first amendment primarily for the more contentious times of high political excitement. But we may not get what we need. The historical record is not terribly encouraging: The Supreme Court affirmed the convictions of opponents of U.S. involvement in World War I, upheld some efforts to suppress the Communist Party in the 1920s, affirmed the convictions of leading Communists in 1951 and 1961, backed away from a direct confrontation with McCarthyism in the 1950s. There are some bright spots—a few reversals of convictions for seditious speech and a general acceptance of protests against the Vietnam War—but overall the picture is not one of a Court actively protecting speech.[71]

Contemporary free speech doctrine need not provide that protection either. Chapter 2 described some parts of that doctrine. Legislatures may not prohibit speech because of its content, and they may prohibit political speech because of its connection to social harm only if the causal connection is quite strong. If public officials desire to suppress speech these doctrines may do little more than force them to search for different ways of doing so: the desire to suppress migrates, so to speak, but does not disappear.[72] Under existing law people can be convicted of creating social harms, such as public disorder or difficulty in mobilizing the resources to support a war. Free speech law obviously does not preclude prosecutions for engaging in a riot or blowing up a munitions plant. It does, however, make it difficult to establish that speech caused the riot. As the metaphor of migration suggests, during the Vietnam era prosecutors discovered a different method of suppressing speech. They argued that certain speeches did not themselves cause riots and the like but were merely evidence of conspiracies to cause riots. Conspiracies are agreements to act in concert, and obviously the agreements can be manifested in words. Liberals tried hard to develop first amendment theories that limit the use of speech as

71. For a good, short historical overview, see Laurence Tribe, *Constitutional Choices* 190–91 (1985).

72. Contemporary first amendment law distinguishes between low-value speech and high-value speech. See Stone et al., *Constitutional Law,* pp. 1058, 1169, for a general discussion of the distinction. Low-value speech receives substantially less protection than high-value speech. There is a remote possibility that oppositional speech could be reclassified as "low value" during times of political stress, which would further undermine the argument that the general structure of free speech law provides strong protection for oppositional speech.

evidence of conspiracy, and they achieved some fragile victories in the lower courts.[73] The analytic contortions in these decisions make it clear that the next time around—with a somewhat different set of judges on the lower courts and the Supreme Court—the decisions need not impede those who would suppress dissent.

Another part of the core of contemporary free speech doctrine involves public protest demonstrations. Dissidents typically lack substantial financial resources but are sometimes able to mobilize their supporters for marches that show how many people agree with them. Without resources other than numbers demonstrators have to use someone else's resources—that is, they must use public property. Contemporary doctrine divides public property into several categories.[74] Some, such as streets and parks, are traditional "public forums" in which demonstrations have historically taken place with some frequency. Officials can also decide to dedicate other public property, such as auditoriums, to speech activities. The Supreme Court has held that demonstrators can use traditional and dedicated public forums if they comply with reasonable time and manner restrictions. A third category includes "limited purpose" public forums, which are dedicated to nonspeech activities but which can sometimes be used for speech without causing too much difficulty; schools and public libraries may fall into this category.[75] States must allow demonstrators access to limited purpose forums so long as the demonstrators' activities do not substantially interfere with the normal uses of the forums. Finally, there are nonpublic forums; dissidents can be kept out of these completely, and administrators can let these facilities be used only by people who have the required stamp of approval.[76]

---

73. See Kent Greenawalt, "Speech and Crime," 1980 *American Bar Foundation Research Journal* 645, for a discussion of the problems associated with developing a constitutional basis for challenging the use of speech as evidence of conspiracy to cause harm.

74. See Perry Educators' Ass'n. v. Perry Local Educators' Ass'n., 460 U.S. 37 (1983).

75. See Tinker v. Des Moines Independent Community School Dist., 393 U.S. 503 (1969) (school); Brown v. Louisiana, 383 U.S. 131 (1966) (library).

76. Several points must be noted about this scheme. The lines between the categories are ill-defined. A facility dedicated to speech can be changed into a limited purpose forum by redefining the activities to which the area was deliberately opened. For example, a public auditorium can become a theater for entertainment and commercial conventions without any change in the activities its managers want to allow. Further, the Court has never defined how we are to distinguish between limited purpose and nonpublic forums. Finally, the "substantial interference" test is plainly subject to considerable manipulation. Some recent decisions treat public property as having symbolic functions. See Greer v. Spock, 424 U.S. 828 (1976) (access to military base denied in part on ground that access would interfere with symbolic separation of military and politics). See also United States v. Albertini, 472 U.S. 675 (1985). Once interference with symbols becomes a sufficient reason to restrict access,

Public forum doctrine unequivocally protects access only to streets and parks. This has some political significance; demonstrations in the streets provide important opportunities for people to come together, see how many they really are, and begin to overcome their political alienation. Recent experience has shown that street demonstrations are not enough, though. Drama is required to attract public attention.[77] Given the structural demands of press coverage, drama means either engaging in or being the victim of violence, which tends to discredit the movement, or developing some novel form of protest, such as sleeping in tents across from the White House. Yet precisely because effective types of protest must be novel, they are not protected by public forum doctrine.

In the free speech area, then, liberals can take only a little comfort from the general framework of first amendment law if they consider it in purely pragmatic terms. We cannot perform a complete pragmatic survey of constitutional law here. One point, though, seems worth emphasizing. Liberals tend to think that judicial review, no matter how unsatisfactory it has been recently, cannot hurt their interests. They are wrong. They tend to assume that legislatures will not advance their political program; courts cannot hurt if legislatures do not do anything that liberals like. However, much of the liberal program, on matters of racial and gender equality, for example, has been accomplished in our legislatures. A pragmatic liberal ought to remember that courts can invalidate affirmative action programs as well as segregation.[78] Once again the case for inductive generalization seems strong.

Finally, what about the Warren Court itself? Liberals repeatedly say that *Brown v. Board of Education*, the reapportionment decisions, the abortion cases, and the Warren Court's criminal justice decisions pragmatically vindicate judicial review.[79] However, this justification attributes too much social power to the Supreme Court. Frequently the Court intervenes to support existing trends. For example, the number of abortions was increasing significantly before the Court's decisions in 1973, and the decisions may have only accelerated slightly the trend toward *legalizing* abortions, not the trend toward having them.[80] Police

---

the game is over. Schools can be treated as symbolic temples of disinterested learning, and so on.

77. See, e.g., David Garrow, *Protest at Selma* (1978); Todd Gitlin, *The Whole World Is Watching* (1980); Robert Vandeveer, "Coercive Restraint of Offensive Actions," 8 *Philosophy and Public Affairs* 175, 187 (1979).

78. See Wygant v. Jackson Board of Education, 106 S. Ct. 1842 (1986).

79. See, e.g., Perry, *Courts, Constitution, and Human Rights,* pp. 1–2.

80. See Allan Hutchinson, "Tribal Noises," 1986 *American Bar Foundation Research Journal* 79, 89, and n. 38; Choper, "Consequences of Supreme Court Decisions," pp.

agencies were becoming more professional during the 1960s, and the Court's criminal justice decisions may only have helped police administrators who were already trying to eliminate the abuses that concerned the Warren Court. (See Chapter 8.)

In addition, the pragmatic justification ignores the complex interplay between ordinary political action and Court decisions. Consider the story of race relations.[81] For several decades before *Brown* the black community had engaged in a struggle on all fronts: it had supported litigation to undermine segregation, it had lobbied for a federal law against lynching, it had threatened a massive march on Washington to secure fair employment legislation. Coupled with changes in the American economy, which led to large-scale black migration to the North, and the start of the Cold War, which made the existing system of race relations a global embarrassment, these activities had increased the political power of the black community. Southerners, however, remained powerful enough in Congress to block the legislation that blacks desired. *Brown* galvanized black communities not so much because schools were desegregated—except in the border states substantial segregation continued for more than a decade after *Brown*—but because it showed that one branch of the national government was on their side. Two years later the Montgomery bus boycott was the first episode in the development of the modern civil rights movement, whose sit-ins and marches prodded Congress to enact important civil rights acts in 1964, 1965, and 1968. The Court's response to the movement was hesitant and indirect. It never ruled that sit-ins were protected by the Constitution, but it did allow demonstrators to invoke the powers of the federal courts to limit the worst sort of harassment, and it upheld innovative efforts by the executive branch to convict white terrorists under old statutes.[82] Overall the courts played a distinctly subordinate role in the post-1960 struggle for civil rights. It seems fair to wonder whether the pattern of race relations in 1970 or 1980 would have been dramatically different had blacks been forced to use only political methods.

Finally, the pragmatic justification overlooks the fact that a pragmatic assessment must take a rather long view, for it would be silly to praise a court for issuing a judgment that turned out to be unenforced and uninfluential. Yet a longer view will have to take into account not just *Brown*

186–89; Rosalind Petchesky, *Abortion and Woman's Choice: The State, Sexuality, and Reproductive Freedom* 103, 113 (1985).

81. For a general discussion of these developments, see Harvard Sitkoff, *The Struggle for Black Equality, 1954–1980* (1981).

82. See Mark Tushnet, "Commentary," in *The Civil Rights Movement in America* 117 (Charles Eagles ed. 1986).

or the 1973 abortion decisions but what the Court itself did thereafter. The moral messages of those cases become less clear once they are seen as part of a body of complex doctrine. Probably the firmest judgment one can come to is that the courts helped some segments of the community, which were already using the ordinary processes of politics, to place their interests higher on the political agenda than they could have otherwise. This is not a trivial accomplishment, but it is much less than the pragmatic justification appeared to offer at the outset.

Like the case against systematic moral philosophy as a theory of judicial review, the case against judicial review as a pragmatically useful instrument is not conclusive. Here too, though, cautious skepticism seems justified by history and the current composition of courts and legislatures.[83]

The Moral Philosophy of the Community

The pragmatic justification of judicial review builds on the experience of the Warren Court in promoting justice. Earl Warren had humane instincts, not a systematic philosophy.[84] Those instincts, as we have just seen, resonated strongly with the best values in American society. Warren's example suggests a different role for philosophy in constitutional theory. Instead of looking to systematic moral philosophy in the abstract, theory might direct its attention to the philosophy of justice implicit in our community. By historicizing the values to which constitutional theory appeals, this approach would avoid some of the difficulties that we found with the appeal to systematic moral philosophy. Ronald Dworkin has offered the most sophisticated version of this theory, but before examining it we should put aside some other theories of the same general sort.[85]

Cases like *Moore v. City of East Cleveland* provide the model for one type of appeal to community morality.[86] East Cleveland had a zoning ordinance that limited the ability of people who were not part of the same family to live in a single home. Such ordinances are not uncommon, but

83. The pragmatic argument must of course be bound to particular historical contexts. For discussions of skepticism on the British left concerning the pragmatic utility of "rights," see Gerry Danby, "The Use and Abuse of Rights," 12 *Journal of Law and Society* 375 (1985); Alan Hunt, "The Future of Rights and Justice," 9 *Contemporary Crises* 309 (1985); Hugo Steinert, "The Amazing New Left Law and Order Campaign," 9 *Contemporary Crises* 327 (1985); David Nelken, *The Limits of the Legal Process: A Study of Landlords, Law, and Crime* (1983).

84. See generally G. Edward White, *Earl Warren: A Public Life* (1982).

85. A comprehensive survey of these theories is in Wojciech Sadurski, "Conventional Morality and Judicial Standards," 73 *Virginia Law Review* 339 (1987).

86. 431 U.S. 494 (1977).

East Cleveland defined *family* in a way that prohibited a grandmother from establishing a home for two grandchildren who were born of two different daughters. It seems easy enough to claim that this ordinance was so far out of line with values widely shared among the public of the United States as a whole as to be unconstitutional. As Richard Posner puts it, the courts should hold unconstitutional laws that violate "a fundamental social norm held by most of the nation."[87]

This appeal to common values does have inherent limits. It would seem unable to justify the invalidation of recently enacted federal statutes[88] or of statutes, such as those restricting the availability of abortion or—in the 1950s—enforcing segregation, that many states have adopted. Even within its limits the appeal to common values faces a number of well-known problems.

First, the judges must identify both what the common values are and what these values imply for the resolution of the issue they face. Judges could rely on surveys or on their consciences. Yet surveys consistently show great sensitivity to variations in the way questions are phrased. A majority regularly opposes "abortion on demand" and a majority regularly supports a woman's right to choose, in consultation with her doctor, whether to bear a child.[89] The courts, unlike respondents to surveys, are not faced with "the abortion issue" at large. They must decide whether specific statutes, often written in great detail, are constitutional.[90] Public views on such statutes are likely to be unformed and unavailable to the courts. The difficulty in asking the judges to consult their consciences to determine what common values are is that, as we have seen, judges are drawn from a narrow stratum of our

87. Richard Posner, *The Federal Courts: Crisis and Reform* 194 (1985) (emphasis omitted).

88. Courts could invalidate older statutes on the ground that they were inconsistent with contemporary common values.

89. See Petchesky, *Abortion and Woman's Choice*, pp. 365–66; Benjamin Barber, *Strong Democracy: Participatory Politics for a New Age* 181 (1984). Petchesky and Barber note that the precise phrasing of survey questions conveys political messages and may affect the answers respondents give. Petchesky, *Abortion and Woman's Choice*, p. 374; Barber, *Strong Democracy*, p. 181.

90. See, e.g., Thornburgh v. American College of Obstetricians and Gynecologists, 106 S. Ct. 2169 (1986) (considering constitutionality of statute that [1] required informing woman at least twenty-four hours before abortion of operating physician's name; possible physical and psychological effects of abortion; medical risks of specific procedure to be used; probable gestation age of fetus; medical risks of carrying fetus to term; availability of prenatal, childbirth, and neonatal care; and father's legal liability for child support; [2] required reporting the operating physician's name, the grounds for determination that the fetus was not viable, and detailed information regarding woman's age, race, address, and prior history of pregnancy; and [3] required that a second physician be present to care for the fetus after the abortion procedure).

society and what they consider to be common values may instead be the reflection of their personal experience.[91]

Second, as we saw in Chapter 1, the level of generality on which the common values are identified is open to substantial manipulation.[92] Suppose we agree in the abstract on some set of common values. Those values will generally have ambiguous implications for the questions posed to the courts. The solution lies in specifying the level of generality on which we are to consider our common values. Consider the Supreme Court's analysis of the statute challenged in *Bowers v. Hardwick*, which made it a criminal offense to engage in homosexual sodomy in private.[93] The majority upheld the statute, devoting much of its opinion to an enumeration of the statutes against sodomy and the historical tradition of making it a criminal offense. It concluded, "Against this background, to claim that a right to engage in [homosexual sodomy] is 'deeply rooted in this Nation's history and tradition' . . . is, at best, facetious."[94] The four dissenters pointed to a more general commitment in the society to privacy in sexual matters. This commitment derives from protection afforded to "certain *decisions* that are properly for the individual to make . . . [and] to certain *places* without regard for the particular activities in which the individuals who occupy them are engaged."[95] This amounts to an implicit challenge to the description of the conduct at issue as "merely homosexual sodomy" and offers instead a description of the conduct as "sexual activity in private." They found a strong tradition of protecting that sort of conduct from state regulation. The alternative formulations of our common values make transparent the manipulation that the approach licenses and demonstrate that it does not adequately constrain judicial discretion.[96]

91. Justice Blackmun once suggested, in a majority opinion, that poor people regularly spend their money going to the movies. United States v. Kras, 409 U.S. 434 (1973). This reveals a great deal about the image of poor people held by someone who is not so poor and suggests that we should be skeptical about claims that the Justices have a finely tuned sense of what common values are.

92. See Tribe, *American Constitutional Law*, p. 944 ("Insofar as the right of personhood is limited to liberties long revered as fundamental in our society, it makes all the difference in the world what level of generality one employs to test the pedigree of an asserted liberty claim") (footnote omitted). See also Philip Bobbitt, *Constitutional Fate: Theory of the Constitution* 159–62 (1982) (deriving constitutional limits on state power to restrict availability of abortions from "ethos" barring government from coercing intimate acts).

93. 106 S. Ct. 2841 (1986). In view of the quotation in note 92, it may be worth noting as well that Tribe argued the case against the constitutionality of the statute before the Supreme Court in *Bowers*.

94. 106 S. Ct., at 2846.

95. Id., at 2850–51 (Blackmun, J., dissenting).

96. Tribe, *American Constitutional Law*, pp. 944–46, argues that, because "the history of homosexuality has been largely a history of disapproval and disgrace, . . . it is crucial, in asking

Third, one undeniable value in our society is federalism. Federalism allows and indeed encourages localities to step to a different drummer and impose on themselves regulations that outsiders find distasteful.[97] Any apparently aberrational regulation can be defended as the expression of some complex common value, such as "Privacy, taking federalism into account." In this view a locality can prohibit sodomy precisely because its intrusion on privacy is justified by the fact that homosexuals can move to cities and states more tolerant of the practice.[98]

Finally, in any constitutional case courts have before them one indisputable item of evidence about common values, the regulation at issue. They also have their sense, developed from their participation in the society, of what our common values are. It is not obvious why the courts should rely on their sense of common values rather than the regulation at issue. In *Furman v. Georgia* Justice Marshall provided an explanation for his view that the death penalty is unconstitutional because it is inconsistent with the values of the American people. He argued that the general population is unaware of the way in which the death penalty is actually administered, that judges are in a position to know how it is administered, and that if the public knew what the judges did, it would oppose the death penalty.[99]

---

whether an alleged right forms part of a traditional liberty, to define the liberty at a high enough level of generality to permit unconventional variants to claim protection along with mainstream versions of the protected conduct." This approach ingeniously allows the courts to disapprove regulation of activities that are conceded to be unconventional, on the ground that such regulation is inconsistent with conventional morality. A useful pre-*Bowers* discussion is Richard Saphire, "Gay Rights and the Constitution: An Essay on Constitutional Theory, Practice, and *Dronenburg v. Zech*," 10 *University of Dayton Law Review* 767 (1985).

97. Precisely because they are outsiders critics have voted with their feet to express their distaste for the regulations. See the Introduction and Chapter 2. Richard Posner argues that federalism can be ignored in this context because "most new ideas are bad, and the new ideas that are good, or at least that reflect powerful forces in the society, will hang on tenaciously." Posner, *Federal Courts*, pp. 195–96. This seems inadequate. If the courts slap down innovations as soon as they crop up, it is not easy to see how those innovations "will hang on"; one would think that their supporters would get discouraged at the spectacle of repeated political victories followed by repeated judicial defeats. Perhaps Posner means that supporters of good innovations will eventually prevail in the political process, not in getting their innovations adopted but in getting enough judges appointed that the new judges will no longer obstruct the innovations. This is rather indirect and imposes substantial interim costs on those who support innovations. See Chapter 6. In addition, there is no general reason to think that people who support innovation, even sound innovation, with respect to one or two issues will have enough political power to become part of a winning coalition that will make changing the shape of the judiciary an important political task.

98. The fact that antisodomy statutes are generally unenforced, as in fact they were in Georgia, where *Bowers* arose, suggests that this dimension of federalism is an important one.

99. 408 U.S. 238, 360–69 (1972).

This response to the evidentiary objection to the appeal to common values is questionable on its face. The response appears to be making an empirical claim,[100] and as an empirical claim it is vulnerable to the reply Justice Stewart made later. Justice Stewart said that *Furman* had brought the issue to the attention of the public, which had responded by reenacting death penalty statutes.[101] Invalidating a statute on the ground that it is inconsistent with common values might be justified as a means of testing public support for a statute that, to the judges, seems inconsistent with what they understand to be those values. That is peculiar form of judicial review.[102]

The appeal to common values as a basis for invalidating legislation faces a difficulty that is inherent in efforts to base judicial review on the community's values. The enterprise is caught between an apologetic thrust, because it must refer to the values of the community, and a critical thrust, because the community's values are somehow supposed to explain why legislation adopted by the community is inconsistent with the community's truest values. Ronald Dworkin has grappled with the dialectical interplay between criticism and apologetics more carefully than anyone else. His efforts, which involve several attempts to work around the difficulty, have led him to formulations that retain the critical intention but lack substantial content. Even so, his most recent work helps to illuminate directions in which constitutional theory might develop.[103]

Dworkin has offered, and then modified, several approaches to adjudication, but all are premised on some sort of appeal to community values. For example, taking as a given our community's commitment to the proposition that constitutional adjudication must rest on constitutional interpretation, Dworkin argues that the proper interpretation of a constitutional provision involves application of the provision's animating "concept" rather than its drafters' specific "conception." As we saw in Chapter 1, this argument is vulnerable to two objections: concepts may be no more than the aggregation of conceptions, and in any event we need some method to identify which of several possible concepts actually animates the provision at issue. Dworkin's answer to both objections is to

100. For an examination of the empirical question, see Austin Sarat and Neil Vidmar, "Public Opinion, the Death Penalty, and the Eighth Amendment: Testing the Marshall Hypothesis," 1976 *Wisconsin Law Review* 171.

101. Gregg v. Georgia, 428 U.S. 153, 179–80 (1976).

102. For a discussion of a related approach, see Chapter 6.

103. For evaluations of Dworkin's earlier formulations, see *Ronald Dworkin and Contemporary Jurisprudence* (Marshall Cohen ed. 1983), discussed in Allan Hutchinson, "Of Kings and Dirty Rascals: The Struggle for Democracy," 9 *Queen's Law Journal* 273 (1984). Hutchinson notes that, "as with [those of] all important thinkers, Dworkin's ideas have not stood still." P. 274.

invoke systematic moral philosophy. The proper concepts to be applied are those identified by the best moral theory we have.[104] Notice, however, that moral philosophy enters Dworkin's scheme not because it is good in itself that courts invoke moral philosophy but rather because moral philosophy is the only way to make sense of our commitment to interpretation.

Moral philosophy plays a similar role in another approach that Dworkin has proposed. Here the datum of community values is its commitment to a precedent-oriented system of adjudication, in which the cases decided in the past provide substantial guidance for deciding cases today. Chapter 1 described the central problems in such a system: the decided cases do not tell us what they mean for our present purposes, and alternative interpretations of the cases can yield divergent results.[105] Again *Bowers v. Hardwick* is exemplary. The precedent-based argument that sodomy statutes are unconstitutional relied on two sets of cases, one primarily involving abortion and the other providing some degree of protection for the privacy of the home. The argument claimed that these cases established a rule protecting sexual conduct, of whatever sort, in the privacy of one's home.[106] The majority disagreed, saying that those cases really protected only private decisions related to "family, marriage, or procreation," none of which are involved in sodomy.[107] Dworkin argues that the proper basis

104. Dworkin, "Forum of Principle," p. 500.

105. For discussions that deal with these issues in connection with Dworkin's work, see Andrew Altman, "Legal Realism, Critical Legal Studies, and Dworkin," 15 *Philosophy and Public Affairs*, 205, 216–20, 223–27 (1986); John Farago, "Intractable Cases: The Role of Uncertainty in the Concept of Law," 55 *New York University Law Review* 195 (1980).

Dworkin's formulations tend to take the form of requiring judges to decide novel questions by giving the answer offered by the best moral theory consistent with most of the most recently decided cases. See, e.g., Dworkin, *Taking Rights Seriously*, pp. 122–23. This notion of "best fit, allowing for mistakes in the past" allows a judge to do almost anything. It is a celebrated theorem in mathematics that, given a finite number of points, an infinite number of curves can be drawn linking them. See Kripke, *Wittgenstein on Rules*, p. 18. Some of the curves would be simple, others bizarre, others interestingly complex. Saying that one fits the points "best" involves adopting a substantive theory of what counts as a "best fit." The analogy to Dworkin's analysis is that the best moral theory consistent with the decided cases is simply the best moral theory, so long as we use moral theory to provide the criterion for deciding what "consistency" is. The point is even stronger when we recognize that we are allowed to discard some decisions as mistakes precisely because they do not fit well, given our notions of consistency, with the rest of the decisions in light of our moral theory.

106. See 106 S. Ct., at 2851–53 (Blackmun, J., dissenting).

107. Id., at 2844. The majority treated Stanley v. Georgia, 394 U.S. 557 (1969), as a first amendment case rather than as a privacy case. In doing so it may have betrayed the approach attributed to it here, although the majority opinion is structured so as to make the linkage to the first amendment the relevant point when *Stanley* is discussed. A better formulation in the terms used here would be that *Stanley* protected a form of privacy closely

for choice between these conflicting interpretations of the prior cases lies in moral philosophy: courts should choose the interpretation that is more consistent with the best moral theory.[108]

Bowers shows that this approach does not resolve our difficulties. The dissenters argued that privacy with respect to family and procreational decisions is valuable because it enhances dimensions of the human personality that are equally enhanced by protecting the homosexuals' decision to engage in sodomy.[109] The majority responded indirectly, but its opinion can be read to rely on moral philosophy too. It might be read to argue that family values are worthy in themselves, so that no further justification, such as relying on the connection between family values and personality, is needed. Alternatively, the opinion's extensive discussion of the historical record of intolerance of homosexual activity can be understood as an argument that protecting family values helps to maintain a valuable social order, whose contribution to the development of human personality is morally worthy.[110] Dworkin's methodological prescription simply tells us to rely on moral philosophy. It does not tell us what moral philosophy to rely on, and we have already seen in this chapter that we will have difficulty in assuring that the courts will figure out what the best moral theory is.

Several authors, relying at least in part on some aspects of Dworkin's analysis, have suggested a third way to invoke a community's commitments as the basis for judicial review.[111] Instead of relying on "common values" widely shared in the society at the time of decision, courts could invalidate statutes because they are inconsistent with an enduring consensus about fundamental values, as reflected in the language of the Constitution, decided cases, and our society's cultural heritage. Like the preceding approaches this one has the advantage over systematic moral

---

related to cognition, not all forms of privacy in the home. Neither the majority nor the dissenting opinions made much of the fact that some of the abortion cases involved protecting the rights of the pregnant woman against efforts by the state to include her parents in the abortion decision. See, e.g., Planned Parenthood of Central Missouri v. Danforth, 428 U.S. 52 (1976). Presumably this is because these cases could have been treated by the majority as involving the definition of the family whose decisions are to be protected: One candidate for "the family" is "the pregnant woman and the parents," but another candidate is "the pregnant woman and the fetus."

108. Dworkin, Taking Rights Seriously, pp. 67–68, 116–18, 126–28, 340–41.

109. 106 S. Ct., at 2851 (Blackmun, J., dissenting).

110. See Bruce Hafen, "The Constitutional Status of Marriage, Kinship, and Sexual Privacy—Balancing the Individual and Social Interests," 81 Michigan Law Review 463 (1983); Elizabeth Wolgast, Equality and the Rights of Women (1980).

111. See, e.g., Simon, "Authority of the Framers," pp. 1505–8 (Constitution "represents a deeply layered consensus toward certain basic values").

philosophy of linking the inquiry to the historical experience of a real society. It has the disadvantage of assuming that the underlying consensus, if it exists, is an attractive one. Too often writers who adopt this approach describe the enduring consensus in terms reminiscent of the rhetoric of Motherhood and Apple Pie—that is, as consisting solely of entirely unobjectionable, and therefore vacuous, platitudes. These authors have difficulty explaining why motherhood and apple pie invalidate unenforced antisodomy laws or have any other determinate consequences.

One might fairly wonder why we are not told that the deepest values of our society require us to adopt a form of Christian socialism.[112] Or perhaps the enduring values of our society are what some would describe as racist, sexist, and generally inegalitarian and intolerant. Certainly there is historical support for that description in the Constitution,[113] in the case law—including some recent cases [114]—and in our practices, as the discus-

---

112. Dworkin dismisses this suggestion out of hand, Ronald Dworkin, *Law's Empire* 382, 403 (1986), but there is a long tradition of socialist thought in the United States, reflected to some extent in the political practice of absorbing third-party challenges to major-party dominance. In the context of constitutional law the Supreme Court's decisions about the requirements of equal protection, when coupled with its complex jurisprudence of "state action," would authorize a Dworkinian judge to conclude that the Constitution authorizes the judge to impose socialism if that is the best political theory around.

Griffin v. Illinois, 351 U.S. 12 (1956), and related cases, see Stone et al., *Constitutional Law*, pp. 791–802, establish that the state has an obligation to provide access to important resources even if people have been unable to secure enough money through the market to purchase those resources. Cases such as Ross v. Moffitt, 417 U.S. 600 (1974), which refused to require that states provide lawyers to indigents who sought discretionary review of their convictions, can be explained as involving resources that are not important enough. Another line of cases, beginning with Shapiro v. Thompson, 394 U.S. 618 (1969), see Stone et al., *Constitutional Law*, pp. 808–15, can be understood as defining "important resources" as the necessities of life. Contrary cases, such as Dandridge v. Williams, 397 U.S. 471 (1970), and Lindsey v. Normet, 405 U.S. 56 (1972), can be rejected as simple mistakes or as mistakes predicated on the Court's refusal to adopt a properly Dworkinian theory of constitutional adjudication. Finally, the state action cases, see Stone et al., *Constitutional Law*, pp. 1467–1536, can be read to stand for the proposition that the state has the duty to regulate the outcomes of "private" or "market" transactions where the public interest in regulation outweighs the private interest in retaining discretion over the decision, an interest otherwise limited only by whatever regulations states choose to impose.

See also Charles Black, "Further Reflections on the Constitutional Justice of Livelihood," 86 *Columbia Law Review* 1103 (1986).

113. See U.S. Constitution, art, I, §2 (representatives to be apportioned by "number of Free persons" plus "three fifths of all other Persons," i.e., slaves); id., art. IV, §2 (requiring that persons "held to Service or Labour in one State, under the Laws thereof," be returned to "the Party to whom such Service or Labour may be due").

114. See, e.g., Dred Scott v. Sandford, 60 U.S. (18 How.) 393 (1857); Plessy v. Ferguson, 163 U.S. 537 (1896); Washington v. Davis, 426 U.S. 229 (1976). Washington v. Davis is a

sion earlier in this chapter of the history of free speech suggests. Or perhaps our culture can best be described as relentlessly pragmatic, oriented toward the resolution of immediate problems without being committed to any enduring values. Or finally, perhaps there is no "deep consensus" in the United States because the United States is simply the adventitious collection of people whose primary relationship is coresidence in an arbitrarily defined territory. That is, the appeal to consensus assumes that we live in a community that has a consensus, which may not be true.[115] If either of the final two characterizations of this country's culture is correct, the critical thrust of this approach would disappear.

The Dworkinian approaches combine an attractive method—an appeal in one or another form to the values held by real communities—with a pervasive inability to specify what those values are.[116] This combination arises from some systematic defects in the approaches.

Dworkin explains his view that law is a culture's interpretation of itself by using a striking metaphor. As we saw in Chapter 1, he asks us to consider the enterprise of writing a collaborative novel.[117] One person writes a chapter and sends it on to the next author, whose obligation is to write another chapter that will make the novel the best it can be, given what has gone before. This enterprise has a normative component—the obligation to make the novel the best possible one—and a historical component—the prior chapters. In Dworkin's presentation the historical component places some constraints on each author. Dworkin argues that it would probably undermine the novel's integrity, and therefore its quality, for an author to change the personality traits of the novel's characters drastically, although over time new events may gradually reshape those traits. Dworkin argues that adjudication is like writing this sort of novel: judges should try to make the law the best it can be, given the way that it has developed up to this moment.

The metaphor of the collaborative novel is indeed illuminating but not quite as Dworkin intends. Dworkin's central examples of novels are *A*

---

case involving what some would call institutional racism, which is why I inserted a qualifying phrase in the formulation in the text.

115. The essays in Symposium, "Law and Community," 84 *Michigan Law Review* 1373 (1986), discuss this possibility, each expressing some ambivalence about it.

116. In his most recent work, e.g., Ronald Dworkin, "What Is Equality?" 10 *Philosophy and Public Affairs* 185 (Part I), 283 (Part II) (1981), Dworkin has set his examination of substantive moral philosophy apart from his jurisprudence. The most convincing and interesting parts of Dworkin, *Law's Empire*, for example, deal with the question that used to be formulated as What is law?

117. Dworkin, *Law's Empire*, pp. 229–38.

Christmas Carol and similar nineteenth-century classics.[118] Consider a few alternatives. There is the novel of Christian faith, in which an experience of transcendent grace dramatically alters a character's personality and life. Then there is the picaresque novel, in which a character whose only personality trait is naiveté blithely moves through a world in which all manner of events occur around him, none of which affects him in the slightest. Finally, there is the novel of the bizarre, in which character traits shift randomly from one episode to the next, calling into question the stability of our understanding of the world.[119] Each of these novels can be good, although they all lack the continuity and constraint that Dworkin finds essential to goodness in a novel and by implication in the law.

The difficulty is that Dworkin has taken the classical novel as his exemplar. Suppose instead that we took modernist works as our models. Discontinuity pervades modernist novels, in part precisely to raise questions about the category of "the novel." One view of modernist art holds that its aim is to force upon readers and viewers an awareness of the artificiality of the artist's creation, which it does by taking the artistic enterprise as its subject. In this way modernist art denies that it has connections to "the real world" or, more strongly, denies that there is a real world beyond the constructions we choose to make.[120] This view has unsettling implications for Dworkin's approach, for it denies that there are standards of goodness of the sort that Dworkin seeks.

The modernist challenge can be fended off by saying that, whatever may be the case about modern art in general, Dworkin uses the metaphor of the collaborative novel to explain a practice within a community that accepts a stipulated understanding of what a novel is: We could not fairly expect Charles Dickens to collaborate on a novel with James Joyce; we

118. In *Law's Empire* Dworkin cites *Moby Dick* (p. 44) and discusses *A Christmas Carol* in some detail (pp. 232–37).

119. Lief Carter directed my attention to a fantasy series called Thieves' World. See also Lief Carter, *Contemporary Constitutional Lawmaking: The Supreme Court and the Art of Politics* 123 (1985). This series consists of stories written by a number of authors, who receive instructions to use the same set of characters and to give them attributes that are roughly consistent from one story to the next. Because of the fantasy genre, however, some rather dramatic changes in attributes occur between stories. I must confess that I found the series not terribly impressive, which might support Dworkin's views about artistic quality, except for the fact that I am not at all sure that I would recognize high quality in the fantasy genre anyway. And the point that fantasy forms a distinct genre seems to undermine Dworkin's effort to analogize law to a unitary novelistic form.

120. See Richard Hyland, "A Defense of Legal Writing," 134 *University of Pennsylvania Law Review* 599, 611–13 (1986) (describing relation between literary style and vision of the world); Erving Goffman, *Forms of Talk* 50–54, 73–74 (1981) (describing discontinuities in ordinary conversation as form of creative activity in which social setting can determine structure of interaction).

therefore cannot undermine the metaphor's utility merely by pointing out that the interpretive community is not universal. It is sufficient that the interpretive community includes enough of the people who would be called upon to write and read the collaborative novel.

Unfortunately for this defense modernism challenges even the more limited claim about interpretive communities. Discontinuity pervades modernist art only in part to raise questions about our concepts of art; it does so in part also to capture the modernist sensibility that our communities have shattered around us.[121] If in the face of this understanding of the world judges nonetheless form a single interpretive community, that would appear to be a sociological fact of some interest, deserving analysis. Dworkin, however, strenuously resists the effort to engage in such analysis.[122] Further, as we will see in more detail in Chapter 4, it may be misleading to analogize citizens subject to coercive law to readers of novels: Even if people do not want to "read" the law, the judges will make them do so. Once again the existence of a community of interpretation that includes writers and readers, judges and citizens, is exactly what modernism places at issue.

Conclusion

Michael Perry has faced the difficulties of using moral philosophy in constitutional theory by calling on the judges to carry forth the prophetic strand of our political tradition.[123] Our judges should be the Isaiah that Brandeis was to his friends. There are substantial problems with this proposal. Supreme Court Justices, including Brandeis and Warren, are to say the least not without honor in their own country. And the point of the biblical observation is that being a prophet and exercising coercive power are incompatible activities. In one tradition prophets speak truth to power but do not exercise power. Indeed, perhaps prophets can most

121. James White, *Heracles' Bow: Essays on the Rhetoric and Poetics of Law* 99–103 (1985), takes an explicitly conservative view of community in the face of the modernist challenge: "In place of the constituted 'we' that it is the achievement of our past to have given us, we are offered an unconstituted 'we.'" The modernist would respond that one of the ways in which the past has constituted us lies in our ability to reconstitute ourselves. (White's essays use mostly premodernist literature to focus the discussion.)

122. See Dworkin, *Law's Empire*, pp. 13–14, calling this sort of analysis "essential" but condemning all previous efforts as "impoverished" and "depressing." Nonetheless, Dworkin employs an incredibly casual empirical theory of judicial socialization, on which his entire edifice rests. One minor example is his discussion of the appropriate "compartmentalization" of contemporary law, which he asserts "usually match[es] popular opinion." P. 252.

123. Perry, *Courts, Constitution, and Human Rights*, pp. 98–99.

effectively call us to what is right when they have behind them only the moral force of their passion. Obedience to a prophet's call that has some coercion behind it may be unlikely to receive God's blessing, and yet that is what occurs when the justices are our prophets.[124] Nor is there any need to locate prophecy in the Supreme Court. The prophetic voice has indeed been part of the American tradition, but a list of American prophets would include people rather more like William Sloane Coffin, Jr., Martin Luther King, Jr., and Jerry Falwell than like Harry Blackmun or even Louis Brandeis.

Thomas Grey has responded rather acerbically to Perry's proposal by noting that Supreme Court Justices are "officials who are given more job security than other civil servants . . . They are comfortably middle-of-the-road, senatorially confirmable lawyer-politicians . . . Under the robes, federal judges are ordinary members of the comfortable classes."[125] Grey's observation, a version of the sociological inquiry mentioned earlier, raises a final question about the effort to ground constitutional theory in community values. We have seen that modernism denies that there is a community-at-large whose values are to be interpreted. Attaching the general possessive *our* to the word *community* makes a false claim of fact. At most judges can interpret "their" community's values.[126] That immediately directs our attention to who they are.[127] Indeed, who they are and how they are selected are aspects of our legal culture that themselves deserve interpretation.

124. Subject to qualifications about the degree of compliance with judicial orders, discussed in Chapter 6.

125. Thomas Grey, "The Constitution as Scripture," 37 *Stanford Law Review* 1, 23–24 (1984). Another objection is that Perry's religious vision is so conventional—everything converges on the left-liberal wing of the Democratic Party. It would be engaging to find out that God wants us to be vegetarians, or to disarm unilaterally, or to fire a preemptive nuclear first strike.

126. See Lucinda Finley, "Transcending Equality Theory: A Way out of the Maternity and the Workplace Debate," 86 *Columbia Law Review* 1118, 1170 (1986) ("problematic for those in power . . . to put themselves within the perspective of someone they have been taught to view as different"); Susan Okin, "Justice and Gender," 16 *Philosophy and Public Affairs* 42, 65–66 (1987). There is no denying that people in power can attempt to take the perspective of others, but their differences from the others provide reason to be skeptical about their ability to do so successfully. Finley and others have suggested that these considerations should lead judges to be humble in what they do; it would seem that humility might properly take the form of refusing to exercise the power of judicial review.

127. Dworkin recasts objections like this as pointing to "practical problems" about the ability of judges to interpret their society in light of the pressures of heavy dockets and the need to compromise among themselves to reach a decision. Dworkin, *Law's Empire*, pp. 380–81. This allows him to forgo the sociological analysis that he states, but appears not to believe, is essential.

The appeal to community values is a contemporary version of the republican tradition. It is attractive because it explicitly assumes that adjudication should be based on values, and the republican tradition also insisted on the importance of civic values in our governance. It is attractive as well because it implicitly assumes both that those values should be historically grounded in the experience of actual communities—another republican theme—and that we live in a society, valued by conservatives and radicals alike, in which people have unalienated relationships and self-understandings, in short, that we live in a community.[128] The conservative imagines a past in which each person knew and accepted his or her own place. That past, if it ever existed, was destroyed by the dynamic thrust of economic growth. The radical imagines a future in which the separateness of each of us has been overcome by the elimination of class society. That future, if it ever will exist, will have to overcome the other sources of our separateness as well, an unlikely occurrence.

The vision of community that animates the appeal to community values is simultaneously pernicious and inspiring. It is pernicious because it imagines that community now exists, that we simply have to reach for the brotherhood of man in the fatherhood of God. It is inspiring because it tells us that even if community does not now exist, we can begin to create it. We need not await the revolution that will transform society, for by acting on our vision of community we make society different. But the wholesale argument against systematic moral philosophy suggests how difficult it will be to take such action. For although we do know that there is Truth, we cannot now know what it is. When we choose among systematic moral philosophies, we say simultaneously who we are and who we might become. The limits of our social understanding make it difficult for us to recharacterize ourselves and develop utopian visions of who we might become. If Truth is historicized, how are we to live now? Everything is up for grabs, but we ought not grab at everything. We can only do our best, do what we can to transform ourselves and our society so that Truth can be made real. Inevitably we will have to abandon the false security of theory and open ourselves to the risk of tragic error as we take political action.

We can conclude by thinking about the implications of Dworkin's offhanded dismissal of the suggestion that judges in the United States could, under his approach, decree socialism.[129] Of course not—today.

---

128. For a survey of recent discussions of the policy implications of a commitment to republicanism, see David Price, "Assessing Policy: Conceptual Points of Departure," in *Public Duties: The Moral Obligations of Government Officials* 147, 155–67 (Joel Fleishman, Lance Liebman, and Mark Moore eds. 1981).

129. Dworkin, *Law's Empire*, p. 382.

Who would contend that the judges we have now would do that? Consider instead what legal materials would be available were judges ever to be appointed who wanted to decree socialism. The political world would have changed so much that perhaps they would not have to.[130] Once again, the ideas behind the republican tradition may make judicial review based on the values of a true community both possible and unnecessary.

130. In an earlier version of part of the argument of this book, I responded to the What would you do? question by saying that I would "make an explicitly political decision: which result is, in the circumstances now existing, likely to advance the cause of socialism? . . . I would then write an opinion in some currently favored version of [constitutional theory]." Mark Tushnet, "The Dilemmas of Liberal Constitutionalism," 42 *Ohio State Law Journal* 411, 424 (1981). This is a purely Dworkinian proposal. "Advancing the cause of socialism" is not "imposing socialism." Rather the suggestion is to use the materials presently available in the law in the service of a strategic judgment about what incremental step that could be taken in a given case would advance the cause of socialism. Were I a judge political circumstances would have changed dramatically from what they are today, making it rather likely that there would be substantial legal materials available to support decisions that would, in the sense specified, advance the cause of socialism. See also note 112.

Charles Black's appeal for a constitutional right of livelihood, note 112, concludes by acknowledging that the courts as presently constituted are unlikely to recognize such a right but notes that he is addressing law students who, in a generation or so, might be in a position to influence the courts into adopting Black's views. Yet if those students-turned-lawyers are to succeed, they will have to persuade a new generation of judges, who will be open to the argument only because they have been appointed as a result of a change in the political atmosphere which itself might produce legislative movement in the direction Black favors.

4

Antiformalism in Constitutional Theory

THE preceding chapters have examined a number of efforts to explain why a small group of people, called judges, should be allowed to displace the otherwise legally authoritative decisions of a somewhat larger group of people, called legislators, who are selected by processes that seem closer to the normatively attractive mechanisms of democracy than those used to select judges.[1] These efforts attempt to provide "formalist" solutions to the countermajoritarian difficulty with which the liberal tradition is concerned. This chapter examines antiformalist attempts to displace concern with the countermajoritarian difficulty rather than to allay that concern. It argues that these antiformalist tendencies are flawed either because their adherents are sometimes unwilling to confront the implications for social reform of their rejection of the political theory underlying formalism or because their proponents know that under current political circumstances they are unable to pursue the analysis more fruitfully.

As we have seen, judicial review plays a central role, as a method of controlling exercises of legislative power, in the liberal tradition. Constitutional theory plays a similar role, as a method of controlling exercises of judicial power. It constrains judges by providing a set of public criteria by

1. In some versions the normative difficulty arises from concern for efficient government, that is, wholly apart from differences in character between courts and legislatures, judicial review introduces some redundancy in decision making. The costs of redundancy may be worth bearing if redundancy improves the quality of the outcome in some specified sense to a sufficiently significant degree. For a discussion of this issue, see Robert Cover and T. Alexander Aleinikoff, "Dialectical Federalism: Habeas Corpus and the Court," 86 *Yale Law Journal* 1035 (1977). The formalisms discussed in this chapter attempt to specify both the sense in which the quality of outcomes can be improved and the institutional differences between courts and legislators that lead theorists to think that redundancy improves quality in the specified sense. Notice that absolute judgments about the courts', or the legislatures', abilities to address some issue are not in question; rather, comparative judgments about differences at the margin are.

which theorists, interested observers, and the judges themselves can evaluate what the judges do. These criteria have characteristics that lead me to
call them formalisms. Each formalism consists of a relatively limited
number of propositions, ordered in a way that makes it relatively clear
which criterion has priority over others under specified conditions. If the
criteria are to provide the basis for the evaluation that constrains the
judges, we must be able to deploy the criteria in particular cases in
relatively uncontroversial ways: The criteria may have margins about
which there can be argument in specific cases, but they must have relatively well-defined cores about which there can be no question; otherwise
constitutional theory will fail to provide the public constraints that it
demands.[2]

Antiformalist themes have become attractive as the inadequacies of
every available formalism have been exposed. Antiformalist authors do
not criticize some or all formalisms for failing to provide the constraints
on judges that the liberal tradition requires; they reject the search for
constraints as irrelevant. Anarchist antiformalists deny that we need to
constrain coercive power at all, no matter where it is lodged. They contend either that coercive power does not exist or that we need not fear
unconstrained exercises of coercive power. Other antiformalists reject the
search for constraints by denying the premises upon which that search
rests. Specifically, they assume that each of us is able to give our life
meaning only by participating in a community whose actions are guided
by public values that transcend the aggregation of individual preferences.
Both versions of antiformalism draw on the republican tradition. Antiformalists can look to the documents in that tradition, which include the
Constitution, to enhance their rhetoric. They can also appeal to our
immanent understanding that civic republicanism expresses something
important about our communal life that the liberal tradition overlooks.
Perhaps unfortunately we cannot merely adopt or retrieve the republican
tradition. Its vitality depends on a set of social arrangements that are no
longer available to us. To develop antiformalist themes into something
more, we must transform society.

2. I have inserted the word *relatively* in these formulations to indicate that, as used here,
formalism does not mean a theory in which results can be derived from the criteria by
employing standard operations of deductive logic. In short, formalism is not mechanical
jurisprudence. To do what constitutional theory must do in the liberal tradition, though,
formalisms must place some bounds on possible results.

As a matter of personal moral deliberation each of us might accept our ambivalence
about principles, but our resignation would not lead us to accept the imposition by others of
their personal resolution of similar ambivalences.

Anarchist Antiformalism

Formalisms are efforts to establish a governmental structure in which constraints are placed on the exercise of coercive social power at every level. Anarchists deny the normative validity of any exercise of coercive social power. Anarchist antiformalism in recent works has taken two forms: a denial that coercive social power exists, which makes the search for constraints irrelevant, and a denial that exercises of coercive social power have any normative differences from exercises of coercive individual power, which re-creates the state of nature from which the liberal tradition tried to rescue us.

Robert Burt's article "Constitutional Law and the Teaching of the Parables" exemplifies the first strategy.[3] It argues in effect that the concern with constraining judges is seriously misplaced. Burt argues that we mistake what is going on when we think that judges making decisions on constitutional issues are exercising one form of social power while constraining the exercise of another form. Instead, he argues, they are engaged in a continuing dialogue with the legislature and the public, in which the judges invoke the Constitution as a rhetorical device to suggest a better course to us not to coerce us into following their advice.

Burt's essential perception is that sometimes competing claims of right are offered by those who do not see themselves as parts of the same community.[4] Any coercive resolution of their dispute necessarily accepts one side's definition of the community and thereby excludes the other. Thus, Burt argues, these disputes should not be resolved by the coercive imposition of a solution. Instead courts should invite the parties to consider redefining what each believes to be the community by reminding them of the deeper claims—to personal identity, to humanity, to social peace, and the like—to which they say they are also committed.[5] For Burt, the much-criticized decision at the remedial stage of *Brown v. Board of Education* is exemplary.[6] The Court there reached its "proper limit" in "say[ing] . . . that the dispute in its present posture cannot legitimately be

---

3. 93 *Yale Law Journal* 455 (1984).

4. Burt's article is extremely elusive, and I frequently find myself thinking that what it says is inconsistent with Burt's apparent intentions. I suspect that the elusiveness is deliberate, in order to make the article exemplify as well as describe the pedagogical value of parables.

5. Burt, "Parables," pp. 455–56, 471, 479–80, 501.

6. 349 U.S. 294 (1955). The Court directed that desegregation occur "with all deliberate speed" and instructed the federal trial courts to supervise the process. The Court's failure to define more precise guidelines, or to insist on speedy or immediate desegregation, has been widely criticized. For a summary of the criticisms and a different view of the overall process, see Paul Gewirtz, "Remedies and Resistance," 92 *Yale Law Journal* 585 (1983).

resolved and that accordingly the particular resolution . . . that one party has imposed on the other is invalid." It properly "did not [go on to] dictate the scheme that would replace" segregation laws, because that would have been simply to impose the other party's resolution.[7]

Burt's argument gains force from his understanding that it is foolish to believe that the Court has "power . . . to secure obedience in practice." At least in contentious cases, "every action of [the Court] carries the same fundamental implication" and "weakness," of "vulnerability [and] . . . dependence on others."[8] The courts are weak because, although they utter words that usually imply that coercion will follow noncompliance, we know that the degree of compliance varies tremendously. The Court said in 1962 that school-initiated prayer in public schools was unconstitutional,[9] but in the 1980s some schools maintained the practice. Burt's central example in this context is *Brown* itself, which initiated—or more precisely was located in the middle of—an extended process of adjustment; it did not impose a resolution in fact. For Burt, law is dialogue, not coercion. Concern about constraints on the exercise of power is irrelevant because judges do not exercise power. They only invite the rest of us to consider "claim[s] for inclusion in a communal relation."[10]

What we know about compliance with legal commands gives powerful support to Burt's analysis. Still, Burt does not pursue the argument to a full-scale anarchism. By focusing on judges and the Constitution, he suggests that legislative law is something different, that is, coercive in a way that judicial law is not. By confining his attention to a subset of especially contentious cases, he suggests that his anarchism can be similarly confined. Both suggestions are wrong. Finally, by criticizing some recent decisions as closing off the legal dialogue, Burt fails to grasp the implications of his emphasis on the Court's weakness.

Burt insists that courts do not resolve legal disputes; they insert those disputes into an ongoing process of social dialogue and education. The judgment entered by a court in a litigated case does not involve the exercise of coercive social power, because the entry of the judgment determines nothing; it is just another move in the continuing dialogue. Issues are presented to the courts, decisions are made there, commentators in the legal academy and the popular press respond to them, entrepreneurial legislators try to piggyback their own programs onto what the courts have said, other legislators try to get some mileage out of opposing what the courts have done, and so on indefinitely.

7. Burt, "Parables," p. 485.
8. Id., pp. 474, 476.
9. Abington School District v. Schempp, 374 U.S. 203 (1962).
10. Burt, "Parables," p. 500.

Nothing in this version of the argument claims anything special about courts as places where this dialogue occurs in any privileged way.[11] Burt's use of the law of handicapped persons as an important illustration of his argument demonstrates this point. The courts had the limited but important role of initially raising the general rights consciousness of the society. Then Congress and the state legislatures took over, only to find the courts again intervening, and not nearly so sympathetically as those encouraged by the rights rhetoric had probably hoped.[12] The complexity of the interchange between the public, legislators, and the courts is what makes it sensible to treat Burt as offering an account that dissolves coercive social power wherever it appears and not just an account of how courts do and ought to behave.[13]

Nonetheless, Burt is attracted to the idea that he should offer criteria for judicial intervention. He frames his argument around situations in which the parties "define themselves as diametrically and irrevocably opposed to one another, . . . [with] no shared communal interest or value," but he does not specify when those situations arise.[14] He does however state "an elusive criterion" for judicial intervention: "the importance of the dispute, either because of its general social significance or its intense urgency to some few who are directly affected by it."[15]

11. See, e.g., id., pp. 465, 484–85 n. 93. For a discussion of Burt's effort to identify a distinctive judicial role nonetheless, see text accompanying notes 21–33.

12. Id., pp. 489–500. But see id., p. 497 (legislative action rested on prior judicial determinations of unconstitutionality).

13. A similarly complex interchange among citizens, legislators, and courts occurred *before* Brown v. Board of Education. Constitutional theorists' belief that all they need to know is contained in the U.S. Reports leads them to start the story with *Brown*. Before *Brown*, however, there were sustained efforts to secure the passage of antilynching legislation, a threatened march on Washington that led to the creation of a wartime Fair Employment Practices Commission, the desegregation of the armed forces, and the like.

14. Burt, "Parables," pp. 456–57. His argument gains its rhetorical power by its use of two core examples, segregation and the rights of the retarded, with which he correctly assumes most of his readers will be sympathetic. He also slips in a brief discussion of abortion, id., p. 488. The rhetorical force of his argument would have been diminished, I suspect, had it placed the abortion issue at its center. Certainly, though, the social forces that generated the abortion decisions, the decisions themselves, and the social response that followed them would have provided at least as good an example—in my view a better example—of the processes with which Burt is concerned.

15. Id., p. 484. See also id., p. 500 ("the proper occasions for . . . judicial intervention . . . will depend on many complicated considerations"). Burt appears to want to distinguish between people who lose because they are coercively excluded from the community (or who lose in being so excluded) and people who lose even though they have "shared communal interest[s]" with the winners. His use of segregation and the rights of the retarded suggests an affinity with John Hart Ely's concern for representation, with all its attendant difficulties. See Chapter 2. One of those difficulties deserves mention here. Burt

Burt's antiformalism should lead him to eschew the search for criteria for judicial intervention, which are useful only because they serve to constrain the exercise of coercive power. In his analysis because law is dialogue rather than coercion, it simply does not matter when courts intervene. What they do has no final consequences; society chooses what to do by playing out the continuing dialogue. Sometimes decisions appear to be (relatively) final. Yet in Burt's view the finality is illusory. A dialogue may end "by invoking superior coercive force to impose silence" or by "a mutually agreed end."[16] Distinguishing between coerced and agreed-upon silence is impossible in the absence of an understanding of what community is. Until we have that understanding there can be no final decisions.

In this view Burt's argument supports an attitude of indifference to the outcomes of particular cases, because the outcomes are merely temporary positions in a process of continual adjustment. Like most commentators, however, Burt finds some decisions of the Supreme Court deeply disturbing, when they treat "the simple assertion of the wish to avoid association as intrinsically justified without any need to account for, or listen to, competing claims."[17] Rather than leaving the dialogue open, the Supreme Court in these cases closes it off.

Once again Burt betrays his own argument. If all law is dialogue, nothing within the domain of law can terminate the conversation. Consider two examples Burt offers of judicial attempts to impose closure on the conversation; in both the attempt clearly failed. *Dred Scott v. Sandford* "shut off the possibility" that blacks would be heard in the federal courts.[18] But the discussions that constitute the law continued, in the Lincoln-Douglas debates, in Congress, and ultimately on the battlefield. Burt is willing to take the long view of *Brown*, citing actions by the Court

---

would allow judicial intervention when a dispute is "intensely urgent" to some people and is concerned with situations in which people "define themselves" as opposed. This psychologistic emphasis at least raises questions about cases in which people do not urgently feel or define themselves as excluded precisely because they have been so successfully excluded as to make their situation seem natural to them. See Ely, *Democracy and Distrust*, pp. 165–66; Chapter 9. Further, Burt's "elusive criterion" suggests the possibility that what we might call political therapy would lead more losers to begin to see themselves as actually excluded.

16. Burt, "Parables," p. 488.

17. Id., p. 489. His candidates are cases, such as Pennhurst State School v. Halderman, 451 U.S. 1 (1981), invoking state autonomy to deny claims for "mutual engagement and obligatory dialogue."

18. 60 U.S. (19 How.) 393 (1856); Burt, "Parables," p. 489.

and Congress in 1968.[19] Thirteen years after *Dred Scott*, the fourteenth amendment was adopted.[20]

Burt's second example is the initial abortion decision, in which "the Supreme Court wrongly held itself to be the authoritative calculator."[21] The dialogue on the abortion issue has surely intensified since 1972. The Court in *Roe v. Wade* purported to remove from the legal system consideration of the question of the fetus' status as a person.[22] Nonetheless, and perhaps as a result, contemporary discussions of abortion are more concerned with that question, and other associated issues, than were the more pragmatic discussions in the 1960s.[23] All of this certainly confirms Burt's original insight, but it undermines his criticism of the Court for cutting off the conversation.

Burt's arguments lead, perhaps despite his intentions, to the position that law is not coercion and that lawmakers need not be constrained. There is something decidedly odd about this, for it has the effect of denying that the forms of law are implicated in causing suffering. The difficulty is that we know that the legal system indeed places people in positions to do harm. Burt's analysis is troubling because it may lead us to think that at the end of the day nothing can be done. His concern that dialogue be used to create the possibility for community offers a way out.[24]

19. Burt, "Parables," p. 485. See also Milner Ball, "A Letter to Professor Burt," 42 *Washington and Lee Law Review* 27, 31 (1985) (*Brown* "a case of judicial chicken," promoting not "peace [or] ordered conversation but unnecessarily prolonged suffering"); Peter Teachout, "The Heart of the Lawyer's Craft," 42 *Washington and Lee Law Review* 39, 50–52 (1985) (discussing ambiguity of Burt's use of "enslavement" as metaphor for "losing a case").

20. It is possible to distinguish the periods on the basis of the amount of overt violence (directed by some white people at other white people) in each. I would be hesitant, though, to put much weight on such a distinction, because it ignores the routine violence of everyday life, see Barrington Moore, *The Social Origins of Dictatorship and Democracy* 426–30 (1966) (on violence attendant to "peaceful" social transformations in England and United States), and because it is likely to suffer from historical amnesia. On violence during the Second Reconstruction, see Michal Belknap, "The Vindication of Burke Marshall: The Southern Legal System and the Anti-Civil-Rights Violence of the 1960s," 33 *Emory Law Journal* 93, 102–3, 109–10 (1984).

21. Burt, "Parables," p. 488 n. 106.

22. 410 U.S. 113, 156–59 (1973).

23. See Kristin Luker, *Abortion and the Politics of Motherhood* 140–41, 144 (1984). As Luker shows the questions are considerably more complex than the distinction between pragmatic and moral arguments indicates, because the arguments are bound up with stances their proponents take toward a wide range of issues relating to modern life and their place in it.

24. Works in the dialogic vein continue to appear. See, e.g., Carter, "Right Questions." For a discussion of the problem of coercive power in Habermas' dialogic social theory, see

He believes that *Youngberg v. Romeo* understood "the lesson of community" in holding that the Constitution guaranteed Romeo, a resident of an awful state institution for the mentally handicapped, a "minimally adequate" program to prevent the imposition of physical or psychological harm.[25] Once again these beliefs cannot fit into the analysis underlying Burt's express arguments. The Court held that Romeo had certain rights, which he could enforce in an action for damages. It also held that damages would be unavailable if his custodians had failed to provide him with the required program because the state legislature denied them the resources to do so.

Suffering occurs, but in Burt's analysis the law cannot relieve it. What does this imply? Consider again Burt's preferred action in his hard cases. The Court should have kept the dialogue open—but of course the dialogue is always open. Certainly courts—even appellate courts—are places where, sometimes, community and shared values can be brought into being.[26] The sociological critique of theory cautions against an excess of optimism about that possibility: if judges are in fact much like legislators, they will rarely be inclined to promote much more in the way of dialogue than legislators are. Still, we need not rule out in principle the possibility of constructing a community in the courtroom. At the same time, however, we cannot privilege courts over legislatures, zoning boards, and collective bargaining sessions as locations for that effort.[27]

Another proponent of law as dialogue, James Boyd White, has developed the antistatist conception of law by treating law as rhetoric. He argues that we usually understand law as a bureaucracy devoted to issuing authoritative commands designed to achieve our social purposes. He says that we should instead see it as a rhetorical activity which "constitutes both the community and the culture it commends." Lawyers use the language of their audience to urge that it adopt a different understanding of itself; "in this sense legal rhetoric is always argumentatively constitutive of the language it employs." White thus is able to acknowledge "the condition of radical uncertainty in which we live," which includes "uncertainty as to the meaning of words." Finally, law as rhetoric is ethical

---

Koen Raes, "Habermas' Approach to Law," 13 *Journal of Law and Society* 180, 190–93 (1986).

25. 457 U.S. 307, 323 (1982); Burt, "Parables," p. 495. For a different perspective on this case, see Chapter 7.

26. See, e.g., Peter Gabel and Paul Harris, "Building Power and Breaking Images," 11 *New York University Review of Law and Social Change* 369 (1983).

27. See Burt, "Parables," p. 466 (courts have "pedagogic advantage" arising from "their palpable weakness in imposing effective force on the disputing parties").

and communal, creating "for the moment" an "ethical identity" for the lawyers, their audience, and those about whom they speak.[28]

White's arguments are powerful and attractive. They explain much of what lawyers do, without exaggerating lawyers' cultural importance, and they show how a lawyer's work is necessarily bound to the culture in which he or she is located and yet also contains the potential for transforming that culture. Even so, the argument, in White's hands, has some disquieting overtones. As befits the works of a professor of law and English, White's books are filled with examples from classical literature. This suggests to a modernist reader that White believes law's transformative potential to be severely limited. His arguments are not explicitly conservative, but his rhetoric, to which his arguments direct our attention, is conservative. As we have already seen in the discussion of Ronald Dworkin's approach to adjudication, the sense of the argument would be different if the examples White used were James Joyce and Gabriel García Marquez rather than Homer and Milton. And ultimately White, like Burt, must take the long view: law as rhetoric constitutes a culture by means of persuasion; unfortunately law at the point of its application requires or justifies action by means of coercion.[29]

Burt's anarchist antiformalism uses religious metaphors to support its argument. Robert Cover's "Foreword: *Nomos* and Narrative" does so as well.[30] Cover is more thoroughgoing in his anarchism, explicitly refuses to privilege any locus of law creation or community building, and recognizes the role of coercion in law creation, but he holds a romantic view of community. His argument includes the premises that law creation is community building and that law creation involves violence. He fails to discuss the inference that follows from these premises: community building involves violence too.

Explication of Cover's views can usefully begin by contrasting them with some of Owen Fiss's.[31] Fiss has said that in "legal interpretation there is only one school and attendance is mandatory."[32] This metaphor con-

---

28. White, *Heracles' Bow*, pp. 32–44. See also Lief Carter, "'Die Meistersinger von Nurnberg' and the United States Supreme Court: Aesthetic Theory in Constitutional Jurisprudence," 18 *Polity* 272 (1985).

29. White's primary discussion of the coercive dimension of law is confined to an afterword, in which he argues that the coercive power of legal judgments is exaggerated and is not that different from the power of poetry and propaganda. White, *Heracles' Bow* pp. 238–39. See also id., pp. 7–8 (describing lawyers as practicing one of two types of persuasion, but omitting force, which had been included in prior list of types of persuasion).

30. 97 *Harvard Law Review* 4 (1983).

31. Cover discusses another portion of Fiss's views, id., pp. 43–44.

32. Owen Fiss, "Objectivity and Interpretation," 34 *Stanford Law Review* 739, 746 (1982).

veys an image of the legal system as unitary, hierarchical, and, in a sense to be defined in a moment, passive. In contrast, Cover's "Foreword" depicts the law as pluralist, antihierarchical, and active.

As Burt does, Cover denies that the exercise of coercive social power can be justified. He insists that anyone's claim that his or her legal rights have been invaded has the full status that we conventionally accord to what the schoolmasters say.[33] Cover's theory is pluralist and antihierarchical: everyone can make claims of legal right, and no one's claims of legal right, or determinations that legal rights have or have not been invaded, is entitled to privileged status. That is, what you or I say is "The Law" is on exactly the same normative plane as what a majority of the Supreme Court says is "The Law."[34] Once again, this is exactly the anarchists' claim, that no one in a position to exercise coercive power—to be a schoolmaster—has any greater claim than does anyone else to force others to act in one way rather than another. Unlike Burt, Cover need not deny that coercive social power is ever exercised. He can acknowledge that coercion is rampant in the society without repudiating his essential point, that the exercise of that power always requires justifications so strong as to be rarely available.

This image of law is made even more attractive by what I have called its active rather than its passive character. The metaphor of the school suggests an enterprise in which an informed and dominating person instructs people who sit and listen to find out what the law is, absorbing what is offered to them. For Cover, everyone is a lawmaker, a schoolmaster, although at that point the metaphor becomes rather less enlightening. In all our interactions we create law. To put it in Burt's terms, our everyday dialogues directed at each other, and not just the ones directed at those nominally in positions of power, are where we create law. In short, Cover has told us that law is what *we* do not what someone else does to us.[35]

It is important to emphasize that Cover argues that *law* is what we do. He would not give those in positions to exercise coercive social power the normative force that our culture accords to "The Law." What they do has no more claim, no less of course but no more either, to our deference than anything we do.

33. See, e.g., Cover, "*Nomos* and Narrative," p. 43.
34. Id., pp. 46–53.
35. See also White, *Heracles' Bow*, p. 40–41 ("Law might come to be seen as something that lawyers themselves make all the time, . . . not as something that is made by a political sovereign"), pp. 123–24 (describing law as embodying "the radical equality of all people . . . in a life of composition and reading").

Indeed, Cover devotes a great deal of attention to what he sees as the problem of state violence, the coercive use of the state's version of law to suppress competing versions. His exposition slips when he romanticizes the communities from which those competing versions emerge. In discussing how communities with deviant versions of law might respond to efforts to suppress them, Cover writes, "In interpreting a text of resistance, any community must come to grips with violence. It must think through the implications of living as a victim or perpetrator of violence in the contexts in which violence is likely to arise. Violence [is] a technique either to achieve or to suppress interpretations or the living of them." The passage seems to imply that the community of resistance will be the victim of violence directed at it by the dominant community or will itself perpetrate violence against that *other* community.[36]

That is acceptable enough as far as it goes. But Cover's assumption that communities, even communities of resistance, can be constituted without violence directed at their own members betrays the "theory of radical autonomy of juridical meaning" he proposes in this article. There are a number of ways to show this. For Cover, juridical meaning is created at every moment of social interaction. What if my friends and I wander off? The community cannot guarantee that the meaning we create will be consistent with the "stable social understandings" that constitute the community of which we nonetheless remain a part. Our community must therefore hold in reserve the possibility of coercion, not to suppress other communities but to assure the continuity of our own. To put it even more strongly, the threat of instability is the condition for the existence of stable understandings: Only if we know that coercion is available should someone create new legal meanings can we choose to adhere to existing ones—or, perhaps better, can we choose to re-create old ones—or, perhaps best of all, can we *choose* to adhere to old ones.[37]

36. Cover, "*Nomos* and Narrative," p. 50. This reading is supported by the footnote to the passage quoted. In it Cover says that he is speaking of "communities that already have an identity[,] . . . [whose] members are . . . already bound by . . . stable cultural understanding . . . Violence may well be a particularly powerful catalyst . . . in the chemistry by which a collection of hitherto unrelated individuals becomes a self-conscious revolutionary force . . . The persistent effort to live a law . . . presupposes a community already self-conscious and lawful by its own lights . . . Although resistant groups affirming their own laws need not realize themselves in violence, they always live in the shadow of the violence backing the state's claim to control." Id., n. 137. The sense of violence as external to the community comes through with increasing clarity as the footnote proceeds.

37. One might respond that if *radical autonomy* means anything it means that when my friends and I wander off, we create a new community, in regard to which external violence is relevant but internal violence is not. Then, however, a second difficulty arises. The metaphor of "wandering off" is dramatic but inaccurate. Cover's radical autonomy means that every social interaction constitutes a community for those involved in it. Thus, treating the

Cover's vision of communities of resistance confronting problems of external violence captures some but not all of the interesting phenomena of law creation. Cover describes situations in which communities of resistance say, "Our law is as good as, or better than, your law." But there are situations in which such communities say, "Our law *is* your law." They are then not communities of resistance at all. They may appeal to the deeper commitments embodied in state law, as against the particular expressions of state law.[38] Or they may attempt to convert the rest of us to their views. Throughout, they insist that our effort to treat them as outsiders, to exclude them from our community, must fail because they are no different from us. In these situations violence is internal to the community. Completing Cover's theory requires us to return to Burt's.

The anarchisms of Burt, White, and Cover demonstrate that constitutional theory requires a theory of community. Such a theory would displace the liberal tradition's concern for placing constraints on individual power. Burt and Cover suggest that an appropriate theory would treat community as created and dissolved at every moment of social life, and they would understand social life as shared values and violence, each dependent for its meaning and existence on the other.[39]

Intuitionist Antiformalism

Chapter 3 argued that systematic—formalist—moral philosophy fails to provide the constraints on judges that the liberal tradition requires. The field of moral philosophy contains antiformalist elements as well. These elements are usually described as intuitionist theories. Intuitionistic moral philosophies identify moral principles but do not specify how conflicts are to be resolved.

Steven Shiffrin has defended intuitionistic moral philosophy and has defended balancing in first amendment cases as an application of intuitionism.[40] Even if his defense of intuitionism succeeds, however, it cannot provide the foundation for judicial review in the liberal tradition. Intuitionism may be a sensible way for each of us to arrive at our judgments so

creation of new legal meanings as a secession from an existing community actually denies the possibility of community in the first place.

38. Compare the discussion of concepts and conceptions in Chapter 1.

39. See the appendix to this chapter for a discussion of the use of community in constitutional theory.

40. Steven Shiffrin, "Liberalism, Radicalism, and Legal Scholarship," 30 *UCLA Law Review* 1103 (1983); Steven Shiffrin, "The First Amendment and Economic Regulation: Away From a General Theory of the First Amendment," 78 *Northwestern University Law Review* 1212 (1983).

that we may seek to convince others that we are right, but standing alone it cannot tell us *whose* intuitions ought to prevail in the end. Specifically, it cannot explain why the intuitions of a majority of the Supreme Court rather than the intuitions of state judges or of legislators should control.

Consider first a relatively pure situation. The law of libel, which implicates first amendment values, is almost entirely a creation of state judges in their common law capacity. If an intuitionistic balancing is appropriate here, we need a rather strong theory of institutional differences between state courts and the Supreme Court to justify reliance on the intuitions of the Supreme Court.[41] Such differences lie in the guarantees of article III. The most careful recent examination of those differences concedes that they are relatively small when the rulings of state supreme courts are compared with those of the U.S. Supreme Court and that they have their primary impact in cases where expeditious disposition or accurate determination of the historical facts is particularly important.[42] It is unlikely that a very robust intuitionist theory of the first amendment could be built on these institutional differences.[43]

The problem of comparative institutional capacity to make intuitionistic judgments affects review of legislative action as well. Here the balancers have attempted to augment their balancing by invoking a supplementary substantive principle, a presumption against governmental restrictions on speech.[44] Once balancing enters the picture, however, that presumption cannot justify committing final judgment to the Supreme Court. The rhetoric of hostility to governmental restrictions obscures the fact that courts are agencies of "the government" too. So long as a balancer acknowledges that there is some interest that weighs against speech in the premises,[45] the choice is always between one govern-

41. Frederick Schauer, "Public Figures," 25 *William and Mary Law Review* 905, 926 and n. 95 (1984), notes the problem but discusses only "legislators" as "the governors who enjoy the power ... of public office." See also Gerald Ashdown, "Of Public Figures and Public Interests," 25 *William and Mary Law Review* 937, 949–51 (1984).

42. Burt Neuborne, "The Myth of Parity," 90 *Harvard Law Review* 1105, 1120, 1119 (1977).

43. This argument can be generalized to non–common law areas. The "case or controversy" requirement of article III means that every case the Supreme Court decides has been processed by another court, even if the case implicates some substantive legislation. Further, Congress could channel all these cases to state courts. (But see Theodore Eisenberg, "Congressional Authority to Restrict Lower Federal Court Jurisdiction," 83 *Yale Law Journal* 498 [1974].) If it did the Supreme Court would always be reviewing the intuitionist balancing a state court had engaged in.

44. See Vincent Blasi, "The Checking Value in First Amendment Theory," 1977 *American Bar Foundation Research Journal* 521; Frederick Schauer, *Free Speech: A Philosophical Enquiry* 80–86 (1982).

45. If there is none, a pure due process, minimal rationality requirement will do.

mental restriction on speech that strikes one balance between speech and other interests and another equally governmental restriction that strikes a different balance.

Once again, what intuitionists require is an institutional theory about the quality of intuitions.[46] Typically one gets a few sentences that compare the ideal judge in the ideal adjudication with real-world legislators in the "dance of legislation."[47] Usually this approach involves too much cynicism about legislators and not enough cynicism about judges.[48] The sociological critique of theory suggests a more fundamental point. We should not expect that, brief periods aside, judges are going to be much different from legislators. Life tenure and the conditions of adjudication may produce some small differences in the quality of their intuitions, but it would be surprising to find large differences persisting over extended periods.

In an odd way intuitionism leads us back to Burt's position. Intuitionism cannot justify judicial review because it cannot explain why the Supreme Court's intuitions should be dispositive. One of the reasons for that inability is that the Court's intuitions are unlikely to differ substantially from those of other institutions. This means that judicial review does not matter much one way or the other.

Public Values, Practical Reason, and Antiformalism

Owen Fiss, Frank Michelman, and Cass Sunstein have attempted to ground constitutional theory in what they call public values. Their efforts recall a nonliberal approach to moral discourse, the Aristotelian view that we have a moral-intellectual capacity called the faculty of practical reason.[49] That faculty allows us to perceive situations raising moral issues as

46. This is not to say that hostility to governmental restriction cannot ground a formalist or systematic approach to the problems, only that it cannot ground an intuitionist one.

47. See, e.g., Perry, *Constitution, Courts, and Human Rights*, pp. 100–101. Compare Komesar, "Taking Institutions Seriously" (criticizing most constitutional theory for ignoring careful analysis of actual institutions).

48. Arthur Maass, *Congress and the Common Good* (1983), is a useful though undoubtedly overstated corrective to the usual cynical view of congressional politics. The romanticized view of the judicial process typified the response to Bob Woodward and Scott Armstrong, *The Brethren: Inside the Supreme Court* (1979), although an interesting undertone along the lines "We knew it all the time" also pervaded the response. See Victor Navasky, "The Selling of the Brethren," 89 *Yale Law Journal* 1028 (1980).

49. This sketch is drawn from conversations with Warren Lehman and his article "Rules in Law," 72 *Georgetown Law Journal* 1571 (1984). The leading recent discussion in which practical reason plays a central part is Alisdair MacIntyre, *After Virtue* (1981). See also Richard Bernstein, *Beyond Objectivism and Relativism: Science, Hermeneutics, and Praxis* (1983); Anthony Kronman, "Practical Wisdom and Professional Character," 4 *Social Philosophy and Policy* 203 (1986).

a whole and, more important, to apprehend the appropriate action in the situation. In this tradition apprehension comes close to its literal meaning of "grasping." That is, the faculty of practical reason is not exercised by deductive reasoning from premises or by clearly articulated analogical reasoning from similar circumstances; it is exercised more directly, by responding to situations without the intervention of those modes of reason we now call logical or analytical.

Courts may be thought well suited to the task of exercising practical reason. They must passively await cases to be brought to them, and passivity may encourage the apprehension of a situation taken as a whole. In contrast, the active, analytic mode of reason may encourage its user to believe that what his or her activity has disclosed encompasses all that needs to be known. Similarly, the concreteness of real cases provides the occasion for viewing a situation as a whole.[50]

This may be a sound description of how an ideal court in an ideal society would behave.[51] It fails, however, as a description of courts today. The difficulty is that the faculty of practical reason, like all human faculties, depends for its sound exercise on appropriate training and discipline. Practical reason can be exercised by good citizens in a good society.[52] Under other circumstances, people will assume that they have exercised practical reason when they have merely come up with partial solutions to imperfectly understood situations.

Unfortunately, at least for constitutional theory, the Aristotelian tradition is hardly vibrant.[53] The idea of a faculty of practical reason is, if not entirely foreign to us, at least far enough removed from our way of thinking to require some effort to understand. That itself suggests that we do not live in the Aristotelian good society. Further, the social divisions to which the sociological critique of theory draws attention undermine the

50. R. Lea Brilmayer, "The Jurisprudence of Article III: Perspectives on the 'Case or Controversy' Requirement," 93 *Harvard Law Review* 297 (1979), and the recent work of Henry Monaghan describe the task of the federal courts as exercising practical reason under a set of rules of justiciability designed to facilitate its sound exercise. To the extent that the idea of practical reason grounds arguments for traditional notions of justiciability, it is particularly pernicious in supporting rules for a real society on the basis of a utopian vision of an ideal one.

51. It is not obvious, however, that under similarly ideal circumstances legislatures would behave otherwise.

52. I draw this statement from comments by Michael Sandel at the conference "Undergraduate Education and Legal Education," held at the Georgetown University Law Center, May 25, 1984. I take it to be a measure of my education that I am confident that the statement has a more standard citation and that I am ignorant of what it is.

53. Without having done a systematic survey, I would guess that serious discussions of the relation between that tradition and law have occurred only in journals sponsored by Roman Catholic institutions. Cf. note 49.

capacity to develop the faculty of practical reason. Once we abandon Aristotle's view that some people are by nature slaves, and instead treat practical reason as a truly human capacity, it becomes clear that differences in life chances, education, security, independence from domination by others, and the like will significantly affect the degree to which that capacity will develop.[54]

These observations lead in the direction of a revival of the republican tradition. The recent attention to "public values" in constitutional theory may foreshadow such a revival. As we saw in Chapter 3, constitutional theory cannot rely on common values as a basis for adjudication. Thus, public values must be different from ones that merely happen to be commonly shared.[55] In public values jurisprudence, legislation can be "justified [only] by reference to some public value."[56] Frank Michelman writes: "Politics is a process . . . for making the self-defining choices that constitute our moral freedom. As social beings in a social world, we have such choices to make regarding . . . the moral ambiance of the social world we can only inhabit together. Such choices by their nature have to be made jointly, that is to say politically. Public values, then, are a necessary accompaniment of the moral freedom of the individual . . .

54. An obvious response is elitism: those who, in our society's terms, are better educated, more independent, and the like are likely to have the faculty of practical reason better developed. Although this conclusion is consistent with elements of republican thought, it is not encouraging. Any revival of Aristotelianism will have to come to terms with the intellectual legacy of the Enlightenment, which makes moral-intellectual elitism extremely suspect. See MacIntyre, *After Virtue*.

55. The concept of public values expresses a vision of politics that contrasts with an alternative vision of politics as a process in which private interests are aggregated. Compare Justice Rehnquist's opinion for the Court in United States Railroad Retirement Board v. Fritz, 449 U.S. 166 (1980), finding it sufficient to support a statute's constitutionality to note that the parties disadvantaged by its operation had simply lost a political battle. Here politics is an arena where private interests struggle to secure the benefits of public power. This vision of politics generates a minor doctrinal embarrassment, because it makes it impossible to find any legislation irrational. Every statute is just the right— that is, the politically feasible—compromise among contending forces. See Richard Posner, "The DeFunis Case and the Constitutionality of Preferential Treatment of Racial Minorities," 1974 *Supreme Court Review* 1. The embarrassment is minor because rationality review by the present Supreme Court is superficial at best. For critiques, see Cass Sunstein, "Public Values, Private Interests, and the Equal Protection Clause," 1982 *Supreme Court Review* 127, 130–31; Robert Bennett, " 'Mere' Rationality in Constitutional Law: Judicial Review and Democratic Theory," 67 *California Law Review* 1049 (1979).

56. Sunstein, "Public Values," p. 131. See also Cass Sunstein, "Deregulation and the Hard-Look Doctrine," 1983 *Supreme Court Review* 177, 183 (administrative law involves effort to "implement the public values at stake in regulatory choices").

Values . . . are public as well as private in origin, originating in political engagement and dialogue as well as in private experience."[57]

Cass Sunstein and Michelman explicitly link their vision to the republican tradition.[58] In that tradition public life is not just the reflex of private interests. It is a place where citizens conceive of themselves as acting to advance something they think of as the public interest and where they come together to discuss, deliberate on, and ultimately decide on the course their society will take.

Thus, a public values jurisprudence might support a popular democratic politics. Citizens would be reminded that their public life is not simply a forum in which they can advance their private interests. They would act in their public lives in ways that express their conscious accommodation of their private preference to their knowledge that public decisions affect others whose preferences are different. (For an example, see Chapter 8.)

The contours of a constitutional politics among the citizenry are quite ill defined at present.[59] It seems likely that such a politics would avoid what Robert Nagel calls "the formulaic Constitution."[60] That is, public discussion of problems of equality and free speech would not invoke formulas such as "level of scrutiny" or "four-part test." Those terms are peculiarly appropriate for judicial review, as attempts to devise sufficiently formal methods by which judges will be constrained. They are inappropriate for informed public debate, which should deal openly with competing underlying values. What we need is a more "legible" constitutional discourse, one that makes these underlying and constitutive values clear to the citizenry.[61] Perhaps the most important point about a constitutional politics, though, is that it is a politics.[62] To the extent that a

---

57. Frank Michelman, "Politics and Values or What's Really Wrong with Rationality Review?" 13 *Creighton Law Review* 487, 509 (1979).

58. Id.; Sunstein, "Deregulation," p. 183 n. 25.

59. The major discussion is Paul Brest, "The Conscientious Legislator's Guide to Constitutional Interpretation," 27 *Stanford Law Review* 585 (1975), which, as the title indicates, focuses on legislators not citizens.

60. Robert Nagel, "The Formulaic Constitution," 84 *Michigan Law Review* 165 (1985).

61. I take the term *legible* from William Harris, "Bonding Word and Polity: The Logic of American Constitutionalism," 76 *American Political Science Review* 34 (1982).

62. The existence of judicial review may have inhibited the development of such a politics. Perhaps the women's movement has been weakened by its reliance on the courts to defend the right to reproductive choice. Their opponents have been able to frame the issue as one pitting the undemocratic courts against the will of the people; that distracting overlay to the real questions about the lives of women and men would be removed in a constitutional politics among the citizenry.

politics is involved, specialists in constitutional law have nothing distinctive to offer to the discussions.[63]

Another form of public values jurisprudence *would* address the courts. To Owen Fiss, "adjudication is the social process by which judges give meaning to our public values."[64] The difficulty of retrieving the republican tradition suggests caution in elevating the antiformalist appeal to public values into a full-scale constitutional theory. Several more specific criticisms deserve particular mention.

First, it is all too easy to assume that the proper form of popular discussions of constitutional questions can be transferred directly to the courts. Problems of developing institutional methods of constraining coercive institutions are irrelevant to popular discussion about what the polity ought to do. A direct transfer might lead to a populist antiintellectualism that glosses over the reasons why the Constitution that the courts apply may look different from the one citizens discuss.[65]

Second, the appeal to public values rarely gives content to the public values it invokes. Sunstein's versions have a charming diffidence to them. He concludes one article with this footnote: "It is of course a premise of this whole enterprise that such values at least potentially exist and that the regulatory process may serve to define them. That premise may be questioned by those who believe that, at least under current conditions, the result will not be dialogue but domination."[66] Michelman is equally tenta-

63. People often dismiss appeals to the public interest as political rhetoric designed to mask a self-interested effort to advance a narrow goal. See generally Note, "The New Public Interest Lawyers," 79 *Yale Law Journal* 1069 (1970) (public interest lawyers explain their activities in a purely procedural way as representing the unrepresented, injecting a neglected private interest into the bargaining processes of public life). This stance allows public interest lawyers to deflect—or at least force into more subtle forms—charges that they are elitists seeking to impose their vision of the public interest on an unwilling public. For a discussion of the subtlest version of the charges, see Deborah Rhode, "Class Conflicts in Class Actions," 34 *Stanford Law Review* 1183 (1983).

64. Owen Fiss, "Foreword: The Forms of Justice," 93 *Harvard Law Review* 1, 2 (1978). See also id., p. 58 (judge "straddl[es] . . . the world of the public value and the world of subjective preference, the world of the Constitution and the world of politics").

65. Nagel, "Formulaic Constitution," p. 212 (likening courts to "the arrogant modern painter or composer, whose roles also are to uplift an unappreciative and uncomprehending mass sensibility"), makes this mistake. See also Theodore Lowi, "Book Review," 63 *Texas Law Review* 1591, 1597–98 (1985) (describing asserted "legal integrity"—clarity and closeness to direct sense experience—of nineteenth-century statutes).

66. Sunstein, "Deregulation," p. 213 n. 135. See also Sunstein, "Public Values," pp. 144–45. Sunstein's most extended discussion, "Naked Preferences and the Constitution," 84 *Columbia Law Review* 1689 (1984), is devoted entirely to defending the negative proposition that statutes are unconstitutional if they rest only on naked (Hobbesian) preferences. To survive, statutes must have at least one public value that justifies them. But again Sunstein does not spell out what such values are. See id., p. 1694 ("A public value can be

tive.[67] Fiss provides a list of public values suggesting that he would pre-fer—but cannot commit himself to—an appeal to systematic moral philosophy, thus restraining his antiformalist impulses.[68] The emptiness of the appeal to public values indicates its utopianism—under current conditions, as Sunstein carefully puts it.

Third, Fiss explicitly intends that judges articulate and enforce public values. He does so in part to combat a nihilist challenge that would "drain [the Constitution] of meaning . . . [The Constitution] would no longer be seen as embodying a public morality to be understood and expressed through rational processes like adjudication . . . This nihilism . . . threat-ens our social existence and the nature of public life in America; and it demeans our lives."[69] This passion for the judges as they now are is mistaken in several ways. It is predicated on the view that a "public life" now exists to be threatened, a view that the relative unavailability of the republican tradition suggests is wrong. It assumes that today's judges are the kinds of people who can articulate public values, an assumption that the sociological critique of theory brings into question. Indeed, Fiss's approach is infected by an intellectual antipopulism that is the mirror image of the populist antiintellectualism that can also weaken a public values jurisprudence.

Most important, Fiss's desire for authoritative determination of public values leads him to ignore the emphasis in the republican tradition on deliberation in shaping values. Here Fiss's hierarchical view of the law undermines his commitment to the republican tradition. That view leads Fiss to conclude that adjudication cannot be a process by which public values are created unless it authoritatively determines them. Yet there are many ways in which political action can take place in courtrooms.[70] Instead of seeing the judge as determining public values, we might see litigants creating them as they consider their situation, determine strategy, work out arguments, and the like. In this view the public values are created in litigation—and in demonstrations, lobbying efforts, fund-rais-ing activities, churches, and the like—as well as in the adjudication,

defined as any justification for government action that goes beyond the exercise of raw political power").

67. See Frank Michelman, "Political Markets and Community Self-Determination: Competing Judicial Models of Local Government Legitimacy," 53 *Indiana Law Journal* 145, 149 (1977–78) (public interest model of government depends on "belief in the reality—or at least the possibility—of public or objective values").

68. See Fiss, "Forms of Justice," p. 11. See also id., p. 9 (the judge "searches for what is true, right, or just"). The citation, id., p. 9 n. 24, is to Dworkin. But that may simply be recourse to any port in a storm.

69. See generally Fiss, "Objectivity and Interpretation"; quotation on page 763.

70. For a catalog with examples, see Gabel and Harris, "Building Power."

authoritative for the moment, by the Supreme Court. Fiss rightly regards *Brown v. Board of Education* as a triumph for public values. To him, the hero in *Brown* is Earl Warren.[71] In the alternative view there are no heroes of that sort. Rather we would do well to attend to what Melvin Alston, Lucille Bluford, Linda Brown, Charles Hamilton Houston, and Thurgood Marshall did to create public values through litigation.[72]

The final critique of the appeal to public values generalizes the emphasis that the others place on the utopianism of the appeal in light of who today's judges actually are. To the extent that the appeal seeks to revitalize the republican tradition, it asks for a great deal. At least as it was imagined in the tradition the framers knew, republicanism had a social base. Citizens need secure economic positions, allowing them to avoid personal domination by individuals on whom they depend, in order that they be able to develop public values in public life without fear of retaliation in their other activities. They need sufficient education in public matters and in their republican traditions, to understand the virtues of the republican polity, in order that they be able to resist its subversion from within and without. They have to have a sympathetic understanding of the life situations of people occupying social positions different from their own, in order that the values they develop be fully public. If these social conditions are satisfied, it might be sufficient to think of public values as those that emerge from a process of political discussion; if they are not, there is little to commend the view that we should act as if they were.

Creating the social conditions for republicanism calls for rather large transformations in our present social arrangements. Consider only the decisions of the Supreme Court in recent decades that would have to be repudiated if the courts were to attempt to create the social conditions on which public values could rest: *Board of Regents v. Roth*, denying a presumption in favor of a person's right to a government job;[73] *San Antonio Independent School District v. Rodriguez*, denying that educa-

---

71. See Fiss, "Objectivity and Interpretation," p. 758.

72. Melvin Alston, a black teacher in Norfolk, Virginia, became the lead plaintiff in the first case that reached a court of appeals on the issue of whether it was constitutional for a city to pay its black and white teachers different salaries. See Alston v. School Board of Norfolk, 112 F.2d 992 (4th Cir.), cert. denied, 311 U.S. 693 (1940). Lucille Bluford, a black journalist, was the plaintiff in a series of cases challenging Missouri's failure to provide a graduate program in journalism for black students. See Bluford v. Canada, 32 F. Supp. 707 (W.D.Mo. 1940); State ex rel. Bluford v. Canada, 153 S.W. 2d 12 (Mo. 1941). She later had a distinguished career as editor of a major black newspaper; a relative, Guion Bluford, was the first black astronaut. On Houston, see Genna Rae McNeil, *Groundwork: Charles Hamilton Houston and the Struggle for Civil Rights* (1983).

73. 408 U.S. 564 (1972).

tion is a fundamental interest for purposes of equal protection analysis;[74] *Lindsey v. Normet,* denying that housing, and more broadly the necessities of life, are fundamental interests for the same purposes.[75]

Of course the proponents of public values would welcome the reversal of these decisions.[76] There is plenty of reason to think that today's judges would not. After all, they decided the cases that would have to be repudiated to create the conditions for republicanism. They have said explicitly that, in their view, the Constitution cannot be the vehicle for the creation of the conditions under which there could be public values. *Washington v. Davis* adopted the rule that the equal protection clause was violated only when the state actor involved had a discriminatory intent. Justice White included among the reasons for rejecting the alternative "effects" rule a fear that the effects rule would require radical revision of policies in a wide range of areas.[77]

Consider finally what sort of political changes our society would have to undergo before it would have a group of judges willing to make such decisions. To get judges like that we would already have to have seen substantial changes in ordinary politics. Indeed, the changes would have to have been so substantial that the judges probably would not have to do very much anyway. This may simply be another version of the republican tradition's perception that a republican society does not need a vigorous judiciary. By the time judges were the kinds of people who would promote a jurisprudence of public values, the citizenry would have a politics of public values and would therefore rarely generate the sort of legislation that republican judges would want to correct.

In the end the appeal to public values is radical. The suggestions that courts today do in fact sometimes appeal to such values and that they should do so more often are unlikely to fool many people or judges for very long.[78]

The works discussed in this chapter have more than their antiformalism in common. Unlike other works in constitutional theory, they rarely take the decisions of the Supreme Court to define the subject matter. Cover, Fiss, and Michelman have written forewords to annual reviews of the Supreme Court's work in which decided cases are dragged in by the heels. White has written about lawyers and citizens, not about judges. Even where decided cases play a larger role, the degree to which they are taken

74. 411 U.S. 1 (1973). But see Plyler v. Doe, 457 U.S. 202 (1982).
75. 405 U.S. 56 (1972).
76. See, e.g., Michelman, "Process and Property," pp. 584–85, 590–92.
77. 426 U.S. 229 (1976). Justice White's reasoning appears at 248.
78. This is not to deny that some progress can be made in the courts. It would take the form of "nonreformist" reforms, as discussed in the Conclusion.

to define the subject matter is a measure of the degree to which antiformalist themes have been subordinated.

That is an encouraging sign. Antiformalism requires a radical decentralization of law, as in anarchist antiformalism, coupled with social transformation to create the conditions for republicanism, as in the appeal to public values. It is one version of contemporary legal utopianism.

Appendix: Conservative and Neotraditionalist Constitutional Theories

Proponents of the theories discussed in Part I uniformly fall on the liberal side of the conventional political spectrum. This appendix considers approaches to constitutional theory that either are conservative or make the sorts of appeals to tradition that typify classical Burkean conservative thought. These approaches are unavailing or unnecessary.

CONSERVATIVE CONSTITUTIONAL THEORY

Today's conservative constitutional theories fall into two main groups. There are the almost self-consciously unsystematic theories invoked by conservative popularizers and publicists. For reasons that will appear, I call these anticonstitutional majoritarianism and nostalgic originalism. In addition, there are conservative versions of liberal theories: Invoking systematic moral philosophy, conservatives turn to libertarian thought and Robert Nozick rather than to social welfare liberalism and John Rawls; invoking the economic theory of public choice, they reinforce the representation of groups John Hart Ely ignores.[79]

The most readily accessible conservative constitutional theory is a straightforward majoritarianism, which criticizes the Supreme Court's school prayer and busing decisions on the ground that they contravene the will of the majority. Although this theory might be elaborated in fruitful ways, an unelaborated majoritarianism suffers from several flaws: it is anticonstitutional, noncomparative, and inconsistent (in its usual incarnations).

An unelaborated majoritarianism is anticonstitutional because constitutions must place limits on majority rule. A coherent theory might be developed by explaining why a political process subject to no external

---

79. Because I have addressed the second group of approaches in other chapters, they receive little attention here. A compendium of conservative approaches, and a reasonably accurate indicator of their general intellectual level, is Richard Morgan, *Disabling America: The "Rights Industry" in Our Time* (1984).

checks such as judicial review might nonetheless be restrained by its internal operations. For example, if voters deliberated carefully, exposed their views to public discussion, engaged in civic debate themselves, and routinely subordinated their private interests to their vision of the public good, the results of majority rule might never be troubling. The republican tradition embodies these assumptions. But the liberal tradition is skeptical about the formation of the views each voter has at the moment of casting the vote. It seeks to remedy defects in a majoritarianism that pays attention only to that moment and not to the antecedent processes by which the voter's views were shaped.

A democrat might attempt to revitalize majoritarianism as a constitutional theory. Such a theory would examine the processes of civic education, for example, the sloganeering of political campaigns aimed at getting sixty seconds on the evening news or capturing a viewer's attention with a snappy thirty-second spot commercial. (See Chapter 9.) It is unlikely that that theory would be conservative, as that term is used in contemporary politics.

The fundamental issue for any theory of judicial review is a comparative one: will the judicial enforcement of the limitations the theory proposes to place on legislative action yield "better" results than judicial enforcement of some other limitations or no judicially enforced limitations at all? Simple majoritarianism fails to make the necessary comparative judgment, which would require us to measure the fit between the political program of today's conservatives and the results likely to accrue from simple majoritarianism as compared with an interventionist theory of judicial review.

In the past conservatives developed a powerful prima facie case against majoritarianism. They understood that the domain of public policy unaffected by judicial review is much larger than that affected by it. The courts have essentially nothing to say, at least in the language of constitutional law, about the size of the national budget, its distribution between social welfare and military programs, the scope of public regulation of enterprise, or foreign policy. To a conservative, majoritarian mistakes in these areas will be serious and large. Even if majoritarian errors are rare, conservatives might want to develop an antimajoritarian theory to catch the few but extremely grave mistakes that the majority might make.

Conservatives therefore should have a presumption against simple majoritarianism. They have been attracted to simple majoritarianism because they believe that today's majorities, and tomorrow's, are likely to be more conservative than the courts will be. As we have seen though, courts are unlikely to remain substantially out of line with the majority's views for very long.[80] Majoritarianism is thus not so much wrong as it is beside the point.

Finally, majoritarianism does not fit comfortably with much of the political program of contemporary conservatives. When majoritarian processes produce, or seem likely to produce, results of which conservatives disapprove, they applaud if the courts place obstacles in the way of those results and groan if the courts accede to the majority.[81] Contemporary conservatives adopt majoritarianism to attack public power but willingly accept judicial review that invalidates populist regulation of private power. Thus they are not heard to complain about the restrictions the Court has placed on efforts to regulate campaign finance,[82] but they do complain about the Court's abdication from the task of restricting experiments in social control over investment,[83] and they applaud restric-

80. For example, after a brief experiment in the other direction, the Supreme Court has now deregulated the process by which the death penalty is imposed. See Robert Weisberg, "Deregulating Death," 1983 *Supreme Court Review* 305. This makes Raoul Berger, *Death Penalties: The Supreme Court's Obstacle Course* (1982), which proceeds on the assumption that the Court has somehow effectively blocked the imposition of capital punishment, a truly bizarre document in the conservative attack on the Supreme Court. It is noteworthy, too, that careful conservatives make a moral rather than a majoritarian critique of the abortion decisions, because their more extreme positions are pretty clearly not shared by a majority of the country. See Charles Johnson and Bradley Canon, *Judicial Policies: Implementation and Impact* 12–13 (1984).

For present purposes I leave aside complications arising out of the possibility that the Court's decisions have helped to shape public attitudes and out of differing intensities of the views held by supporters and opponents of the Court's decisions. It is worth mentioning again, however, that legislative liberalization of restrictive abortion laws was underway in 1973, as was widespread evasion of existing restrictive statutes.

81. This ambivalence about judicial review is characteristic of transitional eras. As Martin Shapiro has argued, liberals faced the same issues during the New Deal. Martin Shapiro, "Fathers and Sons: The Court, the Commentators, and the Search for Values," in *The Burger Court: The Counterrevolution That Wasn't* 218 (Vincent Blasi ed. 1983). They had gained control of Congress and the presidency in the 1932 elections, but for six years some of their legislative initiatives were thwarted by a conservative Supreme Court. Once they gained control of the Court too, liberals had to decide whether to dismantle the institution of judicial review entirely, for example by adopting a majoritarian theory of the Constitution (the position associated with Justice Frankfurter), or to use judicial review to promote their goals in the face of resistance by some conservative legislatures (the position associated with Justice Murphy). Today's conservatives are faced with the same choice, made more difficult by the fact that their control of the legislature and the presidency seems less secure than was the Democrats' control in the late 1930s and by the fact that their control of the courts is not yet complete.

82. See, e.g., Buckley v. Valeo, 424 U.S. 1 (1976); First National Bank of Boston v. Bellotti, 435 U.S. 765 (1978). See also Chapter 9.

83. See Hawaii Housing Authority v. Midkiff, 467 U.S. 229 (1984); "Lords of the Manor" (editorial), *Wall Street Journal*, June 1, 1984, p. 24, col. 1; James J. Kilpatrick, "When the Government Takes Your Property," *Washington Post*, July 30, 1984, p. A–11,

tions the courts place on affirmative action programs.[84] They criticize the abortion decisions even though those decisions may have the support of the majority, and they took advantage of the supermajority requirements of the amendment process to thwart the adoption of the Equal Rights Amendment, which the surveys indicated had majority support.[85]

It is hard to take conservative majoritarianism seriously. In a way that is too bad. Because political liberals have in recent years been concerned with imposing limits on what they conceive of as the actual excesses of existing democratic processes, they have not paid careful attention to the conditions under which majoritarianism might not threaten liberal values. Conservative majoritarianism does at least insist on the importance of majoritarian processes. But if it paid attention as well to the social conditions under which majoritarian opinion is formed, it could not be conservative.

The second popularized conservative theory of judicial review is a nostalgic appeal to the meaning of the Constitution and the intent of the framers. This theory allows conservatives to preserve their majoritarianism while retaining their constitutionalism. They acknowledge that majoritarian decisions can be limited by courts that apply the words of the Constitution as the framers understood them. Unfortunately this sort of originalism has not survived critical scrutiny, and one can continue to adhere to it only out of nostalgia for a past which never existed and is now forever lost. (See Chapter 1.)

---

col. 1. See also Charles Fried, "Exit," *New Republic*, Oct. 31, 1983, p. 10 (criticizing certain tax bills and plant relocation legislation on the ground that they deny fundamental right to vote with your feet).

84. See Wygant v. Jackson Board of Education, 106 S. Ct. 1842 (1986).

85. See Deborah Rhode, "Equal Rights in Retrospect," 1 *Law and Inequality* 1, 2 n. 3 (1983). Most dramatically, conservatives have taken to heart the proposed Balanced Budget Amendment. If adopted the amendment would place limits on what Congress can do in the national budget. On its face the amendment is plainly antimajoritarian. If conservatives expect the courts to enforce it, they must abandon simple majoritarianism. If they expect the courts to refrain from enforcing it, they treat the amendment as either unnecessary, because political forces will assure congressional compliance with its requirements, or ineffective, because they will not. See Note, "The Balanced Budget Amendment: An Inquiry into Appropriateness," 96 *Harvard Law Reveiw* 1600, 1610–19 (1983). Some, not only conservatives, have argued that constitutional provisions dealing with the structure of the government need relatively less interpretation than provisions dealing with individual rights. See, e.g., Carter, "Constitutional Interpretation." Much turns on the strength of "relatively" in this formulation; Carter's presentation is, as noted earlier, so strongly qualified that it does not eliminate the underlying concern that licensing judges to interpret the Constitution actually licenses them to do what they wish. In the present context the various versions of the Balanced Budget Amendment are all so loosely phrased that substantial interpretation would be required.

This nostalgia seems particularly to infect the work of some conservative political scientists interested in constitutional law, such as Walter Berns and his students.[86] In general their works combine a sensitive appreciation of the structural guarantees of liberty, such as federalism and the separation of powers, and complete incomprehension of judicial review. They invoke the thought of the framers as a guide to the decisions the courts should make. Their use of the framers' thought, however, is both tendentious and empty. Apparently the only framers who count are those in 1789, with Abraham Lincoln somehow thrown in on occasion. It is as if the fourteenth amendment had not changed the Constitution because it was written by lesser men than the original framers. Further, these conservatives' idea of the thought of the framers has rather little relation to what the framers actually thought; it is a construct of what they should have thought if they had been as sensible as today's conservatives.[87] In the end these conservatives tell us that judges should do the sensible thing, which reduces to doing what the conservatives think is the sensible thing. One would have thought that sensitive conservatives would have discerned in our history the lesson that they can pretty well count on that not happening.

Nostalgia of this sort is particularly damaging to conservative thought. Most conservative originalists treat the critique of originalism as a thesis about language meaning and properly point out that where institutions are stable enough so too is language meaning as determined by examining the intent of the framers. Yet one part of the attack on originalism is the claim that language meaning always depends on existing institutional arrangements. This claim makes the stability of language meaning depend on the stability of institutions, which exposes what historically has been the central weakness of conservative social theory: its inability to account for the coexistence of stability and change.[88] That weakness is especially

---

86. See "Symposium on Constitutional Law," 13 *Teaching Political Science* (1985); Harry Clor, "Judicial Statesmanship and Constitutional Interpretation," 26 *South Texas Law Journal* 397 (1985); Christopher Wolfe, *The Rise of Modern Judicial Review: From Constitutional Interpretation to Judge-Made Law* (1986).

87. This manner of discovering the true meaning of the framers' thought seems to derive from the distinctive, and widely criticized, approach taken by Leo Strauss. One difficulty is that Straussians insist that the Court should enforce natural rights but are unconvincing in their narrow specification of what those rights are. See, e.g., Gary Jacobsohn, *The Supreme Court and the Decline of Constitutional Aspiration* 46–48 (1986) (arguing that courts should protect property as a natural right because that was within framers' contemplation but failing to give any indication of awareness of complexity of idea of property). See also Carter, *Contemporary Constitutional Law-Making*, p. 41.

88. A useful discussion of the conservative and liberating effects of historical consciousness is Dorothy Ross, "Historical Consciousness in Nineteenth Century America," 89 *American Historical Review* 909 (1984).

poignant for conservatives who support a dynamic capitalism whose chief characteristic is unconcern for tradition and existing institutions except insofar as they serve present interests. Originalism is thus nostalgic in two senses. It looks back to a theory whose premises have been demolished almost completely, and it looks back to a stable society whose institutions have been destabilized by the very economic system to which contemporary conservatives are committed.

As usual there are ways to make sense of conservative thought of this sort. The conservative arguments might be effective if one of two things happened: a revival of civic virtue, so that judges and legislators would do the right thing spontaneously or unthinkingly, or a revival of a millenarian view that God is omnipresent in the affairs of the United States. In neither case would there be much reason to criticize whatever the courts or legislatures did. Nor, it should be clear, is the social change that either course would require something that a conservative should be completely comfortable with.

Conservative efforts to appropriate liberal theories are no more successful. Consider the use of moral philosophy. Conservatives might agree with Ronald Dworkin that constitutional law must be developed from the best moral theory consistent with most of the recently decided cases. They would argue that libertarianism satisfies Dworkin's criteria better than any version of social welfare liberalism.[89] Surely there is something to that claim. The very cases that embarrass simple majoritarianism—the campaign finance cases *and* the abortion cases—are at the least consistent with libertarianism.[90] The present Court's right-wing activism is its effort to make the Constitution a libertarian document.[91]

Libertarianism faces serious problems as it attempts to become a conservative constitutional theory. Although some of the Court's decisions are consistent with libertarianism, many of them are not.[92] Statist ele-

89. See, e.g., Richard Epstein, *Takings: Private Property and the Power of Eminent Domain* (1985); Richard Epstein, "Toward a Revitalization of the Contract Clause," 51 *University of Chicago Law Review* 703 (1984); *Rights and Regulation: Ethical, Political, and Economic Issues* (Tibor Machan and M. Bruce Johnson eds. 1983).

90. For a more elaborated account, see John Nowak, "Foreword: Evaluating the Work of the New Libertarian Court," 7 *Hastings Constitutional Law Quarterly* 263, 284–311 (1980).

91. L. Michael Seidman, "Book Review: ABSCAM and the Constitution," 83 *Michigan Law Review* 1199 (1985).

92. The Court has allowed governments to do pretty much what they wish in the investigation of crime. See, e.g., United States v. Russell, 411 U.S. 423 (1973); Hudson v. Palmer, 468 U.S. 517 (1984). See also Silas Wasserstrom, "The Incredible Shrinking Fourth Amendment," 21 *American Criminal Law Review* 257 (1984). I doubt that a libertarian theory of criminal procedure would be completely comfortable with the extremes to which the Court has gone, although I confess that I do not know what a libetarian theory of

ments predominate in the Court's analysis of constitutional limits on state regulation of enterprise; while libertarian theory generally takes most of its examples of improper state actions from just that area, the Court has essentially abandoned the field.[93]

Here too the problems of conservative constitutional theory open important issues to view. Conservatives understood that moral skepticism and the claim that values are subjective lay at the heart of the project of classical liberalism, to which they saw themselves as heirs.[94] That project required that the social order be constructed on the premise that no one's view of the good has a stronger claim to acceptance than anyone else's.[95] Conservatives' critique of contemporary liberals was that they had abandoned the project of classical liberalism. That project precludes a libertarian constitutional theory too. Further, and more interesting, the conservative critique of contemporary liberals might lead us to wonder about how and why classical liberalism became transformed into contemporary liberalism. The usual answer is along the lines that some such transformation was necessary if capitalism, itself transformed by its own dynamic, was to retain some acceptable ideological underpinnings.[96] Once again we see why conservative constitutional theory may fail to pursue the implications of its arguments.[97]

---

criminal procedure would look like, given that criminal procedure is predicated on the conflict between what libertarians would see as private intrusions on private interests (crime) and public intrusions on private interests (its investigation).

93. See especially Siegan, *Economic Liberties and the Constitution*.

Libertarians might respond by advising the Court to be more active in these areas. But eliminating the theory's reliance on recently decided cases and requiring a wholesale repudiation of almost fifty years of decisions would convert a conservative theory into a reactionary one.

94. See Roberto Unger, *Knowledge and Politics* 76 (1975).

Conservatives reacted to liberal constitutional theory by claiming that values are inevitably subjective and that judges who purport to invoke any moral theory are simply imposing their personal views on an unwilling public. See Bork, "Neutral Principles," p. 30 (defining "political truth" as "whatever result the majority reaches and maintains at the moment"). By resting their critique of liberal constitutional theory on this moral skepticism, conservatives disabled themselves from substituting libertarianism for social welfare liberalism as the moral philosophy on which judges should rely. For a useful discussion, see Sotirios Barber, "The New Right Assault on Moral Inquiry in Constitutional Law," 54 *George Washington Law Review* 253, 256–66 (1986); Jamie Kalven, "Round Two for Judge Bork," *Nation*, June 16, 1984, p. 731 (explaining why Bork erred in rejecting the label "moral skeptic" as applied to his position).

95. For a recent expression, see Ackerman, *Social Justice*.

96. For an overview, see Dunn, *Western Political Theory*.

97. For a discussion of conservative versions of representation-reinforcing review, see Chapter 2. One additional problem with these conservative versions was not discussed there. The theory provides an account of flaws in the legislative process, but it does not

CENTER-LEFT BURKEANISM: NEOTRADITIONALIST THEORY

When someone asks us to consider traditional values, we ordinarily would guess that we are being addressed by a conservative. Recently, however, liberals have offered traditionalist defenses of judicial review.

Michael Perry relies on a form of textualism in which the Constitution's text connects the present community to its tradition by "mandat[ing] the form of life to which the community and tradition aspire" and by "symboliz[ing] that mandate."[98] Laurence Tribe adopts a traditionalist's skepticism about the utility of highly rationalized theories of judicial review and insists that in making constitutional choices we must "choose without losing the thread of continuity that makes us whole with those who came before."[99] Anthony Kronman rehabilitates Alexander Bickel's Whiggish "prudentialism," which cautions against rationalist efforts to make our institutions conform to a program and celebrates the "aspirational component[s]" of complex institutions and traditions.[100] The apparent political anomaly of liberals invoking tradition is resolved once we understand that the tradition or aspiration to which appeal is made is the tradition of the New Deal and its judicial embodiment, the Warren Court.

Center-left Burkeanism faces the enormous difficulty posed by the fact that all traditions are complex. Perry takes Abraham Lincoln and Earl Warren as his models. Yet within "our" tradition are William Lloyd Garrison and W.E.B. Du Bois, each of whom had a relation to "the

---

account for flaws in the judicial process. In particular, the courts have abstained from intervening in precisely the area to which the conservative version of the theory directs attention, that of economic regulation. Instead of offering some systematic explanation for this behavior, conservatives provide pure normative criticism of the courts, or vague invocations of sheer judicial preference or ignorance, or mutterings about the new class. See generally *The New Class?* (Barry Bruce-Briggs ed. 1979).

That will not do. If the flaws in the judicial process are systematic, fulminating against them is pointless. If they arise from institutional arrangements substantially controlled by the legislature, as the sociological approach to constitutional theory suggests, no alternatives are likely to be adopted. For what conservatives desire here are controls on the legislature, which is flawed in particular ways. Those flaws do not disappear when the legislature turns from considering economic regulation to considering institutional design, at least where the implications of institutional design for specific results are fairly clear.

98. Perry, "Authority of Text," p. 558. See also Daniel Conkle, "The Legitimacy of Judicial Review in Individual Rights Cases: Michael Perry's Constitutional Theory and Beyond," 69 *Minnesota Law Review* 587 (1985) (advocating review based on "pattern of American moral development").

99. Tribe, *Constitutional Choices*, pp. 6, 267. For a more extended discussion, see Mark Tushnet, "Book Review," 21 *Harvard Civil Rights–Civil Liberties Law Review* 285 (1986).

100. Anthony Kronman, "Alexander Bickel's Philosophy of Prudence," 94 *Yale Law Journal* 1567, 1602–4, 1608–10 (1985).

Constitution" very different from those of Lincoln or Warren.[101] And of course on the other side lie John C. Calhoun and Andrew Carnegie.[102] Further, we cannot identify a single past with which we are continuous. Rather we *choose* the past with which we are continuous. That choice must be defended on some ground other than that it, and only it, is our past. It might be that the "excesses" of the New Deal, and their exacerbation by the Warren Court, were deviations from the real tradition, with which they almost broke. Or it might be that the humanitarian dimensions of the welfare-administrative state were a politically necessary compromise to assure the domestic stability of the American empire. Thus, there are three pasts with which we are continuous: capitalism tout court, welfare-state capitalism, and imperialist technocracy. Even a center-left Burkean cannot tell us which one is really ours.[103]

Perry and Tribe do not overcome the difficulty that the existence of a plurality of traditions poses for their traditionalism. If traditions are irreducibly plural, Perry's appeal to the text as something symbolizing a mandate of "a" form of life that resides in the traditions becomes much less interesting. It turns out that his judges are not to call us to the form of life that resides in the traditions in all their complexity; they are to call us to the true and just form of life. The text of the Constitution does no analytic work in Perry's vision. Instead it provides the rhetorical modes that are sometimes useful, but sometimes harmful, in bringing us closer to the realization of truth and justice.

Further, Perry's effort to predicate judgment only on what is valuable in "our" traditions deprives us of the richness that can be found in them. Perry seems to read this richness out of the Constitution by acknowledging the pluralism of tradition and then relegating to the dustbin of history everything that seems inconsistent with truth and justice. There may be a different lesson in the pluralism of our traditions: One cannot envision within those traditions a form of life that expresses only the good and the true.[104]

101. On Garrison, see William Weicek, *The Sources of Antislavery Constitutionalism in America*, 1760–1848, 228–48 (1977). On Du Bois, see B. Joyce Ross, *J. E. Spingarn and the Rise of the NAACP* 187–98 (1972).

102. See John Calhoun, *A Disquisition on Government* (1853); Joseph Wall, *Andrew Carnegie* (1970).

103. For a general discussion of the relation between tradition and morality, see Daniel Callahan, "Tradition and the Moral Life," 12:6 *Hastings Center Reports* 23 (Dec. 1982). The rationalist theories that Burkeans disdain might be seen as efforts to explain which of the many pasts we have ought to be the one with which we maintain continuity.

104. Perry's argument is flawed as well by his insistence that our tradition is a rosy one. I take it that part of the adverse reaction to the visit of President Reagan to the cemetery at Bitburg rested on the view that Germans ought to make their present continuous with a past

Finally, the traditions to which we are heirs take their life from far more than the Constitution. The Constitution speaks to a group of people located within the geographic boundaries of the United States, who are a sort of community. That community is composed in an ill-defined way by people who orient themselves to many other traditions as well. As a result, the most one can do with tradition is choose among the many one has available. Like all choices in our society, the choice of "a" tradition is open.

The emphasis that Kronman and Perry place on a tradition's aspirations may be designed to narrow the range of choice. We then must decide what the tradition's aspirations are. Kronman and, more clearly, Perry say that its aspirations are to the achievement of the good and the just. Chapter 2 argued that such criteria are too vacuous to be useful in theory, even when deployed by center-left Burkeans. Sensitivity to history shows that there has always been a gap between the aspirations that we are told to follow and the dismaying performance that we are told to ignore. It seems obvious to wonder whether the aspirations just *are* the combination of verbal commitment and persistent shortcomings. Burkeanism can move either way if that description is correct: It can move to the right, taking the view that practices express aspirations better than words do, or it can move to the left, taking the view that the verbal statements are worthless. It probably cannot remain comfortably on the center-left.

These efforts to use tradition and aspiration as a basis for a center-left defense of judicial review founder on two facts: traditions are irreducibly complex, and aspirations are intertwined with actual practice. The appeals to tradition and aspiration are deeply antihistorical. The history of the United States is just not center-left enough to sustain a center-left Burkeanism. One way to make the point is this: Earl Warren was Chief Justice for the sixteen years between 1953 to 1969. Warren Burger was Chief Justice for the seventeen years between 1969 to 1986. Which one better represents the true traditions and aspirations of the United States?

BURKEAN CONSTITUTIONALISM

A truly Burkean approach to the Constitution would avoid the search for theory. Theories are systematic efforts to impose order on aspects of the world, but the Burkean tradition rejects the rationalism of theories about political life. Burkeans believe that politics is too varied to be captured by any system. For them efforts to impose theoretical order inevitably lead to

---

that includes the experience of Nazism. So too with slavery in the United States. See Remarks of Thurgood Marshall at the Annual Seminar of the San Francisco Patent and Trademark Law Association, May 6, 1987.

the forcible imposition of the theorists' vision of the good society simply to make the world conform to the theory. Further, they believe that an unsystematic politics promotes efficiency as well as liberty; by encouraging politicians to muddle through in an ad hoc way, it reaches better results in the face of inevitably changing circumstances than any system could. When translated into a theory of law the Burkean strand of conservative thought is hostile to legislation; it asks that judges decide only the cases before them and that they not systematically consider the relation between the result in the present case and those in others, past or future. This justifies a strict view of the "case or controversy" requirement but otherwise has no implications for substantive outcomes—which is precisely its merit.

One can be comfortable with ad hoc decision making, in law as well as in politics, only if one is comfortable with the decision makers. Burkeans explain why we should indeed be comfortable with the decision makers. They insist that consensus and community rather than conflict are the basis of social order and that conflict can be tolerated only within the bounds our community agrees on. The dissolution of consensus over the past two centuries has of course made the conservative view of social order fantastic. Within the Burkean tradition, however, the imagined consensus means that no decision maker, legislator or judge, can possibly deviate in any interesting way from the community's views. Since constitutional theory aims at specifying limits on legislators and judges, conservatism has no need for it.

Finally, if the consensus is imaginary in regard to the society as a whole, it is rather more real in regard to the judges themselves and the politically active generally. Here Burkean thought converges with the politics of today's conservatives. The judges today are increasingly conservatives, and conservatives can trust them to act appropriately even without an overarching theory. Because the courts are part of the society's governing coalition, if that coalition turns conservative so inevitably will the courts.

Perhaps constitutional theory develops only under the pressure imposed by the need to defend results in a hostile environment. An increasingly conservative Court may face a receptive environment. Its product would then be unlikely to receive a systematic defense because it would be unlikely to be subjected to criticism that its admirers would regard as worthy of response. That is too bad. Burkean social thought, for all its defects, illuminates dimensions of our lives that, for all its strengths, liberalism leaves unexamined. Conservative constitutional theory might be interesting, but it isn't.

5

Intuitionism and
Little Theory

THE preceding chapters have explained the important role that grand theory plays in the liberal tradition. They have also suggested that grand theory cannot be made coherent today because of the erosion of the republican tradition. So far, though, we have considered only one theory at a time. Perhaps the theories could be combined so that their strengths reinforce each other and the strengths of one cancel the weaknesses of another. Unfortunately that strategy will not work. In discussing each grand theory I made two general kinds of arguments. First I developed an internal critique of the theory. That critique identified the premises of the theory and exposed the maximum coherent content of a theory with those premises. The internal critiques establish that each theory's maximum content is rather limited. Then I brought to bear a standard external critique of each grand theory, exposing its content as *too* limited: We can readily identify forms of dictatorship or tyranny that are likely to occur and are permitted by the theory once it is shorn of its insupportable claims. Each grand theory is thereby placed in a situation that might be thought of as an unstable equilibrium. Within quite narrow confines the theory yields interesting results, but it collapses in complete disarray when we make the slightest move outside those confines. Unfortunately for grand theorists such moves are inevitable once we recall that the aim of the Constitution is to prevent tyranny.

Most of my criticisms of specific theories are relatively conventional, but instead of accepting the criticisms of one or two theories on the way to proposing a different theory, I have argued that no grand theory survives the combined internal and external critiques. I have tried to be fairly comprehensive in covering the candidates for grand theory of the era, and I believe that the arguments I present severely impair each one.[1] I cannot

1. In the interests of keeping the text and notes to a reasonable length, I have usually addressed only the main lines of argument within a grand theory. Each theory's devotees

guarantee that the liberal tradition can no longer provide a defense of judicial review. I believe that I have done enough to support an inductive generalization to that conclusion, but two obvious challenges to my strategy of argument must be addressed.

The first claims that proponents of judicial review need no grand theory but can rely on a group of little theories, each dealing with some specific subject. The second claims that, all things considered, grand theories and little theories together rule out enough judicial misbehavior to reduce the risk of judicial tyranny to an acceptably low level. Examining these claims requires us to understand the structure of grand theory.

Generally a grand theory's proponents will concede that some other analysis or even theory will handle some provisions of the Constitution but will contend that their pet theory is the only way to handle the truly important provisions. For example, John Hart Ely devises his theory to yield interesting results when questions arise under the first amendment and the equal protection clause of the fourteenth amendment but assumes that questions under the criminal justice provisions of the Bill of Rights can be dealt with through originalism.[2] Charles Black says that originalism will do for the first amendment but that something more is needed for privacy and gender discrimination.[3]

These examples illustrate the pervasive strategy of the challenge to my single-minded focus on each grand theory and also illustrate the strategy's main defect. The strategy is to allocate specific areas of the Constitution to different grand theories: privacy to moral philosophy, criminal justice to originalism, the first amendment to representation reinforcement, and so on. The defect is that the grounds for the allocation, when specified, suffer from the flaws of the theories themselves. That is, when asked why a certain allocation is appropriate, the theorist responds by invoking a metatheory. For example, Ely calls his approach "the ultimate interpretivism."[4] The problem of constraining judges by constitutional theories has

---

have developed refinements in the nature of Ptolemaic epicycles, but I believe that little is gained by paying attention to the refinements when the main arguments present such great problems. In addition, I have not discussed a variety of approaches to constitutional law in which the Constitution figures as a symbol of national unity and the like. Such approaches provide no substantive content to the Constitution and are therefore beyond the scope of the kind of analysis I wish to pursue.

2. Cf. Ely, *Democracy and Distrust*, p. 76 ("interpretivism is *incomplete*: there are provisions in the Constitution that call for more") (emphasis added).

3. Black, *Decision according to Law*, pp. 65–66, 71–76.

4. Ely, *Democracy and Distrust*, pp. 11–41, criticizes a "clause-bound" interpretivism as applied to problems of equal protection or free speech but accepts that version of interpretivism as applied to problems of criminal procedure. He justifies this by invoking a metaprinciple, interpretivism tout court, "the ultimate interpretivism," p. 88.

simply shifted to another level. Thus, although it is possible to dream up an allocation of areas to theories, that allocation will have to be justified by a comprehensive metatheory. But invoking metatheories introduces serious instability into the enterprise.

Grand theories are what I will call unitary theories of constitutional law.[5] Any theory identifies a set of principles from which its results follow, but unitary theories are special in two related ways. First, there are no conflicts among their principles. Some may appear to conflict with others, but the appearance is misleading because somewhere in the theory there is a metaprinciple that explains why the conflict does not really arise. Some metaprinciples attempt to define the area within which some principle operates. I will therefore call the strategy of invoking that kind of metaprinciple, and allocating certain substantive areas to specific principles, a strategy that pervades constitutional theory, a territorial strategy. Conflicts among the principles cannot arise because each has its own territory of application, mapped out by the relevant metaprinciples. Alternatively, conflicts may be resolved by invoking a metaprinciple that gives one rule priority over another.[6] The second special aspect of unitary theories is that their results follow from their principles in a reasonably rigorous way. Because the set of principles in a unitary theory is self-consistent, standard operations in elementary logic or at least standard uses of the rhetorical devices of legal reasoning can be employed to identify the precise scope of the theory.

The fact that unitary theories of constitutional law have dominated recent discussions provides the preceding chapters with a structure that otherwise would be at least curious. There I examined proposed theories one at a time. This internal critique identified the fundamental principles of a theory and worked out its maximum content. I called this exercise a critique because at the end, I argued, it is impossible to resist skeptical questions, either "If that's all that's unconstitutional, the theory isn't worth much" or "If all that is unconstitutional, the theory goes way too far." The chapters then ended, leaving unanswered some obvious responses. We could augment or restrict the theory by adding new principles. Thus, if Ely's theory does not adequately handle problems implicating the constitutional dimensions of criminal procedure, we can

5. See also Book Review, "Liberalism, Separation and Speech," pp. 81–85 (distinguishing "monist" from "pluralist" theories).

6. For example, Rawls, *Theory of Justice*, pp. 42–44, provides two principles, one of which is "lexically prior" to the other: the second principle selects certain social arrangements out of a set determined by the first. See also David Richards, *Toleration and the Constitution* 203 (1986) (balancing is not "intuitional adjustment of independent values" because "all the values in question express an integrated underlying ideal").

throw in a little originalism there. Or if his theory seems to imply that nonresidents of the United States, such as Central Americans, ought to have some say in determining "American" foreign policy, we can point to the Preamble's reference to "We the People of the United States," and the definition of citizenship "of the United States" in the fourteenth amendment, and use textualism to limit the theory.

This strategy, which is what I have called a territorial one, is bound to fail for two reasons. The first is that we are asked to augment or restrict theory A with principles drawn from theory B. If theory B is inadequate on its own terms, we will not have solved our initial problems. Another way of putting the difficulty is this: the territorial strategy requires that we have some metaprinciples to explain why theory A's domain is one thing and theory B's is another. Yet the only available metaprinciples are themselves parts of some other theory that is criticized in some other chapter.

The second reason for the failure of the territorial strategy goes deeper and is my subject here. By invoking principles from another theory, we have destroyed the unitary character of the one we started with.[7] There would be nothing wrong with that so long as what I will call pluralist theories are acceptable. The principles in a pluralist theory need not be self-consistent. They may conflict in ways not resolved by territorial allocations or rules that give one priority over the other in cases of conflict.

Pluralist theories have a respectable philosophical pedigree,[8] but they cannot be the foundation of the theory of constitutional law. Pluralist theories tell those whom they address to think carefully and balance the relevant considerations before arriving at a judgment. That judgment, however, cannot in the end be defended by more than what John Rawls and other philosophers call intuitionism.[9] It is perfectly all right, and perhaps inevitable, that I rely on my intuitions in deciding what to do and in attempting to persuade others to join me. But, as we have seen, the situation is different within liberal constitutional theory, where the issue is who can exercise coercive power over another. Pluralist theories give judges an unreviewable discretion to force on the rest of us what their intuitions tell them is correct, and that discretion is unacceptable in the liberal tradition.[10]

7. Subject to the possibility of embedding the combination in a unitary metatheory, which would then be open to the first critique.

8. See James Fishkin, *Justice, Equal Opportunity, and the Family* 169–91 (1983).

9. See Rawls, *Theory of Justice*, pp. 34–40; W. H. Shaw, "Intuition and Moral Philosophy," 17 *American Philosophical Quarterly* 127 (1980).

10. The argument that follows is developed in detail in Tushnet, "Anti-Formalism," pp. 1508–19. See also T. Alexander Aleinikoff, "Constitutional Law in the Age of Balancing," 96 *Yale Law Journal* 943 (1987).

Discussions of intuitionism in constitutional law have focused on the issue of "balancing the interests" as a method of arriving at decisions. The most useful text for present purposes is an article by Gerald Gunther written at the completion of Justice Lewis Powell's first term on the Court. Gunther compares Powell to Justice Harlan, whom Gunther regards as a first-rank practitioner of balancing.

> In the finest manifestations of Justice Harlan's approach to first amendment problems, . . . he viewed balancing . . . as a mandate to perceive every free speech interest in a situation and to scrutinize every justification for restriction of individual liberty. Moreover, . . . Justice Harlan strove for unifying principles that might guide future decisions. The Harlan legacy . . . is rich in sensitive, candid, and articulate perceptions of competing concerns, and in overarching approaches which retain their capacity to instruct.[11]

Gunther thus regards balancing as requiring candor and sensitive perception, and generating "unifying principles."

In one view of the approach as Gunther describes it, balancing demands only that judges do their best to see and describe what is at stake "in a situation." Balancing then really does not constrain the judges. Indeed, balancing so conceived does not even provide a critical observer with grounds for evaluating what judges have done, because this analysis asks only that judges describe the interests they see fully and articulately—even though other observers might discern other interests at stake.

The vision of unifying principles might provide more critical leverage and constraint. Two difficulties intrude, however. Principles are to be generalized beyond the facts "in a situation" so that they have a "capacity to instruct." Precisely because they go beyond the facts at hand, the principles necessarily obscure the interests that will in fact be at stake in the case that may arise later. (See Chapter 1.) Also, Gunther nowhere tells us what counts as an acceptable unifying principle. His approach rules out ad hoc balancing but provides no positive criteria for identifying what else is all right.

There is more to Gunther's approach, though. His sentences parse well enough and seem to be saying something, and yet they turn out to have almost no content. Their tone and manner of presentation *do* say something, though not perhaps what Gunther consciously intended. The article is very much written for insiders, who are assumed to share a way of looking at the world and the laws that ought to regulate it. Gunther implicitly says that we can finesse the difficulties of choosing a level of generality in describing a situation or characterizing interests, and of

11. Gerald Gunther, "In Search of Judicial Quality on a Changing Court: The Case of Justice Powell," 24 *Stanford Law Review* 1001, 1013–14 (1972).

selecting what amount of unification a principle must provide, because all of us know what good judges ought to do. And in this he may well be correct, if "all of us" is defined in a certain way. Yet it is hard to see why those who lose in the courts should regard the decisions of such judges as binding—why, that is, they should believe that the Hobbesian problem has been overcome. For losers may well think that all good judges know what to do because judges are chosen by methods and according to criteria of goodness that give their decisions no authority. Of course, insiders will not think that their methods and criteria are narrow. But outsiders will look at who judges are—mostly male, mostly highly secularized, mostly white, mostly rich, mostly old, all lawyers, mostly owners of stock, almost never members of labor unions, mostly tolerant of moderate use of some mind-altering drugs but not others, mostly heterosexual, and so on—and may take a different view.[12]

The sociological defense of intuitionism may be useful for a project like Gunther's where one insider is talking to another. Justice Powell was clearly Gunther's primary audience, and Gunther was trying to reduce Powell's conservative tendencies in favor of Gunther's liberal ones. But as a general strategy for constitutional theory it is sure to fail. Douglas Laycock's efforts to revive balancing as a liberal strategy are instructive.[13] Starting from a textualism that raises its own problems (see Chapter 1, appendix), Laycock identifies a few basic values in the Constitution. The process of identifying those values reveals Laycock's sympathies with conventional liberalism and, not so incidentally for my purposes, shows that they do not coincide closely with those of the present Court. Under the circumstances the conclusion that balancing is appropriate is vapid and politically curious. The more general problem is that the sociological defense of balancing assumes that all insiders agree on certain fundamental points and assumes that there are no fundamental differences between insiders and outsiders. This is probably false as a matter of fact in the contemporary United States and in any event is basically inconsistent with the liberal tradition's premise that in the world of social interaction we

12. For a conservative response to this observation, see Phillip Johnson, "Do You Seriously Want to Be Radical?" 36 *Stanford Law Review* 247, 280 n. 88 (1984), arguing that intellectual elites in the law schools have provided substantial support for programs contrary to the "class" interests identified in the text. See also Chapter 4 (appendix). The empirical evidence, though, does not support the inferences Johnson wishes to draw. See, e.g., Thomas Walker and Deborah Barrow, "The Diversification of the Federal Bench: Policy and Process Ramifications," 47 *Journal of Politics* 596 (1985) (female and black judges appointed by President Carter do not differ in their decisions from white male appointees).

13. Laycock, "Taking Constitutions Seriously."

are all outsiders at one time or another, as conspiracies of those who wish to exploit us seek to employ the coercive power of the state against us.

To the extent that the coherence of intuitionism depended on insiders' self-assurance, it was an approach fitting for the decade of the American Century and the End of Ideology. Philosophers may find pluralism acceptable, although even in the realm of philosophy intuitionists are assailed by utilitarians, Rawlsians, and others offering unitary theories. The subjects of a liberal state, however, cannot accept pluralism in the courts. It is bad enough that legislatures can oppress them, but at least they may hope that judges will keep legislatures in check. Pluralism in constitutional theory makes it impossible to keep judges in check.[14]

Territorial strategies to allocate theories to specific areas are initially attractive because they correspond to our sense of how we make our own decisions[15] and because they seem to be a lawyer's version of philosophical intuitionism.[16] Their attractions fade once we see that the issue is not how we should decide to live our own lives, or what a good metaethical theory is, but is instead a question of institutional design. How can we organize institutions that exercise power over us but do not oppress us? Because we rule our own lives, and because philosophers do not exercise the relevant kinds of power, the analogies to private decision making and to philosophy are inapt. Given the characteristics that courts have, territorial strategies do not eliminate the risk of tyranny.

The second general challenge to my concentration on grand theories one at a time begins by suggesting that the requirement that the risk of tyranny be eliminated is too stringent. All we need, the challenge continues, are approaches that exclude enough extreme judicial behavior to make judicial review an acceptable institution for the exercise of power. Exclusions can occur through the use of grand theories, or of territorial strategies, or of many little theories directed at discrete constitutional problems.[17] Like balancing, an exclusionary approach to constitutional law has an affinity with some philosophical analyses of liberalism,[18] but unlike balancing, it can in principle be used as a tool for institutional design. The difficulty is that the exclusionary approach is too unwieldy a tool to be of much help.

14. See "Commentary." 78 *Northwestern University Law Review* 1025, 1028 (statement of Steven Shiffrin: "It depends all [*sic*] upon who does the balancing").

15. But see Lehman, "Rules in Law."

16. Cf. Shiffrin, "Liberalism, Radicalism, and Legal Scholarship" (defending "eclectic liberalism").

17. Frederick Schauer, "An Essay on Constitutional Language," 29 *UCLA Law Review* 797, 830 (1982), calls these "horizontally clause-bound" theories.

18. See, e.g., Amy Gutmann, "Communitarian Critics of Liberalism," 14 *Philosophy and Public Affairs* 308, 310–14 (1985).

A defensible exclusionary approach has to place a great deal of weight on its notion that it excludes "enough" extreme judicial behavior. Perhaps any of today's competing theories would invalidate Stalinism or apartheid, but because neither is on the presently foreseeable political agenda it is hard to understand what the theories actually accomplish in doing so.[19] I propose the following test: determine the best and worst politically feasible outcomes you can imagine from legislatures in the ten years following the time that you are applying the test. An approach to constitutional law, be it a grand theory or an exclusionary one, is indefensible if it would allow judges to uphold the worst and invalidate the best politically feasible programs that legislatures are likely to devise in the near future. I submit that the preceding chapters have shown that constitutional theory fails this test.[20]

The framers' attempt to reconcile the liberal and republican traditions has failed for the reasons that the sociological critique of balancing identified. The framers did not understand that courts are inevitably part of a society's governing coalition, and they failed to appreciate the extent to which the dynamics of private property would transform their society and thereby its governing coalition. Constitutional theory today suffers from

19. I have already suggested that if they were on the political agenda, the resources would be available to explain why they were permitted by the Constitution. See, e.g., Chapter 1 (appendix) and Chapter 3. When apartheid was politically feasible the Court found it constitutional. Plessy v. Ferguson, 163 U.S. 537 (1896). Its invalidation may not have occurred *because* it was no longer politically feasible, but it certainly was not compelled by any theory prevalent in 1954.

20. Because proponents of exclusionary approaches have yet to specify their terms, they have only occasionally provided examples that they say illustrate the utility of these approaches. What examples there are, are not encouraging. Schauer, "Easy Cases," p. 431 n. 83, argues that the abortion cases were wrongly decided to the extent that they relied on a theory of substantive due process, because they "exceeded the separate boundaries established by the distinct clauses of the Constitution." He acknowledges that this conclusion is "rendered . . . problematic" by a long tradition of substantive due process adjudication in the Supreme Court. Thus, he agrees that his "horizontally clause-bound" theory must be supplemented by a theory of precedent. Because that theory is unspecified, it is impossible to know what his overall approach really excludes.

Gutmann, "Communitarian Critics," p. 321, asserts that "we can respect the right of free speech by opposing local efforts to ban pornographic bookstores . . . but still respect the values of community . . . by supporting local (democratic) efforts to regulate the location and manner in which pornographic bookstores display their wares." This "combines— uneasily—liberal and communitarian commitments." Gutmann's combination suggests a balance in which certain rules, such as one prohibiting an outright ban on pornographic bookstores, are excluded. Yet Gutmann does not explain why in a federal system it is impermissible for a suburb of Seattle to ban the sale of materials readily available across the city line. See City of Renton v. Playtime Theatres, Inc., 475 U.S. 41 (1986) (city may confine adult theaters to an area where continued operation of theaters is unlikely to be economically feasible).

the same problems. Each theory identifies a moment of republican community—contemporaneous in the case of moral philosophy, historical in the case of originalism—within a period of liberal fragmentation. The task of constitutional theory ought no longer be to rationalize the real in one way or another. It should be to contribute to a political movement that may begin to bring about a society in which civic virtue may flourish.

II

THE CONSTITUTION
OF SOCIETY

6

The Constitution
of Government

MANY of the criticisms developed in Part I are familiar to constitutional scholars. The presentation here is distinctive only because it accepts *all* the familiar criticisms. This skepticism about "the rule of law" characterizes Legal Realism, a school of thought from which my arguments are descended. The first section of this chapter describes Legal Realism's attack on the theory of the rule of law at the heart of the liberal tradition and introduces a discussion of some jurisprudential responses to the Realist challenge. The second section examines a recent development in constitutional theory—structural review—that is another heir to Legal Realism. Structural review attempts to bring the insights of empirical political science to bear on normative constitutional theory. Although structural review does not solve the liberal tradition's problems, the examination of its defects introduces the approach taken in the remainder of this book.

Legal Realism as Jurisprudence and Sociology

Legal Realism was both a jurisprudence and a sociology. As a jurisprudence Realism attacked the idea that legal doctrine provides an objective basis for decisions in specific instances. When the Realists looked at doctrine, they saw that it never disposes of particular problems.[1] The materials of legal doctrine are almost measureless, and the acceptable techniques of legal reasoning—distinguishing on the basis of the facts, analogizing to other areas of law where cognate problems arise, and the

---

1. See Chapter 1, where the argument is developed in the specific area of constitutional law.

like—are so flexible that they allow us to assemble diverse precedents into whatever pattern we choose.[2]

The Realists understood that this jurisprudential argument has an air of unreality about it. They knew that certain lines of argument were in fact accepted at some times and places, while others not less inherently acceptable were not in fact accepted. This perception converted the claims of classical jurisprudence about the nature of law into facts about ideology that needed a sociological explanation.

The Realists drew their explanation of the fact that people in power find some arguments more acceptable than others from the tradition of debunking scholarship associated in the United States with the Progressive impulse of the early twentieth century.[3] As Progressives most of the Realists delighted in establishing the partisanship or class bias of purportedly neutral rules of law, but, as the Progressive impulse became the basis for the New Deal, the Legal Realists found themselves in a position to influence the development of public policy. The opportunity to manipulate the instruments of public policy proved hard to resist.[4]

The Realists' reformist program also influenced their intellectual one. The Realists developed a twofold attack on classical legal rules. In one branch of the argument they pointed out the high level of abstraction— "free will," "freedom of contract," and the like—on which the classical rules operate. The Realists claimed that it is absurd to think that a simple abstract concept can properly regulate the multifarious forms of social reality. The Realists believed that the general law of contracts should be replaced by a law of consumer transactions, a law of insurance, a law of marriage agreements, and the like. They argued that the large abstractions have to be replaced by middle-sized ones.[5] This attack required that the Realists explain why they selected the particular middle-sized abstractions on which they pinned so much. Just as the basis for the attack was a

2. For example, Karl Llewellyn gave us a catalog of paired and contradictory maxims of statutory construction, presenting the flexibility of standard techniques. Karl Llewellyn, *The Common Law Tradition: Deciding Appeals* 521–35 (1960). The great casebook by Friedrich Kessler and Malcolm Sharp is organized precisely around the contradictory substantive elements in contract law and presents the variety available in the existing set of precedents. Friedrich Kessler and Malcolm Sharp, *Cases and Materials on Contracts* (1953).

3. John Nowak, "Realism, Nihilism, and the Supreme Court: Do the Emperors Have Nothing But Robes?" 22 *Washburn Law Review* 246 (1983), is a direct descendant of the purely debunking strand of Legal Realism.

4. As the title of a recent study indicates, the Realists were reformers as well as iconoclasts. Robert Jerome Glennon, *The Iconoclast as Reformer: Jerome Frank's Impact on American Law* (1985). The reformist impulse limited the impact of the Realists' iconoclasm.

5. For a recent version of this argument, see Bruce Ackerman, *Reconstructing American Law* (1984). For my evaluation of this version, see Mark Tushnet, "Book Review," 78 *Northwestern University Law Review* 857 (1984).

commonsense incredulity at using large abstractions in a complex world, common sense was part of the justification for stopping points: Certain categories seemed to emerge out of a mature reflection on social reality, and those categories provided the midlevel abstractions.

In the second branch of the attack on classical legal rules, the Realists argued that the large abstractions not only fail as appropriate regulations of social reality, they also fail as descriptions of what courts in fact do. The Realists argued that the choices courts make among the abstractions are guided implicitly or explicitly by the judges' views of what proper public policy should be. They concluded that the middle-level abstractions should be based on policy considerations. For example, rules regulating consumer transactions should differ from those regulating business deals because consumers are in general less sophisticated and less able to negotiate terms than businesspeople are.

The difficulty with the program of relying on common sense and policy is that it does not explain why we stop at midlevel abstractions rather than continuing in an ever more particularistic direction. Consider the first branch of the attack. Common sense tells us that, as a matter of social reality, consumer transactions differ from business deals. But if we think about it some more, we will realize that a consumer transaction involving a car is different from one involving a video recorder, that a car purchase by a Hispanic-American is different from one by an Anglo-American, and so on indefinitely. As a matter of social reality, all interactions in society are unique. If followed this far the attack on abstract classical legal rules becomes an attack on all legal rules and on any abstractions, but only a few Realists went that far.[6]

More commonly Realists invoked the policy branch of the attack to halt the slide from total abstraction to complete particularity. Eventually, though, an analytic problem arose. The Realists had discovered that abstractions can be manipulated to achieve policy goals. They came to understand that policies can be manipulated to achieve desired levels of abstraction. For example, suppose one Realist urged us to adopt a midlevel abstraction that creates a law of consumer transactions as an appropriate accommodation between interests in freedom of action and actual limitations on freedom such as consumer ignorance. Another more "progressive" Realist could counter by invoking exactly the same policies to show that our midlevel abstraction should distinguish "big-ticket" consumer purchases like cars from more routine purchases, perhaps on the ground that consumers rapidly gain experience with their routine

6. Grant Gilmore, *The Ages of American Law* 80–81 (1977), says that Wesley Sturges did so. I believe that Arthur Leff did so as well. See Chapter 3.

purchases and so lose their ignorance.[7] A third more "conservative" Realist would tell us to move in the opposite direction, invoking market processes to show that consumer knowledge is great enough to justify more deference to freedom of action.[8] There are therefore no neutral stopping places between abstraction and particularity.

Of course the Realists knew that from the beginning—or at least their program committed them to that view. Their criticisms of classical rules forced out into the open the policy choices embodied in legal rules. For example, some Realists argued that when a court has to decide whether a person has "created" a contract by behavior that should be treated as "accepting" an offer, the court should structure its result around the perceived commercial needs of traders. Once arguments like this are accepted, law is transformed into policy, and lawmaking into policy-making.[9] The policy emphasis of Legal Realism amounted to a repudiation of the liberal tradition's theory of the rule of law. Law was supposed to be the way in which the warring interests of private individuals can be disciplined. If law is only policy it is simply the continuation of the war of all against all by other means.

For a while the threat Realism posed to the liberal tradition could be contained. Policy analysts faced no difficulties so long as they could plausibly claim that they were concerned with the most effective ways to implement uncontroversial goals. The move to policy analysis ultimately failed because difficulties in executing the program of policy analysis revealed that American society did not have enough uncontroversial goals for policy analysts to implement.

Policy analysis must start with a postulated goal, and early policy analysts thought they could systematically apply common sense to find out how to reach that goal. But their expertise in social analysis also led them systematically to challenge common sense. Sometimes they argued that the commonsense route may not get us to the postulated goal as effectively as some other route.[10] Sometimes the policy analysts examined the side effects of the commonsense route, showing that in a world as

7. See Howard Beales, Richard Craswell, and Steven Salop, "The Efficient Regulation of Consumer Information," 24 *Journal of Law and Economics* 491, 505–6 (1981).

8. Cf. Duncan Kennedy, "Form and Substance in Private Law Adjudication," 89 *Harvard Law Review* 1685 (1976).

9. The classic expression is Harold Lasswell and Myres McDougal, "Legal Education and Public Policy: Professional Training in the Public Interest," 52 *Yale Law Journal* 203 (1943). The concern for policy accounts in part for the attractions the New Deal had for the Realists, although of course much more than ideas—for example, the allure of power and the availability of government jobs to those excluded from elite legal practice—was at work.

10. For example, when greater corporate responsibility is the goal, the analysis draws on economic theory to show that such responsibility is maximized by market, rather than

perverse as ours following the commonsense route to the postulated goal will produce a conflict with some other desirable objective.[11] The policy analyst then searches for a way to reach the original goal while attempting to intrude as little as possible on other values. At the end of the line, of course, the policy analyst often concludes that, in light of all the constraints, we really cannot reach the original goal at all. Or, in one of the classic versions, if you require that apartments be kept in a habitable condition, the landlord will just raise the rent (and reduce the availability of apartments to relatively poorer people, who were the intended beneficiaries of the warranty).[12] It was no simple thing to identify in specific contexts the policies that had to be promoted. It was one thing to talk about the "commercial needs of traders"; it was quite another to find out how clothing manufacturers dealt with their suppliers and how that differed from the way in which automobile makers dealt with their dealers.[13]

If analysis was difficult, application was dispiriting. Law and policy are located in an extremely complex social order. One could tinker at one point only to find the problems migrating elsewhere.[14] Reforms that called for governmental intervention occurred in the face of adaptable and politically powerful private interests.[15] Reforms directed at the operations of government were absorbed and trivialized. The policy analysts prided themselves on their pragmatic "realism," but the power of private interests stringently limited what was politically acceptable and so made even the pragmatists' proposals for reform seem utopian.

---

political, processes. For a summary of these arguments, see Daniel Fischel, "The Corporate Governance Movement," 35 *Vanderbilt Law Review* 1259 (1982).

11. For example, eliminating discrimination based on gender might require imposing and enforcing limits on the hours that professional men can work. See Kathryn Powers, "Sex Segregation and the Ambivalent Directions of Sex Discrimination Law," 1979 *Wisconsin Law Review* 55.

12. There is a large literature on this issue. See, e.g., Richard Markovits, "The Distributive Impact, Allocative Efficiency, and Overall Desirability of Ideal Housing Codes: Some Theoretical Observations," 89 *Harvard Law Review* 1815 (1976) (summarizing the discussion). The conclusion seems to be that it all depends on the shape of the demand curve.

13. See Stewart Macaulay, "Non-Contractual Relations in Business: A Preliminary Study," 28 *American Sociological Review* 55 (1963); Stewart Macaulay, *Law and the Balance of Power: The Automobile Manufacturers and Their Dealers* (1966).

14. A classic discussion, Albert Alschuler, "Sentencing Reform and Prosecutorial Power: A Critique of Recent Proposals for 'Fixed' and 'Presumptive' Sentencing," 126 *University of Pennsylvania Law Review* 550 (1978), deals with the reduction of judicial discretion and the likely compensating rise of prosecutorial discretion.

15. See Paul Starr and Gosta Esping-Anderson, "Passive Intervention," 7 *Working Papers for a New Society* 15 (July–Aug. 1979).

The problems of analysis and application provided grounds to question the move to policy analysis. These problems gave an increasingly conservative cast to policy analysis, which tended to conclude that reasoned interventions in complex processes are unlikely to have desirable effects.[16] This conservatism highlighted the increasingly obvious political dimensions of policy analysis. For almost a generation, roughly from 1935 to 1965, most of the serious intellectuals among American legal scholars, as among American academics generally, were aligned with the Progressive–New Deal tradition. Given that uniformity of political perspectives in the relevant community, it was entirely natural for legal scholars to think that what they personally preferred coincided with what a policy analyst would prescribe. The convenient congruence between rational policy and the platform of the Democratic Party became openly problematic as soon as serious conservative and radical critiques of the program of the Democratic Party developed. Policy analysis thus became politicized, and the temporary resolution of the dilemmas of the liberal tradition ended.

Legal Realism began as a description of how rules of law actually operate. Its description posed a challenge to the theory of the rule of law, because the Realists demonstrated that rules of law can only be applied if judges make value choices. Policy analysis attempted to transform the description of the legal system as it actually is into a normative justification of specific results. It embraced the Realist conclusion that judges make value choices but failed to understand the depth to which that conclusion threatens the liberal tradition.

Policy analysis did leave an important residue in a continuing effort by some legal academics to use disciplines such as sociology and political science to understand how legal rules operate in practice. For it seemed that one has to understand law as a phenomenon before one can sensibly choose how to implement one's policy goals. In this way the positivist impulses of social scientists were turned to assist the normative aims of policy analysts.[17]

Political Science and Structural Review

The Realist emphasis on description affected constitutional theory in ways related to, but somewhat different from, the development of policy

16. See, e.g., Bruce Ackerman and William Hassler, *Clean Coal/Dirty Air* (1981).

17. Today the major form of policy analysis of interest is Chicago-style law-and-economics, discussion of which is beyond the scope of this book. I note only that the recent development of a liberal reformist law-and-economics rather openly reproduces the general problems of policy analysis just described.

analysis. Legal academics are primarily concerned with advising legislators about how to develop public policy, advising lawyers about how to litigate cases, and advising judges about how to decide them. The descriptive aspects of Legal Realism may help academics provide their audiences with a more subtle understanding of what kinds of interventions can actually produce desired results. They cannot assist in coming to judgment, particularly in the field of constitutional law, where the focus has rarely been on what legislators ought to do.[18] In addition, the threat Realism posed to the rule of law was most apparent in constitutional law. If judges deciding contract cases get out of line and impose their values on an unwilling populace, the legislature can always intervene to set things right.[19] If the Justices of the Supreme Court decide to write their personal values into law—which, according to the Realists, they necessarily do—there is nothing, at least formally and in the short run, that the rest of us can do about it. Somehow constitutional lawyers had to domesticate Legal Realism if they were to preserve their enterprise.

Lawyers absorbed Legal Realism in two steps. First they relegated its descriptive thrust to political science departments; then they reappropriated the political scientists' insights.[20] Robert Dahl provided the most important insight in this process.[21] When he examined Supreme Court decisions holding federal statutes unconstitutional, he discovered that most often the Court invalidated statutes enacted many years before its decision; the countermajoritarian thrust of the decisions was weakened because the statutes might not have retained majority support when the Court acted.[22] When the Court blocked recently enacted federal legislation, its decisions tended to erode rapidly. Dahl noted the limits of his study: it concentrated on invalidation of federal rather than state legislation, and it focused on a period when the courts applied doctrines limiting access to constitutional rulings more rigidly than they do today. Still, the central thrust of Dahl's analysis is clear and remains compelling: in the

18. Even Brest, "Conscientious Legislator's Guide," is concerned primarily to establish *that* legislators should sincerely consider the constitutional dimensions of what they do, not *what* they should conclude.

19. Subject, of course, to constitutional constraints enforced by the courts—a formulation that suggests the ultimate circularity of the endeavor.

20. The primary contributors to this process were Bickel, *Least Dangerous Branch*, and Charles Black, *The People and the Court: Judicial Review in a Democracy* (1960). An assessment of the state of the field in political science is "Whither Political Jurisprudence: A Symposium," 36 *Western Political Quarterly* 533–69 (1983).

21. Robert Dahl, "Decision-Making in a Democracy: The Supreme Court as a National Policy-Maker," 6 *Journal of Public Law* 282 (1957).

22. For a recent example, see Bolger v. Youngs Drugs Products Corp., 463 U.S. 60 (1983), invalidating a provision enacted in 1873 at the urging of Anthony Comstock.

medium-to-long run judicial review doesn't matter very much.[23] Most of the time judicial review does little more than ease the burden on those who wish to take obsolete statutes off the books; they can turn to the courts instead of having to overcome legislative inertia.[24] Even this conclusion is weakened by studies of the impact of Supreme Court decisions.[25] Although the evidence is not uniform, the general conclusion of these studies is that controversial Supreme Court decisions will be implemented fully only under special circumstances, for example, when sympathetic bureaucracies are charged with the task of implementation. It seems that Supreme Court decisions make a difference when contemporary majorities or near-majorities want them to make a difference.[26]

The conclusion that judicial review doesn't matter was probably implicit in the Realist program. If law is only power dressed up in ways that satisfy our demand for neutrality, ultimately the powerful will prevail no matter what a few eccentric judges occasionally say. In this view judges are constrained not by constitutional theory but by political reality. Yet it seems unsatisfactory to eliminate concern about the risk of judicial tyranny by invoking the realities of the political world. Once we understand how political realities actually do constrain the judges, we may wonder if

23. David Barnum, "The Supreme Court and Public Opinion: Judicial Decision Making in the Post–New Deal Period," 47 *Journal of Politics* 652 (1985), updates Dahl's study and concludes that Supreme Court invalidation of legislation was often "supported . . . by at least the trend—and in some cases even the distribution—of nationwide public opinion." Id., p. 662. Slightly more qualified, but still broadly consistent with Dahl's analysis, is John Gates, "The American Supreme Court and Electoral Realignment: A Critical Review," 8 *Social Science History* 267 (1984).

24. Of course we still must explain why the burdens of overcoming inertia should be allocated in that way. For a discussion of a related issue, see Chapter 2.

25. See generally *The Impact of Supreme Court Decisions* (Theodore Becker ed. 1969); William Muir, *Prayer in the Public Schools: Law and Attitude Change* (1967); Johnson and Canon, *Judicial Policies*. See also Dudley Clendinen, "Ten Morals, A Mistake, No Leaks," *New York Times*, Nov. 25, 1985, p. A-16, col. 1 (five years after Supreme Court held practice unconstitutional, school board refuses to remove poster of Ten Commandments from classroom walls).

26. Black, *People and Court*, p. 52, argues that the Court's "most necessary function . . . has been that of validation," by which it "satisf[ies] the people that [the government] has taken all steps humanly possible to stay within its powers." As Black recognizes, however, "the power to validate is the power to invalidate." Id., p. 53. Thus, the legitimating function of the Court can be performed only if it at least occasionally invalidates a statute. If it invalidates a significant statute, the significance of its action goes beyond the invalidation's contribution to the legitimating function and requires additional and independent justification. If the Court invalidates only insignificant statutes, we need a social theory that explains how people can come to believe that the government is operating under significant constraints when the evidence of those constraints consists of decisions that enforce only insignificant constraints. For some skeptical observations about the availability of such a theory, see Chapter 1.

we have simply reinstituted the tyranny of the majority, or alternatively whether the political methods of controlling judges are ineffective during a short-run period that we must still care about. Ordinarily three mechanisms of political control are invoked: constitutional amendment, control of the jurisdiction of the courts, and appointments of new Justices.[27]

A decision can be overturned by constitutional amendment, as when the twenty-sixth amendment, guaranteeing the right to vote to those over eighteen, was adopted within six months of a Supreme Court decision holding unconstitutional a congressional statute that sought the same end.[28] The amendment process, though, is insufficient to allay concern about judicial tyranny even on the formal level. The process requires supermajorities, two-thirds of the national legislature and three-quarters of the states. A minority, larger to be sure than five Justices of the Supreme Court but still a minority, may block the adoption of an amendment.[29]

Charles Black and Michael Perry have recently attempted to rely on the second mechanism of political control, restricting the jurisdiction of the

27. Impeachment is also mentioned sometimes, but it has fallen into disuse. See Richard Ellis, *The Jeffersonian Crisis: Courts and Politics in the Young Republic* 69–82, 96–107 (1971) (on early impeachments); Charles Warren, *The Supreme Court in United States History* 292–95 (1926) (describing long-term effects of acquittal of Justice Samuel Chase).

More recently several authors have been attracted to the idea that at least some constitutional decisions should be treated as nonfinal, in the sense that legislators should be allowed, and sometimes encouraged, to reenact laws that the Court has held unconstitutional in order to communicate to the Court their continuing rejection of its position. See, e.g., John Agresto, *The Supreme Court and Constitutional Democracy* (1984); Daniel Conkle, "Nonoriginalist Constitutional Rights and the Problem of Judicial Finality," 13 *Hastings Constitutional Law Quarterly* 9 (1985) (a more moderate version of the argument). Whatever its merits as a normative suggestion, the argument seems strikingly unrealistic: Expressions of direct defiance seem unlikely to influence the judges who made the decision that is being defied; indeed, they may stiffen the judges' backs. See, e.g., Wallace v. Jaffree, 472 U.S. 38, 48 (1985) (castigating trial judge who had expressly rejected controlling Supreme Court decisions); Thornburgh v. American College of Obstetricians and Gynecologists, 106 S. Ct. 2169 (1986). Defiance might influence one or two Justices to join with those who dissented in earlier cases when later ones provide the opportunity for narrowing the decisions. This seems to have been the effect of congressional opposition to some decisions in the late 1950s regarding the rights of members and former members of the Communist Party. See Walter Murphy, *Congress and the Court* (1962). The broader effects of defiance seem likely to occur by means of new appointments to the Court.

28. Oregon v. Mitchell, 400 U.S. 112 (1970).

29. The best contemporary example is the failure of the Equal Rights Amendment to receive ratification. Polls indicated that a majority of the American people, but less than two-thirds, supported the amendment. See Rhode, "Equal Rights in Retrospect," p. 2 n. 3. The outcome is thus consistent with the constitutional scheme, in that an amendment that lacked supermajority support failed, but it is also an example of the inability of the amendment process to serve the majority's will.

courts, to allay concern about judicial overreaching.[30] Congress has the power to regulate the jurisdiction of the federal courts. According to Black and Perry, if Congress disagrees with some constitutional ruling by the Supreme Court, it may remove cases raising similar issues from the Court's jurisdiction. Reliance on congressional power to regulate jurisdiction, however, suffers from serious political problems. The position taken by Black and Perry is opposed by the substantial weight of scholarly opinion. Most scholars argue that Congress may not selectively restrict the Court's jurisdiction to keep it from deciding a class of cases based on Congress' prediction of how the Court would decide those cases. They say that selective restriction of jurisdiction interferes with the role of the Court in the constitutional scheme.[31] In the world of pure constitutional theory, the fact that most scholars disagree with Black and Perry might not matter, because Black and Perry might be right and everyone else wrong. What matters here, though, is not constitutional theory but how politics operates. The scholarly consensus is a political force that keeps Congress from enacting jurisdiction-restricting legislation; the proposals fail to be adopted because some members of Congress who think the Court overreached itself think, despite Black and Perry, that it would be unconstitutional to restrict the courts' jurisdiction.[32]

Appointments to the Court, the final political mechanism to control judges over the middle-to-long run, are the most important method of control. The Supreme Court is an enduring institution with a regularly changing membership. The President and the Senate determine over time what the composition of the Court is and so determine what constitutional law is. Although the appointment mechanism may reduce the risk of judicial tyranny over the long run, it does not eliminate the theoretical problems. First, the President and Senate can influence constitutional law only indirectly through appointments. When appointing a judge for a life term, the President and Senate must predict how that judge will behave in

30. Black, *Decision according to Law*; Perry, *Constitution, Courts, and Human Rights*. Perry relies on this mechanism only for cases in which the court exercises noninterpretive review. Even apart from those who question the coherence of the underlying category, see Chapter 1, most of those who have discussed Perry's work question the ability to distinguish clearly between interpretive and noninterpretive review. See, e.g., Ira Lupu, "Constitutional Theory and the Search for the Workable Premise," 8 *University of Dayton Law Review* 579, 601–9 (1983).

31. See Perry, *Constitution, Courts, and Human Rights*, pp. 128–39, and sources cited therein; Mark Tushnet and Jennifer Jaff, "Why the Debate over Congress' Power to Restrict the Jurisdiction of the Supreme Court Is Unending," 72 *Georgetown Law Journal* 1311 (1984).

32. For a more complete discussion of Congress' power to restrict jurisdiction, see Tushnet and Jaff, "Debate over Congress' Power."

a wide range of cases over a long career. The issues that arise over a Justice's career will change: What will the conservative position be on the constitutional issues of 2008? The appointee's background may provide a fairly good basis for predictions about her position on most of the foreseeable issues, but inaccurate guesses about the future are inevitable. Such mistakes may be disastrous from the point of view of those who want to eliminate judicial tyranny. Perhaps the best recent example is the appointment of four proponents of judicial restraint and conservatism by Richard Nixon, three of whom voted to restrict the power to regulate abortions.[33]

In addition, the appointment mechanism is effective only over the middle-to-long run. Yet the costs to the public between the time a tyrannizing decision is made and the time it is repudiated by a new majority on the Court can be quite high. Again the abortion cases serve as an example. If one thinks that abortion is murder, the Supreme Court has licensed murder, and it is cold comfort that because of new appointments the license may be withdrawn after fifteen or twenty years and millions of murders.

Finally, relying on the appointment process to check the courts simply reintroduces the problem of legislative tyranny. All that it can accomplish is the creation of repeated oscillation between a regime in which judges defer to legislative will and allow the legislature to tyrannize over those who lack sufficient political power and a regime in which judges do not defer and themselves tyrannize on behalf of the parties defeated in the legislature. After a time one regime may be converted into the other, but neither solves the problems of the liberal tradition.[34]

The insights of political science cannot allay concern about judicial tyranny. A recent development in constitutional theory embraces the political scientists' conclusion that judicial review basically doesn't matter and attempts to give it a different kind of normative content. This

33. It is possible to make too much of this caution. Overall, careful attention to ideology in the selection process can provide the basis for rather good, but probably not perfect, predictions about future decision-making behavior by the appointee. But sometimes considerations other than ideology affect the selection of appointees. And in any event the appointee straying from the reservation only once or twice, but in particularly important cases, can be disastrous from a political point of view.

34. Put somewhat differently, the argument that in the long run judicial review does not make a difference raises severe questions about the utility of constitutional theory as anything other than a weapon in a political struggle. Because constitutional arguments can sometimes lead one of the Justices to take one position rather than another, such arguments can be a form of political action, like a street demonstration or lobbying in a city council. It is, of course, interesting to try to figure out why some Justices respond to certain arguments and others do not. See Earl Maltz, "The Concept of the Doctrine of the Court in Constitutional Law," 16 *Georgia Law Review* 357 (1982) (calling this "atomistic analysis"). But that enterprise is rather remote from the theoretical concerns of grand theory.

theory, sometimes called structural due process, has not yet been systematically defended as a general theory of judicial review.[35] Instead commentators have noticed that the Court seems to be doing something novel in a few areas and have given the label *structural review* to the phenomenon without articulating its basis.

Structural review has two aspects. It counsels judges to pay attention to *who* makes decisions and *how* they are made rather than paying attention to the substance of the decisions. Governmental actions will be unconstitutional under structural review if they were made by agency A—an administrative agency or the courts, for example—when they should have been made by agency B—the executive or the legislature. Or they will be unconstitutional if the proper decision maker used inadequate methods of making decisions. Structural review faces two related questions: First, why should agency A rather than agency B be required as the source of the action, and why should certain decision-making methods be required? Second, how can structural review satisfy the requirement that the Constitution constrain the government if it places no limits on the substance of what the government does? The answers to these questions reveal that structural review attempts to remake the legislative process into the image of the judicial process. That deduction foreshadows the methods and conclusions in the remainder of this book.

The modern era of structural review began with *Hampton v. Mow Sun Wong*.[36] The Civil Service Commission had adopted a regulation barring resident aliens from employment in the federal competitive civil service. The plaintiffs included aliens who sought jobs as postal workers, janitors, file clerks, and typists—positions in which their citizenship status would seem irrelevant. The plaintiffs challenged the regulation on the ground that it discriminated against aliens without adequate justification. The Court analyzed the problem differently. Justice Stevens' majority opinion acknowledged that "overriding national interests" *might* justify restricting federal employment to citizens. For example, such a restriction might encourage aliens to become citizens, or, more plausibly, its existence might provide the President with a bargaining chip in treaty negotiations: "If you relax your tariff restrictions, we'll let your citizens get federal jobs." But, according to the Court, those interests were in the domain of Congress and the President, not in the domain of the Civil Service Commission. The Commission was a management and employment agency, which had neither the mandate nor the expertise to impose regulations that would serve foreign policy interests.

---

35. See Tribe, *American Constitutional Law*, pp. 1137–46, and Supp. 103–4 (1979).
36. 426 U.S. 88 (1976).

Two preliminary observations about *Hampton* define some of the important aspects of structural review. First, the Court suggested that the regulations would have been constitutional if they had been promulgated by the President instead of the Civil Service Commission. Certainly the structural ground on which the Court relied would have been unavailable if the President had done so. And indeed, immediately after the Court's decision the President did promulgate the same regulations. The federal courts then upheld them against constitutional challenges.[37] *Hampton* thus demonstrates that structural review does not impose substantive limits on governmental action.

Second, the Court did not invalidate the regulation because Congress had failed to authorize the Commission to take foreign policy into account in formulating its employment policies. If the Court had relied on that argument, *Hampton* would be an ordinary case in administrative law, a case about an agency that exceeded the bounds of its statutory authority. Rather the Court said that Congress' attempt to authorize the Commission to worry about foreign policy was constitutionally impermissible.[38]

Hampton's approach finds unconstitutional the delegation of some authority to the wrong agency. We still need to know, though, why these delegations might be unconstitutional.[39] Other examples of structural

37. Mow Sun Wong v. Campbell, 626 F.2d 739 (9th Cir. 1980). The Supreme Court decided *Mow Sun Wong* on June 1; the regulation was repromulgated on September 2.

38. *Hampton* revived a tradition of imposing limits on the tasks Congress can give to an administrative agency. Earlier versions prohibited the delegation of "legislative" authority to administrative agencies and had been invoked most recently in 1935 to invalidate the National Industrial Recovery Act. A.L.A. Schechter Poultry Corp. v. United States, 295 U.S. 495 (1935). The growth of the welfare state and its associated administrative bureaucracies inevitably meant that the nondelegation doctrine would fall on hard times. In the administrative state the legislature confers substantial discretionary power on bureaucracies to handle problems as yet undefined when they arise. Using a strict definition of *legislative authority* in the nondelegation doctrine would seriously impede the necessary operations of the welfare state. The doctrine thus fell into disuse until recently.

National Cable Television Ass'n. v. United States, 415 U.S. 336 (1974), construed a statute narrowly to avoid a delegation problem; the statute authorized agencies to collect "fees," but if "fees" were defined broadly the statute would let agencies impose general taxes, a job for the legislature. In Industrial Union Dep't. v. American Petroleum Institute, 448 U.S. 607 (1980) (Rehnquist, J., concurring in judgment), and American Textile Manufacturers Inst. v. Donovan, 452 U.S. 490 (1981) (Rehnquist, J., dissenting), Justice Rehnquist would have held portions of the Occupational Safety and Health Act unconstitutional because Congress had failed to specify what it meant when it told the agency to set standards that assure "to the extent feasible" that workers will not suffer from health problems after being exposed to toxic materials.

39. A careful survey of areas in which the Supreme Court has engaged in something like structural review is Burt Neuborne, "Judicial Review and Separation of Powers in France

review suggest a rationale for the theory. *Regents of the University of California v. Bakke* involved an affirmative action plan for admission to one of the University's medical schools. Justice Powell thought the plan was unconstitutional, but he recognized that similar plans had gained wide acceptance in related areas. For example, in many cases the federal courts had approved plans designed to eliminate the results of discriminatory practices, and administrative agencies had imposed such plans in the same situation. Justice Powell agreed that affirmative action was permitted to eliminate "the disabling effects of identified discrimination." Anticipating the University's claim that its affirmative action plan was designed to do just that, Justice Powell said that the University "does not purport to have made, and is in no position to make . . . findings [of past discrimination]. Its broad mission is education, not the formulation of any legislative policy or the adjudication of particular claims of illegality . . . Isolated segments of our vast governmental structures are not competent to make those decisions, at least in the absence of legislative mandates and legislatively determined criteria."[40]

Similarly, when the Court upheld a provision of the 1977 Public Works Employment Act that reserved 10 percent of the funds for businesses owned and controlled by members of certain minorities, Justice Powell and Chief Justice Burger examined the legislative history in detail.[41] They concluded that, although the act itself contained no specific statements that Congress had found widespread discrimination in construction projects, the legislative history demonstrated that such discrimination existed and that Congress had enacted the "minority set-aside" to remedy that discrimination. Thus, in contrast to *Bakke*, the remedial decision was made by a "competent" body.

Washington v. Seattle School District is similar. In 1978 the Seattle school board adopted a desegregation plan that used busing to integrate its schools. Two months after the plan went into effect, a statewide initiative was passed; the initiative barred school boards from assigning students to schools outside their neighborhoods, although it allowed courts to require such assignments. The Supreme Court held that the initiative violated the Constitution. Justice Blackmun's opinion said that

---

and the United States," 57 *New York University Law Review* 363 (1982). Neuborne acknowledges that the contours of this sort of review are not well-defined and concludes that "much work remains before a developed separation of powers based [a structural] theory of judicial review can be said to exist," because the bases for allocating decisions to various decision makers "must be tested at greater length" and "more precisely defined." Id., p. 437.

40. 438 U.S. 265, 307–9 (1978) (opinion of Powell, J.).
41. Fullilove v. Klutznick, 448 U.S. 448 (1980).

the initiative violated the principle that states cannot use "the *racial nature* of a decision to determine the decisionmaking process."[42]

These cases are tied together by structural review's concern for allocating decision-making authority to the proper agencies of government. How do we know what the "proper" agency is? Justice Powell said that the mission of the University of California was education, not making findings of and then remedying past discrimination. As the analysis of *Hampton* suggests, he did not say that the University had exceeded the authority the people of California had granted to it in adopting the affirmative action plan. Nor could he have done so without repudiating generally accepted principles of constitutional law. Ordinarily states can allocate decision-making authority to various bodies in whatever way they want; the federal Constitution is usually irrelevant to their choices about who is to make what sorts of decisions. If the people of California want to eliminate the post of Governor, or establish a system of neighborhood governments completely autonomous from one another, they can do so.[43] Similarly, one would have thought before *Bakke* that the people of California could create a University with two missions: one broadly educational and the other narrowly to find and remedy discrimination in education. In the Seattle case the difficulty is that Washington did not have to give school boards the power to assign students in the first place; it could have adopted statewide criteria from the outset. Nor were the criteria it ended up adopting cast in racial terms, although of course Washington's voters were provoked into rethinking the proper allocation of authority because of Seattle's race-related policy. It is hard to see what is wrong with restructuring the process by which students are assigned to schools so long as the process that results could have been used from the start.

Perhaps Justice Powell believed that the people of California really didn't give their University a dual mission. This branch of structural review may be designed to ensure that certain decisions be made by agencies of the government that are more responsive to the electorate than other agencies are. As Justice Rehnquist put it, the nondelegation doctrine "ensures to the extent consistent with orderly government administration that important choices of social policy are made by . . . the branch of our

42. 458 U.S. 457, 470 (1982). See also Wygant v. Jackson Board of Education, 106 S. Ct. 1842, 1869–70 (1985) (Stevens, J., dissenting) (affirmative action plan negotiated by union of which adversely affected teachers were members, and approved "overwhelmingly" by membership, was constitutional in part because of "fairness of the procedures used to adopt" plan).

43. Subject to the judicially unenforceable clause guaranteeing to each state a republican form of government.

government most responsive to the public will."[44] This notion makes sense of *Hampton's* distinction between the President, who is elected in part precisely to make foreign policy decisions, and the Civil Service Commission, whose members are not selected to do that, and of Justice Powell's distinction between Congress and state legislatures, which can adopt affirmative action plans, and state universities, which can't. There will inevitably be problems of classification,[45] but the central idea is clear enough.[46]

The idea that structural review should be concerned with allocating authority to responsive agencies is beset by several difficulties. Two difficulties are empirical. The view that appointees to the Civil Service Commission cannot make foreign policy decisions as well as the President can misconceives the policy-making process.[47] The regulation barring aliens from the civil service did not emanate from "the Commission" or "the President." It was undoubtedly produced after a study by members of the Commission's staff, who most certainly consulted both formally and informally with members of other staffs knowledgeable about foreign policy. A "presidential" regulation would be produced through similar

44. Industrial Union Dep't. v. American Petroleum Institute, 448 U.S., p. 607 (Rehnquist, J., concurring in judgment). See also Eugenia Toma, "State University Boards of Trustees: A Principal-Agent Perspective," 49 *Public Choice* 155 (1986) (examining hypothesis that structure of boards of trustees reflects costs to politicians of allowing shirking by their agents).

45. See generally Comment, "Principles of Competence: The Ability of Public Institutions to Adopt Remedial Affirmative Action Plans," 53 *University of Chicago Law Review* 581 (1986).

46. Peter Aranson, Ernest Gellhorn, and Glen Robinson, "A Theory of Legislative Delegation," 68 *Cornell Law Review* 1 (1982), urge that the nondelegation doctrine be revitalized. They argue that delegations diminish the political costs that legislators must bear when they enact statutes that benefit concentrated groups and that delegations increase the cost of supervising the execution of policy to determine whether the policies actually implemented accord with the legislators' goals. As they recognize, this argument depends on the normative judgment that "reduc[ing] the use of regulation to produce private benefits and to satisfy high demanders at collective cost" is desirable. Id., p. 63. In this sense the proposal is one version of the effort to use public choice theory to explain why some form of substantive due process is desirable. For a more complete discussion of this normative premise, see Chapter 2. .

47. *Hampton* might rest on the view that members of the Civil Service Commission are appointed to be personnel managers and not makers of foreign policy. Perhaps they lack competence to make personnel decisions in light of foreign policy considerations. Members of the Commission might be chosen primarily because of their managerial qualities. Yet within the pool of qualified personnel managers there will inevitably be people qualified to make an occasional foreign policy decision. There is no reason to think that the selection process will systematically exclude those who could competently and of course only occasionally think about the relation between personnel and foreign policies.

staff efforts.[48] This identifies a general difficulty with structural review in a complex policy-making system: in this branch of the theory structural review is predicated on a vision of an imaginary policy-making process, in which rational deliberation has a large place, and attaches constitutional consequences to the judges' efforts to distinguish between one imaginary process and another.

The second empirical difficulty with structural review identifies a different point where an imaginary democratic process is substituted for the real one. Justice Powell may have believed that the affirmative action plan in *Bakke* was made up by the faculty of the University's medical school, was only formally ratified by the University's governing board, and was paid not the slightest bit of attention by the California legislature, the institution most responsive to the people of California.[49] That belief might be accurate in some contexts, but it seriously underestimates the degree of political attention that university affirmative action plans, especially for professional schools, receive from state legislatures.[50] Notably, in the Seattle case the initiative was adopted directly by the people in the election; no complex empirical arguments are needed to demonstrate that it resulted from as democratic a process as we have.

Again the point is general. All agencies of government, except the federal courts, are either directly or indirectly responsible to the people. As a general matter there is no reason to think that indirect responsibility leads to weaker controls over the agencies than direct responsibility provides. Bureaucrats may be protected by civil service regulations, but incumbents have an automatic electoral advantage against opponents. Both are insulated from political accountability. This is especially true where such politically sensitive issues—in Justice Rehnquist's terms such "important choices of social policy"—as affirmative action are involved. Indeed, the distinction between indirect and direct responsibility is likely

48. The distribution of expertise in the two staff processes might differ; for example, the Commission's staff process would probably give more weight to personnel considerations and less to foreign policy ones than the President's staff process would. But it is hard to see as marked a difference as *Hampton* suggests.

49. See Terrance Sandalow, "Racial Preferences in Higher Education: Political Responsibility and the Judicial Role," 42 *University of Chicago Law Review* 653, 695–96 (1975).

50. The offices of administrative officials regularly receive calls from irate parents of applicants and letters from legislators whom those parents have called as constituents, complaining about the adverse impact of the affirmative action plan on a particular child's application. University administrators everywhere have spent a great deal of time defending affirmative action plans to skeptical legislators. Within the university the message is clear: the administrators acknowledge faculty responsibility for and autonomy in developing those plans but repeatedly point out that some plans will be more controversial than others.

to be weakest precisely in areas where the social policy is most important and controversial.

Political sensitivity helps to identify the third difficulty with structural review. No one has yet specified when structural review is appropriate. *Hampton* argued that the regulation in question would have been unconstitutionally discriminatory against aliens had it been adopted by a state legislature. Structural review was triggered by the fact that the national government's special power over foreign policy was the only thing that could save an otherwise obviously unconstitutional provision. It is hard to see how this triggering mechanism is justified or how it could be generalized into an entire theory of structural review. In every constitutional case an otherwise unconstitutional rule is justified by some purported policy. On the model of *Hampton*, then, we would always have to ask whether the policy was made by the "right" agency of government. Structural review would then indeed be a comprehensive theory of judicial review, but because of the empirical difficulties already discussed, it would leave the judges wholly unconstrained in their determination of what the "right" agency is.[51]

Structural review also fails to specify how much attention an issue must get in the legislature. Justice Powell could not treat silent acquiescence in an administrative policy as enough attention, because that is what happened in *Bakke*, but he was willing to accept a detailed legislative history as sufficient in the minority set-aside case. In contrast, Justice Stevens would have required that the set-aside statute itself contain legislative findings of fact regarding past discrimination.[52] Yet in another case, involving the interpretation of a congressional enactment in light of constitutional concerns over federalism, Justice Stevens accepted statements in committee reports as providing a clear indication of Congress' intention to make states liable for attorneys' fees if they lost civil rights cases against state employees, while Justice Powell wanted the states to be named explicitly in the statute as potentially liable for those fees.[53]

These examples show that the proponents of structural review have failed to confine the Court's discretion both in deciding when to invoke structural review and in deciding when its requirements are satisfied.

51. That is why the nondelegation doctrine has rarely been invoked since the 1930s and the growth of the welfare state. See note 38. Even Justice Rehnquist's formulation, which allows delegation "to the extent consistent with orderly government administration," left room enough for seven other Justices to find a permissible delegation. (Chief Justice Burger joined Justice Rehnquist's dissent in Textile Manufacturers Inst. v. Donovan, 452 U.S. 490 [1981].)

52. Fullilove v. Klutznick, 448 U.S. 448, 549–54 (1980) (Stevens, J., dissenting).

53. Hutto v. Finney, 437 U.S. 678 (1978), and id., at 704–10 (Powell, J., dissenting).

Thus, the first branch of structural review, concerned that the "right" body make decisions, fails to do what the liberal tradition requires.

A second branch of structural review tells us to be concerned that the proper agency make the decision using proper processes. This branch has been developed most forcefully by Justice Brennan in a series of cases involving the equal protection clause, which requires that there be justifications for treating two classes of individuals differently. This branch of structural review is concerned with the method by which courts discover those justifications. The traditional view is that the courts can make up justifications: "Legislatures are presumed to have acted constitutionally even if source materials normally resorted to for ascertaining their grounds for action are otherwise silent, and their statutory classifications will be set aside only if no grounds can be conceived to justify them."[54] Justice Brennan believes that statutory classifications can be found constitutional by examining whether they are justified by policies articulated in the legislative history or otherwise apparent from the statute's terms.[55]

---

54. McDonald v. Board of Election Comm'rs., 394 U.S. 802 (1969). One structural approach is not entirely inconsistent with this statement. In Kassel v. Consolidated Freightways Corp., 450 U.S. 662, 682 n. 3 (1981) (Brennan, J., concurring in judgment), Justice Brennan argued that the courts should not ignore unconstitutional reasons that are found in the legislative history even if they could dream up reasons that would make the statute constitutional.

55. A series of cases involving the Social Security Act presents reasonably clearly the choice between inventing reasons and relying on only those apparent in the "source materials usually referred to." Weinberger v. Weisenfeld, 420 U.S. 636 (1975), involved a provision allowing widows with children in their care, but not widowers with children in their care, to receive benefits based on the earnings of the deceased spouse. In Califano v. Goldfarb, 430 U.S. 199 (1977), the statute allowed all widows to receive benefits, but widowers could receive them only if they had been receiving at least half of their support from the deceased wife.

If one were allowed to invent justifications for these discriminations, there is one strong candidate. The provisions might serve to reduce the income inequalities between working men and working women over their lifetimes. Because of discrimination in the workplace, women as a class receive less income while they work than men do. After women die their spouses receive less than the surviving spouses of males. If we look at the income of the unit [family plus surviving spouse] over its entire course, providing less to widowers than to widows equalizes payments to that unit. Further, the Court has indeed held that different treatment of men and women can be justified if it is designed "to compensate for particular economic disabilities suffered by women." Califano v. Webster, 430 U.S. 313 (1977).

The Court held the statutes in *Weisenfeld* and *Goldfarb* unconstitutional despite the possible compensatory rationale. Justice Brennan examined the history of the provisions in both cases. In *Weisenfeld* he found that the purpose was "to provide children deprived of one parent with the opportunity for the personal attention of the other" and in *Goldfarb* that the purpose was "to equalize the protection given to the dependents of women and men." Thus, because the statutes were not in fact intended to compensate women—or family units—for discrimination in the work force, the Court would not consider whether the statutes were reasonably capable of accomplishing a purported compensatory goal.

This second branch of structural review might be developed in two directions. One would be to require that the reasons for a statute always be clearly articulated.[56] Such a requirement would destroy the legislative process as we know it. Much legislation is adopted by city councils and state legislatures, which keep quite rudimentary records of what precedes formal enactment. Although the situation is changing in many states and in a few cities, there still are relatively few committee reports, few records of debates, and the like. A general requirement of articulated reasons would invalidate much of what is on the books. Moreover, frequently— perhaps usually—there are no reasons for legislation except that the legislators who voted for it thought that they would win votes by doing so or that this statute seemed a fair compromise between contending political forces.[57] Thus, it seems unsound to develop structural review in this direction.

The alternative direction is suggested by the fact that the main cases all involved what traditionally have been thought of as suspect or quasi-suspect groups, ones about which we think the legislature may be prejudiced. Structural review says that legislatures may do things to or for those groups—exclude them from jobs, compensate for past discrimination—but we should be sure that that is what the legislature really wants. The anomaly in this direction of development is clear once we bring *Bakke* to mind. Structural review would force into the legislative arena precisely those issues on which we are skeptical of the legislature's ability to act fairly.

Taken together, these critiques of structural review in all of its versions suggest that it cannot serve as a theory of constitutional law. Even more, in form structural review is only suspensory. It does not bar the government from taking some action but only seeks to ensure that the government take that action in an appropriate way. Structural review appears to

---

Three weeks after it decided *Goldfarb* the Court found constitutional a provision of the Social Security Act that resulted in higher benefits for retired women than for retired men. Califano v. Webster, 430 U.S., p. 313. The provision allowed women to exclude more years of low pay from the base upon which Social Security benefits are calculated. It thus was directly responsive to the reality that women receive lower pay than men: "Allowing women, who as such have been unfairly hindered from earning as much as men, to eliminate additional low-earning years from the calculation of their retirement benefits works directly to remedy some part of the effect of that discrimination." Further, the legislative history showed that the disparity was "purposely enacted . . . to compensate for past employment discrimination."

56. This line can be developed from the implications of Justice Brennan's views in Kassel v. Consolidated Freightways Corp., 450 U.S. 662 (1981), and United States Railroad Retirement Board v. Fritz, 449 U.S. 166 (1980).

57. See Linde, "Due Process of Lawmaking"; Posner, "DeFunis Case," pp. 26–31.

avoid the problem of judicial tyranny by avoiding decision on what actions government may take. If the appropriate agency decides that the policy at issue is sound after a second look, the policy will go into effect. Structural review thus directly translates the political scientists' argument that judicial review doesn't matter into constitutional law. This translation fails for two related reasons: the suspensory nature of structural review is usually illusory, and where structural review's "second look" is not an illusion, the process conflicts with the premises of constitutional theory.

As we have seen, the President immediately repromulgated the regulation at issue in *Hampton* after the Court's decision. The repromulgation happened so fast that it is clear that neither the President nor his staff had given any more thought to foreign policy than the Civil Service Commission had. Once more the point is general. In the real world of politics we can predict with great accuracy what the effect of suspensory decisions will be. Sometimes we can predict that the regulation will be readopted, in which case structural review has given the illusion but not the reality of constraint on legislatures. Sometimes we can predict that the statute will not be reenacted, in which case structural review has given the reality of constraint on legislatures and the illusion of freedom for legislatures to do what they want. Clever judges will invoke structural review when they predict that the legislature will be unable to enact legislation that contravenes the judges' personal preferences; they will invoke other modes of review in other cases.

Suppose the judges guess wrong and use structural review in cases where the legislature will take the opportunity it has been given to rethink a particular problem. Then structural review is not constitutional review at all. Because structural review, when it works, is suspensory, it imposes no substantive limitations on legislative activity. That means that the legislature can do whatever it wants, which is what the Constitution is supposed to protect us against. Structural review does not satisfy the demands of constitutional theory that both legislators and judges be constrained. We have already seen that structural review does not constrain judges, and now it appears that it does not constrain legislators either.

Commentators have done no better than the Court in making sense of structural review. Charles Black and Douglas Laycock have sketched a grander version of structural review.[58] In this version we inspect the provisions of the Constitution and discover that they create a governmen-

---

58. Charles Black, *Structure and Relationship in Constitutional Law* (1969); Laycock, "Taking Constitutions Seriously," discussed also in Chapter 1 (appendix).

tal structure embracing some values that go beyond the specific provisions themselves. Both Black and Laycock emphasize provisions that express the value of national unity. Laycock also finds rights to individualism, personal autonomy, and private association in the Constitution, by piecing together the implications of such provisions as the prohibition on forfeiture of estates, the ban on cruel and unusual punishment, the fourth amendment, and the like. The method resembles Justice Douglas' approach in *Griswold v. Connecticut,* in which, as we have seen, he provided an interpretive basis for the right to privacy by arguing that specific constitutional provisions have penumbras that overlap to create a constitutional right to privacy.[59]

The difficulty here is familiar, best put by Vincent Blasi in reviewing Black's presentation: Black "offers no guidelines for the eager law student who would master the methodology of structural inference . . . The inferences, it would seem, can radiate from the structures and relationships in a number of ideological directions, depending on who is doing the inferring."[60] The particular rock on which this version of structural review founders is state sovereignty, which Black and Laycock acknowledge as an important component in the structure of American government. Black discusses *Carrington v. Rash,* in which the Court held unconstitutional a provision in state law that barred military personnel from voting in county elections unless they had been residents of the county before entering the service.[61] The Court relied on the equal protection clause. Black would have preferred that it invoke a structural principle, that "no state may annex any disadvantage simply and solely to the performance of a federal duty."[62] Blasi asks quite sensibly why that principle should not be accommodated to the equally structural principle of state sovereignty to yield a rule that no state may annex unreasonable disadvantages.[63]

A similar problem occurs in Laycock's discussion of the abortion cases. He says that they are "extraordinarily difficult" because they force the Court to "str[ike] a balance among competing constitutional values" respecting the woman and the fetus. Surely state sovereignty makes the cases easy. Laycock finesses that response by defining the value of state sovereignty as "assum[ing only] that states will continue to exist and function as governments."[64] Yet disabling states from acting on as sensi-

59. See Vincent Blasi, "Book Review: Creativity and Legitimacy in Constitutional Law," 80 *Yale Law Journal* 176, 182 (1970).

60. Id., p. 183.

61. 380 U.S. 89 (1965).

62. Black, *Structure and Relationship,* pp. 10–11.

63. Blasi, "Creativity and Legitimacy," p. 183.

64. Laycock, "Taking Constitutions Seriously," pp. 376, 364.

tive an issue as abortion could plausibly be characterized as so diminishing their authority that it makes them not governments at all but mere executives of judicial directions. The structural values thus do not have the obvious content that Black and Laycock attribute to them. When they come into "tension," as Laycock puts it, all that is left is for the courts to "resolve" the tension by "balancing" values, which cannot rescue a defective theory.

Structural review may fail as theory. The effort to develop it is illuminating nonetheless. I have suggested that structural review would transform the legislative process. What would it be transformed into? The structural review cases offer us the image of a judicialized legislature, in which interests are openly articulated and fairly balanced against each other. A judicialized legislature is as much a contradiction as is a legislative judiciary. In the legislative judiciary, judges who are supposed to use reason to constrain the exercise of will by the legislature impose their own will on the society. In the judicialized legislature, legislators who are assumed in general to be creatures of will are supposed to be transformed into beings of reason. Some might find it nice if it were so, but the liberal tradition is deeply suspicious of efforts to combine reason and will in a single institution. After all, we have courts so that judicial reason will constrain legislative will and constitutional theory so that reason will constrain judicial will.

Structural review offers a description of courts that is, in one way, a legacy of Legal Realism. The Realists read decisions in which judges said that they were being guided by values or policies that were independent of the judges' will. The Realists knew that the judges had to have been wrong. Something else had to have been at work. Some Realists also knew that judicial willfulness alone is not enough to explain the law, because they saw patterns of decision that could not arise unless something underlay them all. For the Realists this unseen force was social power.

The remainder of this book tries to develop that perception by examining the processes by which power operates to shape our understanding of the social world. The suggestion that structural review offers a particular description of a judicialized legislature is an example of the kind of analysis used. Instead of treating the judicialized legislature as a normative ideal, and criticizing it as inconsistent with the liberal tradition, I treat the emergence of that ideal as a social phenomenon, the expression of a technocratic vision of society. Succeeding chapters further describe the vision of technocratic rationality that we find in contemporary constitutional law. The descriptive enterprise lays the foundation for the normative one with which the book concludes.

7

The Constitution of
the Bureaucratic State

SINCE 1970 the Supreme Court has been grappling with the constitutional aspects of the welfare state. It held in *Goldberg v. Kelly* that the Constitution guarantees a relatively formal hearing to any recipient of public assistance whose benefits are threatened with termination.[1] *Goldberg* was the Court's recognition that the growth of the welfare state required some response from those who regard enforcing the Constitution as a primary method of regulating government conduct.[2] Prior to the 1950s benefits received from the government were taken to be privileges, not rights, and were therefore immune from regulation under constitutional norms.[3] Yet it seemed to make little sense to treat the massive governmental activities of the welfare state as equivalent to the relatively limited activities of its predecessor in the ideology of liberalism, the night-watchman state.

In an influential article relied on by the Court in *Goldberg*, Charles Reich called the benefits provided by the welfare state "the new property," serving for their beneficiaries the same social purposes as land and stocks served for their owners and deserving the same kinds of protection against arbitrary government action.[4] This chapter explores the meaning the Court has given to the new property. The Court's decisions have a logic that expresses the Court's vision of welfare state bureaucracies, which sees them as rationalized and professionalized.

The central argument of this chapter requires an informal sociology of bureaucracies. All welfare state bureaucracies face serious problems of control, because the "street-level" bureaucrats who actually deliver goods

1. 397 U.S. 254 (1970).
2. Justice Black's dissent in *Goldberg* explicitly links the decision to the growth of the welfare state. 397 U.S., at 271–72 (Black, J. dissenting).
3. See William Van Alstyne, "The Demise of the Right-Privilege Distinction in Constitutional Law," 81 *Harvard Law Review* 1439 (1968).
4. Charles Reich, "The New Property," 73 *Yale Law Journal* 733 (1965).

or services to recipients ordinarily have a great deal of discretion regarding the granting of benefits, their size, and their timing.[5] Superiors in the bureaucracy need to control these discretionary decisions in order to assure that general state policies—that just the right amount of goods and services be provided to the right people—are advanced. For present purposes we can distinguish among three types of welfare state bureaucracies according to the methods by which superiors assert control.[6] First, both analytically and historically, superiors in *politicized* bureaucracies assert control by guaranteeing that subordinates adhere to a political program set by the superiors. Superiors in *rationalized* bureaucracies assert control by promulgating and enforcing rules that regulate the subordinates. Finally, superiors in *professional* bureaucracies assert control by participating jointly with subordinates in developing a project, with both material and ideological components, to extend the scope of professional norms with a base outside the bureaucracy.

The distinction among types of bureaucracies plays a central role in what follows. The prototypical politicized bureaucracy is the classic urban machine, which dispensed jobs on city projects, assistance to the needy, and relaxation of rules that otherwise restricted the citizenry's pleasures, all to the end of securing the political allegiance of recipients and street-level bureaucrats.[7] The prototypical rationalized bureaucracy is the Social Security Administration, which dispenses benefits according to a rigid set of rules defining exactly what contributions entitle recipients to how much in benefits.[8] The prototypical professional bureaucracy is the child welfare agency, in which social workers are supposed to act on their judgment about what is in the best interest of the child.[9]

---

5. See Michael Lipsky, *Street-Level Bureaucracy: Dilemmas of the Individual in Public Service* (1980); Eliot Friedson, *Doctoring Together: A Study of Professional Social Control* (1975), for general views of the problems of hierarchical control in bureaucracies where subordinates must have substantial discretion. William Simon, "Legality, Bureaucracy, and Class in the Welfare System," 92 *Yale Law Journal* 1198 (1983), develops an argument that converges with the one offered here, although Simon's argument is based on the actual administration of public assistance programs and this one is based on Supreme Court doctrine.

6. It is worth noting the bureaucracies I discuss all involve persons in situations of dependency. A formal definition of welfare state bureaucracies might focus on their role in distributing various benefits, provided from tax dollars, to recipients who thereby become dependent on the bureaucracies.

7. See Daniel Bell, *The End of Ideology* 141–50 (rev. ed. 1962).

8. See generally Jerry Mashaw, *Bureaucratic Justice: Managing Social Security Disability Claims* (1983).

9. Even though no real bureaucracy truly exemplifies these pure forms, it will help to treat some mixed types as falling in only one category. In particular the discussion treats an agency in which the superiors use professional norms as a basis for developing rules that they impose on their subordinates as a rationalized bureaucracy. For some theoretical

The main theme of this chapter is that the Court envisions the welfare state as composed primarily of rationalized and professional bureaucracies. This is emphatically not to say that the welfare state is in fact made up of such bureaucracies or that a "sound" law of due process can be developed by taking account of modern social science regarding the modes by which superiors in bureaucracies control their subordinates. Rather the Court is constituting the welfare state by articulating its vision of bureaucracies; the constitution of the welfare state occurs almost subliminally as the Court uses what seem to be natural categories in an entirely unselfconscious way, yet the categories—and therefore the constitution of the welfare state—are not at all natural.

The Court has made the Constitution applicable to rationalized and professional bureaucracies by treating the rules of a rationalized bureaucracy as creating propertylike entitlements and by adopting professional norms as constitutional ones.[10] Further, although the Court has developed doctrines that prevent beneficiaries from securing judicial control over politicized bureaucracies through the due process clause, it has developed other doctrines that provide incentives to both superiors and subordinates to convert politicized bureaucracies into rationalized or professional ones. The bulk of this chapter is devoted to explaining how one can reorganize the usual categories of analysis so that these themes come to the fore.[11]

---

justifications for this approach, see Charles Derber, "Managing Professionals: Ideological Proletarianization and Post-Industrial Labor," 12 *Theory and Society* 309 (1983).

10. Two distinctions should be noted. First, street-level bureaucrats engage in relations in two directions, one with their superiors and one with the recipients of benefits. The argument here is that efforts by superiors to control subordinates affect the relations between subordinates and recipients as well. Second, superiors can assert two kinds of control. They may try to control the internal operations of the bureaucracy, through rules that regulate hiring and firing, and they may try to control the relations between subordinates and recipients, through rules that specify who should get what. Rodney Smolla, "The Reemergence of the Right-Privilege Distinction in Constitutional Law: The Price of Protesting Too Much," 35 *Stanford Law Review* 69, 119 (1982), hints at this second distinction in an effort to justify the Court's decisions.

These two kinds of control can be exercised in different institutional forms. Most dramatically, superiors may (be forced to) share control over internal operations with public-employee unions while retaining control over substantive rules. Again the argument concerns the *form* of control: politics, rules, or professional norms. It seems likely that no matter what the institutional mechanisms, the forms of control will be the same in any particular bureaucracy.

11. As the analysis develops we will see that the image of the rationalized bureaucracy dominates the cases involving deciding when process is due, whereas that of the professional bureaucracy dominates those involving deciding what process is due. This division is probably an artifact of the decided cases, but it may reflect something systematic that I have overlooked.

The conclusion discusses scholarly efforts to justify the Court's scheme or to provide an alternative that uses traditional categories more attractively. Justification and alternatives cast in traditional terms are impossible because the welfare state bureaucracies, as they actually exist, serve functions of social containment that belie the promises of rules and professional norms. Alternatives are defeated by their acceptance of the hierarchy of superiors, subordinates, and recipients. A better alternative is a repoliticized bureaucracy of a certain sort. Rationalized and professional bureaucracies can be repoliticized in different ways. Politics can be reinserted in rationalized bureaucracies by injecting mechanisms of community control and in professional ones by insisting on participation by clients in the bureaucrats' decisions. These modes blur into each other as the community that controls becomes the organized client constituency. The Court's disapproval of politics in bureaucracies indicates how radical these suggestions are.

When Does the Constitution Apply?

It seemed easy to decide when the Constitution applied before the welfare state mushroomed. The due process clauses provide that governments may not deprive people of life, liberty, or property without due process. If a government took some stuff away from you, it had to use fair procedures. And *stuff* was meant almost literally. The operative image was that you had some land, or some cash in your pocket, and a government official wanted to take it away.[12] As governments began to regulate the use of property, this image became harder to sustain. Property began to seem not some tangible "stuff" but a group of rights to use tangible stuff subject to various kinds of regulation. Still, an owner might be thought of as someone who had a bunch of those rights in his or her pocket, and then the image of deprivation could work—for a while.

All of this broke down over the course of the twentieth century. In constitutional law one key moment came in 1972, two years after *Goldberg*. *Goldberg* had treated public assistance as a form of property but without extensive analysis. The Court said, "Such benefits are a matter of statutory entitlement for persons qualified to receive them. Their termination involves state action that adjudicates important rights."[13] As Justice Black pointed out in dissent, the first sentence conceals a serious problem. The recipient is entitled to the benefits only if she or he satisfies the statutory requirements, but in the case at hand the state officials had claimed exactly that the recipient did not satisfy the require-

12. See generally Bruce Ackerman, *Private Property and the Constitution* (1977).

13. 397 U.S. 263 (1970) (footnote omitted). The footnote quotes from and cites articles by Charles Reich.

ments and so was not entitled to the benefits.[14] Justice Black argued further that the second sentence, invoking the importance of the rights, has some troublesome implications.[15] Black noted that "the operation of a welfare state is a new experiment for our Nation." He did not want these "new experiments in carrying out a welfare program . . . [to] be frozen into our constitutional structure."[16]

Two years after *Goldberg* the Court adopted a position that met the concerns Black had expressed. In *Board of Regents v. Roth*, an untenured professor at the University of Wisconsin was not rehired when his contract expired.[17] He sued the Regents, claiming that due process required them to give him at least a statement of the reasons for their decision.[18] The Court rejected Roth's due process claim. The Constitution protects liberty and property against deprivation without due process, but not every interest that a litigant regards as important is liberty or property. Property interests "are not created by the Constitution. Rather, they are created and their dimensions are defined by existing rules or understandings that stem from an independent source such as state law." A person like Roth is entitled to due process only if state law creates "a legitimate claim of entitlement."[19] Thus, what mattered was not the importance of the interest affected but whether state law recognized the interest as one deserving protection. Experimentation in the welfare state could continue so long as states figured out that they should define the interests affected by experiments in ways that did not create legitimate claims of entitlement.

Justice Black's other concern was implicitly addressed by *Roth*'s reliance on state law. Justice Rehnquist later made the point explicit in *Arnett v. Kennedy*, which involved a nonprobationary federal employee who worked in a regional office of the federal poverty agency.[20] Kennedy was fired by his superior on the ground that he had falsely stated in public that the superior had attempted to bribe a grant recipient into signing a statement against Kennedy. As civil service statutes required, Kennedy

14. Id., pp. 274–75 (Black, J., dissenting).

15. He also criticized the Court for its comments about the "desperate" situation of a recipient "deprived of the very means by which to live while he waits," which it made to distinguish *Goldberg* from prior cases involving "blacklisted government contractor[s and] discharged government employee[s]." Id., p. 264. Black regarded "importance" and similar standards as inadequate to control willful judges. See Tushnet, "Anti-Formalism," pp. 1508–12.

16. 397 U.S., p. 279 (Black, J., dissenting).

17. 408 U.S. 564 (1972).

18. Roth also claimed that he had not been rehired because of certain speeches he had made, but that issue was not before the Court, which noted that Roth might still prevail on it. Id., pp. 574–75 and n. 14.

19. Id., p. 577.

20. 416 U.S. 134 (1974).

received a notice of the proposed firing and was given an opportunity to appear before his superior to answer the charges. Under the statutes a triallike hearing was available only after the firing. If Kennedy prevailed on appeal from the firing in that hearing, he would be reinstated and receive back pay. Kennedy claimed that due process required a triallike hearing before removal and a decision by an impartial decision maker, not by the very person whom he had charged with bribery. The Supreme Court rejected Kennedy's claim.

Justice Rehnquist, in a plurality opinion joined by two others, argued that the due process clause was irrelevant under the circumstances. *Roth* established that Kennedy had to have a legitimate claim of entitlement, grounded in a source like positive state or federal law, in order to have a property interest protected by the due process claim. But, according to Justice Rehnquist, when one looked at the relevant positive law, one saw in it a combination of substantive provisions giving civil service employees various rights and procedural provisions describing the manner in which those rights can be terminated. Reviewing the history of the civil service system, Justice Rehnquist concluded that the combination of substantive and procedural provisions forms an unbreakable package: "Where the grant of a substantive right is inextricably intertwined with the limitations on the procedures which are to be employed in determining that right, a litigant in the position of [Kennedy] must take the bitter with the sweet."[21] In an argument that echoes Black's concerns in *Goldberg*, Justice Rehnquist pointed out that the package embodied a compromise in which those who fear that a civil service system will be rigid and inefficient are pacified by provisions allowing quicker action than people in Kennedy's position will like.

If *Roth* is correct in saying that positive law is the source of entitlements, the analytic force of this argument is difficult to resist.[22] The difficulty, as the Court later held, is that relying on positive law to define a package containing entitlements and procedures would "reduce[ ]" the due process clause "to a mere tautology."[23] In Justice Rehnquist's view, when the legislature creates an entitlement, the procedures it creates (or

---

21. Id., pp. 153–54 (opinion of Rehnquist, J., for plurality).

22. It cannot be confined to situations in which the legislative history explicitly reveals a compromise between substance and procedure. Assume that a legislature enacts a substantive entitlement and relies on existing law, such as a long-established administrative procedure act, to provide the procedures for divesting the entitlement or commits to an agency the decision about what procedures to employ. The argument from compromise is that the legislature gave the entitlement the scope that it did, and not a narrower one, because it knew what the procedures were or trusted the agency, not the courts, to come up with appropriate ones.

23. Cleveland Board of Education v. Loudermill, 470 U.S. 532 (1985).

relies on) satisfy due process by definition.[24] Nonetheless, no one has been able to develop an alternative to the positivist approach that retains *Roth*'s reliance on positive law to create substantive entitlements.[25]

Roth thus left the law regarding when process is due in conceptual disarray. Not surprisingly, though, the Court has chugged along making decisions in the area every year. These decisions appear to be quite arbitrary within the express terms of the analysis, as indeed they must be so long as one takes those terms as the only relevant ones.[26] A different perspective on the cases, however, begins to make sense of them.[27]

24. Douglas Laycock has pointed out that the positivist trap conflicts with the syntax of the due process clause, which reads as if people first have property which they then cannot lose except by fair procedures. Douglas Laycock, "Due Process and Separation of Powers: The Effort to Make the Due Process Clauses Nonjusticiable," 60 *Texas Law Review* 875, 879–82 (1982).

25. For a discussion of two commonly suggested but unsatisfactory approaches, see Mark Tushnet, "The Constitution of the Bureaucratic State," 86 *West Virginia Law Review* 1077, 1085–87 (1984). The approaches rely on tradition and natural law to distinguish between new and old property.

26. Liberty is treated only slightly differently by the Court. Compare Santosky v. Kramer, 455 U.S. 745 (1982) (relying on "historical recognition that freedom of personal choice in matters of family life is a fundamental liberty interest" to impose procedures beyond those required by state law for terminating parental rights), with Meachum v. Fano, 427 U.S. 215 (1976), and Olim v. Wakinekona, 461 U.S. 238 (1983) (prisoner's right to remain in institution near home is protected only if positive law confers that right). The remainder of this chapter relies indiscriminately on property and liberty cases for several reasons.

The prisoners' rights cases involve matters such as transfers between penal institutions, parole, and probation. Instead of absolute deprivations of liberty, they are conditional ones, analogous to conditional rights to public assistance and, importantly, products of the Progressive impulses that also generated the welfare state. See, e.g., David Rothman, *Conscience and Convenience* (1980). Further, these forms of conditional liberty are models for other ways in which the welfare state erodes traditional liberties. For example, Wyman v. James held that a social worker need not obtain a search warrant before visiting the home of a recipient of public assistance. 400 U.S. 309 (1971). According to the Court, the visit was not a search, in part because the social worker's purpose was to determine whether children were being treated well and in part because it was fair to condition public assistance on relinquishing some privacy. In other cases the Court has held that government agents need no warrants to search the premises of highly regulated businesses such as liquor sales, gun sales, and mining. Colonnade Catering Corp. v. United States, 397 U.S. 72 (1970); United States v. Biswell, 406 U.S. 311 (1972); Donovan v. Dewey, 452 U.S. 594 (1981).

These cases show that the welfare state can operate in ways that implicate traditional or core liberties and that the doctrinal tools to exert pressure on core liberties are as available here as were similar tools in the case of core property. Perhaps those tools have not been employed widely in liberty cases because those most protected by core liberties have enough political power to avoid the problems. Seen in this way, the positive law approach to liberty can be used to explore the Court's vision of the Constitution in the welfare state.

27. It does not make sense of them all. See, e.g., Memphis Light, Gas & Water Div. v. Craft, 436 U.S. 1 (1978).

One way of looking at the cases is this: when the Court wants to impose procedural requirements, it finds entitlements in positive law *and* natural law guarantees of liberty and property; when it does not want to impose such requirements, it finds no entitlements and ignores natural law arguments for liberty and property under the circumstances. In this perspective the interesting question becomes When does the Court want to impose procedural requirements?[28] The answer is that it does so when it is dealing with rationalized or—less significantly in this setting—professionalized bureaucracies. In the Court's view the Constitution regulates modern bureaucracies but not old-fashioned ones. As we will see, there are collateral doctrines that ameliorate the apparent perverseness of the incentives this view gives decision makers.

Two years after *Roth* the Court decided *Wolff v. McDonnell.*[29] Prisoners in Nebraska had been disciplined for violating prison rules and as a result lost "good time credit" that would have reduced the time they had to serve in prison. According to written regulations adopted by prison authorities, good time credits could be revoked only for serious misconduct. The prisoners claimed that the procedures for determining whether they had engaged in serious misconduct were inadequate. En route to agreeing with most of the prisoners' claims, the Court had to face the *Roth* question. It gave two reasons for holding that the prisoners had a liberty interest in good time credit. The state had "specifie[d] that [good time] is to be forfeited only for serious misconduct," and the prisoners' interest in shortening their sentences "had real substance." Thus, although "the liberty itself is a statutory creation of the State," due process was required in determining whether serious misconduct had occurred. Although the Court emphasized the state's creation of the interest in its positive law, the close relation between good time credit and the traditional liberty to walk the street allowed the Court to juxtapose the positive and natural law approaches.[30]

28. The positive law approach does have independent force, however, in cases where as a matter of state law entitlements are (more or less) clearly created. See, e.g., Greenholtz v. Inmates, 442 U.S. 1 (1979); Hewitt v. Helms, 459 U.S. 460 (1983). Yet the rhetoric of *Greenholtz* betrays a reluctance to find state law entitlements. See 442 U.S., pp. 9–11. Compare Bishop v. Wood, 426 U.S. 341 (1976) and Olim v. Wakinekona, 461 U.S. 238 (1983), in which the Court declined to interpret state law to create entitlements. Early comments on *Bishop* treated it as adopting the positivist approach, see, e.g., Monaghan, "Of 'Liberty,' " pp. 442–43. But the Court has instead treated it as relying on the trial court's bizarre interpretation of state law. It has therefore become a sport.

29. 418 U.S. 539 (1974).

30. See also Goss v. Lopez, 419 U.S. 565 (1975) (short-term suspension from schools subject to due process clause because state law created legitimate claim of entitlement to public education and because students' liberty to pursue higher education might be impaired). See Franklin Zimring and Rayman Solomon, "Goss v. Lopez: The Principle of the

Vitek v. Jones involved the transfer of a prisoner from a prison to a state mental institution. The prisoner had been convicted of robbery; shortly after he arrived at the prison he set his mattress on fire, and prison officials, believing him suicidal, transferred him to a mental hospital. The Court found that state statutes created a liberty interest in remaining in a prison when they identified specific grounds for transfer to a mental hospital: the state "grant[ed] ... a right or expectation that adverse action will not be taken against him except upon the occurrence of specified behavior."[31] In addition, even prisoners have a liberty interest in avoiding the further stigma that is imposed by being labeled mentally ill.[32]

In the cases discussed so far the Court holds the due process clauses applicable where it views decision makers as constrained by rules or professional norms and holds it inapplicable where it views decision makers as unconstrained.[33] Internal regulatory methods by which superiors control the discretion of subordinates gave rise to rights held by persons outside the bureaucracy. A series of cases in criminal procedure

Thing," in *In the Name of Children: Advocacy, Law Reform, and Public Policy* 449 (Robert Mnookin ed. 1985), for an interesting discussion of the background of the litigation.

31. 445 U.S. 480, 490–91 (1980).

32. Compare these cases with the prisoners' rights cases discussed in note 26. It would not have been difficult in the prisoners' rights cases to find natural law liberties. Nor would it have been difficult to interpret state law to create positive law entitlements; the statutes interpreted in *Goss v. Lopez* to create entitlements were no more directly relevant to the issue of entitlement than were those creating a system of parole in Jago v. Van Curen, 454 U.S. 14 (1981) (due process clause inapplicable to revocation of announced date for parole).

One popular reading of the distinction between the prisoners' rights cases and *Vitek* makes dispositive the presence of "specified grounds" in *Vitek*. See also Dixon v. Love, 431 U.S. 105 (1977) (summary suspension of driver's license for accumulating points based on traffic offenses, as specified in administrative rules, is constitutional). The idea is that hearings are useful to determine facts, but if the authorities need not make any factual determinations before acting, hearings are pointless.

This reading is flawed in two ways. First, a presentation at a hearing may affect the way a decision maker exercises discretion. See, e.g., Gagnon v. Scarpelli, 411 U.S. 778, 786–88 (1973). See Frank Michelman, "Formal and Associational Aims in Procedural Due Process," 18 *Nomos: Due Process* 126, 130, 143 (J. Roland Pennock and John Chapman eds. 1977). Second, every system of state law and administrative regulations contains enough leeway for the courts to find a "specific grounds" requirement if they want to. The Court could easily have interpreted the statutes in *Vitek* to give officials the discretion to decide whether their information about a prisoner's mental health justified a transfer to a mental hospital. That is only to drive home the point that neither *Roth* nor the alternatives are analytically dispositive.

33. All bureaucracies are to varying degrees politicized, rationalized, and professional. In some cases the Court emphasizes one rather than another facet of the bureaucracy, and in other cases it reverses the emphasis: Parole decisions are rationalized (*Wolff*), but not always (*Van Curen*); prisons are professionalized (*Vitek*) in some of their operations (*Meachum*). But what matters is that it is the idea of bureaucracy to which the Court is reacting.

also makes the existence of rules as a method of hierarchical control relevant to the decision of constitutional issues. Whereas rules give rise to rights that the courts enforce in the due process area, they insulate police agencies from external control in the criminal procedure area. That is, the central constitutional issue concerns the internal operation of bureaucracies not the relation between street-level officials and beneficiaries and clients. In effect the Court sees hierarchical control within the police agency as an alternative to hierarchical control by an external agency, the courts. This reinforces the argument that the Court envisions self-contained bureaucracies governed by internal rules and internalized professional norms.

The criminal procedure cases deal with searches. The hornbook law is that, subject to a limited number of exceptions, the police must obtain a warrant before they conduct a search. Some recent cases, invoking narrow exceptions, suggest a broader principle that no warrant is needed when the search is conducted pursuant to routine procedures whose effect is to place bounds on the discretion otherwise available to police officers. In *South Dakota v. Opperman*, the police towed Opperman's car to the police station after finding it parked in a no-parking zone and then conducted what was called a routine inventory search to determine what was in the car.[34] The bureaucratic rationale for inventory searches is that they protect the police against claims that some valuable object was stolen while the car was in police custody, that they allow the police to determine what actions are appropriate to protect the car from vandalism, and that they assure superiors that subordinates have no temptation to remove items from the car. Thus, the fact that the inventory search was "routine" disposed of Opperman's effort to exclude drugs found in the glove compartment: The drugs were admissible.[35]

In another line of cases the Court has considered a variety of efforts by police agencies to detect crimes that occur intermittently over a large area and for what amount to long periods: drunk driving, importation of undocumented aliens, and drug smuggling. The Court has held unconstitutional random stops of drivers for breath tests[36] and "roving checkpoints" at which officers stop some drivers who pass the point the officers

---

34. 428 U.S. 364 (1976).

35. The role of routine is confirmed by Illinois v. Lafayette, 462 U.S. 640 (1983), in which the Court found constitutional an inventory search of a backpack. Obviously the car search cases were not directly relevant, and securing the backpack unopened would have been simple. See also Colorado v. Bertine, 107 S. Ct. 738 (1987). For a general discussion of inventory searches, see United States v. Lyons, 706 F.2d 321 (D.C. Cir. 1983).

36. Delaware v. Prouse, 440 U.S. 648 (1979).

have chosen.[37] It has permitted stops at fixed checkpoints[38] and has strongly hinted that roadblocks could be established to screen all drivers for sobriety.[39] Although the cases can be reconciled in a number of ways, the discussion so far should make one of them obvious. The pairs of situations differ in the location of the authority to institute the stop. Line officers decide which cars to stop at random and which drivers to stop at roving checkpoints whose location they have chosen. In contrast, superior officers decide where to place a fixed checkpoint. In view of the public attention a sobriety roadblock will inevitably attract and considering their broader view of where drunk drivers are likely to be found, superior officers are also likely to decide where to put up the roadblocks.[40]

Occasionally the police do try to get search warrants. They go to a magistrate—usually but not necessarily a judge—and swear that they have certain information. If that information amounts to probable cause to believe that evidence is at the place the police want to search, the magistrate issues the warrant. The crucial step is the magistrate's evaluation of the information presented by the police. Sometimes the police rely on facts given to them by an outside informant. Over the years a complex set of rules developed to guide the evaluation of police statements relying on informants: The police had to give the magistrate enough information to allow him or her to evaluate the credibility of the informant—for example, that the informant had given information that had proved true in the past—and to evaluate the basis on which the informant rested the information—for example, that the informant had seen drugs at the location described. Further, some deficiencies in the informant's statements could be made up if the police said that they had confirmed the accuracy of some parts, even innocent details, of what the informant had told them.

---

37. Almeida-Sanchez v. United States, 413 U.S. 266 (1973).

38. United States v. Martinez-Fuerte, 428 U.S. 543 (1976).

39. Delaware v. Prouse, 440 U.S., p. 663.

40. Another line of cases involves businesses that are subject to limited regulations such as fire codes or occupational safety laws. See Marshall v. Barlow's, Inc., 436 U.S. 307 (1978). Although warrants are required to inspect these businesses, the Court has recognized that such laws can be enforced effectively only if the enforcement agency is able to make spot checks. It has suggested that the agency could use special kinds of warrants. For example, the agency could establish a program of inspecting business places in industries where the rate of accidental injury is highest. That is, the warrant would be issued not on the ground that there was probable cause to believe that the law had been violated but on the ground that the enforcement agency had a set of rules saying, in effect, that it was time for the place to be inspected. Notice that such rules, whatever their effect on business, allow superiors to check on the work of enforcers at the street level: They are, or at least can be used as, production quotas or measures for inspectors.

In *Illinois v. Gates* the Court did away with this elaborate rule structure.[41] The detailed rules, it said, should do no more than point out to magistrates some things they should think about before issuing warrants. Their decisions should be guided not by rules at all but by a general standard of reasonableness: Given what you know, the Court said to magistrates, decide whether as a commonsense matter it is reasonable to think that the evidence is where the police want to search. It further emphasized the deference appellate courts should give to the magistrate's initial determination of probable cause.

Rules and standards are alternative ways of regulating the activities of street-level bureaucrats such as police officers and magistrates. The pattern here treats the police force as a rationalized bureaucracy in which superiors have to control relatively unsophisticated line officers through relatively crude rules and the judiciary as a professionalized bureaucracy in which superiors can trust subordinates to exercise discretion appropriately because they all share a common ethos. *Gates* announces the Court's new understanding that magistrates are enough like judges to make it appropriate to subject them to control by professional norms rather than by rules whose use would be appropriate if magistrates were really like police officers.

Of course this pattern may be an artifact. The majority of the present Court does not like to restrict the activities of the police in conducting searches or in much else. It may simply be using whatever tools are within easy reach to validate what the police have done in the cases before the Court. Yet the pattern here can also be seen as part of a patchwork of doctrines from a large number of areas whose design is built upon the Court's preference for rationalized and professional bureaucracies.

If the Court has that preference, the criminal procedure cases make some sense. But the due process cases seem strange. They say to the politicized bureaucracy that its activities will be free of constitutional restraints and to the partially rationalized or professional one that because it has taken a few steps in adopting substantive rules, the Constitution forces it to go further and provide more procedures. This appears to create an incentive not to adopt substantive rules, which seems perverse in light of the Court's apparent preference for modern bureaucracies.[42] The perversity may not be real.

The process of modernizing bureaucracies—rationalizing or professionalizing them—may well be propelled by such strong forces that positive law creates legitimate claims of entitlement in all but minor backwaters of the

---

41. 462 U.S. 213 (1983).

42. For a judicial comment on the perversity of the incentive structure, see Miller v. Henman, 804 F.2d 421 (7th Cir. 1986).

welfare state. After all, the rules that create such claims often serve the interests not of recipients alone but of superiors in the bureaucracies who want to control their subordinates.[43] If the process of modernization goes far enough, the Court will ratify the procedures adopted by a fully modernized bureaucracy by holding that although process was due under *Roth*, the process provided was all that the Constitution required.

In addition, even old-fashioned bureaucracies must comply with the substantive provisions of the Constitution. The Court has gone further and has held that when such bureaucracies violate the Constitution they may be required to do more than modernized ones must do to make up for their deficiencies. *Hutto v. Finney* was a late stage in protracted litigation challenging as "cruel and unusual punishment" the dreadful conditions in the Arkansas prison system.[44] The trial court had directed that various changes be made in the system. The Supreme Court had before it only one part of that comprehensive order, a direction that no prisoner serve longer than thirty days in punitive confinement. The Court recognized that thirty days is not an unusually long period for punitive confinement in the abstract. Still, it expressly stated that the remedial order was appropriate in the context of the Arkansas case, precisely because the system had been so terrible before the courts acted. We might test the implications of *Hutto* by comparing Arkansas and a hypothetical neighboring state. In Arkansas prisoners cannot be placed in punitive confinement for more than thirty days. In the neighboring state prisons are minimally decent and have a rule allowing sixty or ninety days in punitive confinement. *Hutto* implies that a challenge to that rule would fail. Prison administrators in the neighboring state can therefore do things that those in Arkansas cannot solely because the Arkansas bureaucrats had not exercised sufficient control over their prisons. *Hutto* thus provides incentives to modernize in order to have the freedom accorded administrators of modern prisons but denied those of retrograde ones.[45]

---

43. It seems to me significant that immediately after the *Roth* decision the Regents of the University of Wisconsin adopted a detailed code establishing numerous procedures for notice and administrative review of decisions not to renew contracts. They did so not because the Constitution required them to but because the University had grown so large that rationalization of employment procedures was necessary if the University was to operate smoothly and because the professoriat at the University was disturbed at the Supreme Court's endorsement of the Regents' claim that they were free to act arbitrarily. The desire to rationalize employment procedures also lies behind the willingness of sophisticated university administrators to deal with faculty unions. Cf. Katherine Stone, "The Post-War Paradigm in Labor Law," 90 *Yale Law Journal* 1509 (1981).

44. 437 U.S. 678 (1978).

45. In addition, judges developing plans to remedy unconstitutional conditions are likely to look to professional standards such as those developed by the American Correctional

Finally, there are two important doctrinal devices that provide incentives to modernize. The first gives incentives to depoliticize the bureaucracy, the second incentives to rationalize it.

During the 1820s and 1830s Andrew Jackson and his political allies created the American spoils system, in which government jobs down to the lowest level were given to political supporters of those in power. After the Civil War middle-class reformers, concerned in part about the inefficiency of the spoils system and in part about the fact that new political forces dominated by immigrants had taken over the system, fought to establish a professional civil service. Government jobs were to be allocated on the basis of merit, and civil servants would be protected against dismissal on the basis of their political affiliations. Almost a century later the Supreme Court discovered that this program was part of the Constitution. In *Elrod v. Burns* the newly elected Republican Sheriff of Cook County, Illinois, dismissed a number of deputies because they were Democrats.[46] A divided Supreme Court held that such patronage dismissals violated the first amendment: Political affiliation could not be used as a ground for governmental action of that sort. It could justify patronage dismissals of policy-making bureaucrats, although that class might be narrowly defined,[47] but not of ordinary street-level bureaucrats.[48]

Elrod disqualifies adherence to a common political program as a mechanism by which superiors can control the exercise of discretion by subordinates in an established bureaucracy.[49] As soon as the "outs" displace the "ins," other methods of control—rules or professional norms—will have to be developed. Indeed it is probably significant that *Elrod* arose in Cook County, where the dominance of a single party had prevented that displacement for many years; elsewhere the rotation of ins and outs proba-

---

Association. Such standards provide ready-made criteria in areas with which the judges may not be familiar. *Hutto* and related lower-court cases, e.g., Ramos v. Lamm, 639 F.2d 559 (10th Cir. 1980), cert. denied, 450 U.S. 1041 (1980); Williams v. Edwards, 547 F.2d 1206 (5th Cir. 1977), imply that it is within the trial court's discretion to require that those standards be met. Yet failing to meet any individual standard does not itself violate the Constitution. See text accompanying note 79.

46. 427 U.S. 347 (1976).

47. See Branti v. Finkel, 445 U.S. 507 (1980).

48. The Court suggested that political affiliation might be a permissible basis for initial appointment to a street-level position, which of course gives those temporarily in power an incentive to create new bureaucracies.

49. It also disqualifies a more obvious but less interesting mechanism of control: removal pursuant to the unchecked discretion of a superior. The threat of a lawsuit based on a claim that the removal was motivated by impermissible political concerns will induce superiors to develop a more rule-oriented system.

For a discussion of the implications of *Elrod* for politically motivated hiring decisions, see Messer v. Curci, 806 F.2d 667, 670–73 (6th Cir. 1986) (Boggs, J., dissenting).

bly made it almost essential to depoliticize the bureaucracy so that it could operate smoothly during and after political transitions.

The ins in superior positions might be uncomfortable even with *Elrod*'s limited concession to political appointments, for they have no guarantee that their appointees will continue to adhere to what might well be a political program that changes as different factions displace each other. *Elrod* depoliticizes decisions to fire street-level bureaucrats. Superiors would like to depoliticize the daily operation of the bureaucracy as well. Statutes such as the Hatch Act severely limit the kinds of political activity in which street-level bureaucrats can engage. Under this act and its state counterparts, such bureaucrats cannot hold party office, raise money for parties, or run for office under a party label. The Supreme Court has held that these restrictions on political activity do not violate the first amendment rights of street-level bureaucrats.[50]

Taken together *Elrod* and the Hatch Act cases give bureaucratic superiors good reasons to try to regulate the behavior of subordinates by rules and professional norms.[51] They thereby offset to some extent the pressure *Roth* exerts in the opposite direction.

50. Civil Service Comm. v. National Association of Letter Carriers, 413 U.S. 548 (1973). Its rhetoric suggests that the restrictions are not only permissible but are also wise and sensible attempts to depoliticize the bureaucracy: The decision "confirm[s] the judgment of history . . . that it is in the best interest of the country, indeed essential, that federal service should depend upon meritorious performance rather than political service, and that the political influence of federal employees on others and on the electoral process should be limited . . .

"It seems fundamental in the first place that employees in the Executive Branch of the Government, or those working for any of its agencies, should administer the law in accordance with the will of Congress, rather than in accordance with their own or the will of a political party. They are expected to enforce the law and execute the programs of the Government without bias or favoritism for or against any political party or group or the members thereof. A major thesis of the Hatch Act is that to serve this great end of Government—the impartial execution of the laws—it is essential that federal employees, for example, not take formal positions in political parties, not undertake to play substantial roles in partisan political campaigns, and not run for office on partisan political tickets. Forbidding activities like these will reduce the hazards to fair and effective government . . .

"A related concern, and this remains as important as any other, was to further serve the goal that employment and advancement in the Government service not depend on political performance, and at the same time to make sure that Government employees would be free from pressure and from express or tacit invitation to vote in a certain way or perform political chores in order to curry favor with their superiors rather than to act out their own beliefs." Id., pp. 557, 564–65, 566.

51. Under Pickering v. Board of Education, 391 U.S. 563 (1968), and Givhan v. Consolidated Sch. Dist., 439 U.S. 410 (1979), subordinates can complain both inside and outside the bureaucracy about their superiors' substantive policies. Apparently the Constitution does not require that they be allowed to complain about personnel policies or to organize co-workers to oppose their superiors. See Connick v. Myers, 461 U.S. 138 (1983). That is,

If the civil service cases provide incentives to depoliticize bureaucracies, another set provides incentives to regularize their operations. A federal civil rights statute says that people whose constitutional rights have been taken from them by state officials may recover money damages from those officials. As the Supreme Court has developed the law of damages, two elements make it sensible for officials to follow routines. Individual bureaucrats have to pay damages only if they did not act in good faith.[52] *Good faith* is defined as a reasonable belief that the actions were constitutional. A bureaucrat would be well positioned to assert the good faith defense if he or she had acted in accordance with preestablished rules, especially if those rules had been cleared with legal counsel to the agency.[53]

In addition, a person whose rights were violated must show that the violation had caused his or her injuries. For example, *Mt. Healthy School District v. Doyle* involved a teacher who had been fired.[54] The teacher was a union activist who had criticized the school board quite vociferously. There also was evidence that he had physically abused some students and disobeyed reasonable orders given him by his principal. The Court held that he could recover damages for the firing if he showed that his union activities, protected by the first amendment, had been one reason for the firing, but that the school board would win if it showed that he would have been fired anyway because of his disruptive behavior. In the latter instance the violation of rights would not have caused any injury. This rule of causation gives bureaucrats reasons to develop "paper trails" that will allow them to establish the "it would have happened anyway" defense. An important part of a paper trail will be a set of procedures that the bureaucrat followed before acting. Further, the defense will be easier to establish if bureaucrats have at hand a set of previously developed substantive standards against which the subordinate's performance can be measured.

The Supreme Court undoubtedly does not think of these various rules as providing incentives to depoliticize, rationalize, and professionalize the bureaucracies of the welfare state. Nor is it important to establish that

---

subordinates are not protected by the Constitution when they engage in "office politics," thus giving their superiors an even stronger hand in their control.

52. Harlow v. Fitzgerald, 457 U.S. 800 (1982).

53. Under Monell v. Department of Social Services, 436 U.S. 658 (1978), and Owen v. City of Independence, 445 U.S. 622 (1980), the city or agency—that is, the taxpayers—might be liable to pay damages for adopting unconstitutional rules. Such liability indirectly affects bureaucrats' incentives to adopt better rules to the extent that they fear the consequences of a taxpayer revolt.

54. 429 U.S. 274 (1977).

bureaucracies respond to these, or any other, incentives. Rather these rules help fill in the patchwork that is the Court's vision of the welfare state bureaucracy. In that vision the Constitution does not disrupt the operation of bureaucracy; it may even facilitate it, because bureaucracy is already depoliticized and rationalized or professionalized.

What Process Is Due?

Goldberg v. Kelly decided two issues. It held that due process was required when a state sought to terminate public assistance payments, and it defined the process that was due. The state in *Goldberg* had a formal system of appeals, in which the beneficiary could present oral evidence and cross-examine witnesses, that could be taken after assistance payments were ended. The issue in *Goldberg* was therefore what the state had to do before ending the payments. Under state law the recipient was given notice of the reasons for termination at least seven days before the payments were to end and could submit a written statement about why the payments should continue. Although the Supreme Court said that "the pretermination hearing need not take the form of a judicial or quasi-judicial trial," it actually imposed almost all of the characteristics of such trials.[55] Just as the notion of new property rested on an appeal to tradition in defining what interests are important, so here the Court reverted to the only model at hand, the traditional judicial trial, to define the characteristics of the process that was due.

The traditional trial provided a checklist that the Court could work through in any new property situation. Thus, in *Morrissey v. Brewer* the Court considered the procedures required to revoke parole. It analogized the preliminary decision to the pretermination hearing in *Goldberg* and required notice, the opportunity to appear in person and present evidence, and a decision "by someone not directly involved in the case."[56] At the revocation hearing itself more elaborate procedures were required.[57]

55. 397 U.S., p. 266. The hearing did not have to produce "a complete record and comprehensive opinion," but the beneficiary had to have "an effective opportunity to defend by confronting any adverse witnesses and by presenting his own arguments and evidence orally," with the assistance of an attorney "if he so desires," and the impartial decision maker should state the reasons for the decision. Id., pp. 267–71.

56. 408 U.S. 471, 485–87 (1972).

57. Again the two-step of disclaiming reliance on the judicial trial and then requiring it occurred: "We cannot write a code of procedure . . . Our task is limited to deciding the minimum requirements of due process. They include (a) written notice of the claimed violations of parole; (b) disclosure to the parolee of evidence against him; (c) opportunity to be heard in person and to present witnesses and documentary evidence; (d) the right to confront and cross-examine adverse witnesses (unless the hearing officer specifically finds

In both *Goldberg* and *Morrissey* the Court said that it was reluctant to require judicial trials because, as *Morrissey* put it, "creat[ing] an inflexible structure ... [would] impose a great burden" on the state's new property and liberty systems. That is precisely the motivation that led to the adoption of *Roth*'s entitlement theory. And just as *Roth* limited the scope of the due process clause out of concern for stifling the development of new property systems, so *Goldberg*'s reliance on the judicial trial as a model succumbed to pressures arising from the same concerns. The Court wrote: "As the scope of governmental action expands into new areas creating new controversies for judicial review, it is incumbent on courts to design procedures that protect the rights of the individual without unduly burdening the legitimate efforts of the states to deal with difficult social problems. The judicial model for factfinding for all constitutionally protected interests, regardless of their nature, can turn rational decisionmaking into an unmanageable enterprise."[58]

These pressures led to *Mathews v. Eldridge*.[59] Eldridge received disability benefits from the Social Security system. In 1972 he filled out a questionnaire regarding his present medical condition. On receiving Eldridge's answers, the agency administering the benefits obtained reports from his doctor and from a psychiatric consultant. This information led the agency to decide that Eldridge was no longer disabled. It notified him of its proposed termination of benefits, which he disputed in a letter. The agency then made the termination of benefits final. Eldridge challenged the agency's procedures, claiming that *Goldberg* required a pretermination evidentiary hearing. The Court rejected the challenge[60] and adopted as an alternative the following test:

> Identification of the specific dictates of due process generally requires consideration of three distinct factors: First, the private interest that will be affected by the official action; second, the risk of an erroneous deprivation of such interest through the procedures used, and the probable value, if any, of

good cause for not allowing confrontation); (e) a "neutral and detached" hearing body such as a traditional parole board, members of which need not be judicial officers or lawyers; and (f) a written statement by the factfinders as to the evidence relied on and reasons for revoking parole. We emphasize that there is no thought to equate this second stage of parole revocation to a criminal prosecution in any sense." Id., pp. 488–89.

58. Parham v. J.R., 442 U.S. 584, 608 n. 16 (1979).

59. 424 U.S. 319 (1976).

60. The Supreme Court distinguished *Goldberg* on a number of grounds: disability benefits are not based on need, and their termination would therefore not drive former recipients over the edge of subsistence-level income; disability decisions are based primarily on medical evidence usually contained in written materials not subject to serious challenges to credibility that in-person presentation and cross-examination can expose. Id., pp. 333, 340.

additional or substitute procedural safeguards; and finally, the Government's interest, including the function involved and the fiscal and administrative burdens that the additional or substitute procedural requirement would entail.[61]

Eldridge adopted an explicitly utilitarian test of due process.[62] This test is entirely consistent with the essentially technocratic vision of bureaucracies that the Court holds. The traditional model of the judicial trial provided the Court with some guidance in deciding what process was due. One would begin with that model and ask whether particular departures were justified by the circumstances. For example, the Court held that the right to confront adverse witnesses could be limited in prison disciplinary hearings where there was reason to think that the witnesses might be physically harmed by retaliation.[63] In contrast, the utilitarian approach gives the Court no such guidance.[64] The Court is then driven to seat-of-the-robes assessments of the way the world operates and would operate if things were different. These assessments lead in turn to a pair of characteristic judgments: that the professionals making the street-level decisions can be trusted, and that the professionals in charge of the system as a whole can be trusted to adopt procedures that the courts should acknowledge as all the Constitution requires.

Heckler v. Campbell illustrates the second point.[65] The Social Security Administration operates the federal disability system. Under that system people are defined as disabled if they have medical or physical impairments that make them unable to perform substantial gainful work "which exists in the national economy." The Administration processes an enormous number of claims. Prior to 1978 it relied on evidence introduced at hearings to determine whether work existed in the national economy for people with the disabilities the claimants had. "Although this testimony often was based on standardized guides, vocational experts frequently were criticized for their inconsistent treatment of similarly situated claimants." In 1978 the Administration replaced the use of testimony with a set of guidelines in the form of a grid. After identifying the claimant's disability, age, education, and work experience, the administrative law judge

61. Id., p. 335.

62. See Frank Easterbrook, "Substance and Due Process," 1982 *Supreme Court Review* 85, 122; Jerry Mashaw, "The Supreme Court's Due Process Calculus for Administrative Adjudication in *Mathews v. Eldridge*: Three Factors in Search of a Theory of Value," 44 *University of Chicago Law Review* 28, 47 (1976).

63. Wolff v. McDonnell, 418 U.S. 539 (1974).

64. Cf. Mashaw, "Three Factors," p. 55 (analogous problem in justifying departures from traditional model where there is no guidance as to which traditional procedures are apposite to the novel problem).

65. 461 U.S. 458 (1983).

consults the relevant box in the grid to find out whether there are jobs in the national economy for such a person. The Supreme Court upheld the grid as a reasonable form of rule making regarding "general factual issue[s]." The grid introduced uniformity in an overburdened system and, notably, rationalized the behavior of administrative law judges in accordance with expert determinations made at higher levels of the bureaucracy.

The Court's judgments play out as deference to professionals in bureaucracies. They are not expressed, as a general theory of judicial restraint might suggest they would be, as deference to the will of the majority as embodied in the decisions of the representative legislatures that established the bureaucracies that adopted the procedures at issue.[66] The imagery of professionalism, not that of democracy, makes more sense of the situation.

The link between the utilitarian test of *Eldridge* and deference to professional judgments can be seen in cases involving the rules of evidence in bureaucratic hearings and the right to counsel at such hearings.[67] *Richardson v. Perales* makes the professionalism of bureaucratic decision makers important with respect to rules of evidence.[68] Perales applied for disability benefits. After he filed his claim the agency arranged for an examination by an orthopedic specialist, whose report, according to the Court, "was devastating from [Perales'] standpoint." The report said that Perales was "obviously holding back" and "exaggerat[ing] his difficulties." Relying on this report and rejecting evaluations by Perales' own doctor, the agency denied Perales' claim. When Perales requested reconsideration, the agency arranged for an examination by a psychiatrist, who found that Perales had a paranoid personality but was not disabled by a psychiatric illness. At Perales' request a hearing was held. The hearing examiner considered these medical reports over Perales' objection that he had no opportunity to cross-examine the doctors. The examiner called the reports, and other reports introduced by Perales, "objective medical evidence" and concluded that Perales was not disabled.

---

66. The chain between the electorate and the rules is far too long to make a generalized theory of judicial restraint at all plausible under the circumstances. But see Easterbrook, "Substance and Due Process," pp. 118–19. See also Withrow v. Larkin, 421 U.S. 35 (1975) (upholding power of state examining board to investigate, prosecute, and decide cases of professional misconduct; combination of functions does not violate due process; issue is "substantial" but wide variety of solutions is necessary given "the incredible variety of administrative mechanisms in this country").

67. See also Schweiker v. McClure, 456 U.S. 188 (1982) (upholding system in which hearing officers were chosen by, and most had previously been employed by, insurance companies whose decisions were being challenged by patients).

68. 402 U.S. 389 (1971).

Justice Blackmun's opinion for the Supreme Court found that it did not violate due process to rely on these documents to deny the claim. The Court enumerated "a number of factors" to support its conclusion. The first was that the reports were prepared by doctors who examined Perales. Although some of the doctors were paid by the agency, the Court could not "ascribe bias to the work of these independent physicians, or any interest on their part in the outcome of the administrative proceeding beyond the professional curiosity a dedicated medical man [*sic*] possesses." Their reports were detailed and rested on standard procedures. Further, to require oral testimony by the doctors would, in light of the size of the disability system, "be a substantial drain ... on the energy of physicians already in short supply."[69]

Lassiter v. Department of Social Services shows how seat-of-the-robes judgments of fairness get made, in connection with the right to counsel.[70] Lassiter's son William had been placed in foster care in 1975 after a court found that she had not provided him with proper medical care. A year later Lassiter was convicted of second-degree murder; the death had occurred during a fight between Lassiter's mother and the victim, in which Lassiter joined. While she was in prison the Department filed a petition to terminate Lassiter's parental rights because she had not had contact with William since 1975 and had not tried to strengthen her relationship with him or plan for his future. A hearing was held at which the Department was represented by a lawyer and Lassiter was not. The Department presented one witness, who described Lassiter's case by relying on agency records and repeated comments about Lassiter that her neighbors had made. The judge offered to allow Lassiter to cross-examine, but Lassiter, unfamiliar with the rules of evidence, found it impossible to do so. Lassiter and her mother testified that Lassiter's mother was willing to raise William. During the hearing the trial judge was occasionally impatient with Lassiter's labored efforts to show that she had indeed planned for William's future.

Lassiter claimed that she should have been provided counsel at the termination hearing. Rejecting that claim, the Court divided its analysis into three steps. First, it reviewed the precedents on the right to counsel and concluded that an unconditional right exists only if the litigant might lose his or her physical liberty at the conclusion of the hearing. Second, it evaluated the general class of termination cases in light of *Eldridge* and

---

69. Id., pp. 402–6. See also Califano v. Yamasaki, 442 U.S. 682 (1979) (oral hearing required when claimant requests that recoupment of overpaid benefits should be waived because claimant was not at fault and recoupment would be "against equity and good conscience").

70. 452 U.S. 18 (1981).

the presumption against a right to counsel. The parent had a "command-ing" interest in retaining parental rights and avoiding criminal charges predicated on the activity giving rise to the proceeding; the state had an interest in the child's welfare and so "share[d] the parent's interest in an accurate and just decision"; the state's interest in keeping costs down by not paying counsel was legitimate but not very strong; finally, the issues in termination proceedings were sometimes complex, and often had to be developed through the testimony of parents "with little education . . . thrust into a distressing and disorienting situation." Sometimes these interests would come out on balance to favor the appointment of counsel, but they would not always be "distributed" so that the balance came out that way. Thus there was no unconditional right to counsel in termination cases. Rather the issue was to be decided on a case-by-case basis.[71]

The Court's third step was to analyze whether in the case before it Lassiter should have been provided counsel. It concluded that "the trial court did not err in failing to appoint counsel." The case was procedurally and substantively simple.[72] By speaking of the state's interest in child welfare and by treating the social worker's evidence as substantial, the Court acted on an implicit understanding that child welfare bureaucracies operate as professional norms say they should.[73]

71. Id., pp. 27–31. If this analysis is taken seriously, *Eldridge* eliminates the possibility that the Constitution requires that any procedures, not just counsel, be provided in an entire class of cases. It will never be true that the *Eldridge* factors are distributed in every case in any class so that the balance inevitably tips in favor of providing the procedure at issue. This point is driven home by the rhetorical skill with which Justice Stewart's opinion for the Court avoided the usual trap of balancing tests, into which *Eldridge* itself fell, of manipulat-ing the characterization of interests to determine the result. Instead the opinion gave maxi-mum weight to the parent's interest and minimized the state's. If an unconditional right cannot be justified under these circumstances, it never could be. See id., pp. 49–51 (Black-mun, J., dissenting).

72. Hearsay evidence was admitted, and some arguments were not developed as well as a lawyer might have developed them. But the arguments would have failed because the contrary evidence, though controverted, was substantial. Id., pp. 32–33.

73. In Walters v. National Association of Radiation Survivors, 473 U.S. 305 (1985), the Court upheld a statutory limitation on fees that attorneys can charge for representing claimants before the Veterans Administration. Its opinion emphasized the "rational pater-nalism" of the bureaucracy and the values of informal representation in the mass processing of claims. In Smith v. OFFER, 431 U.S. 816 (1977), the Court upheld procedures for the removal of children from foster homes. A footnote in the opinion stated, "In assessing the likelihood of erroneous decisions by the agency in the absence of elaborate hearing proce-dures, the fact that the agency bears primary responsibility for the welfare of the child and maintains, through its caseworkers, constant contact with the foster family is relevant." The natural parents and children could be excluded from the hearing "since the foster parents and the agency, through its caseworkers, will usually be most knowledgeable about condi-tions in the foster home." Id., pp. 850–51 n. 58.

Of course not every due process case since *Eldridge* has relied explicitly on the view of bureaucracies as professionalized, nor has a strong version of that view been implicit in every case. Further, some of the references to professional norms are undoubtedly a little quirky. For example, *Perales'* emphasis on trusting doctors rather obviously stems from Justice Blackmun's well-known sympathy with doctors, derived from his experience as counsel to the Mayo Clinic. Nonetheless, the general pattern is clear enough to warrant identifying it as a significant part of the Court's general view of the world.

That pattern leads to decisions that whatever due process requires, it was provided by the agency. That is not because utilitarian balancing is such a complicated process as to be beyond the competence of the courts but within the competence of majoritarian legislatures. Rather the agency's procedures satisfy due process because the agency is a professionalized bureaucracy. Notice how these cases combine with the *Roth* line of cases to yield the conclusion that no procedures are required beyond those chosen by the agency: Either there is no entitlement and therefore no right to any additional process or there is an entitlement protected by the procedures already provided. If the approach to the problem through positive law was forgone explicitly, it was followed in another form.

Parham v. J.R. is illustrative.[74] There the Court rejected claims that Georgia's procedures by which parents and state agencies with custody over children committed them "voluntarily" to mental institutions were unconstitutional. Under state law guardians filed applications for hospitalization. The child was observed, and if the superintendent of the hospital decided that the child was mentally ill, the child could be admitted. Although not required to do so by state statutes, most of the institutions conducted periodic reviews of each child to determine whether institutionalization should continue. The reviews were done by the medical and professional staff; less frequent reviews were conducted by a different set of staff personnel.

Chief Justice Burger's opinion for the Court is replete with references to the use of "medical knowledge . . . to ameliorate the human tragedies of seriously disturbed children" and the like. The Court applied the *Eldridge* test and concluded that a "neutral factfinder" had to determine whether the child was mentally ill, taking into account all available evidence, and whether there was a continuing need for commitment. "A staff physician will suffice," and "informal, traditional medical investigative techniques" could be used. "What is best for a child is an individual medical decision

74. 442 U.S. 584 (1979).

that must be left to the judgment of physicians in each case." Although doctors are fallible, "the shortcomings of specialists can[not] always be avoided by shifting the decision from a trained specialist using the traditional tools of medical science to an untrained judge." Some had charged that parents often "dumped" unruly children into state institutions. But "it is unrealistic to believe that trained psychiatrists, skilled in eliciting responses, sorting medically relevant facts, and sensing motivational nuances will often be deceived." The Court acknowledged that medical decision making is not "error-free" but was satisfied that on balance "an independent medical decisionmaking process" protected children enough to satisfy due process. It summarized its views: "The State, through its mental health programs, provides the authority for trained professionals to assist parents in examining, diagnosing, and treating emotionally disturbed children. Through its hiring practices, it provides well-staffed and well-equipped hospitals and . . . conscientious public employees to implement the State's beneficent purposes."[75]

With *Parham v. J.R.* we near the point at which professional behavior coincides with the requirements of the Constitution. Georgia's procedures were adequate precisely because they committed decisions to professionals.[76]

Professional Norms and Substantive Law

So far we have seen the near-merger of professional norms and constitutional rights in the setting of procedural due process. Sometimes the Court has gone further and adopted professional norms as substantive rules of constitutional law.

There is a hint of this further adoption in *Parham v. J.R.* The Court devoted much of its analysis to balancing the *Eldridge* factors, which included the interests of parents. But the litigants there also included a class of children who were wards of the state. The majority held that this fact did not affect the outcome of the balance. Although no adult might care deeply about the children, there was a statutory presumption that the state acted in the children's best interest. This was buttressed by the "extensive written records that are compiled about each child while in the State's custody."[77] Thus, social workers become just like parents.

75. Id., pp. 599, 607–9, 611, 613, 616.

76. See also Barry v. Barchi, 443 U.S. 55 (1979) (summary suspension of horse trainer by state racing board, based on test revealing drugs in horse's blood, constitutional, but prompt postsuspension hearing required).

77. 442 U.S., pp. 618–19.

Another mental health case is more explicit. Nicolas Romeo, a profoundly retarded man, was involuntarily committed to a state institution
for the retarded.[78] At the institution he was injured many times, both by
other residents and by his own actions. Eventually he was transferred to
the institution's hospital, where he was physically restrained for part of
each day. Romeo claimed that involuntary commitment without appropriate treatment and under circumstances leading to both direct physical
harm and deterioration of his mental condition was unconstitutional. A
unanimous Supreme Court agreed in substantial measure. It concluded
that Romeo's right extended to training which served to ensure his safety
and his freedom from undue restraint.

The Court also noted that Romeo's interests had to be balanced
against state interests, for example in restraining him in order to avoid
injury to other residents. In striking that balance the Court held that the
Constitution requires "deference to the judgment exercised by a qualified professional." If such a professional in fact exercised professional
judgment in deciding to restrain him, Romeo's rights were not violated.
This would limit "interference by the federal judiciary with the internal
operations of these institutions." A professional's decision violates a
resident's rights "only when the decision . . . is such a substantial departure from accepted professional judgment, practice or standards as to
demonstrate that the person responsible actually did not base the decision on such a judgment."[79] Here the Constitution requires what professionals think appropriate.[80]

78. Youngberg v. Romeo, 457 U.S. 307 (1982).

79. Id., p. 323. A footnote defined "professional" as "a person competent, whether by
education, training, or experience to make the decision." Long-term decisions should be
made by people with medical or nursing degrees or with appropriate training. Day-to-day
decisions could be made by staff under the supervision of professionals.

80. More precisely, it requires that professionals exercise professional judgment. The
psychiatrists in *Romeo* would not be liable simply because their decisions were at odds with
those recommended by a majority of psychiatrists. Only decisions so extreme as to be
unprofessional give rise to liability. Where professional judgment is constrained by politicians' failure to provide resources, *Romeo* held that psychiatrists who do not exercise
professional judgment are not individually liable for damages. Id., p. 323. Here the bureaucracy is seen, in one version, as a professional agency unfortunately at the mercy of external
political forces and, in another version, as an agency composed of deskilled professionals.
See text accompanying note 88. If the psychiatrists themselves were political hacks, that is, if
the bureaucracy had been a politicized agency, they would have been individually liable.

Similarly, the Court has rejected the contention that a prison violates the Constitution by
imposing "cruel and unusual punishment" simply because it fails to comply with standards
developed by the professional association of prison administrators. Rhodes v. Chapman,
452 U.S. 337 (1981). (One reason to reject that contention was discussed by Justice Rehnquist in staying an order to remedy prison conditions in Atiyeh v. Capps, 449 U.S. 1312
[1981]: Professional standards are to some extent efforts by the profession to secure re-

The Supreme Court's rules in abortion cases also incorporate the judgments of professionals and indeed of their associations. The basic abortion decisions held that states had only a narrow authority to protect the health of the woman who chose to have an abortion.[81] They allowed the states to do so, in 1972, by requiring that abortions in the second trimester of pregnancy be performed in hospitals. That requirement was consistent with the positions taken at that time by the American Public Health Association and the American College of Obstetricians and Gynecologists.[82] Eleven years later the Court considered a ban on second-trimester abortions performed in clinics rather than hospitals.[83] During the intervening years the two professional associations had changed their positions and by 1983 found no health purpose served by a hospitals-only requirement.[84] The Court relied heavily on the recommendations of these professional associations in finding unconstitutional a hospitals-only ordinance that fit the requirements the Court had laid down just eleven years before.

This section does not offer a universal explanatory theory for these cases but rather identifies a theme, latent in some cases and openly expressed in others, of deference to professional judgments. The material to this point strongly suggests that the Court has a vision of the welfare state in which professional and rationalized bureaucracies are the norms, both in the sense that most bureaucracies are professional and rationalized and in the sense that bureaucracies ought to be so. It remains to reflect on that vision.

The Repoliticized Bureaucracy as an Alternative

Some of the normative force behind the Court's vision comes from the fact that the vision evokes a sense that things are really like that vision and that the law has to accommodate reality. Yet things are often not like that at all. The bureaucracies of the welfare state are indeed heavily rule

---

sources beyond those available through the usual political process. Prison administrators who wish to upgrade their institutions can use such standards to beat their Governors with or to shame the Governors into increasing the prison budget.)

Yet neither of these rules repudiates professionalism as a constitutional norm. They refuse to impose the norms established by an external body but still treat the psychiatrists and jailers at the institutions involved in the litigation as professionals not political hacks.

81. Roe v. Wade, 410 U.S. 113 (1973); Doe v. Bolton, 410 U.S. 179 (1973).

82. City of Akron v. Akron Center for Reproductive Health, 462 U.S. 416 (1983).

83. Id.

84. Indeed, the American College of Obstetricians and Gynecologists had changed its position after the Akron ordinance had been passed and a challenge to its constitutionality initiated.

governed, but they operate without substantial regard to professional norms.[85] The Court has thus developed a constitutional law for an imaginary society and has sought to persuade us that the imaginary world is our own.[86]

One theme resounds through the literature on street-level professionals in bureaucracies.[87] They are regularly constrained—by inadequate resources, the incredible numbers of decisions they are therefore required to make, and the complexity of the decisions were professional norms honored—to process cases routinely and to forget about trying to do the job they were taught to do in school. Their jobs have become deskilled and they have been made into proletarians.[88] Mental health professionals in public hospitals are reduced to administering drugs and retain their connection to their professional roots by calling doing nothing at all, which is all they can do, "environmental therapy." Indeed the Court in *Romeo* recognized all this when it held that a professional could not be held liable for monetary damages where his or her failure to exercise professional judgment resulted from inadequate resources.[89] These conditions characterize what social workers do in public assistance agencies, what teachers do in schools, and even what police officers do in keeping the peace.[90]

On one level the image the Court offers us is entirely accurate. Bureaucracies are shot through with deskilled employees; superiors make decisions based on personalities; beneath the surface of bureaucratic rules lies a dense network of personal associations that is what really lets the

85. For a discussion in the context of child welfare programs, see W. Norton Grubb and Marvin Lazerson, *Broken Promises: How Americans Fail Their Children* 114–26 (1982). An examination of the legal setting that has strong parallels to the discussion in this chapter is Burt, "Constitution of the Family," although Burt is concerned with a different normative program than I. For a consideration of Burt's program, see Chapter 4.

86. Because the Court endorses the decisions of actually existing institutions, its actions cannot be defended as attempts to bring those institutions into alignment with some ideals the Court holds.

87. Samuel Beer, "Political Overload and Federalism," 10 *Polity* 5, 9 (1977); Douglas Yates, *Bureaucratic Democracy: The Search for Democracy and Efficiency in American Government* 71–72, 95–96 (1982).

88. See, e.g., Harry Braverman, *Labor and Monopoly Capital: The Degradation of Work in the Twentieth Century* (1974); *Case Studies on the Labor Process* (Andrew Zimbalist ed. 1979). The courts are not immune from these tendencies. See Wolf Heydebrand, "The Technocratic Administration of Justice," 2 *Research in Law and Sociology* 29 (1979).

89. 457 U.S., p. 323.

90. See, e.g., James Wilson, *Varieties of Police Behavior: The Management of Law and Order in Eight Communities* 16–34 (1968); William Westley, *Violence and the Police* 56–61 (1970).

bureaucracy operate. On the level of cultural understanding, though, rationality and professionalism seem to characterize modern society. Translated into systematic theories, that understanding produces cost-benefit analysis and the utilitarian ways of thinking that pervade the law of due process.

Important commentators regard the utilitarian and technocratic way of thinking as unattractive. Jerry Mashaw and Frank Michelman have offered an alternative in which the provision of due process is a value in itself.[91] This alternative treats procedures as giving people chances to participate in the operation of the institutions that affect them. In Mashaw's view participation recognizes the dignity and autonomy of the individual; in Michelman's view it is a form of association that promotes the values of fraternity. Neither version of the participatory alternative is satisfactory.

Michelman and Mashaw could defend their alternatives as protecting the utilitarian individual interest in being treated in ways that those subjected to the procedure believe are fair.[92] The idea is that people who lose (and those who win) will feel better after losing (or winning) if they believe that the results were generated by a process in which they had a fair shot at winning (or losing).

As a formal statement of what utilitarianism requires this seems correct. That it will have any effect on outcomes under *Eldridge* is questionable. It seems likely that the interest in winning will usually be overwhelmingly larger than the interest in good feeling. Occasionally losers will walk away feeling less bad if they lost after a full hearing than they would have if they had lost after a summary proceeding; they are unlikely to feel *much* "less bad," and winners are unlikely to feel worse winning in a summary proceeding. Thus the increment that the participatory interest contributes to the *Eldridge* balance seems likely to be small.[93]

91. Mashaw, "Three Factors"; Jerry Mashaw, "Administrative Due Process: The Quest for a Dignitary Theory," 61 *Boston University Law Review* 885 (1981); Michelman, "Formal and Associational Aims"; Martin Redish and Lawrence Marshall, "Adjudicatory Independence and the Values of Procedural Due Process," 95 *Yale Law Journal* 455, 481–91 (1986).

92. See, e.g., Laycock, "Due Process," pp. 885, 887 ("sense of unfair treatment"); Mashaw, "Three Factors," p. 48. This follows Mashaw's criticism of the Court's balancing of the interests it did identify, id., pp. 38–45. See also Michelman, "Formal and Associational Aims," p. 147. Mashaw, "Dignitary Theory," argues that the premises of liberal political theory support only an extremely thin theory of participatory governance. See, e.g., id., pp. 887. 922, 926–29.

93. This account may also trade on an intuition that is misplaced here. Perhaps a utilitarian could get somewhere by including the participatory interest in deciding whether

In contemporary bureaucracies, however, informal procedures are likely to serve ends other than dignity and association anyway. There is, first, the problem of the "wired" procedure, the one in which the outcome is predetermined not by "the facts" but by the imperatives of the bureaucracy. Consider prison disciplinary hearings. Guards sometimes charge prisoners with violating rules where the rules have not been violated or have been broken in a way that rarely elicits a response. The guards may be hot and tired, or may not like the inmate, or whatever.[94] To keep peace in the prison, superiors must back up the guards and find that punishable offenses occurred. The inmate receives an explanation of the outcome that he or she knows is false. A utilitarian might think that patent arbitrariness would be better under the circumstances than fictitious fairness.[95]

In addition there are what might be called the realities of informality. The Court has come closest to endorsing informal procedures in *Goss v. Lopez*, where it required "less than a fair-minded school principal would impose upon himself" in suspending students from schools.[96] The principal simply had to discuss the incident "informally" with the student shortly after it occurred. One can be fairly confident about what such a discussion would be, given the disparities in power between principal and student. The principal has to back up his or her teachers; young people lack credibility. The message in most instances will be, "Don't go away mad; just go away." And a utilitarian would be satisfied by that result.

---

process was due or not. The issue in *Eldridge*, however, is not the "all or nothing" one; it is the marginal task of adding one or two new procedures to an existing scheme. Utilitarian calculations could in principle yield "all or nothing" results: Unless everything is provided, the weight added by the participatory interest is too small to make a difference. Mashaw clearly wants to be able to make smaller moves, see, e.g., Mashaw, "Dignitary Theory," pp. 922, 926–29, and Michelman, with his emphasis on associational values, explicitly prefers to be able, under appropriate circumstances, to require something different from either summary procedures or a full judicial trial. Michelman, "Formal and Associational Aims," pp. 149–53.

94. Cf. James McClure, *Cop World: Inside an American Police Force* 40 (1984) (describing "attitude tickets" given to motorists who, when stopped by police, fail to demonstrate appropriate attitude).

95. The point here is fairly general. As we have seen, although an "impartial" decision maker is often required, impartiality does not mean that the decision maker not be part of a social network that will make him or her sensitive to the bureaucracy's requirements. Not all proceedings are "wired," for sometimes the decision maker will know that the guard is a bad actor who should not be backed up and will think that other guards ought to be sent a message. And sometimes decision makers will be far enough removed from the line officers to be able to be truly impartial. The Constitution seems to require neither arrangement.

96. 419 U.S. 565, 583 (1975).

This process is sometimes called "cooling out the mark."[97] Due process here becomes a technique of conflict "management."[98]

Thus, building participatory and associational values into the utilitarian calculation does not make it any more attractive: The values are unlikely to alter many results, and whatever changes they produce are likely to serve ends that ought not be served.

Michelman and Mashaw could also defend their alternatives by treating them as nonutilitarian limits on the results of a utilitarian calculation. The obstacles to a successful defense along these lines, however, seem huge. The problem of determining which procedures are nonutilitarian limits on what utilitarian processes arises again and needs no additional discussion. Further, Justice Black pointed out in his dissent in *Goldberg* that procedures are costly. The bureaucracies of the welfare state are doing things: locking up inmates, providing material assistance to some of the needy, and the like. If more procedures are required, less of those things will be done, and many of them serve nonutilitarian ends. It is not obvious how one could properly resolve the conflict between doing more nonutilitarian stuff and providing more nonutilitarian procedures.[99]

The most fundamental difficulty is that under no sensible moral theory is process of the sort at issue in these cases in itself a value.[100] The utilitarian version of the participatory alternative treats "feeling good" as the end that the process serves. Nonutilitarian versions in the end defend process as serving democratic values, by giving people a say in the decisions that affect them.[101] That is precisely something that due process does

97. See Arthur Leff, *Swindling and Selling* 44 (1976).

98. For a discussion of criminal procedure as a conflict management device, see John Griffiths, "Ideology in Criminal Procedure, or, A Third 'Model' of the Criminal Process," 79 *Yale Law Journal* 359 (1970).

99. Cf. Mashaw, "Three Factors," p. 52 (claim to "non-alienation" does not "rank ahead of all other social values"); Mashaw, "Dignitary Theory," pp. 915–16 (Kantian theory allows claimant to use others, i.e., taxpayers, as means to his or her ends).

See Smolla, "Reemergence of Right-Privilege Distinction," pp. 93–94. Smolla attributes the trade-off between procedures and material benefits as a political bargain struck with recipients of public assistance. Id., pp. 114–15. This is, to say the least, a curious characterization of the politics of public assistance, in which various elites purport to represent the interests of recipients. It is not obvious that a trade-off that those elites bargain for is fairly attributable to the recipients themselves. See text accompanying note 66 for a similar criticism of a related argument.

100. Of course process writ large may be a value in the sense that the processes by which we govern ourselves are valuable at least in part because they let us get along with one another. The right to confront adverse witnesses or to have counsel at administrative hearings does not seem to have that kind of intrinsic value.

101. See Mashaw, "Dignitary Theory," pp. 930–31; Michelman, "Formal and Associational Aims," pp. 127–28.

not do. None of the procedures give the client any authority over the ultimate decision. They give clients a say, in the sense that they are allowed to utter words in the presence of the decision maker, but nothing requires that the decision maker listen, or listen seriously, or believe that the client's say has added anything to what the decision maker as a well-intentioned and sensitive person would have done anyway. Occasionally procedures will enhance democratic participation, but they are indirect and often ineffectual ways of empowering the clients of the welfare state.

Perhaps empowerment could be accomplished more directly. This chapter has argued that the Court's due process decisions embody a vision in which welfare state bureaucracies are professionalized and rationalized and in which politics is not a proper basis for control within the bureaucracy. It might make sense to invert this vision, to embrace politics and reject professionalism and its routines.[102] If professional norms guide the bureaucracy, the interests of clients could be promoted by making it a professional norm that client autonomy be respected.[103] For example, we could install a serious commitment to informed consent in schools and mental institutions. This course is likely to prove illusory, though, because professional norms do not in fact guide the bureaucracy at the street level. If deskilling has progressed as far as it seems, altering or enhancing the commitment to professional norms will not in itself have much effect. We could take as a political program making the bureaucracy truly professional, but that is not a modest course. It is instead a call for a revolution by the newly proletarianized.

We could also direct our attention to the clients as well as to the deskilled bureaucrats. Consider some of the problems already discussed. In *Goss v. Lopez*, instead of trying to work out the right procedures for kicking kids out of school, we might give the students charged with misconduct, or their parents, the power to veto any proposed disposition. Then the conversation between the student and the principal would be a real one, not a disguised "cooling out the mark." We might hold in reserve an incredibly formal system of hearings as an inducement to the student and principal to work out a mutually satisfactory disposition and

---

102. Of course politics was driven out of the bureaucracy for what seemed good reasons: established elites thought the politicized bureaucracies, dominated by the minions of immigrant political machines, were corrupt and diverted resources from valuable social goals to the pockets of brash upstarts. Professionalism was the elite's response. The political bureaucracy need not be romanticized. The elite's criticisms were frequently well-taken; urban political machines perpetuated bigotry and tolerated violent crime where it was profitable to do so. But knowing that we may find it possible to develop a politics that avoids those evils. See Samuel Hays, *Conservation and the Gospel of Efficiency* (1959).

103. See Joel Handler, *The Conditions of Discretion: Autonomy, Community, Bureaucracy*, ch. 5 (1986).

as a resource if their conversation breaks down. In the hearing, of course, both the student and the principal would have to be at risk. There are tough kids who ought to be kicked out of school, but they still could be. And although the proposal is modestly utopian, we ought to consider that the conversation it promotes might be at least as educationally valuable as what goes on in schools today.[104] Even the utopianism is manageable, for it is undoubtedly true that, should any group find it politically sensible to take my proposal as its program, the group would modify it in the process of struggling for its adoption.

A second proposal is even more utopian, again with the qualification just mentioned. In many areas the police see themselves and are seen as an occupying army. Things might be better in some places if responsibility for domestic tranquillity were radically decentralized and deprofessionalized. Where it is possible to handle through politics the inevitable issues of class and race that will arise, we might try to establish neighborhood patrols as police forces.[105] Again wherever it makes sense to try to struggle to that end, the issues of class and race will immediately be placed on the agenda. To succeed the group seeking neighborhood patrols would have to handle them.

Finally, we could rethink *Goldberg v. Kelly*. That case was designed to increase the resources available to the poor by making it harder to deny them public assistance. Even if it did so by retaining some technically ineligible people on the welfare rolls for a while longer, *Goldberg* could be defended on the ground that most of the technically ineligible were nonetheless grindingly poor. In an era when public assistance budgets were expanding, *Goldberg* served a useful redistributive purpose. When ceilings were imposed on those budgets, it began to achieve only redistri-

104. See Robert Burt, *Taking Care of Strangers* (1979). For a discussion of dialogic theories of constitutional law, see Chapter 4. Mashaw uses the term *conversation* in describing what recipients want from the administrative process itself. Mashaw, "Dignitary Theory," pp. 930–31. He regards this as a demand to dismantle the administrative state. Id., p. 904.

Because the vast majority of benefits are disbursed routinely and without controversy, the sense in which participatory values threaten the administrative state must be carefully specified. If it were possible simply to add participatory values in disputed cases to routine respect for entitlements in all the others, no threat would occur. The conceptual bases of participation and of entitlement are incompatible. Entitlements rest on the view that recipients are set apart from society and must be protected against it by a set of rights, whereas participation rests on the view that recipients and the society form an integral whole. Thus, recognizing participatory values threatens the conceptual underpinnings of the contemporary welfare state.

105. For discussions, see Richard Kinsey, John Lea, and Jock Young, *Losing the Fight against Crime* 88–104 (1986); Jerome Skolnick and David Bayley, *The New Blue Line: Police Innovation in Six American Cities* 13–50 (1986).

bution from the abysmally poor to the merely poor. Thus, *Goldberg* aids the poor, if at all, only indirectly. We might seek instead to establish a comprehensive income maintenance scheme that would redistribute wealth in a way that would permanently eradicate large disparities between the rich and the poor.

Of course the Supreme Court is unlikely to adopt any of these proposals in cases soon to come before it, although as Part I argued nothing stands in the Court's way if it wants to require that my proposals be adopted. Still, utopian thinking may be the best way to begin fulfilling the promise of due process.

8

The Constitution
of Religion

THE constitutional law of religion is "in significant disarray."[1] States may subsidize the purchase of books by students at religious schools, but they may not subsidize the purchase of globes.[2] States may engage in ritualistic invocation of religious norms, but they may not attempt to inculcate the norms that give sense to the rituals.[3] Exempting from the Social Security system those who oppose participation for reasons based on religious belief threatens the integrity of the tax structure,[4] but exempting the same people from the education system does not substantially affect *its* integrity.[5] Forms of aid to nonpublic schools that are indistinguishable in economic terms are distinguished in legal terms, with the Court taking the position—rejected in other contexts—that here form matters more than

1. Stephen Pepper, "The Conundrum of the Free Exercise Clause—Some Reflections on Recent Cases," 9 *Northern Kentucky Law Review* 265, 303 (1982). See also Phillip Johnson, "Concepts and Compromise in First Amendment Religion Doctrine," 72 *California Law Review* 817, 839 (1984) ("a mess"). For compilations of the confusions in the law, see Note, "Rebuilding the Wall: The Case for a Return to the Strict Interpretation of the Establishment Clause," 81 *Columbia Law Review* 1463, 1463–66 (1981); Jesse Choper, "The Religion Clauses of the First Amendment: Reconciling the Conflict," 41 *University of Pittsburgh Law Review* 673, 680–81 (1980).

2. Compare Board of Education v. Allen, 392 U.S. 236 (1968) (books), with Meek v. Pittenger, 421 U.S. 349 (1975) (globes). A distinction between loans and purchases seemed viable until Committee for Public Education v. Regan, 444 U.S. 646 (1980), which for the first time approved a direct financial grant to religious schools.

3. Compare Marsh v. Chambers, 463 U.S. 783 (1983) (prayers in legislature constitutional), with Stone v. Graham, 449 U.S. 39 (1980) (posting of Ten Commandments in schoolrooms unconstitutional).

4. United States v. Lee, 455 U.S. 252 (1982).

5. Wisconsin v. Yoder, 406 U.S. 205 (1972). See William Marshall, "Solving the Free Exercise Dilemma: Free Exercise as Expression," 67 *Minnesota Law Review* 545, 548–53 (1983).

substance.[6] The list could go on, especially if one were to include the tests commentators have offered to impose order on the subject, but the general point is clear enough: contemporary constitutional law just does not know how to handle problems of religion.

This chapter examines the sources of this ignorance and the resulting disarray. It argues that the social relations of our society do not now provide the support needed for a concept of politics into which religion would comfortably fit. Religion poses a threat to the intellectual world of the liberal tradition because it is a form of social life that mobilizes the deepest passions of believers in the course of creating institutions that stand between individuals and the state.[7] The liberal tradition in constitutional law cannot accommodate itself to such intermediate institutions, which are seen as alliances for self-defense. The liberal tradition tolerates intermediate institutions because they serve these defensive purposes not because they have intrinsic value. Contemporary constitutionalists do appreciate the passions that animate believers, and they know that religion was sufficiently special to the framers that the framers singled out religious belief from all other types of belief for special constitutional protection. Under the circumstances constitutionalists in the liberal tradition are committed to developing a law of religion even though they do not understand why they have to do so. They have lost that understanding because the liberal tradition has so increased its cultural authority that it is difficult to retrieve the republican tradition, which does make sense of the religion clauses, for purposes of grasping the meaning of the Constitution.[8] Given that both traditions actually pervade the Constitution, intellectual disarray is the unsurprising result.

6. Compare Mueller v. Allen, 463 U.S. 388 (1983) (one form of tuition tax credit constitutional), with Committee for Public Education v. Nyquist, 413 U.S. 756 (1973) (another form of tuition tax credit unconstitutional). Compare also Flast v. Cohen, 392 U.S. 83 (1968) (taxpayer has standing to challenge donation of money to religious organization), with Valley Forge Christian College v. Americans United, 454 U.S. 464 (1982) (taxpayer lacks standing to challenge donation of land and buildings to religious organization).

7. Note, "Reinterpreting the Religion Clauses: Constitutional Construction and Conceptions of the Self," 97 *Harvard Law Review* 1468 (1984), adopts a position like that taken here. The note locates the source of the tensions in an enduring psychological dualism, whereas I argue that its source lies in a particular confluence of political thought and action. See also John Garvey, "Free Exercise and the Values of Religious Liberty," 18 *Connecticut Law Review* 779 (1986) (for purposes of constitutional analysis, analogizing religious belief to insanity). The note also takes a normative stance, whereas I do not. See note 9.

8. If my argument is correct we should be able to discover analogous tensions in the law of other intermediate institutions such as families and education. I believe that such tensions can be found. For example, see Note, "Peaceful Labor Picketing and the First Amendment," 82 *Columbia Law Review* 1469 (1982) (labor unions and picketing); Note, "Labor Picket-

This chapter first surveys the contemporary constitutional law of the religion clauses to describe the existing doctrinal confusion. It identifies two principles that appear to underlie the Supreme Court decisions: the *reduction* principle, in which religious belief is reduced to ordinary belief, protected by the free speech guarantees of the first amendment but given no further protection because of its special character as religious belief; and the *marginality* principle, in which religion is protected to the point where providing protection is seen to have social consequences.[9] As the labels suggest, these principles express the difficulty that constitutional law has in fitting religion into its categories. Then the chapter links these principles to the structure of liberal thought, to show how they express an effort to domesticate impulses that the liberal tradition cannot accommodate directly. The conclusion suggests some ways in which a reconstituted law of religion might provide nonbelievers as well as believers with a view of the law that affirms the impulses to connectedness that religious belief mobilizes and that fits uncomfortably in the liberal tradition.

Confusion in the Law of Religion

Perhaps it is not surprising that the Supreme Court has not developed a satisfactory case law of the religion clauses. Membership on the Court changes, as do the issues presented to it by litigants responding to the legislative product of shifting political coalitions. Still, it is surprising that no one has been able to make overall sense of the religion clauses by developing a unifying doctrinal or theoretical approach to them.

Doctrinal development falls between two polar positions, strict neutrality and strict separation. These positions are weakened both by their lack of doctrinal coherence and by their extremely unattractive consequences; intermediate positions lack coherence largely because their proponents have been unable to identify in a noncontroversial way what it is

---

ing and Commercial Speech: Free Enterprise Values in the Doctrine of Free Speech," 91 *Yale Law Journal* 938 (1982) (same); Robert Burt, "The Burger Court and the Family," in *The Burger Court*, p. 92 (families); Gerald Frug, "The City as a Legal Concept," 93 *Harvard Law Review* 1057 (1980) (federalism).

9. Two preliminary cautions are appropriate. First, these principles should be taken as ones that provide order to the description of the Supreme Court's decisions rather than as ones that I believe are normatively desirable. With one notable exception, see note 31, I have tried to exclude from my discussion arguments in favor of or against the fundamental normative merit of these principles, although I do indicate analytic difficulties they create. Second, these principles may not be analytically distinct. Once religion is largely reduced to ordinary belief, what is left may necessarily be marginal. Using two labels makes exposition easier.

that makes various outcomes desirable or unattractive to substantial numbers of people.

Philip Kurland has proposed a doctrine of strict neutrality, under which "religion may not be used as a basis for classification for purposes of governmental action, whether that action be the conferring of rights or privileges or the imposition of duties or benefits."[10] Strict neutrality prohibits governments from accommodating their secular programs to the objections of religious believers. A state may not exempt people from military service or jury duty even if those obligations severely intrude on a believer's sense of the proper balance between secular demands and divine commands. Nor may a state enact antidiscrimination laws that require nonbelievers to adjust their behavior to take account of the religious beliefs of others. The difficulty is that it is hard to see why a legislature cannot be nice to believers at least to the extent of exempting them from severe burdens.[11]

Further, facial neutrality is insufficient because there are no nonarbitrary ways of defining the categories over which we will assess neutrality.[12] Legislatures can create identical programs in either of two ways: they can use a single facially neutral statute or they can use two statutes,

10. Philip Kurland, "Of Church and State and the Supreme Court," 29 *University of Chicago Law Review* 1, 5 (1961). Kurland admits that it has not been adopted by the Court, although the rhetoric of neutrality is widely used by commentators. See Philip Kurland, "The Irrelevance of the Constitution: The Religion Clauses of the First Amendment and the Supreme Court," 24 *Villanova Law Review* 3, 24 (1978) ("met with almost uniform rejection").

11. The Court has indeed required exemptions in some cases. See Sherbert v. Verner, 374 U.S. 398 (1963); Wisconsin v. Yoder, 406 U.S. 205 (1972). The scholarly consensus is that the accommodations prohibited by strict neutrality are sometimes compelled by the Constitution, at least when the adjustments of secular programs are modest and the burdens on conscience severe, and are often permitted by it. See, e.g., J. Morris Clark, "Guidelines for the Free Exercise Clause," 83 *Harvard Law Review* 327, 345 (1969); Donald Gianella, "Religious Liberty, Nonestablishment, and Doctrinal Development: Part I. The Religious Liberty Guarantee," 80 *Harvard Law Review* 1381, 1399–1402 (1967); Joseph Dodge, "The Free Exercise of Religion: A Sociological Approach," 67 *Michigan Law Review* 679, 706 (1969); Paul Marcus, "The Forum of Conscience: Applying Standards under the Free Exercise Clause," 1973 *Duke Law Journal* 1217, 1235–36; Leo Pfeffer, "Religion-Blind Government," 15 *Stanford Law Review* 389 (1963). Contra Choper, "Religion Clauses," p. 691; John Garvey, "Freedom and Equality in the Religion Clauses," 1981 *Supreme Court Review* 193, 198.

12. In addition, a doctrine of neutrality must be framed so as to prohibit statutes that either use religious classifications explicitly or are not neutral in their effects. Experience has shown that it is easy to draft facially neutral statutes that raise serious questions about religious freedom. See, e.g., Epperson v. Arkansas, 393 U.S. 97 (1968) (invalidating a state law prohibiting the teaching of evolution). As a religion case *Epperson* seems best explained on the ground that its subject matter was a religiously sensitive one and that legislation on such sensitive matters is highly suspect.

one of which is not neutral on its face. The problem is most evident in the law of aid to nonpublic education. *Mueller v. Allen* upheld a facially neutral program of tax credits for expenses associated with going to school.[13] Everyone knew that this meant, in the main, tuition for nonpublic, largely sectarian, education. A state could achieve the same result by enacting a program of tax credits only for tuition in nonpublic schools. This nonneutral statute could be defended on the ground that the total package of state programs supporting education is neutral: One part of the program is the tax-credit statute, and another is the system of tax-financed subsidies given to public schools. Yet this course was held unconstitutional in *Committee on Public Education v. Nyquist*, in which, despite the existence of a massive state subsidy for public schools, the Court struck down a statute providing tax credits to parents of children in private, primarily sectarian, schools.[14] No one has successfully explained why splitting the package into its components, one of which is not neutral on its face, makes it unconstitutional.[15]

At the pole opposite strict neutrality, the doctrine of strict separation suffers from similar defects. This doctrine prohibits any interaction whatever between the institutions of government and those of religion. The difficulty here is that careful definition of subject matter inevitably produces such an interaction. Again the usual example is aid to education,

---

The category of religiously sensitive issues is open-ended, though, and its content is likely to be affected by quite subjective evaluations: Why should statutes authorizing schools to have a moment of silence not be treated as religiously sensitive? or statutes restricting the availability of abortions? Laurence Tribe initially offered a version of this approach, "Foreword: Toward a Model of Roles in the Due Process of Life and Law," 87 *Harvard Law Review* 1, 21–25 (1973), but later retracted his analysis, arguing that it failed to give enough weight to the interest that religiously motivated people have in participating in politics to advance their religiously based views. See Tribe, *American Constitutional Law*, p. 928. It might be possible, however, to reconstruct the analysis by isolating a particular category of "religion-sensitive" cases to which it applies. The abortion example suggests one serious problem with the category: it may have been true that abortion was a religion-sensitive subject in 1973, but with the rise of organized secular opposition to abortion it has become difficult so to confine the topic.

13. 463 U.S. 388 (1983).

14. 413 U.S. 756 (1973).

15. See Donald Gianella, "Religious Liberty, Nonestablishment, and Doctrinal Development: Part II. The Nonestablishment Principle," 81 *Harvard Law Review* 513, 519–20 (1968); Johnson, "Concepts and Compromise," pp. 822–23.

The example of aid to education illustrates the general source of the emptiness of the concept of neutrality in the setting of impact as well. To assess impact we must identify the relevant subject on which the program at issue has an impact. But the subject matter can be described narrowly or broadly, whichever is needed to produce the desired impact: If "aid to nonpublic education" is too narrow, then try "aid to education" or "aid to socially beneficial nonprofit organizations."

reduces the economic incentives to send children to sectarian schools.[16] That reduction is a form of interaction. Even more troubling than this analytic difficulty are some practical consequences of the doctrine. It would seem to preclude incidental and indirect support for churches, even when this support—such as providing police and fire services at subsidized rates—is widely available to everyone else. And, like the doctrine of strict neutrality, the doctrine of strict separation does not permit, much less require, the adjustment of secular rules to believers' requests for exemptions.

Between the polar positions of strict neutrality and strict separation is the typical doctrinal form of all legal compromises: decision makers are to balance all the relevant factors, such as the values of neutrality and separation, burdens on conscientious religious belief, altruistic desires to accommodate religious belief, the costs of accommodation, and whatever else they want to put into the balance. Although precise formulations may vary these intermediate approaches have the defects of all balancing tests.[17] The "relevant considerations" are defined so generally that the weight a decision maker gives to any particular consideration is left almost entirely open. The effect is that balancing tests are inevitably driven by the results sought.

General theoretical analyses of the religion clauses are as unhelpful as doctrinal ones. Consider the three most prominent theoretical analyses, which are applications of originalism, moral philosophy, and political pluralism, in the context of the religion clauses.

At least since *Everson v. Board of Education*,[18] the dominant originalist position has been that historical evidence provides support for strict separation: the framers of the first amendment wanted strict separation, and the framers of the fourteenth amendment applied that approach to the states. Yet as with all originalist arguments, there is other evidence of the framers' intent that would give a different meaning to those clauses. (See Chapter 1.) Originalist strict separation cannot account for the indisputable fact that most framers explicitly understood that the religion clauses were designed to bar the national government from certain actions, among which was interference with existing establishments of religion in the states. Nor can it explain actions by the framers and their contemporaries, shortly after the adoption of the first amendment, in

16. See Gianella, "Nonestablishment Principle," pp. 574–75; Johnson, "Concepts and Compromise," pp. 822–23.

17. See Tushnet, "Anti-Formalism," pp. 1508–16.

18. 330 U.S. 1 (1946).

linking government and religion by subsidizing missions to Native Americans, authorizing days of thanksgiving, and the like.[19]

These difficulties with originalist strict separation have led others to urge a different originalist position. As we saw in Chapter 1, Justice Rehnquist's dissent in *Wallace v. Jaffree* argued that the best originalist analysis views the religion clauses as authorizing governments to take a stance of what has been called benevolent neutrality toward religion. This proposal too suffers from the standard problems of any originalist position.[20] Social change has made the institutions of government today very different from those the framers knew. We therefore cannot infer from the fact that they endorsed benevolent neutrality by the institutions of 1789 that they would endorse benevolent neutrality by today's institutions. For example, the framers might think that the reach of government is so much greater now that benevolent neutrality poses greater risks to important values than it did in 1789. In addition, religious pluralism has become so much more pervasive that the very notion of neutrality among denominations may no longer make sense. For example, because denominations differ on what counts as a prayer, there may be no such thing as a nondenominational prayer under modern conditions.[21]

A second theoretical analysis of the Constitution looks to moral philosophy to tell us what rights the Constitution protects. A rights-based theory of the religion clauses fairly readily produces some version of the free exercise clause, because religious belief is something that a right to conscience or intellectual freedom ought to protect. No one, however, has produced a persuasive rights-based defense of the establishment clause that is not parasitic upon free exercise: Establishment claims, in this view, are disguised versions of claims that the practice at issue will coerce people into adhering to or abandoning some religious beliefs. For exam-

19. Apart from the general difficulties with the originalist theory of incorporation of the Bill of Rights into the fourteenth amendment, there are some problems specific to the absorption of the religion clauses. The due process clause protects people against deprivations of life, liberty, and property. Its terms are not well suited to encompass the interests protected by the establishment clause; although the right to free exercise of religion is a "liberty," the guarantee against establishment does not protect anything readily characterized as a personal liberty or as property.

These difficulties are most apparent in the Court's decisions on standing in establishment clause cases. See, e.g., Doremus v. Board of Education, 342 U.S. 429 (1952). In addition, to the extent that the framers of the first amendment sought to protect state establishments against national action, it is not entirely coherent to say that the amendment is now applicable to the states.

20. Most of the points were made in Abington School Dist. v. Schempp, 374 U.S. 203, 237–42 (1963) (Brennan, J., concurring).

21. See Marsh v. Chambers, 463 U.S. 783, 819–21 (1983) (Brennan, J., dissenting).

ple, the rights-based analysis says that the vice of school prayers is that children will be forced to pray.[22]

There are several difficulties with the rights-based theory. It is unclear how we are to use a rights-based theory to decide how much coercion is too much; we need to supplement it with a persuasive sociopsychological theory of coercion. Also, a rights-based approach seems likely to deprive the establishment clause of any meaning independent of the free exercise clause.

A third theoretical analysis of the religion clauses relies on the interaction between the religious pluralism of the United States and its pluralistic political system.[23] The theory begins with the observation that there is a tension between the free exercise and establishment clauses. A legislature that exempts people from some general regulation because of their religious beliefs might violate the establishment clause,[24] but its failure to exempt them might violate the free exercise clause. Similarly, in a society pervaded by government subsidies to secular activities, failure to subsidize the alternative desired by religious believers might violate their free exercise rights.[25] The pluralist theory, which has been offered most recently by Justice White, argues that where religion is involved legislatures have a relatively broad range of discretion from within which they can select a policy that reasonably promotes free exercise values at the expense of establishment clause ones and vice versa.[26] Thus, a university may prohibit prayer meetings, or allow them, as *it* chooses; a state may subsidize religious education but need not do so.

22. One might challenge this argument by asking for evidence that coercion actually occurs (which converts the argument into a direct free exercise argument), as did Justice Stewart in *Schempp*. 374 U.S., at 316–20 (Stewart, J., dissenting). But the rights-based defense might respond to that challenge with the assertion that detecting the presence of coercion on a case-by-case basis is so difficult that we can be sure that too much undetected coercion will occur unless the practice is flatly prohibited. In this manner the rights-based theory treats the establishment clause as a prophylactic against free exercise violations.

23. For a discussion of pluralism and constitutional theory in general, see Chapter 2.

24. See Douglas Laycock, "Towards a General Theory of the Religion Clauses: The Case of Church Labor and the Right to Church Autonomy," 81 *Columbia Law Review* 1373, 1414–15 (1981), arguing that the exemption in *Sherbert v. Verner* caused non-Sabbatarians to subsidize Seventh-Day Adventists through their contributions to the unemployment compensation fund; Choper, "Religion Clauses," pp. 691–92. See also 26 U.S.C. §1402(g).

25. See Gianella, "Nonestablishment Principle," pp. 522–26.

26. See, e.g., Widmar v. Vincent, 454 U.S. 263, 288–89 (1981) (White, J., dissenting). See also Sherbert v. Verner, 374 U.S. 398, 418 (1963) (Harlan, J., joined by White, J., dissenting); Thomas v. Review Board, 450 U.S. 707, 720 (1981) (Rehnquist, J., dissenting).

On limits to reasonableness, see Widmar v. Vincent, 454 U.S., p. 287 (White, J., dissenting) (University could not bar students from saying grace before meals).

Pluralism justifies this conclusion by arguing that in a religiously diverse society the contention among religious groups and between religious groups and secular ones, with shifting alliances and overlapping cleavages, will produce a public policy that is unlikely to pose serious threats to the values promoted by the religion clauses.[27] Courts need only police the perimeters of public policy affecting religion to guard against unreasonable deals that work to the severe detriment of one segment of a religiously diverse society.[28]

Pluralist theories of constitutional law are subject to powerful empirical challenges. Problems arise because communities in the United States are not homogeneous as to religion, nor are religious groups represented in substantial numbers in every community.[29] If communities were homogeneous, no one would bother to question a community's decisions, and if there were enough adherents of each religion in every community, the pluralist bargaining process might work well. But the distribution of denominational membership is lumpy, with concentrations of groups in different communities, from which migration is costly. Where there is only a small minority on some issue regarding religion, and if that minority believes that other issues are more important to it, the minority can be

27. Alternatively, the religion clauses might be treated as creating broad outer boundaries for a set of values, and their proper interpretation would require that each generation be allowed to decide for itself how to accommodate those values within the limits set by the clauses. In this view pluralism assures that the accommodation respect those limits.

28. The pluralist theory also offers a justification for the establishment branch of Kurland's religion clause theory. Religious pluralism would require legislatures to structure their programs using criteria that are neutral as to religion. The outcomes of such a process are unlikely to threaten serious erosions of establishment clause values. A more likely result is legislative paralysis, an inability to come up with a neutral program at acceptable levels of cost.

The Equal Access Act, P.L. 98–377, 98 Stat. 1303 (Aug. 11, 1984), provides a useful example, although the operative political constraint was not concern over costs. This act was designed to ensure that student religious groups would be allowed to use school facilities. The act as adopted provides that schools that create "limited open forums" as defined in the act may not discriminate against students who wish to conduct meetings "on the basis of the religious, *political, philosophical, or other content* of the speech at such meetings" (emphasis added). The emphasized words were added to reduce the political opposition to the act; they also dilute its particularly religious content. See Douglas Laycock, "Equal Access and Moments of Silence: The Equal Status of Religious Speech by Private Speakers," 81 *Northwestern University Law Review* 1 (1986).

29. Federalism might reinforce pluralism if adherents of specific denominations came to reside in religiously homogeneous communities; religious communities could be strengthened by allying them with a parallel secular authority, from which dissenters could remove themselves by migration. Of course, formal religious control over local government raises a host of constitutional questions. For a discussion, see Note, "Church Control of Municipality: Establishing a First Amendment Institutional Suit," 38 *Stanford Law Review* 1363 (1986).

disregarded in the pluralist bargaining: Its members will be outnumbered on the religious issue and will be unwilling to withhold their votes on other issues to extract concessions on the religious one.[30] In the context of the religion clauses, the empirical challenge to a pluralist theory seems well-founded. Christians outnumber adherents of other religions by a wide margin, and even expanding our view to include the Judeo-Christian tradition, if that can be considered a coherent concept, leaves much outside the pluralist process.[31]

30. I take this to be a description of the political stance of many American Jews. Bargaining would also fail if the group was completely marginal to the community, so that no one else would find it politically profitable to trade support for the group's position on religious issues in exchange for its support on other issues: engaging in such a deal would be the kiss of death. I take this to be the political position of organized secularists and such outcast "cults" as the Reunification Church ("Moonies"). See generally *The Brainwashing/ Deprogramming Controversy: Sociological, Psychological, Legal and Historical Perspectives* (David Bromley and James Richardson eds. 1983).

31. See Douglas Laycock, "A Survey of Religious Liberty in the United States," 47 *Ohio State Law Journal* 409, 432–33 (1986) (political process adequate to protect "adherents of mainstream religions" but not "small numbers of idiosyncratic believers"). Justice O'Connor has begun to develop a version of the pluralist theory. She advocates inquiring into whether governmental action "sends a message [of endorsement of religion] to nonadherents that they are outsiders, not full members of the political community, and an accompanying message to adherents that they are insiders, favored members of the political community." Lynch v. Donnelly, 465 U.S. 668, 688 (1984) (O'Connor, J., concurring). Norman Dorsen and Charles Sims, "The Nativity Scene Case: An Error of Judgment," 1985 *University of Illinois Law Review* 837, 859–60, generally endorse Justice O'Connor's approach but criticize its application in *Lynch*.

This emphasis on symbolic messages is problematic. It would have judges decide what symbolic content the government's messages have. Because judges will always be broadly representative of the general population, they will be susceptible to all the distortions of interpretation that membership in the majority entails. For example, Justice O'Connor articulated her approach in concurring with the Court's decision to find no establishment clause violation in the public sponsorship of a crèche; she concluded that the practice "cannot fairly be understood to convey a message of government endorsement of religion." Id., p. 614 (O'Connor, J., concurring). This came as a surprise to most Jews, whose judgments on this issue turn out to be "unfair" in Justice O'Connor's eyes. See Laurence Tribe, "Constitutional Calculus: Equal Justice or Economic Efficiency?" 98 *Harvard Law Review* 592, 611 (1985) ("One cannot avoid hearing in *Lynch* a faint echo of the Court that found nothing invidious in the Jim Crow policy of 'separate but equal' "). One could use stronger words.

I find it impossible to avoid expressing my own views on the case. It seems to me difficult to believe that the majority could have reached the result it did had there been a Jew on the Court to speak from the heart about the real meaning of public displays of crèches to Jews. At the same time, of course, Jews have always known that they were stangers in the land and have taken some succor from that fact. See Jacob Neusner, *Stranger at Home: "The Holocaust," Zionism, and American Jewry* 122–23 (1981). *Lynch* just reminds us of that status, and, distressing though it may be to have it brought to light, we may profit from learning the lesson again. See also William Van Alstyne, "Trends in the Supreme Court: Mr. Jefferson's

Order in the Law of Religion

The introduction to this chapter identified the reduction and marginality principles. These principles explain much of what the Supreme Court has done about religion. Most of the Court's religion clause decisions embodying these principles rest on a set of ideas that do not take religion seriously as a form of human endeavor.

We begin with the reduction principle. Religious belief is of course a kind of belief. The free expression clause of the first amendment protects the general class of beliefs and thus necessarily protects religious belief as well. The reduction principle insists that religious belief is indistinguishable from other types of belief, so that neither the free exercise nor the establishment clause constrains governmental action any differently than the free speech clause does.

The reduction principle divides religious beliefs and activities into three components: the belief itself, the body of ritual activities that accompany belief, and the impact of belief-motivated actions—including observance of rituals—on secular interests. Then, for deciding free exercise cases, the reduction principle applies to each of these components the tests that have been developed to deal with problems of free speech. For example, just as the government may not burden "mere" political belief unconnected to otherwise undesirable social consequences,[32] it may not burden religious belief standing alone.[33] Moreover, according to the reduction principle, the rituals associated with belief are forms of symbolic speech and are to be tested by the standards developed in symbolic speech cases. Finally,

---

Crumbling Wall—A Comment on *Lynch v. Donnelly*," 1984 *Duke Law Journal* 770, 781–87; Philip Kurland, "The Religion Clauses and the Burger Court," 34 *Catholic University Law Review* 1, 13 (1984) (*Lynch* is "sleazy"). ACLU v. Birmingham, 791 F.2d 1561, 1572 (6th Cir.) (Nelson, J., dissenting), cert. denied, 107 S. Ct. 421 (1986), addresses this issue expressly, as Justice O'Connor did not, but ultimately concludes that it is enough that crèches are not motivated by "anti-Jewish animus." This does not seem to be a fair application of Justice O'Connor's approach.

In addition, it is not clear why symbolic exclusion should matter so long as "nonadherents" are in fact actually included in the political community. Under those circumstances nonadherents who believe that they are excluded from the political community are merely expressing the disappointment felt by everyone who has lost a fair fight in the arena of politics. Symbolic exclusion following actual inclusion might matter if the nonadherents become so disheartened by their losses that they withdraw from politics altogether. This prospect seems remote enough under presently foreseeable circumstances to make a prophylactic approach as questionable here as it was in the rights-based analysis of the establishment clause.

32. See Yates v. United States, 354 U.S. 298 (1958) (Smith Act construed not to penalize abstract belief as distinguished from advocacy of unlawful action).

33. See U.S. Constitution, art. IV (no religious test to be imposed for public office); Torcaso v. Watkins, 367 U.S. 488 (1961).

advocates of the reduction principle point out that all speech has some effect on governmental interests unrelated to the suppression of speech[34] and that the Supreme Court has developed a number of rules that require governments to accommodate those interests to the interest in free expression. The reduction principle applies similar rules when actions motivated by religious belief affect secular governmental interests.[35]

The reduction principle had its origins in the 1940s, when the Court, emerging from its confrontation with the President over New Deal economic legislation, began to develop a new constituency by enforcing limitations on government that were attractive to civil libertarians.[36] In a series of cases involving local efforts to regulate proselytizing by Jehovah's Witnesses, the Court articulated a set of rules about what governments could do.[37] When the Court addressed the free exercise clause, it drew on a distinction to which it was attracted in free speech cases.[38] In *Cantwell v. Connecticut*, Justice Roberts wrote, free exercise "embraces two concepts—freedom to believe and freedom to act. The first is absolute, but in the nature of things, the second cannot be."[39] This distinction is exactly the one being drawn contemporaneously in labor picketing cases.[40]

A later example of the operation of the reduction principle is provided by the Sunday closing cases.[41] In upholding Sunday closing statutes against a free exercise challenge, Chief Justice Warren's plurality opinion in *Braunfeld v. Brown* distinguished between direct and indirect burdens on religion, a distinction again part of the law of free expression at the

34. See, e.g., Kovacs v. Cooper, 336 U.S. 77 (1949) (noise); Schneider v. Irvington, 308 U.S. 147 (1939) (littering).

35. For articulation and defense of the reduction principle, see Marshall, "Solving the Free Exercise Dilemma," the most extensive discussion; Jesse Choper, "Defining 'Religion' in the First Amendment," 1982 *University of Illinois Law Review* 579, 581–82; Clark, "Guidelines," pp. 336–37.

36. See Robert Cover, "The Origins of Judicial Activism in the Protection of Minorities," 91 *Yale Law Journal* 1287 (1982).

37. See Lovell v. Griffin, 303 U.S. 444 (1938); Cox v. New Hampshire, 312 U.S. 569 (1941); Martin v. Struthers, 319 U.S. 141 (1943).

38. In additon, the Court in these early cases did not distinguish between the protections provided by the free speech clause and those provided by the free exercise clause. Instead it invoked the entire first amendment as the basis for its decisions. See Marshall, "Solving the free Exercise Dilemma," pp. 562–64; Kurland, "Church and State," pp. 36–44.

39. 310 U.S. 296, 303–4 (1940).

40. See, e.g., Thornhill v. Alabama, 310 U.S. 88 (1940).

41. McGowan v. Maryland, 366 U.S. 420 (1961); Two Guys from Harrison v. McGinley, 366 U.S. 582 (1961); Braunfeld v. Braun, 366 U.S. 599 (1961); Gallagher v. Crown Kosher Super Market, 366 U.S. 617 (1961).

time.[42] More interesting is Warren's formulation of the general test for free exercise claims: "If the State regulates conduct by enacting a general law within its power, the purpose and effect of which is to advance the State's secular goals, the statute is valid despite its indirect burden on religious observance unless the State may accomplish its purpose by means which do not impose such a burden."[43] Minor stylistic alterations aside, this test is structurally the same as the one stated for symbolic speech in *United States v. O'Brien*: "A governmental regulation is sufficiently justified if it is within the constitutional power of the Government; if it furthers an important or substantial governmental interest; if the governmental interest is unrelated to the suppression of free expression; and if the incidental restriction on alleged First Amendment freedoms is no greater than is essential to the furtherance of that interest."[44]

There are two prominent cases that seem irreconcilable with the reduction principle.[45] In *Sherbert v. Verner*, a Seventh-Day Adventist lost her job when she refused to work on Saturdays.[46] Finding that her refusal constituted "cause" for her discharge, the state unemployment compensation board denied her claim for benefits. The Supreme Court held that this denial violated her rights under the free exercise clause. Similarly, in *Wisconsin v. Yoder*, the Court held that the free exercise clause required states to exempt from the operation of their compulsory education laws

---

42. 366 U.S., pp. 599, 605–6. See, e.g., Konigsberg v. State Bar, 366 U.S. 36 (1961); Adler v. Board of Education, 342 U.S. 485 (1952).

43. 366 U.S., p. 607.

44. 391 U.S. 367, 377 (1968). The reduction principle may have reached its fullest flower in Widmar v. Vincent, 454 U.S. 263 (1981), in which, in a case crying out for free exercise treatment, the Court adopted a free expression analysis instead. There the University of Missouri denied a group of students permission to conduct its prayer meetings in University buildings even though the buildings were available to nonreligious organizations for their meetings. A free exercise analysis would treat this as a simple case of discrimination against religion. The Court's free speech analysis treated it as a content-based restriction on speech, which could be justified only by a compelling state interest. Religion entered the Court's analysis by the back door, as the Court rejected the University's claim that it had a compelling interest in avoiding the appearance of an establishment of religion. As William Marshall has said, "Because few activities are more profoundly religious than prayer, *Widmar* suggests that there is no core religious activity exclusively protected by the free exercise clause." "Solving the Free Exercise Dilemma," pp. 559–60. Much here depends on the scope one gives to notions of symbolic speech: A ritual sacrifice might or might not be symbolic speech but perhaps could receive free exercise protection no matter how it was regarded. See Frank v. State, 604 P.2d 1068 (Alaska 1979).

45. See Kent Greenawalt, "Religion as a Concept in Constitutional Law," 72 *California Law Review* 753, 777–88 (1984).

46. 374 U.S. 398 (1963), followed in Thomas v. Review Board, 450 U.S. 707 (1981); Hobbie v. Unemployment Appeals Comm'n., 107 S. Ct. 1046 (1987).

the children of Amish parents whose religion forbade attendance at school after the eighth grade.[47]

In these cases the free exercise clause required states to create exemptions from general regulatory statutes. The free speech clause requires states to create exemptions as well; a person seeking to use a park for her company's softball tournament may be subjected to requirements that could not be imposed on a person seeking to use the park for a demonstration.[48] Yet it seems unlikely that, in a free speech version of *Sherbert*, that clause would be held to require unemployment compensation for a person whose political beliefs caused her to be fired and prevented her from finding further employment in the private sector.[49] Similarly, the Court in *Yoder* carefully emphasized that the Amish had a long tradition of opposition to advanced education, precisely to distinguish them from "hippie" types whose opposition to such education was political.[50] Thus the reduction principle does not account well for *Sherbert* and *Yoder*.

Proponents of the reduction principle can handle these cases in either of two ways. First, they can argue that *Sherbert* and *Yoder* were wrongly decided. Because *Yoder* so openly relied on an invidious comparison between religious beliefs and other beliefs, repudiating it might not be unattractive. Repudiating *Sherbert* is more difficult, perhaps because the burden on belief seems both severe and unnecessary.[51] Thus, the second way to salvage the reduction principle is to expand the class of exemptions under the free speech clause. If a Seventh-Day Adventist is entitled to unemployment compensation notwithstanding that her beliefs gave her employers cause to fire her, a person whose political beliefs gave *her* employers cause would be also.[52] Yet tinkering with free speech law to preserve the reduction principle is a bit disquieting, because the reduction

47. 406 U.S. 205 (1972).

48. See Murdock v. Pennsylvania, 319 U.S. 105 (1943); Martin v. Struthers, 319 U.S. 141 (1943) (exempting those engaged in religious and speech activities from requirements imposed on those engaged in commercial activities).

49. The employers might be liable under the civil rights acts for a private conspiracy to deprive her of her political rights. Arguably the state's decision to construe its unemployment statutes to make political grounds "cause" for discharge would be unconstitutional under the circumstances hypothesized. But that was unlikely when *Sherbert* was decided and is even more unlikely now. See, e.g., Rendell-Baker v. Kohn, 457 U.S. 830 (1982).

50. See Philip Kurland, "The Supreme Court, Compulsory Education, and the First Amendment's Religion Clauses," 75 *West Virginia Law Review* 213, 237–38 (1973).

51. This is the consensus of the commentators. See, e.g., Clark, "Guidelines," pp. 337–38.

52. See Marshall, "Solving the Free Exercise Dilemma," pp. 586–87. The fuzziness of the law of exemptions under the free speech clause is such that this expansion would entail no major doctrinal revisions. The courts could tinker a bit with the characterization of the interests that go into the balance and create exemptions that are at present unavailable.

principle denies what the text of the first amendment affirms, that there is a distinction between religion and other forms of expression.[53] Justice White, dissenting in *Widmar*, attempted to describe the distinction. He would have distinguished, as the Court did not, between "verbal acts of worship and other verbal acts," so that "the Religion Clauses [would have] independent meaning in circumstances in which religious practice took the form of speech." Verbal acts of worship include "offering prayers, singing hymns, reading scripture, and teaching biblical principles."[54]

Justice White described the distinction between worship and speech but did not examine it in detail. The key is the distinction between proselytizing and worshiping. Proselytizing is directed from within a community of believers to outsiders, whereas worship occurs among the community of believers. Proselytizing invites others to join an already constituted group; worshiping is the means by which the group affirms its existence as a group. Similarly, praying and singing hymns are means by which believers affirm to one another and to their god their participation in a community set apart from others. Teaching scripture differs from teaching about the Bible because participants in the former activity open themselves to inspiration and participation in a church in ways that participants in the latter need not. Worship differs from speech, then, by manifesting a commitment to a community less encompassing than the whole society.[55]

53. In part the suggestion is troubling because it is unlikely that the Court as presently composed will expand free speech exemptions, except perhaps in largely innocuous situations. See, e.g., Brown v. Socialist Workers '74 Campaign Committee, 459 U.S. 87 (1982).

54. 454 U.S., pp. 285, 284, 283 (White, J., dissenting). The majority criticized the distinction between worship and speech on three grounds. It did not explain when verbal acts such as singing, reading, and teaching acquire religious content so as to transform them from speech into worship. Further, courts could not intelligibly "inquire into the significance of words and practices" to determine whether a reading from the Bible is speech or worship. Finally, Justice White conceded that "religious speech designed to win religious converts" was protected by the free speech clause; there was no distinction between such speech and "religious worship by persons already converted." Id., pp. 269–70 n. 6. Marshall, "Solving the Free Exercise Dilemma," p. 579, argues that, in a Meiklejohn-type theory of free expression, see Chapter 9, religious speech is at least not entitled to greater protection than political speech, because it does not directly contribute to the process of political deliberation.

55. The perspective here is essentially that of Durkheim, but in order to make my major points I need adopt only such a general perspective, without addressing the controversial details of Durkheim's own work. For similar perspectives on recent religious phenomena in the United States, see Alan Tobey, "The Summer Solstice of the Healthy-Happy-Holy Organization," in *The New Religious Consciousness* 5, 14–15, (Charles Glock and Robert Bellah eds. 1976); Gregory Johnson, "The Hare Krishna in San Francisco," id., pp. 31, 41, 44–45; Robert Bellah, "The New Religious Consciousness and the Crisis of Modernity," id., p. 333. For similar perspectives in legal commentary, see William Valente, "Aid to

This distinction captures something deeply important about religion. Yet the reduction principle rejects any such distinction. This principle is attractive precisely because it allows the law of religion to gloss over the fact that religious communities necessarily stand apart from, and in many ways stand in opposition to, the wider community of which they are simultaneously a part.[56] That fact threatens some fundamentals of the liberal tradition.

The operation of the reduction principle in free exercise cases has frequently been noted.[57] Its operation in establishment clause cases has only recently emerged.[58] In establishment clause cases the reduction principle means that the government's support of religion may go as far as its support of speech.[59]

The prevailing view is that government speech should be free of substantial judicial control.[60] This view relies on a pluralist analysis of American politics. According to that analysis, contending interest groups shape the development of public policy, including public policy about government speech. Given a rough balance of forces in the pluralist struggle, troubling forms of government speech are unlikely to occur with sufficient frequency to constitute a problem to which courts can profitably

Church-Related Education—New Directions without Dogma," 55 *Virginia Law Review* 579, 604–5 (1969); Note, "The Sacred and the Profane: A First Amendment Definition of Religion," 61 *Texas Law Review* 139, 158–59 (1982).

56. This description of religion's distinctiveness can be challenged from two directions. It might be said that it ignores religious traditions emphasizing the direct contact between the believer and God, religious traditions celebrating isolated monastic existence, and the deist tradition in which communal worship is replaced by rationalist appreciation of God's role in the world. Yet the anchorite's isolated worship is religious rather than eccentric because it is located in a tradition of discourse to which other believers have access. See Brown v. Pena, 441 F.Supp. 1382 (S.D. Fla. 1977) (worship entailing consumption of cat food not a religion); Africa v. Pennsylvania, 662 F.2d 1025 (3d Cir. 1981) (pantheism not a religion). Talk about a person's relation to God can be coherent only in a socially located discourse making such talk sensible. The second challenge then becomes forceful. All speech, not just religious worship can be coherent only in socially located discourses. Religion should then be treated as exemplary rather than distinctive. I agree with this challenge. See note 8.

57. See note 11.

58. But see Choper, "Defining 'Religion' in the First Amendment," 1982 *University of Illinois Law Review* 579, 610–12; Laycock, "General Theory," pp. 1383–84.

59. Of course it may go no further. But as will be shown, that turns out to be no significant limit on the government's power. Under these circumstances the reduction principle here might be called an escalation principle.

60. Steven Shiffrin, "Government Speech," 27 *UCLA Law Review* 565 (1980); Mark Yudof, *When Government Speaks: Politics, Law and Government Expression in America* (1983). For a review of Yudof, *When Government Speaks*, see Mark Tushnet, "Book Review," 1984 *Wisconsin Law Review* 129.

direct their attention. In the establishment clause context pluralist theories reduce the constraints on the establishment of religion to the level set by pluralist politics.

Mueller v. Allen illustrates this reduction in operation.[61] Ten years before *Mueller* the Supreme Court had held unconstitutional a New York statute that provided tuition tax credits to parents who sent their children to private schools, the vast majority of which were affiliated with religious organizations.[62] *Mueller* upheld a Minnesota statute that allowed parents to deduct certain expenses of sending their children to school, whether public or private. This deduction was limited to actual expenses for tuition, textbooks, or transportation, up to $500 or $700 per child. Because parents whose children attend public school rarely have substantial actual expenses, the primary beneficiaries of the statute were parents with children in private schools, and, as in New York, the large majority of these were sectarian. The Supreme Court distinguished the New York statute on the ground that the Minnesota statute "neutrally provide[d] state assistance to a broad spectrum of citizens."[63]

Of course the New York statute was also neutral on its face. It provided its tax benefits not only to parents in sectarian schools but to those with children in any private schools. What distinguishes the case is not neutrality but the breadth of the statutory classification. It remains to be shown why the classification *parents* is broader in some relevant sense than the classification *parents with children in private schools*.[64] The breadth of the neutral statutory classification appears to be determined by the Court's intuitive theory of the interaction between religious pluralism and the political process. The Court in *Mueller*, after distinguishing the New

61. 463 U.S. 388 (1983).

62. Committee for Public Education v. Nyquist, 413 U.S. 756 (1973).

63. 463 U.S., pp. 398–99. The Court also stated that aid provided through parents rather than directly to the schools "reduced the Establishment Clause Objections." Ibid. But see Committee for Public Education v. Regan, 444 U.S. 646 (1980). It acknowledged that the New York and Minnesota statutes were indistinguishable on this ground.

64. Obviously there are more people in the former class. New York, however, provides massive subsidies through its expenditure system to parents whose children attend public schools. Thus, both forms of subsidies taken together constitute a system of subsidies to parents, just as in Minnesota. Further, the relevance of numbers alone is obscure. In New York enough parents of children in public schools were willing to subsidize the smaller group of parents with children in private schools to create a majority in favor of the statute. The Court in *Mueller* expressly rejected an alternative measure of breadth, refusing to look beyond the face of the statute to the actual fiscal impact of the benefits provided. Id., p. 401. It argued that tracing benefits through the tax system is difficult and that the results would vary from year to year depending on how carefully parents with children in public schools keep records supporting their claimed deductions. Further, the Court was concerned that it could not develop standards to distinguish broad from narrow fiscal impacts.

York statute, stated that "the attenuated benefits flowing to parochial schools [did not threaten] . . . the evils against which the Establishment Clause was designed to protect." Those evils were strife based on religion. But, the Court said, the issues must be kept "in perspective," and it quoted an earlier statement by Justice Powell that today "we are quite far removed from [those] dangers . . . The risk . . . of deep political division along religious lines is remote."[65] The risk is remote because of religious pluralism. A statute whose classifications are neutral is likely to provide benefits to a relatively large number of people as religious and nonreligious interests bargain in the political process. Such benefits are likely to have a significant fiscal impact. That impact in itself is likely to reduce the number of occasions on which statutes that threaten establishment clause values can be enacted.[66]

The deepest irony of the reduction principle is its very existence. It eliminates from the first amendment any specific concern for religion as a distinctive human activity. The marginality principle has much the same effect. It holds that the law must recognize religion only to the extent that religion has no socially significant consequences. It may not do so if religion is indeed socially significant. This does not mean that the constitutional law of religion treats religion as insignificant to its adherents or that our society's bows in the direction of religion are insignificant. It does mean that religion is recognized in ways that constitutional doctrine itself says are unimportant.

The marginality principle in free exercise cases is expressed in the rule that emerged from *Sherbert v. Verner*: the state must accommodate its general regulatory programs to the religious beliefs of its citizens.[67] The

65. Id., p. 399 (quoting Wolman v. Walter, 433 U.S. 229, 263 [1977] [opinion of Powell, J.]).

66. The pluralist analysis is filled with judgments about how the political process is likely to work, and the Court's refusal to examine actual fiscal impact in *Mueller* indicates that it is unwilling to entertain empirical challenges to the wider set of political judgments involved. Yet there is something to be said in favor of the pluralist analysis. Some states might adopt statutes like Minnesota's, and in a federal system that might well be acceptable. In contrast, devising a national tuition tax-credit system that uses sufficiently neutral terms, and that can attract enough political support, may be quite difficult, precisely because of the rather large fiscal impact of such a program. Discussions of proposals to adopt a national tuition tax-credit plan illustrate the problem. See Hearing on S. 2673, Senate Committee on Finance, 97th Cong., 2d Sess. (July 16, 1982). To keep the fiscal impact within acceptable bounds, the Reagan Administration's proposals were scaled back, primarily by eliminating a provision making the credit refundable to those whose incomes are so low as to make them unable to benefit from a pure tax credit. Eliminating that feature, though, makes the program beneficial only to the relatively well-to-do, which undermines the political attractiveness of the proposal.

67. Note that this rule cannot readily be accounted for by the reduction principle.

required degree of accommodation is to be determined by balancing the religious interest against the regulatory interest, each measured in an appropriate way. The effort to measure and balance these interests produces the rhetoric of the marginality principle.

The rhetorical strategy of proponents of free exercise exemptions is to minimize the impact of the exemption on the governmental interest. They do this by emphasizing that the religious practice has trivial social consequences.[68] According to proponents of exemptions, the relevant measure is the incremental impact of the exemption at issue on the governmental interest.[69] Careful definition of the incremental impact will always show that the religious practice plays a marginal role in the accomplishment of social goals.

Opponents of free exercise exemptions engage in a related manipulation of the balance. Instead of focusing on the incremental impact of the particular exemptions sought, their argument focuses on the cumulative impact of these and analogous exemptions. The cumulative impact can always be made significant, particularly if one throws into the balance difficulties in administering a scheme with numerous exemptions.[70] Thus, in *United States v. Lee* the Court refused to exempt Amish employers from the Social Security tax, saying that "it would be difficult to accommodate the comprehensive social security system with myriad exceptions flowing from a wide variety of religious beliefs."[71] This kind of manipula-

68. In Sherbert v. Verner, for example, the Court carefully noted how few Seventh-Day Adventists there were in the locality and suggested that only rarely would a Sabbatarian be unable to get a job which could accommodate her schedule. 374 U.S., p. 399 n. 2.

69. See, e.g., Clark, "Guidelines," pp. 331–33.

70. This is one of the concerns expressed in Goldman v. Weinberger, 475 U.S. 503 (1986), in which the Court rejected a claim by an Orthodox Jew that the free exercise clause required that he be exempted from the military's stipulation that soldiers on duty wear only approved headgear; the applicable regulations did not allow him wear his yarmulke.

71. 455 U.S., pp. 259–60. An alternative explanation of the Court's distinction between *Yoder* and *Lee* is that it believed that exemptions from taxes give people incentives to misrepresent their religious beliefs in ways that exemptions from public education do not and that determining the sincerity with which a religious belief is held is administratively difficult in the tax context. See Mayer Freed and Daniel Polsby, "Race, Religion, and Public Policy: Bob Jones University v. United States," 1983 *Supreme Court Review* 1, 22–26. I find the second of these propositions implausible, given the Court's willingness in other contexts—such as that of religious-based conscientious objection to compulsory military service—to authorize inquiries into sincerity. Note also that the first proposition imposes a rather rationalistic frame on assertions of religious belief.

Cases involving statutory accommodations of religious belief express similar judgments. Once again, law can take religion into account only because, and to the extent that, it is not socially significant. Thus, the Court interpreted Congress' requirement that employers accommodate their practices to the religious beliefs of their employees to demand only de minimis adjustments, that is, accommodations that had only the most minor impact on the

tion is endemic to balancing tests. In the free exercise context it has the particular effect of producing the marginality principle: an exemption will be provided if doing so has no socially significant consequences but not if it does.[72]

Like the reduction principle, the marginality principle emerges less directly in establishment clause cases. Even so, the marginality principle lies at the heart of standard establishment clause doctrine. One of the Court's "tests" to detect an establishment clause violation is that legislation may not have the purpose of advancing or inhibiting religion.[73] The purpose test means that if enough people take religion seriously, they cannot enact their program, but if they favor the same program for other reasons, they can enact it. It seems fair to say that this rule does not accept the view that religion should play an important part in public life.

Mark DeWolfe Howe identified another place where the marginality principle operates, although he did not give it that label or endorse its operation. He called a number of practices de facto establishments of religion.[74] De facto establishments are practices that our society tolerates even though they would be characterized as establishments of religion under any sensible test for establishment. Such practices include tax exemptions for church property[75] and legislative prayer.[76] Difficulties in determining how to identify de facto establishments while distinguishing them from true establishments produce the marginality principle in establishment clause cases.[77]

employers' business decisions. Trans World Airlines v. Hardison, 432 U.S. 63 (1977). See also Thornton v. Caldor, Inc., 472 U.S. 703 (1985) (statute requiring employers to give "Sabbath" off unconstitutional because it failed to take account of the hardships such an accommodation would cause employers and co-workers).

72. This is not to deny that exemptions are significant in alleviating the pressures felt by individual believers; it is to claim simply that the Constitution requires the alleviation of individual burdens only if doing so is not socially significant.

73. Lemon v. Kurtzman, 403 U.S. 602, 612–13 (1971). For an application of the purpose branch of the test, see Stone v. Graham, 449 U.S. 39 (1980) (invalidating statute requiring that Ten Commandments be posted in schoolrooms). Using this test the Court invalidated Alabama's "moment of silence" statute because its examination of the legislative history persuaded it that the sole motivation for the statute was to promote religious observance in the public schools. Wallace v. Jaffree, 472 U.S. 38 (1985).

74. Mark DeWolfe Howe, *The Garden and the Wilderness: Religion and Government in American Constitutional History* 11 (1965).

75. Walz v. Tax Commission, 397 U.S. 664 (1970).

76. Marsh v. Chambers, 463 U.S. 783 (1983).

77. *Marsh v. Chambers* suggests that de facto establishments might be those created contemporaneously with the Constitution. The Court in this case upheld the practice of paying the salary of a chaplain who opened legislative sessions with a prayer. Instead of relying on its settled three-part test for evaluating establishment clause claims, the Court emphasized the "unique history" of the practice, noting for example that three days after

Lynch v. Donnelly, the Court's decision upholding the constitutionality of municipal crèches, illustrates these difficulties, and the Court's analysis suggests that the solution lies in the use of the marginality principle.[78] The Court could not rely on a "contemporaneous interpretation" approach directly because Christmas began to be widely observed as a national holiday after the middle of the nineteenth century.[79] Still, the Court did invoke history. The opinion recited a variety of diverse practices—legislative chaplains, Thanksgiving declarations, displays of pictures with religious subjects in art museums—to show that "the role of religion in American life" has been acknowledged by government since 1789. It then turned to an analysis of the issue actually before it. The crèche had to be evaluated "in the context of the Christmas season"; although it did not precisely identify what that context was, presumably the Court meant to evoke images of a season of generalized goodwill and commercial promotion.[80] In that context the crèche had the "secular" purpose of "celebrat[ing] the Holiday and . . . depict[ing] its origins."[81]

In this conclusion the word *secular* takes on a curious meaning. The Court did not deny that the crèche has a religious meaning; it could not have done so without making meaningless its use of the word *celebrate*.[82]

Congress authorized the appointment of chaplains, it approved the text of the first amendment. Id., p. 791.

A "contemporaneous interpretation" approach to de facto establishments is likely to be unsatisfactory. Changes in social institutions make it difficult to be confident that a present-day practice is sufficiently similar to one in use at the time of the framing to warrant characterizing the institutions as the same. For example, property tax exemptions for churches are different in a society like ours, when major portions of a state's activities are financed by property tax revenues, from what they were two centuries ago, when public activities were much more limited in scope and financed largely by excise taxes. Walz v. Tax Commission, 397 U.S. 664 (1970), upheld such tax exemptions, relying on a slightly broader historical approach. The Court mentioned general establishment clause tests, but it gave more emphasis to the proposition that "few concepts are more deeply rooted in the fabric of our national life . . . than for the government to exercise . . . this kind of benevolent neutrality." Id., p. 696. This approach sees de facto establishments as certain practices deeply entrenched in our traditions without regard to the precise time of their origin.

78. 465 U.S. 668 (1984).

79. Id., at 720 (Brennan, J., dissenting). For much of the period before the Civil War, the Alabama legislature routinely met on Christmas. See J. Mills Thornton, *Politics and Power in a Slave Society* 82 (1978).

80. 465 U.S., pp. 674–78, 680, 685 ("display engenders a friendly community spirit of good will in keeping with the season"). See also id., p. 727 (Blackmun, J., dissenting) (crèche "has been relegated to the role of a neutral harbinger of the holiday season, useful for commercial purposes.").

81. Id., p. 681.

82. See also id., p. 685 (crèche has "religious implications"); 687 (crèche has "religious significance").

Rather, the crèche is "secular" in the sense that, in its context, it does not really do much to promote one religion over another or even to promote religion in general. The crèche is a "passive symbol," acknowledging religion but otherwise not terribly important.[83] The Court's message is that the crèche's opponents were taking the issue far too seriously.[84] The crèche is religious—but not very. There is a tradition of religiosity—but not of Christianity. It is all intended to be very soothing.

The Court in *Lynch* accomplished its goal of dampening sectarian tensions by invoking the marginality principle.[85] Some of its examples of the acknowledgment of religion, such as paintings with religious themes in museums, can only mean that religion is not in itself terribly important. Other examples involve the ritualistic employment of religious symbols which few take seriously. If the crèche is constitutional because its religious component, although real, resembles the religious components of these other activities, it is constitutional because it is marginal.

In this view de facto establishments are governmental activities that support what sociologists have called the American "civil religion."[86] This civil religion includes among its elements a diffuse religiosity, captured in the law by Justice Douglas' statement "We are a religious people whose institutions presuppose a Supreme Being."[87] As an element of civil religion this presupposition has no greater content than what Justice Douglas said. In our public life we are allowed to, and may be encouraged to,

83. See id., pp. 681–85, 686.

84. This theme is almost explicit in Justice O'Connor's concurring opinion, which makes dispositive "the message the crèche conveyed." Id., p. 690. She concluded that the particular crèche "was [not] intended to endorse [and did not have] the effect of endorsing Christianity." Id., p. 694.

85. The Court's decisions prohibiting the practice of state-sponsored group prayer and Bible reading in public schools pose a problem for this analysis, for the practice would seem to be consistent with a system of public support for diffuse religiosity. It may be that the state's role in composing the prayer in Engel v. Vitale, 370 U.S. 421 (1962), was too obvious an intrusion of the state into religious matters and that the use of the Bible in Abington School Dist. v. Schempp, 374 U.S. 203 (1963), was insufficiently diffuse in its religiosity. As the Court saw it these practices were simply motivated by religion (see text accompanying note 94) and therefore went beyond the bounds of diffuse religiosity in public life.

86. See Bellah, *Broken Covenant*. Bellah's own definition of civil religion is that it is a true religion, not "religion in general" or diffuse religiosity. This definition and its use in the U.S. context are quite controversial and probably lack substantial scholarly support. For a collection of the basic materials, see *American Civil Religion* (Russell Richey and Donald Jones eds. 1974). See also N. J. Demerath and Rhys Williams, "Civil Religion in an Uncivil Society," 480 *Annals of the American Academy of Political and Social Science* 154 (1985); George Kelly, *Politics and Religious Consciousness in America* 209–46 (1984). For another discussion of diffuse religiosity in constitutional law, see Van Alstyne, "Trends in the Supreme Court," pp. 786–87.

87. Zorach v. Clauson, 343 U.S. 306, 313 (1952).

bolster our positions by reference to a deity.[88] We cannot, however, derive policy positions from religion; that would make unacceptably concrete the civil religion's generalized religiosity.[89]

The pluralist theory of the establishment clause supports the definition that unites de facto establishments and civil religion. Religious pluralism can be celebrated as providing innumerable locations in which people can create or verify their relationship to a god whom they imagine in many different ways. When religious pluralism enters a political arena whose mode of action is bargaining among interest groups, little more than public support of diffuse religiosity is likely to result. Sects differ in the policy conclusions they draw from religion, and some sects oppose public support of religion on theological grounds.[90] Pluralist bargaining is likely to eliminate all but the least contentious position, which is precisely the religiosity of the civil religion.[91]

Religion and the Liberal Tradition

Both the analytic survey and the pragmatic one leave us with a law of religion that few should find satisfactory. An examination of the historical and analytic relations between religion and liberal political theory discloses the reasons why the reduction and marginality principles are attractive. We can then contrast the liberal tradition with the republican one to see the implications of taking the republican point of view for our understanding of the role of religion in the constitutional order.

88. Cf. McDaniel v. Paty, 435 U.S. 618 (1978).

89. For an especially dramatic criticism of the influence of concrete religiosity on public life, see Anthony Lewis, "Onward, Christian Soldiers," *New York Times*, p. A27, Mar. 10, 1983.

90. Justice Stevens has emphasized the tradition of religious opposition to public support of religion, based on the view that such support actually undermines religion. See, e.g., Roemer v. Board of Public Works, 426 U.S. 736, 775 (1976) (Stevens, J., dissenting) (noting "the pernicious tendency of a state subsidy to tempt religious schools to compromise their religious mission without wholly abandoning it"); Wolman v. Walter, 433 U.S. 229, 264 (1977) (Stevens, J., dissenting).

91. One potential outcome should be noted, although I think it unlikely to be realized very often. Sects might agree to support public endorsement of what might be thought of as a religious fair, in which the sects openly displayed their diverse views on concrete religious matters. Such a fair might exclude some sects. I assume, for example, that the fair would exclude Jews and Buddhists. Two points should be noted. Sectarian opposition to public support of religion may make it difficult to assemble sufficient support for a religious fair. Further, the message of a fair, even one that excludes some sects, is that religiosity in general is worthwhile. Thus, a fair consisting of many religious "booths" still supports no more than the civil religion.

The modern liberal tradition was shaped by a set of historical circumstances and a set of philosophical problems about the maintenance of social order. Each lent support to efforts, like those embodied in the reduction and marginality principles, to reduce the significance of religion in public life.

The historic origins of the modern liberal tradition lay in philosophers' reflections on the emergence of the unified nation-state. The nation-state was created over centuries of struggle to subordinate and eventually eliminate from public life the influence of personal attachments to institutions operating on an other-than-national scale. For example, the baronies of feudalism consisted of relatively small territorial groupings of people bound together by ritualistically created personal ties of reciprocal duty. Guilds protected local markets against erosion. Feudal bonds and local attachments tied workers to their neighborhoods. The nation-state was designed to break these local monopolies of power, to create a national entity strong enough to act in the emerging world polity, and to establish a market of sufficient breadth to allow the nation's expansion into the world market.[92]

The nation-state emerged by destroying the power of intermediate institutions standing between the individual and the comprehensive state.[93] Religious institutions were themselves intermediate institutions and were closely bound to others. As property owners, churches were actors in the feudal order. The ritual bonds of feudalism were created in conjunction with religious sanctions. As ideological enterprises churches developed theologies to support the maintenance of whatever secular hierarchies they found in the vicinity. Further, the central religious institution in the history on which political philosophers reflected was the Catholic church. It posed a particular obstacle to the nation-state by its claim to universal status. Standing against the secular ruler's claim to loyalty were the priests, and establishing the king's power required diminishing that of the priests.

The philosophical origin of the liberal tradition came from a reaction against the theology of Catholicism, which reproduced the problem posed by intermediate institutions. In that theology the believer's relationship to God had to be mediated through the church. In the religious sphere Catholic theology insisted on a relationship with three elements: the

92. See generally Perry Anderson, *Lineages of the Absolutist State* (1974); Immanuel Wallerstein, *The Modern World-System* (text ed. 1976). For a summary of the argument as made in liberation theology, see Harvey Cox, *Religion in the Secular City* 93–96, 163–64 (1984).

93. The term is obviously metaphorically inappropriate; before the nation-state emerged there was nothing for these institutions to stand as intermediaries against.

believer, the church, and God. In the secular sphere the ideology of the nation-state sought to establish a relationship with only two elements: the subject and the state. Clever thinkers could no doubt have designed ideological systems that explained and justified this incongruity. The availability of a competing theology made it largely unnecessary to do so: Protestant theology insisted also on a two-element relationship. Believers could—indeed had to—communicate directly with their God.[94] Thus, ideologists of the nation-state could begin to think of political life and religious life as two harmonious spheres: the direct relationship between believer and God paralleled the direct relationship between subject and state.

As they developed the liberal tradition political philosophers saw a terrain in which attachment to a universal nation-state had substantially reduced attachment to local institutions, in which local attachments seemed increasingly anomalous, and in which their theology allowed them to remain believers while eliminating the church as an intermediate institution. Their task was to rationalize all this into systematic form.

The liberal tradition accommodated religion by relegating it to the sphere of private life, a sphere whose connections to public life were of essentially no interest within the liberal tradition.[95] According to that tradition, public policy rested on the aggregation of individual preferences. Those preferences were formed outside the public sphere, and the manner of their formation was not a subject of political analysis: Preferences were exercises of private will, while public life consisted of mechanisms to subject private will to the operation of reason. (But see Chapter 9.)

In this picture of public life intermediate institutions play a number of roles.[96] They can provide the matrix within which private preferences are formed. Those preferences are then expressed in public life, where they

94. This is the widely noted significance of the Protestant translations of the Bible into the vernacular. The translations enable believers to grasp their religion without having to learn an esoteric language. See also Sidney Mead, "The 'Nation with the Soul of a Church,' " in *American Civil Religion*, pp. 45, 51 (homology of Protestantism and democracy); Ronald Garet, "Communality and Existence: The Rights of Groups," 56 *Southern California Law Review* 1001, 1031–32 (1983).

95. For a brief discussion of the tensions between religious privatism and religious communalities, see Wade Roof and William McKinney, "Denominational America and the New Religious Pluralism," 480 *Annals of the American Academy of Political and Social Science* 24 (1985).

96. The dynamics of economic growth in the United States had particularly strong effects on undermining the republican tradition, so that the development of the relation between church and state in the United States differed from that in other liberal societies. I therefore do not claim that the constitutional law of religion, as it has developed in the United States, is somehow the necessary working out of the implications of the liberal tradition; rather it is how the liberal and republican traditions evolved in the United States.

are aggregated with the preferences of other citizens, to create public policy. For example, voters take positions on abortion because of their participation in intermediate institutions such as their churches, their families, the voluntary associations to which they belong, and the like. In this role intermediate institutions are exogenous to public policy. They are impenetrable black boxes within which things happen that affect public policy but which cannot be the objects of that policy.[97] In addition, intermediate institutions can be the forms taken by alliances among like-minded people who find that they can advance their preferences by pooling resources in the effort to influence the development of public policy. The individualist assumptions of liberal political theory make these alliances unstable.[98]

Religion is not an important form of human experience in any of this; it has no distinctive role to play in the shaping of public policy. Indeed, by treating individual preferences as outside the scope of political analysis, the liberal tradition excludes religion from public life. It then seeks a theoretical expression for what it has done. The reduction and marginality principles together provide that expression: religion is still largely private, and its intrusion into the public sphere is small and unimportant.[99]

This exclusion cannot be sustained without invoking the competing republican tradition. Nonindividualist values are implicit in religious activities. For example, religious believers come to value their religious affiliation not only because it allows individual preferences to shape public policy more effectively but because it allows the experience of

97. For a classic expression, see George Stigler and Gary Becker, "De Gustibus Non Est Disputandum," 67 *American Economic Review* 76 (1977). Intermediate institutions can also be used as instruments of public policy. Churches will be tolerated so long as, and to the extent that, they induce believers to act in ways congruent with public policies determined without reference to religious values. In this role intermediate institutions are not really intermediate; they are instead parts of the state, like a governmental bureaucracy or a school system.

98. Individuals have preferences that coincide in some matters and conflict in others. Temporary trade-offs may be possible, but long-term alliances are unlikely. Instability is promoted by the fact that such alliances provide opportunities for free riders, who remain outside the alliance but benefit from its activities. Even members of the alliance will sometimes be able to profit from strategic behavior by defecting to another alliance when the right issue comes along. See Olson, *Logic of Collective Action*.

99. The most obvious expression would be a theory of strict separation of church and state. The liberal tradition's long-standing and still deeply felt attraction to strict separationist theories demonstrates that they fit well with that tradition.

solidarity, of mutual action.[100] At this point, however, the individualist predicates of the liberal tradition come under stress. Instead of allowing the more effective expression of exogenously determined individual preferences, intermediate institutions now begin to shape those preferences. Further, the preferences that take shape are necessarily preferences for nonindividualist experiences. Thus, when religion is taken seriously it subverts the premises of the very theory into which it was supposed to fit.

Another view of this instability can be gained by reconsidering Justice White's argument in *Widmar v. Vincent*. There he sought to distinguish worship from speech on the ground that worship is directed within the community of believers whereas speech is directed outside. This distinction indicates that rituals take on their meaning because they occur within an intermediate institution. Vis-à-vis the wider society rituals are a communal activity shared among the believers. They are necessarily not individualist but communal.[101] When the liberal tradition attempts to deal with religion, it faces a phenomenon that its major themes make quite mysterious.

The incompatibility between religion, a necessarily communal activity, and the major themes of the liberal tradition provides one explanation for the separate identification of religion in the first amendment. Another explanation is that the reduction and marginality principles deny the felt experience of believers that their religious beliefs are different in kind from political ones, their own or those of others.[102] By distinguishing between religion and other forms of belief, the first amendment contains a

---

100. See Garet, "Communality and Existence," p. 1009 ("groups are possibilities for religious experience"); Parker Palmer, *A Company of Strangers: Christians and the Renewal of America's Public Life* 20–31 (1981).

101. For definitions of religion that point in this direction, see A. Stephen Boyan, "Defining Religion in Operational and Institutional Terms," 116 *University of Pennsylvania Law Review* 479 (1968); Note, "Toward a Constitutional Definition of Religion," 91 *Harvard Law Review* 1056 (1978); Dodge, "Free Exercise."

102. *In kind* means that religious beliefs are not merely "deeper" or about "more fundamental" things than political ones. For definitions pointing to such considerations, see Note, "Sacred and Profane"; Choper, "Defining 'Religion,' " pp. 581–82. As has been frequently noted, this definition in fact does not distinguish religion from some kinds of political belief, such as those grounded in comprehensive social theories. See Clark, "Guidelines," pp. 339–43. The usual example is Marxism and associated bodies of political thought. Another example is liberalism itself, which asks us to take "on faith" a set of assumptions about human nature and capacity. The most dramatic illustration is Nozick, *Anarchy, State, and Utopia*, p. ix (asserting without defense there or elsewhere in the book that "individuals have rights, and there are things no person or group may do to them [without violating their rights]").

nonindividualist principle.[103] It thus signals that the Constitution is not an entirely individualist document. The Constitution's communitarian commitments take the form of an implicit appeal to a tradition of civic republicanism which was more vibrant in the framers' world than it is in ours. That too helps explain the incoherence of the constitutional law of religion: It is founded on a tradition that the courts no longer fully understand.

Although religious institutions fit uneasily into the liberal tradition, they fit quite comfortably into the republican one. Historically the proponents of republicanism sought to preserve some of the traditional intermediate institutions against the encroachment of liberal ones. In that sense they were conservatives and as conservatives understood the role of religion in stabilizing the social order.[104]

Religious institutions fit into the republican tradition for conceptual as well as historical reasons. Citizens must acquire civic responsibility and a concern for the public interest somewhere; if citizens enter the political arena without the appropriate balance of public and private concerns, they may misuse public power. Intermediate institutions provide a sound location for the inculcation of the appropriate balance of values. Lacking the full panoply of state power, they cannot coerce their members into accepting their vision of the needed balance. Having the characteristics of communal organizations in which members experience their interdependence in the creation of the meanings that give life to the institution, they can provide the experience of acting for the common good. With that experience members can enter the political arena knowing that in addition to their private interests there is such a thing as a public interest to be sought.

The constitutional law of religion is confused because the republican tradition is far less available to us than it was to the framers. Once again I do not mean to suggest that we could rationalize the law of religion by imagining what a revitalized republicanism would do with religion. The republican tradition as a conservative tradition insisted on the historicity of institutions and public policy. That very insistence makes it impossible to impose on today's society solutions drawn from a less-than-vital, indeed to some extent imaginary, tradition.

In addition, the republican tradition claimed that its vision of the polity was completely integrated with its vision of the social order. Citizens in the republican society would have sufficient material wealth to ensure

103. See Garet, "Communality and Existence," p. 1013 (need to recognize "a group face of value").

104. Liberals understood that too, which is why they incorporated a challenge to religion into their efforts. See text accompanying notes 93–94.

their independence from anyone who might seek to control their actions as citizens. They would be sensitive to the need to maintain a proper balance between public and private goals and would develop that sensitivity through a system of civic education. The conservative branch of republican thought assumed that the necessary equality in material and intellectual capacity could be accomplished only if the polity were restricted. The democratic revolutions of the eighteenth and nineteenth centuries have made it impossible to realize the republican vision in its conservative form. Instead they require that the republican vision be revitalized by large transformations in the social order.

Arthur Sutherland's comment on *Engel v. Vitale* suggests one view of the relation between republicanism and the religion clauses.[105] *Engel* held unconstitutional the practice of requiring the recitation in public schools of a "nondenominational" prayer composed by a state agency. As did other commentators, Sutherland thought the case trivial.[106] The conclusion of his article opens the way to a more subtle understanding of the religion clauses. Sutherland discussed the intricate question of standing raised by the case: as it was presented to the Supreme Court, the case involved no coercion of students and at most only trivial expenditures of public money to support the prayer.[107] Thus, it was difficult to discern the deprivation of liberty or property necessary to fit the case within the fourteenth amendment. Sutherland recognized, though, that the law of standing was both technical and flexible enough to accommodate the case. Rather than criticizing the Court for finding standing, he used the difficulties to suggest that the Court should have exercised a sound discretion to avoid deciding the case.

Sutherland then concluded his article by suggesting a brilliant generalization of the question of discretion.[108] Drawing on his experience as a member of a small town's school board, he said that the school board in

---

105. 370 U.S. 421 (1962); Arthur Sutherland, "Establishment according to Engel," 76 *Harvard Law Review* 25 (1962).

106. See, e.g., Ernest Brown, " 'Quis Custodiet Ipsos Custodes?'—The School Prayer Cases," 1963 *Supreme Court Review* 1; Philip Kurland, "The Regents' Prayer Case: 'Full of Sound and Fury, Signifying ... ,' " 1962 *Supreme Court Review* 1, 19–22. The case generated much more public controversy. See Kirk Elifson and C. K. Hadaway, "Prayer in Public Schools: When Church and State Collide," 49 *Public Opinion Quarterly* 317 (1985) (reviewing opinion surveys from 1974 and 1980); H. Frank Way, "Survey Research on Judicial Decisions: The Prayer and Bible Reading Cases," 21 *Western Political Quarterly* 189 (1968).

107. Sutherland, "Establishment," p. 41. See Doremus v. Board of Education, 342 U.S. 429 (1952), suggesting that more than de minimis expenditures are required to support standing to raise establishment clause claims. *Engel* was decided before Flast v. Cohen, 392 U.S. 83 (1968), temporarily restructured the law of establishment clause standing.

108. Sutherland, "Establishment," p. 52.

Engel might have deliberated seriously about the religious contention its use of the prayer caused and might have forgone—as a matter of discretion not of constitutional command—the use of the prayer. The point is of course symmetrical in a way suggested by *Lynch v. Donnelly*: those offended by the prayer might have exercised a wise discretion to forgo the constitutional challenge they were in a strict sense entitled to bring.

In bringing out the possibility of mutual forbearance rather than the Constitution as the basis for resolving issues of the relation between government and religion, Sutherland drew on the tradition of civic republicanism. One consequence of a vital republicanism might well be the kind of culture of mutual forbearance to which Sutherland appealed.[109] Citizens would understand that the polity was intended to advance the public good. They might conclude that civic actions that generate intense hostility are unlikely to advance the public good and forbear from taking them. They might also conclude that civic actions designed to promote intensely held values are likely to advance the public good, even if some think those actions unwise or even troublesome on grounds of conscience. They might then forbear from challenging such actions. A culture of mutual forbearance might result in a pattern of public actions that superficially resemble the current marginality of religion in public life. Marginality would not be a principle; it would be a characteristic that citizens decide, on balance, to give their public life. Sutherland was exactly right to appeal to discretion rather than to the law of standing. That appeal reminds us of what remains valuable in the republican tradition.

109. See also Leonard Levy, *The Establishment Clause: Religion and the First Amendment* 179 (1986).

9

The Constitution
of the Market

Introduction: Institutions and the Formation of Preferences

TODAY'S prevalent political theories describe the task of social institutions, such as the market and the political process, as aggregating the preferences of society's members. (See, for instance, Chapter 2.) Social institutions themselves, however, influence the preferences that they are then supposed to aggregate.[1] It is difficult to understand how the aggregation can coherently take place when preferences are not exogenous to the institutions.

This chapter examines some institutional dimensions of the construction of preferences in the United States by exploring the constitutional law applicable to the regulation of campaign finance, commercial speech, and pornography. The topics are connected, as this chapter argues, because analysis of all three shows that contemporary constitutional law embodies a preference for instrumental rationality. In turn, the idea of instrumental rationality provides important support for a variety of subordinate concepts that limit the play of politics in the United States.[2] For example, instrumental rationality supports the pluralist image of politics as a process in which people participate simply to accomplish their private goals—that is, as a process in which instrumental rationality governs. In addition, instrumental rationality characterizes participation

1. For an introduction to this problem, see Jon Elster, *Sour Grapes: Studies in the Subversion of Rationality* 109–40 (1983). Another set of difficulties, also discussed in Chapter 2, is defining the geographic scope of the society whose members' preferences are to be aggregated and defining the entities who are to count as members of the society for these purposes.

2. See Charles Taylor, *Philosophy and the Human Sciences* 102–3 (1985) (noting that "cultural conditions" allow "a certain form of rationality" to become "a [if not the] dominant value").

in the market, where people are supposed to take their goals as given and then work out the instrumentally best way to accomplish those goals by allocating their time appropriately. Finally, instrumental rationality is what is taken to distinguish the public sphere, which includes both the politics and the market and which is governed by instrumental rationality, from the private sphere, which need not be so governed.[3] This chapter begins with a discussion of an obviously "public" issue and ends with a discussion of an apparently more "private" one in order to expose the underlying structure of the public/private continuum.

Institutions can influence preferences in several ways.[4] They might produce support for particular policies, or they might impose limits on the policies that can seriously be considered, or they might define the ways in which people approach issues of public policy by establishing criteria of rationality, acceptability, and the like. As we will see, most of the recent discussions of campaign finance and commercial advertising focus on the first of these methods. We will also see that the pluralism of our social system makes it difficult to defend regulation of campaign finance and commercial advertising on the ground that, unregulated, those institutions influence the choice of particular policies.[5] Rather the defense must rest on the argument that the existing systems of campaign

3. See generally Frances Olsen, "The Family and the Market: A Study of Ideology and Legal Reform," 96 *Harvard Law Review* 1497 (1983).

4. The issue has a dynamic and a static dimension. Institutions can shape preferences over time. For example, Madison defended federalism on the ground that voters in the states would learn to identify the most civic-minded candidates, whereas voters in large governments would attend only to their individual interests. Similarly, over time the citizens in a plebiscitary democracy will come to prefer different things than those in a representative democracy prefer, perhaps because they will not have the experience of striking political deals that leads people to appreciate and to wish to accommodate the values held by those with whom they differ. (The point here is not just that policy outcomes differ, as might be the case in comparing proportional representation systems with district representation ones. Rather the point is that the preferences themselves differ.)

Institutions also elicit different preferences from people as they are at any one time. Taking people as already shaped in part by existing institutions, we would still expect that policy outcomes in a plebiscitary democracy would differ from those in a representative federal republic populated by the same citizens. (Formalizing this point is quite difficult. For example, plebiscites usually are single-issue elections, which may occur in sequence, whereas representation usually is for a fixed term during which many issues might arise. Representation systems therefore allow long-term deals to be made in a way that is impossible in a plebiscitary system. Perhaps the best comparison would be between a representation system and one in which numerous plebiscites were to take place simultaneously. In the latter system people could coordinate their campaigns, but shirking would be fairly easy and any deals would be unenforceable at the voting booth.)

5. By *unregulated* I mean the present system of regulation or a less extensive one.

finance and commercial advertising place limits on what can be accomplished through political action.

Defenders of regulation in these areas have also argued that regulation is compatible with the first amendment's guarantee of freedom of speech because that guarantee is predicated on a vision of politics derived from the republican tradition and because regulation promotes republican values such as the creation of an informed and rational electorate. This argument does invoke the limits that unregulated institutions place on political discussion. The first two sections of this chapter argue that a successful defense of regulation cannot rest on these grounds either. In part the defense fails because the liberal tradition has so eroded republicanism that it is difficult to believe that the products of today's legislatures could actually revitalize republicanism.

The defense also fails for a more fundamental reason, its commitment to a particular form of rationality. This is shown by confronting the third way in which institutions influence preferences, through establishing criteria of rationality. This is the primary subject of the discussion of pornography. Those in the liberal tradition object to regulation of political campaigns and commercial advertising because they believe that the citizenry has sufficient rational evaluative capacities to accept or reject political and commercial claims on whatever the merits might be. The republican tradition is also committed to the view that public life should be governed by a well-developed instrumental rationality. For present purposes that tradition assumes that the capacity for instrumental rationality is not an immutable characteristic of human nature and that social institutions must be structured to encourage the development of the capacity for instrumental rationality. One method of structuring institutions involves the use of the noncognitive devices that constitute the art of rhetoric. In this way the republican tradition is only ambivalently committed to the importance of instrumental rationality.

By examining the constitutional law of campaign finance and commercial speech, we will see that regulation founders on the assumption that instrumental rationality is the most fundamental or privileged human capacity. The analysis of pornography and its most important feminist critics then shows that both pornography and those critics appeal to a different deliberative capacity. Yet prevailing constitutional doctrine forces efforts to regulate pornography into a framework structured by the very notion of instrumental rationality which advocates of regulation wish to repudiate. The conclusion suggests that the most effective way out of the difficulties posed in all three areas is by means of openly political evaluations of proposed institutional arrangements, including in that category the status quo and moderate reforms as well as fundamental alternatives.

Republicanism, Rationality, and Campaign Finance

Is the regulation of campaign finance consistent with the first amendment? Or must we leave the financing of political campaigns to the "unregulated" market? The argument against regulation is straightforward.

Suppose I have become dissatisfied with existing public policy. I stand on a street corner and give some speeches. Then I realize that I could reach more people if I distributed a leaflet, so I close my savings account and use the money to publish a pamphlet. Some of the people who read the pamphlet are convinced by its arguments and call me to find out how they can help to propagate the arguments. We pool our money and make some advertisments that are broadcast on the radio. But, although I am a decent public speaker, it turns out that I lack the presence to be an effective radio broadcast speaker. One of the people who has read the pamphlet offers to deliver our radio messages. She believes that to be effective she must work at the job of politics full-time, and we agree with her suggestion that we pay her a salary for her political work. The radio advertisments are reasonably successful, and more people give us money to spread the message. In addition, a member of the state legislature calls to say that she has been convinced by our arguments and wants to make them the centerpiece of a campaign for the House of Representatives. We decide that our resources can best be used by dividing them in three ways. Some of us have little money but lots of energy and free time; that group will canvass voters door to door. Another group can write powerful political speeches, and we decide to pay them for their time and to pay to have the speeches published. A final group has few talents but believes deeply in our cause. They decide to contribute money to the legislator's campaign for Congress.

Regulation of campaign finance affects the second and third groups. Typically such regulations attempt to limit the expenditures made by supporters of a candidate or policy and to limit contributions to candidates or groups urging the adoption of a policy.[6] If the first amendment prohibits governmental regulation of my own activity, it is far from obvious that it permits regulation of coordinated activities of the sort I have described.[7]

6. See, e.g., Federal Election Campaign Act of 1971, 86 Stat. 3 (1972), Federal Election Campaign Act Amendments of 1974, 88 Stat. 1263, and Federal Election Campaign Act Amendments of 1976, 90 Stat. 475, and of 1979, 93 Stat. 1339.

7. For general discussions of the state of the law, see Herbert Alexander, "The Future of Election Reform," 10 *Hastings Constitutional Law Quarterly* 721 (1983); Comment, "Legislative Regulation of Campaign Financing after *Citizens against Rent Control v. City of Berkeley*: A Requiem," 36 *University of Miami Law Review* 563 (1982).

The government could not keep me from giving my street-corner talk.[8] Nor could it require me to use what I regard as less effective methods of propagating my message: It could not decide that because I was "too effective" a public speaker I had to deliver my speeches with pebbles in my mouth.[9] It seems to follow that the government cannot interfere with my judgment that my political goals will be best advanced by my keeping my job and using some of my income to hire someone who would be more effective than I in getting my message across.[10] The analysis is the same for a group of like-minded people: each has a set of endowments—talents, money, and the like—and each decides that his or her endowments will be best used to advance his or her political goals by a mixture of some personal political activity and some expenditures to hire others whose more specialized talents will advance the cause.[11] Thus, regulation of campaign expenditures seems inconsistent with the first amendment.[12]

Defenses of efforts to regulate expenditures take a number of forms, but all are linked to the view in the republican tradition that public policy

8. Subject to time, place, and manner regulations not relevant to this discussion.

9. Some regulations deprive speakers of what they believe to be their most effective methods of communication, see, e.g., Kovacs v. Cooper, 336 U.S. 77 (1947), but they do so to promote goals unrelated to communication not because the methods are believed to make the speaker too effective.

10. See L. A. Powe, "Mass Speech and the Newer First Amendment," 1982 *Supreme Court Review* 243, 258–59.

11. See Daniel Polsby, "*Buckley v. Valeo*: The Special Nature of Political Speech," 1976 *Supreme Court Review* 1, 22–23; Sanford Levinson, "Book Review: Regulating Campaign Activity—The New Road to Contradiction?" 83 *Michigan Law Review* 939, 948–50 (1985).

12. Questions about the regulation of contributions to candidates are somewhat different. Contributions to candidates may occasionally verge on bribes, that is, a transfer of money to enhance the candidate's personal wealth in exchange for the legislator's vote. For a comprehensive discussion of bribery, see John Noonan, *Bribes* (1984). Of course bribery is itself a criminal offense. But perhaps some additional methods of reducing the risk of bribery are needed. Disclosure of contributions coupled with a vigorous press interested in investigating corruption might still be thought inadequate. Limitations on contributions to candidates might then be justified on anticorruption grounds. See Buckley v. Valeo, 424 U.S. 1, 24–29 (1976). (The impossibility of bribery in connection with referenda explains the Court's unwillingness to accept contribution limitations in that context. See First National Bank of Boston v. Bellotti, 435 U.S. 765 [1978]; Citizens against Rent Control v. City of Berkeley, 454 U.S. 290 [1981].)

The argument supporting contribution limitations has its weak points; avoiding the appearance of corruption may not be an especially potent reason for limiting an otherwise permissible exercise of free speech, and much in the relevant argument turns on the degree of deference the courts should give to the "expertise" of perhaps self-interested legislators who desire to protect themselves against competition from outsiders. See text accompanying note 28. I will not, however, devote further attention to the issue of contribution limitations.

should serve the public interest rather than private interests.[13] Yet each of the defenses is vulnerable to two challenges: each relies on the notion of civic virtue to resuscitate a politics that, by its own arguments, has been polluted by private interest, and each defines the public interest with reference to the same criteria of instrumental rationality used to define private interests.

One defense of limitations on expenditures takes advantage of the widespread perception among some segments of the intelligentsia that excessive expenditures have led to the thirty-second political commercial and all that that symbolizes. These advertisements, it is said, lead voters to decide not "on the merits" but on the basis of their visceral reactions to images that were created precisely to manipulate viewers.[14] That is, expenditures affect preferences not so much by persuading voters that the policy preferred by those who spend the most is the better policy[15] but, more important, by structuring voters' consciousness so that emotion prevails over reason.[16] By restricting expenditures we could confine the forms of political discussion to those in which the merits figure more prominently.

The preference for instrumental rationality is clear in this argument; the reasons for the preference are not. The preference for instrumental rationality in advancing the public interest overlooks too much about politics even in the republican tradition.[17] The art of political rhetoric consists in framing instrumentally rational arguments in ways that appeal to a citizenry that is not always attentive to the public interest alone. Political rhetoric in its best forms uses nonrational methods to advance

13. See Cass Sunstein, "Interest Groups in American Public Law," 38 *Stanford Law Review* 29, 31–35 (1985); Charles Beitz, "Political Finance in the United States: A Survey of Research," 95 *Ethics* 129, 144–45 (1984).

14. See Archibald Cox, "Constitutional Issues in the Regulation of the Financing of Election Campaigns," 31 *Cleveland State Law Review* 395, 416, 418 (1982).

15. People do make these arguments too, see, e.g., id., pp. 415–16, but they are overdrawn. See Daniel Lowenstein, "Campaign Spending and Ballot Propositions: Recent Experience, Public Choice Theory and the First Amendment," 29 *UCLA Law Review* 505 (1982). In any event persuading people one way or the other would seem to be pretty close to the heart of the first amendment.

16. General studies of this structuring process are Austin Ranney, *Channels of Power: The Impact of Television on American Politics* (1983); Max Atkinson, *Our Masters' Voices: The Language and Body Language of Politics* (1984); Greg Philo, John Hewitt, Peter Behamel, and Howard Davis, *Really Bad News* (1982).

17. In addition, people aggregate their wealth to invest in particular forms of campaign advertising for deeply instrumental reasons: they believe that given their endowments they can accomplish their goals best by that sort of investment. The argument that expenditure limitations promote instrumentally rational decisions "on the merits" of the public interest ignores the instrumental rationality that produces the expenditures in the first place.

rational goals.[18] Thus, the idea that there is a rational decision to be made "on the merits" seems questionable in light of what politics is.

A second set of arguments for limiting expenditures invokes the metaphors of communications and antitrust. Large aggregations of wealth used for political purposes can "drown out" opposing voices. This is not sufficient to justify limiting expenditures, for opposing voices might try to accumulate enough money on their own. But, it is said, they cannot because the "barriers to entry" are so high.[19] The initial response to the "drowning out" argument is that in a pluralist system we expect the competition between ideas to provide the basis for voter choice. It is an empirical question whether some views are drowned out or are simply not widely enough accepted to become important elements in discussions of public policy. On many issues the evidence is fairly strong that drowning out does not occur, although of course some sides of issues spend more than others—perhaps because their adherents care more or because the precampaign distribution of preferences favors them.[20]

Drowning out should be rare in a pluralist system because each side of an issue can appeal for financial support. Here the antitrust analogy appears. Some have argued that the conditions of modern campaigning, which require large investments in television advertising, make it difficult to enter the pluralist discussion in the first place. The difficulty with this argument is that it relies on a performance measure of antitrust: its proponents see that certain policy positions tend to prevail and infer that something must be wrong with the political process. Performance measures are notoriously difficult to use in antitrust analysis because they rely on normative standards for evaluating outcomes; in contrast, a market orientation is attractive precisely because it eliminates the need for such normative standards.[21] The analogue in the political context is obvious: drowning out must occur, in this view, because policies are not adopted on the merits (or, even worse, because the "wrong" policies are adopted).

---

18. One might wonder whether it makes sense to think about the nomination of Geraldine Ferraro in terms of the merits conceived of as instrumentally rational. In some sense "the merits" were obviously involved in her selection, but not in the sense of instrumental rationality; indeed, it may be literal nonsense to speak of evaluating a person, as distinct from a policy, "on the merits."

19. See Cox, "Constitutional Issues," p. 409; J. Skelly Wright, "Money and the Pollution of Politics: Is the First Amendment an Obstacle to Political Equality?" 82 *Columbia Law Review* 609, 609 (1982); Harold Leventhal, "Courts and Political Thickets," 77 *Columbia Law Review* 345, 375 (1977).

20. See generally Yudof, *When Government Speaks*; Beitz, "Political Finance," pp. 139–41.

21. See Lawrence Sullivan, *Antitrust* 28 (1977).

We might use the antitrust analogy differently, focusing on structure rather than performance. The current view of industry structure is that no antitrust problems are raised by the simple fact that a large initial investment is needed before one can enter some field.[22] If production would be profitable, the amounts needed to enter would be made available by a well-functioning market for capital funds. Similarly in politics: Suppose that a policy serves the public interest more than its opposite serves aggregated private interests. Supporters of the policy should contribute enough money to generate political advertising to offset that produced by the private interests. Are there structural barriers to the accumulation of resources for these purposes?

At least three structural barriers might exist. The public interest might not be an aggregation at all; it might indeed conflict with the private interests of many people and be irrelevant to the private interests of others. If people think of their private interests when they make decisions about whether to invest in political activity or personal consumption, there will be systematic underinvestment in advertising to advance the public interest, leading in the extreme to drowning out. But, as we will see, there are good reasons to believe that limitations on campaign expenditures are ill suited to the task of enhancing the public interest components of contemporary political discourse.

A second structural barrier is organizational. As we saw in Chapter 2, if the benefits of a policy are widely diffused and the benefits of the contrary policy are highly concentrated, there is likely to be underinvestment in support for the widely diffused policy. Its supporters will count on others to invest in political activity, and the result will be that less activity will occur than the policy's supporters desire. This may be the condition of policies in the public interest. We also saw that it is difficult to identify real political circumstances in which we can be confident that this problem occurs. Like entrepreneurs in the market, political entrepreneurs— another name for candidates and parties—may be less risk averse than the rest of us and may seek out unutilized opportunities for political advancement. Further, underinvestment in activity to promote particular policies might occur if the returns on those policies are nonmonetary and likely to be undervalued. Political parties aggregate particular policies into general platforms and have an interest in accurately determining the true return on each policy in the platform's package of programs so as to maximize their chances of success given the resources they can secure.[23]

---

22. See Herbert Hovenkamp, *Economics and Federal Antitrust Law* 151 (1985).

23. Political parties may err in their calculations about what the public wants, but there would seem to be no obvious systematic bias about the kinds of mistakes that might occur.

Finally, there is a true structural barrier. The antitrust analogy suggests that we should be unconcerned about drowning out in the presence of a well-functioning capital market. There is, though, one issue on which the capital market is almost sure to malfunction—the value of capitalism itself or, more generally, the value of institutions that systematically benefit the relatively well-to-do. The capital market is likely to malfunction here because people have to choose between spending money on political activity and spending it on personal consumption, and the relatively less well off face a more stringent budget constraint that reduces their ability to invest in political activity. Once again, however, a limitation on expenditures seems ill adapted to remedying that structural problem because it is not correlated with the underlying problem. Subsidies to socialist parties would be the more obvious remedy,[24] and the absurdity of that suggestion in contemporary American politics ought to cast some doubt on the sincerity of the asserted concern with the drowning out problem.[25] Nor are restrictions on expenditures likely to be a sound "second or third best" solution to the problem of income inequality: Adopted by politicians who have benefited from the existing distribution of wealth, such restrictions are quite unlikely to be structured in ways that will over time have the political consequence of significantly altering that distribution.[26]

In sum, the difficulty with the drowning out argument is that it focuses on a problem to which pluralism and fund-raising are responsive and to which limitations on expenditures are not. This suggests that the underlying concern is not that some views are drowned out but that the views that are drowned out should not be. That returns us to a concern for republicanism and rationality.

The third set of arguments for expenditure limitations relies on the idea that such regulations may be useful ways to commit ourselves in advance

24. The Supreme Court has held that, under rather limited circumstances, some political groups may be entitled to exemption from otherwise applicable regulations, which is a form of subsidy. See Brown v. Socialist Workers '74 Campaign Committee, 459 U.S. 87 (1982); Geoffrey Stone and William Marshall, "*Brown v. Socialist Workers*: Inequality as a Command of the First Amendment," 1983 *Supreme Court Review* 583.

25. It may be that cognitive overload occasionally occurs so that people reject additional information simply because the volume of information available to them has become too great. This sort of drowning out would seem to have no systematic effects that would justify regulation.

26. A skeptic might answer that expenditure limitations are a useful way station to adopting egalitarian policies, the direct adoption of which is blocked by the existing system of campaign finance. If such limitations have that instrumental value, it is hard to understand why the well-to-do do not figure this out and act to preempt the threat that might later be realized.

to avoiding decisions that we do not now want to make and that we fear we might (but should not) want to make in the future.[27] Sedition laws are this sort of precommitment: We fear that if people advocate forcible overthrow of the government, our successors, less sturdy folk than we, might be persuaded to overthrow the government; we therefore prohibit advocacy of forcible overthrow. But, as we saw in Chapter 2, the first amendment is itself a sort of precommitment. Our predecessors barred us from being persuaded that it is permissible to prohibit speech on the ground that we fear that our successors will be persuaded by it.

Limitations on expenditures might be a special sort of precommitment. The dynamics of campaign expenditures may be that once one person starts spending a lot on campaigns everyone else has to match the expenditure or lose the election. In ordinary markets such expenditures are constrained by the profit motive, because people cannot spend more than they would receive in return. The political market, however, lacks that constraint. So long as investors are willing to put up the money, in return for influence on matters of private interest or to advance the public interest, someone is willing to spend it. Campaign expenditures thus may spiral upward, at the least diverting money away from activities that have greater social value. Yet no one candidate can stop the spiral. Statutory limitations can coordinate action that all may desire but that none can achieve alone.[28] In this sense more speech may not be socially desirable. Proponents of limitations argue that excessive expenditures degrade public discourse in ways that more modest outlays do not. According to this argument, a precommitment to limit expenditures preserves the rationality of public debate by eliminating the possibility that an upward spiral in expenditures will cause a downward spiral in the quality of debate.

Concern over the quality of debate is a theme in the republican tradition. In Chapter 1 we saw that Bruce Ackerman tried to explain the structure of constitutional law as a precommitment to a republican society. Ackerman argued that some periods, such as the New Deal, saw widespread exercises in "constitutional" politics even though they yielded only legislation. We might treat recent legislation regarding campaign financing as similarly the product of a period of heightened democratic consciousness stirred into action by the abuses that go by the name of

27. See Jon Elster, *Ulysses and the Sirens: Studies in Rationality and Irrationality*, ch. 2 (1979). Note that most laws are aimed at controlling minorities (the losers in the legislative process), but precommitments are imposed by one majority (today's) on another majority (tomorrow's).

28. Even so, the evil attacked here—excessive spending and the ensuing social waste that diverts money from more productive uses—might not be substantial enough to justify regulation.

Watergate. Some of the difficulties with Ackerman's arguments, however, recur in this setting. Watergate may not accurately symbolize the emergence of a new period of constitutional politics. The campaign finance legislation of that period and since has strong effects in protecting incumbents and entrenching the existing parties.[29] These effects look a lot like what ordinary politicians would try to accomplish. Thus, Ackerman's analysis seems unhelpful for the analysis of campaign finance legislation as a precommitment.

The more specific precommitment argument, that campaign finance legislation avoids the degradation of public discourse, is also questionable. It reiterates the republican defense of instrumental rationality in politics. Yet as the Supreme Court has said, the government may not prohibit speech "in order to maintain . . . a suitable level of discourse within the body politic." A state government therefore could not convict a young man who had a jacket with FUCK THE DRAFT on the back. The Court emphasized the fact that "words are often chosen as much for their emotive as their cognitive force" and said that the Constitution, "while solicitous of the cognitive content . . . , [also protects] the emotive function which, practically speaking, may often be the more important element of the overall message."[30]

The final argument for restricting expenditures is that such restrictions direct political activity into more valuable forms. When people cannot spend money on political activity, they will substitute direct discussion, canvassing, and the like.[31] These more personal forms of political activity encourage debate and discussion in ways that political advertising aimed at a passive listener does not and thus are more compatible with the republican tradition and its version of instrumental rationality.[32] Regulating campaign expenditures attempts to break the connection between the economic market, where wealth is accumulated and the private interest prevails, and the political process, in which wealth should not be spent and the public interest should prevail.[33] Given the dominance of market

---

29. See, e.g., Joel Fleishman, "Freedom of Speech and Equality of Political Opportunity: The Constitutionality of the Federal Election Campaign Act of 1971," 51 *North Carolina Law Review* 389, 466–70 (1973); Lillian BeVier, "Money and Politics: A Perspective on the First Amendment and Campaign Finance Reform," 73 *California Law Review* 1045, 1076–77, 1080 (1985).

30. Cohen v. California, 403 U.S. 15, 23, 26 (1971).

31. See, e.g., J. Skelly Wright, "Politics and the Constitution: Is Money Speech?" 85 *Yale Law Journal* 1001, 1012 (1976).

32. This argument ignores the opportunity costs of direct activity; those costs are obviously correlated with wealth and may be correlated with substantive views.

33. See Michael Walzer, *Spheres of Justice* (1983). The use of wealth in politics might be said to differ from cashing in on celebrity or using celebrity in politics because the talents

processes in our society, the connection cannot be broken completely, but limiting expenditures, unlike other devices to limit the importance of markets, might modestly weaken the connection with few troubling implications for a theory of human freedom in other spheres.

This defense of expenditure limitations has two versions. The first is itself instrumental. In this version the pollution of politics by private interests produces a distinctive and unsound set of public policies, which promote private interests and exacerbate or at least preserve inequalities of wealth.[34] Egalitarian policies are desirable but cannot be achieved because wealth dominates the political system. One response is that those who seek equality can reach it by egalitarian policies that raise no constitutional problems rather than by limiting speech.[35] That response overlooks the structural barriers to the full airing of egalitarian policies, which were discussed previously. A more powerful response is that the defense is driven by a substantive commitment to equality, which may itself be perfectly sound but which needs a deeper justification.

That justification can be found in the second, directly and simply republican, version of this defense. The republican tradition stresses the importance of equality in wealth as the basis for independence in political judgment. If the market and the political system are to be kept separate, the market must have a fairly egalitarian structure. The republican tradition also emphasizes the intrinsic value of political activity, so that it is a sufficient defense of a policy that it encourages people to divert attention from the market and private interest to politics and the public interest.

We have examined four general arguments for restricting campaign expenditures. Each rests in the end on a complex of rationalist and republican values. These arguments should puzzle us. If we were a republican society we would not need campaign finance legislation because we would adopt policies with the public interest in mind anyway. If we are not a republican society, it is unlikely that campaign finance legislation will make us one. These reforms are the products of the system that we are attempting to reform, and we have already seen that this gives the reforms a deep orientation toward protecting incumbents and other aspects of the status quo.[36] Perhaps this circle can be broken: A moment of reflection on

that make one a celebrity are not necessarily driven by private interest in the way that economics is. Cf. Levinson, "Regulating Campaign Activity."

34. See, e.g., Wright, "Politics and the Constitution," pp. 1017–20.

35. See, e.g., Powe, "Mass Speech," pp. 282–83.

36. See generally Owen Fiss, "Free Speech and Social Structure," 71 *Iowa Law Review* 1405 (1986). Expenditure limitations are indirect ways of promoting rationality, yet more direct ones, such as a requirement that political claims about opponents be substantiated, are obviously not going to be adopted. This suggests again that arguments drawn from the

the public interest may break through the pervasive absorption with private interest. As the discussion of Ackerman's work suggests, we are entitled to be skeptical.

Further, the rationalism of republicanism is not entirely attractive. It denies the importance of nonrational deliberation as a human capacity. Yet as we will see in a later section of this chapter, recognizing that we have additional, nonrational deliberative capacities is troubling too.

Republicanism, Rationality, and Commercial Speech

Proponents of campaign finance legislation often rely on an expressly republican theory of free speech, which is associated with Alexander Meiklejohn.[37] Meiklejohn argued that the free speech clause guaranteed liberty by structuring the political process.[38] As a regulatory device free speech is designed to protect a particular kind of political system, in which, according to Meiklejohn, rational deliberation on matters of public policy prevailed. Campaign finance legislation is another regulatory device designed, according to its proponents, to serve the same end. It is therefore compatible with the first amendment.

Meiklejohn's emphasis on free speech as an element of the political system led him to question broader theories of free speech that stress its role in arriving at truth or its place in the full development of the human personality. These limitations have been questioned as counterintuitive—for example, Meiklejohn's theory leaves little room for constitutional protection of imaginative literature[39]—and as unprincipled—for example, because we need a theory of the human personality to explain why we want to preserve a rational, deliberative political process.[40] Recent developments in the constitutional law of commercial speech show that, even if

---

republican tradition are not the ones that actually affect political deliberations. See also text accompanying note 24, and note 26.

37. See, e.g., Wright, "Money and Politics," pp. 638–39; Cox, "Constitutional Issues," p. 418.

38. Alexander Meiklejohn, *Free Speech and Its Relation to Self-Government* (1948).

39. Of the recent commentators, only Robert Bork has a full commitment to the narrow Meiklejohn view. See Bork, "Neutral Principles." Lillian BeVier, "The First Amendment and Political Speech: An Inquiry into the Substance and Limits of Principle," 30 *Stanford Law Review* 299 (1978), justifies an expanded version by invoking notions of overbreadth that yield protection for nonpolitical speech on the ground that political speech cannot be adequately protected without protecting some nonpolitical speech. This does not treat nonpolitical speech as having independent first amendment value.

40. See, e.g., C. Edwin Baker, "Scope of the First Amendment Freedom of Speech," 25 *UCLA Law Review* 964, 976–81 (1978).

we abandon Meiklejohn's limited focus on the political process, we are likely to find that arguments for regulation are structured by the republican concern for rational deliberation. Perhaps because the Supreme Court does not believe that our legislatures today are repositories of republican virtue, it has become skeptical of efforts to regulate commercial speech.[41]

Advertising provides information to consumers. Producers would not advertise unless consumers found their advertisements valuable, and advertisers provide advertising in the form that consumers find helpful. In this advertising would appear to resemble any other type of speech: it is something that helps people decide what to do with their lives.

The Supreme Court's earliest decision clearly rejecting regulation of advertising struck down a state's prohibition on advertising prices for prescription drugs. The Court said that consumers had an interest in receiving accurate price information that is "as keen, if not keener by far, than [their] interest in the day's most urgent public debate." For "so long as we preserve a predominantly free enterprise economy, the allocation of our private resources ... will be made through numerous private economic decisions. It is a matter of public interest that those decisions, in the aggregate, are well informed. To this end, the free flow of commercial information is indispensable."[42] The listener's interest in receiving information, a private interest, thus prevails over a more republican vision of politics, in which political discussion is, at least on the level of public norms, "keener by far" than private interest.

Prohibiting advertising of prices may be particularly troubling because it interferes with the consumer's deliberative capacities. How can we decide what to buy if we do not know what it costs? Critics of advertising argue that much advertising is not informational in this way, that it is designed to convey a noncognitive message about the attributes of the type of person who buys the advertised good not about the attributes of the good. Thus, they believe that a republican theory of commercial speech would allow the government to regulate noninformational adver-

41. The Court's current approach is stated in Central Hudson Gas & Electric Co. v. Public Service Comm'n., 447 U.S. 557 (1980), which allowed states to ban advertising for the purpose of decreasing the demand for a lawful product. See also Posadas de Puerto Rico Associates v. Tourism Co. of Puerto Rico, 106 S. Ct. 2968 (1986). The Court did require that such restrictions be narrowly drawn. By emphasizing the public interest in hearing, reading, or seeing the advertisement rather than the speaker's interest, the Court permits the state to ban speech that can reach the public in other ways. It balances the public's interest in hearing the speech against the state's interest in prohibiting it, as well as the probability that the message will reach the public in another way. See Note, "Constitutional Protection of Commercial Speech," 82 *Columbia Law Review* 720 (1982).

42. Virginia State Board of Pharmacy v. Virginia Consumer Council, Inc., 425 U.S. 748, 763, 765 (1976).

tising.[43] Yet even purely informational advertising has the same kind of effect, because it authorizes the reader to construct herself as the kind of person who cares about rationally evaluating the empirically identifiable components of a product. Thus, the republican theory once again asserts its preference for a particular kind of rationality: The well-informed consumer, who is protected against restrictions on the flow of information, cares about prices, verifiable quality, and the like; she does not dream of release from the humdrum by means of fantasies provoked by purchasing goods that have been given noncognitive meanings.

Listeners—that is, all of us—are thus constructed by the social setting in which we find ourselves. The question for a theory of commercial speech is whether or to what extent we can use the institutions of public life to alter who we are. A similar concern with the social construction of personality underlies arguments about commercial speech that examine speakers rather than listeners. The people who write advertisements are creative artists, none more so than those who develop the noninformational advertising that appeals to our emotions. If free speech is valuable because it protects expressions of our personality, why should not the creative expressions of advertisers be protected?

C. Edwin Baker has given one answer. Advertising shapes preferences by appealing to and transforming what listeners already know about themselves. What the writer of advertisements does is therefore guided primarily by what other people want, think, and believe. It is determined by market forces not by the writer himself.[44] This argument may romanticize the creative artist, for many artists do the best they can to find markets for their work so that they can make a decent living, and in searching for buyers they may—indeed, I suspect that most do—shape their art to what potential buyers can be brought to appreciate. The argument may also romanticize politics, which can be as driven by demand as the market.[45] These counterarguments, though, miss Baker's main point, which is normative rather than empirical. It may be true that politics today is like the market and that the world of art is like the world of commerce. For Baker, these are regrettable facts of life, which need not provide the basic framework for our understanding of the Constitution. Instead, in Baker's view we should base our constitutional law on an

43. See, e.g., Daniel Farber, "Commercial Speech and First Amendment Theory," 74 *Northwestern University Law Review* 372, 383–84 (1979).

44. C. Edwin Baker, "Commercial Speech: A Problem in the Theory of Freedom," 62 *Iowa Law Review* 1 (1976).

45. See, e.g., Farber, "Commercial Speech," p. 382; Redish, "The Value of Free Speech," 130 *University of Pennsylvania Law Review* 591, 621 (1982).

evaluation of the degree to which its doctrines will encourage or at least allow us to separate the public and private spheres.

Will allowing governments to regulate commercial speech do that? Prohibiting price advertising disadvantages consumers who are in a position to shop around; as a general matter it aids small corner pharmacies in their competition with large chains. Regulation of advertising, as it is likely to be done in our society, resembles other forms of regulation. It is one way that some producers limit the competition they face from others.[46] The Court was exactly right when it said that regulation of advertising interferes with the free market; the only problem is that the fact that the interference occurs by means of restricting speech is entirely accidental.[47] Perhaps we should be suspicious of claims that regulation of commercial speech promotes a republican separation of the public and private interests. The regulations may represent instead the capture of public institutions by private interests. Yet as the example of the corner pharmacy suggests, they may also represent a social decision that a particular organization of the market, in which small entrepreneurs are protected against the ravages of competition, is the best way to promote a republican society and that promoting such a society is worth the loss in efficiency that regulation entails.

On balance, those who believe that the Constitution allows governments to regulate commercial speech face a severe problem. If their arguments rest, like Meiklejohn's, on a sharp division between public matters to which the Constitution is addressed and private ones about which the Constitution is silent, the arguments are not terribly appealing. If the division is blurred so that the Constitution protects some private matters, the arguments may rest on a largely unrealistic picture of the contemporary political process. Perhaps *largely* is the key word, though. Most of the time regulation of commercial speech is unlikely to serve republican values, but sometimes it will. Perhaps the best we can hope for is a constitutional doctrine that inquires directly whether the regulations serve those values.[48]

46. See Thomas Jackson and John Jeffries, "Commercial Speech: Economic Due Process and the First Amendment," 65 *Virginia Law Review* 1 (1979).

47. Ronald Rotunda, "The Commercial Speech Doctrine in the Supreme Court," 1976 *University of Illinois Law Forum* 1080, 1081–83, argues that restrictions on advertising are subsidies that are concealed from voters. But because all regulatory subsidies are concealed, this argument cannot be the ground for a special first amendment doctrine regarding regulatory subsidies by means of restrictions on advertising.

48. Cf. Pierre Schlag, "An Attack on Categorical Approaches to Freedom of Speech," 30 *UCLA Law Review* 671, 735 (1982) (such approaches "hypostatize the culture" and "underestimate their own power on" it).

Rationality and Pornography

Daniel Farber has said that "advertising [might be called] the pornography of capitalism, intended to arouse desire for objects rather than for persons."[49] This section examines recent feminist arguments for the legal regulation of pornography.[50] Those arguments begin by identifying the appeals pornography makes to what I have somewhat awkwardly called nonrational or noncognitive deliberative capacities. The structure of the feminist arguments itself appeals to those noncognitive deliberative capacities, which is understandable given the subject matter. What is striking is that the best conventional constitutional defense of anti-pornography legislation requires that rational deliberative capacities be more valued than those noncognitive capacities to which the feminist arguments appeal. Thus, the feminist arguments begin by understanding the importance of nonrational capacities and by challenging the priority our culture gives to what it defines as rationality, but they end by relying on that priority.[51]

Feminist critics have identified a number of harms that pornography creates. It harms the women who participate in its production.[52] Some are physically coerced into making pornographic films. Others find themselves situated in a society that makes them depend on men for their financial and emotional support and those men coerce them into participating. Still others find that, all things considered, making pornographic films is the best they can do for themslves, but one of the things that they must consider is that opportunities for women to succeed in this society are severely limited.[53] Women in the first two groups are harmed in the way that coercion in its pure form harms people; those in the third group are harmed by coercion defined more generously.

Pornography also harms women because it is causally connected to violence against women. Some men who view pornography take it as a

---

49. Farber, "Commercial Speech," pp. 383–84.

50. I have refrained from relying on the Report of the Attorney General's Commission on Pornography (1986), because the Commission did not offer serious feminist arguments for the regulation of pornography, and its factual investigations were, by its own account, too limited to be useful here.

51. It is important to emphasize that noncognitive deliberative capacity is not just sloppy rationality or irrationality in a pejorative sense. It is simply a capacity different from cognitive deliberative capacity.

52. See, e.g., Catherine MacKinnon, "Pornography, Civil Rights, and Speech," 20 *Harvard Civil Rights–Civil Liberties Law Review* 1, 32–36 (1985); Note, "Feminism, Pornography, and Law," 133 *University of Pennsylvania Law Review* 497, 517–18 (1985).

53. See Sandra Grove, "Constitutionality of Minnesota's Sodomy Law," 2 *Law and Inequality* 521, 532 (1984) (describing limitations, including "relative economic and psychological powerlessness," on women's ability to consent).

model and act on the images it contains. For example, some rapists are later found to have enacted scenes from pornography they possessed.[54] Some men who view pornography become accustomed to the images of sexuality it contains. When they are called upon to act in situations where they must assess sexual behavior, they may act in a manner consistent with those images. For example, men who view films in which women are portrayed as coming to enjoy being raped are more likely than others to accept claims that women who say they were raped actually consented to intercourse.[55]

More generally pornography harms women because it is causally connected to the general subordination of women in society. Among other influences the availability of pornography contributes to an atmosphere in which men believe themselves entitled to dominate women and in which some women, reacting to the images of women conveyed in pornography, find themselves unable credibly to attack those images.[56]

These three types of harm occur because pornography is causally connected to several types of subordination. A final argument avoids questions of causation. In this view pornography simply is the subordination of women. Pornography may be defined in a way that incorporates subordination.[57] Alternatively, we could make subordination a sufficient condition for pornography: that which subordinates women is pornography.[58]

The first three types of harm involve causal connections between pornography and something else, and so we can examine the evidence offered to show such connections. The fourth harm occurs by definition, and so

54. See, e.g., Margaret Baldwin, "The Sexuality of Inequality: The Minneapolis Pornography Ordinance," 2 *Law and Inequality* 629, 639–40 (1984); MacKinnon, "Pornography," pp. 43–50.

55. The sociopsychological evidence is comprehensively cited in MacKinnon, "Pornography," pp. 52–54 nn. 116–18. A recent collection is *Pornography and Sexual Aggression* (Neil Malamuth and Edward Donnerstein eds. 1984).

56. See generally MacKinnon, "Pornography."

57. The ordinance held unconstitutional in American Booksellers Ass'n. v. Hudnut, 771 F.2d 323 (7th Cir. 1985), aff'd., 475 U.S. 1001 (1986), defines pornography as "the graphic sexually explicit subordination of women . . . that . . . includes one or more of the following: (1) Women are presented as sexual objects who enjoy pain or humiliation; or (2) Women are presented as sexual objects who experience sexual pleasure in being raped; or (3) Women are presented as sexual objects tied up or cut up or mutilated or bruised or physically hurt, or as dismembered or truncated or fragmented or severed into body parts; or (4) Women are presented as being penetrated by objects or animals; or (5) Women are presented in scenarios of degradation, injury, abasement, torture, shown as filthy or inferior, bleeding, bruised, or hurt in a context that makes these conditions sexual; or (6) Women are presented as sexual objects for domination, conquest, violation, exploitation, possession, or use, or through postures or positions of servility or submission or display."

58. See MacKinnon, "Pornography," p. 27.

we can ask what might make that definition one that women (and perhaps men) should accept. I argue next that the feminist argument appeals to noncognitive deliberative capacities in the evidence for the causal claims and reasons for the definitional ones that it offers.

The argument requires us to examine the reasons the feminist argument provides to explain how pornography harms women by means of its effects on men. The reasons have one characteristic that must be identified at the outset. I call this characteristic definitional ambiguity, and it occurs in two forms.[59] First, pornography is defined in one way at the outset of the argument, and then reasons are given that seem to invoke a different definition. For example, the initial definition of pornography may invoke notions of violence and physical pain inflicted on women in sexually explicit ways, where "violence" and "pain" are illustrated by examples calling on our conventional understandings—beatings, whips, chains, and the like.[60] Later the causal connection between pornography and male acceptance of the consent defense to rape charges may be supported by the assertion that pornography is a $7 billion business.[61] The business to which reference is made is the entire system of producing sexually explicit materials, including such magazines as *Playboy* and *Penthouse*, which

59. Others have noted, usually critically, the definitional ambiguity in statements by advocates of feminist efforts to regulate pornography. See, e.g., Kate Ellis, "I'm Black and Blue from the Rolling Stones and I'm Not Sure How I Feel about It: Pornography and the Feminist Imagination," nos. 75–77 *Socialist Review* 105–6 (May–Aug. 1984); Lorna Weir and Leo Casey, "Subverting Power in Sexuality," nos. 75–77 *Socialist Review* 144–45 (May–Aug. 1984); Lisa Duggan, Nan Hunter, and Carole Vance, "False Promises: Feminist Antipornography Legislation in the United States," in *Women against Censorship* 134 (Varda Burstyn ed. 1985); Note, "Feminism, Pornography, and Law," p. 520 n. 119 (noting that some advocates of regulation use "far looser definitions"); Robert Fullinwider, "Feminism and Pornography: Discussion Review," *QQ: Report from the Center for Philosophy and Public Policy* 12 (undated, in author's possession). See also Richard Delgado, "The Language of the Arms Race: Should the People Limit Government Speech?" 64 *Boston University Law Review* 961, 967–77 (1984) (describing linguistic and psychological techniques by which rhetorical devices like definitional ambiguity operate).

60. See note 57.

61. The source for this figure appears to be Martha Langelan, "The Political Economy of Pornography," *Aegis*, Autumn 1981, p. 5. See, e.g., Baldwin, "Sexuality of Inequality," p. 58 (citing Langelan); MacKinnon, "Pornography," p. 58 (citing Langelan; also citing *U.S. News and World Report* for $8 billion figure); Michael Gershel, "Evaluating a Proposed Civil Rights Approach to Pornography: Legal Analysis As If Women Mattered," 11 *William Mitchell Law Review* 41, 58 (1985); "The Place of Pornography," *Harper's*, Nov. 1984, p. 34 (statement by Jean Bethke Elshtain); Note, "Feminism, Pornography, and Law," p. 58. The source for Langelan's figure is an estimate by D.C. Feminists against Pornography. Questions about this figure are raised by an opponent of regulation in Barry Lynn, " 'Civil Rights' Ordinances and the Attorney General's Commission: New Developments in Pornography Regulation," 21 *Harvard Civil Rights–Civil Liberties Law Review* 27, 30–31 (1986).

utilize images of violence and physical pain much less pervasively than the initial definition suggests.[62] Or the causal connection between pornography and rape is supported by evidence that rapists possessed pornography, but no evidence is given to rule out the possibility that the pornography they possessed was *Playboy* and *Penthouse*.[63]

The second form of definitional ambiguity occurs when the initial definition, in terms of violence and physical pain, is explicitly or implicitly modified to take account of objections to arguments similar to those I have just outlined. In the modified definitions the harms to women are not violence and physical pain defined in conventional ways but are phenomena that the critic of pornography argues are just as harmful. This second form of definitional ambiguity has an important rhetorical effect: if a skeptic challenges the claimed causal connection between pornography in its initial definition and rape, for example, definitional ambiguity shifts the discussion to one about the causal connection between pornography in its modified definition and women's subordination. Thus the antipornography argument floats freely from one sort of harm to another and back again, assisted by definitional ambiguity. The argument is therefore effective precisely because it appeals to some noncognitive deliberative capacities.

That appeal can be seen in most of the more particular reasons given to explain how pornography harms women.[64] Empirical evidence is needed

62. See Neil Malamuth and Barry Spinner, "A Longitudinal Content Analysis of Sexual Violence in the Best-selling Erotic Magazines," 16 *Journal of Sex Research* 226 (1980) (examination of *Playboy* and *Penthouse* showed increase of violent pictures to 5 percent of content from 1973 to 1977; no increase in violent cartoons, which remained at 10 percent throughout the period), cited in Note, "Feminism, Pornography, and Law," p. 514 n. 97. Lynn, " 'Civil Rights' Ordinances," p. 105, suggests that levels of violence in pornography have declined recently.

63. See, e.g., "The Place of Pornography," p. 36 (statement by Susan Brownmiller).

64. It seems to be generally agreed that no special problems are raised by prohibitions on coercing women into participating in the production of pornography. See, e.g., American Booksellers' Ass'n. v. Hudnut, 771 F.2d, p. 332. But see note 100 (on singling out pornography for regulation of that sort). The ordinance in *Hudnut* created a cause of action by any person coerced into performing for pornography. This provision enumerated thirteen facts that, "without more," would not "negate a finding of coercion." These facts included that the person "is a woman," "is or has been a prostitute," "has attained the age of majority," is connected by marriage to anyone involved in the production, "has previously had, or been thought to have had, sexual relations with anyone," "has previously posed for sexually explicit pictures," "actually consented to a use of the performance that is changed into pornography," "knew that the purpose of the acts . . . was to make pornography," "showed no resistance or appeared to cooperate actively" in the production, "signed a contract, or made statements affirming a willingness to cooperate in the production," or "was paid." In addition, it does not negate a finding of coercion, without more, to show that "no physical force, threats, or weapons were used in the making of the pornography."

to support claims of causal connection. The type of evidence will vary depending on whether the question is the connection between pornography and violence, on which one might seek relatively "hard" evidence, or the connection between pornography and subordination, on which one would rely on cultural insights. These differences in the type of evidence one can rely on make definitional ambiguity an especially effective rhetorical technique; in particular, when hard evidence is challenged on the ground that it does not establish the connection between pornography and violence, its proponent can respond that the evidence remains good as to the more cultural claims.

What sort of evidence is there? Much of the evidence is anecdotal. Indeed, the anecdotes tend to be drawn from an apparently small pool.[65] To show that production of pornography involves coercion, the story of Linda Marchiano is offered,[66] with no mention made of possible alternative anecdotes or reinterpretations of Marchiano's story.[67] This raises

---

This enumeration appears to be designed primarily to reduce the possibility that facts specific to women's relations with men will unduly influence the determination of the question of coercion. (Whether the provision as drafted would have that effect is a different question, not addressed here.) It is interesting that, with the possible exception of the "physical force" provision, the enumeration does not address the question of whether coercion can be established by showing that participating in the production of pornography was the best option available to the woman. For an interview suggesting that market coercion of this sort plays an important role in the production of pornography, see Laura Lederer, "Then and Now: An Interview with a Former Pornography Model," in *Take Back the Night: Women on Pornography* 45 (Laura Lederer ed. 1980). See also Sheila Jeffreys, "Prostitution," in *Women against Violence against Women* 59 (Dusty Rhodes and Sandra McNeill eds. 1985). For criticism of expanding the concept of coercion to include market coercion, see Lynn, " 'Civil Rights' Ordinances," pp. 101–3.

65. The anecdotal nature of the information on which the argument rests is made apparent in Paul Brest and Ann Vandenberg, "Politics, Feminism, and the Constitution: The Anti-Pornography Movement in Minneapolis," 39 *Stanford Law Review* 607 (1987), a narrative of the legislative process in Minneapolis. Perhaps it is difficult to acquire more than anecdotal information regarding the production and use of pornography, given the nature of the business. Yet there is a substantial body of nonanecdotal information available about prostitution, which would seem to have many of the same characteristics. Lynn, " 'Civil Rights' Ordinances," pp. 74–76, criticizes the anecdotal nature of the evidence on the ground that it tends to have resulted from orchestrated presentations to support attempts to regulate pornography.

66. See, e.g., Gershel, "Evaluating a Proposed Civil Rights Approach," p. 57; Baldwin, "Sexuality of Inequality," pp. 636–37.

67. For possible alternative anecdotes, see, e.g., Bill Zehme, "For Goodness' Seka," *Vanity Fair*, May 1985, p. 45 (interview with "porn queen"); David Friendly, " 'This Isn't Shakespeare,' " *Newsweek*, Mar. 18, 1985, p. 62 (describing filming of pornographic movie); Michael London, "The Death of Colleen," *Los Angeles Times*, May 6, 1984, Calendar section, p. 1 (describing life and suicide of actress in pornographic films). See also Lynn, " 'Civil Rights' Ordinances," p. 100.

questions about the reliability of the sample of behavior from which we are asked to draw causal conclusions. A similar sampling problem arises with anecdotes about rapists' possession of pornography. Social scientists would draw no conclusions about the connection between pornography and rape from evidence that a large proportion of rapists possessed pornography; they would need to know what proportion of nonrapists possessed it too, for if nonrapists possessed it about as often as rapists did, social scientists would not infer a causal connection.[68] Finally, a series of well-known psychological studies establishes some connection between some sorts of violent sexual material and attitudes supporting women's subordination.[69] Again we find definitional ambiguity of two sorts. The material used in those studies was not obviously pornographic, if pornography requires sexually explicit depictions, and the material is causally connected not to violence but to attitudes linked to women's subordination.[70]

What this means is that the empirical arguments do not meet the usual standards applied when one appeals to cognitive deliberation. This is not to say that the empirical arguments are bad arguments, just that they are different arguments. Perhaps the point can be made by drawing together three points made in support of regulating pornography. Testifying at a Minneapolis hearing to establish the empirical basis for regulation, one woman said, "Every time I walk into a neighborhood grocery store or drug store, I am reminded that if I don't watch my step, . . . I could end up like one of the women in that pornographic material being sold in those

---

As a reinterpretation, Marchiano's story might be located in the tradition of lurid, often highly sexualized, exposés of discreditable activities, the most celebrated of which is *The Memoirs of Maria Monk*, about the activities in Roman Catholic institutions. MacKinnon, "Pornography," pp. 35–36, discusses such alternative accounts as additional examples of the way in which pornography silences women. For a discussion of the reception of Marchiano's story by those not committed to the regulation of pornography, see Gloria Steinem, "The Real Linda Lovelace," in her *Outrageous Acts and Everyday Rebellions* 243 (1983).

68. Even evidence that all rapists possessed pornography might not be probative of a connection between pornography and rape, if, as some proponents of regulation argue, pornography is so pervasive that virtually all men possess it. But see MacKinnon, "Pornography," pp. 44–45 (responding to skepticism about probative value of these reports by pointing to underreporting of rape and number of men who commit rape but are not arrested or convicted).

69. See note 55. Lynn, " 'Civil Rights' Ordinances," pp. 65–69, criticizes these studies, as does Marcia Pally, "Ban Sexism, Not Pornography," *Nation*, June 29, 1985, pp. 795–96.

70. When people's attitudes change we can reasonably expect that their behavior will also change in a direction consistent with the attitude change, but obviously the connection between the materials that cause attitude change and the behavioral change is likely to be somewhat looser than the connection between those materials and the attitude change itself.

stores."[71] It would seem that definitional ambiguity plays a large role here. But perhaps not. As Catharine MacKinnon asked about Justice Stewart's standard, "I know it when I see it," "Does he know what I know when I see what I see[?]"[72] And Andrea Dworkin observed that, having studied pornography in detail, she cannot see a hair dryer or a lighting fixture without considering it as an implement to be used, among other things, to inflict pain on women.[73] These are powerful points about how one sees the social world. The usual standards of social science construct the social world in one way, invoking instrumental rationality. The antipornography arguments invite us to construct it in a different way, invoking our noncognitive deliberative capacities.

Noncognitive deliberative capacities play another important role in the arguments examined here. They help explain what is wrong with pornography. We begin by noting that these arguments rest on the view that pornography persuades men to subordinate women. In this sense pornography is itself an argument.[74] How does pornography make its argument? Through its imagery, that is, by methods that appeal to noncognitive capacities.[75]

First, pornography depicts women as available to any man who chooses to take them. The pictures show women in positions that emphasize their sexual availability, displaying and emphasizing their genital

71. See Baldwin, "Sexuality of Inequality," p. 639. See also "The Place of Pornography," p. 35 (statement by Susan Brownmiller that "corner newsstand" has "pictures of women mutilated, tortured, spread into ridiculous postures"). Cf. Lisa Duggan, "Censorship in the Name of Feminism," *Village Voice*, Oct. 16, 1984, p. 11, col. 1 (opponent of regulation describing difficulty in finding pornography in Indianapolis and stating that only *Playboy* and *Penthouse* could be found in city's convenience stores).

72. Catharine MacKinnon, "Not a Moral Issue," 2 *Yale Law and Policy Review* 321, 325 (1984).

73. Andrea Dworkin, "A Woman Writer and Pornography," 6:5 *San Francisco Review of Books* 16–17, col. 1 (Mar.–Apr. 1981).

74. See Lynn, " 'Civil Rights' Ordinances," pp. 49–51. For Lynn this makes the case against regulation conclusive. For additional discussion, see text accompanying notes 98–115.

75. I omit a discussion here of overt depictions of women with animals, being beaten, and the like. Many of these materials could be found obscene under current definitions of obscenity, and, despite their importance in the feminist arguments for the regulation of pornography, they therefore raise no novel questions. In addition, there is sometimes reason to believe that the depictions are intended to be taken in a sense other than that which the antipornography argument attributes to them. See text accompanying notes 88–90 (on irony and detachment in pornography).

Because it is an argument, pornography appeals to a deliberative capacity, but the way in which it makes its argument is not a method that appeals to cognitive capacities.

organs to invite viewers to penetrate them.[76] Sometimes the women look directly at the viewer, posed in what critics call "The Look," with partly open mouth, wet lips, and expectant eyes.[77] Sometimes the women are dreamily self-absorbed, vulnerable to a surprise attack by the man who already is looking at them. Women's sexuality is available to men without consequence to the men.[78]

Second, pornography depicts women as subordinate to men. When men appear with women in pornography, the men are often clothed or partly clothed while the women are completely unclothed or substantially less clothed. The women in pornography are placed below the viewer— on beds, the floor, furniture—so that the viewing male stands over the observed women.[79] And, no matter what the details, the women in pornography are there to be consumed and therefore dominated by men.

Third, pornography depicts women as merely sexual objects. Photographs are framed so as to isolate the genital organs or are printed so that those organs are detached from the rest of the body. These techniques transform women from people into objects.[80] Instead of having relationships with women who (are imagined to) have complex lives as workers, lovers, friends, and so on, the viewer is invited to appropriate the woman's sexuality for his own sexual purposes.

This construction of the way that pornography makes its argument uncovers additional aspects of the use of appeals to noncognitive deliberative capacities. Critics of the antipornography arguments examined here often observe that regulation of pornography for the reasons given in these arguments is both overinclusive and underinclusive.[81] Regulation is overinclusive because at least some of the material to be regulated has rather weak causal connections to violence against women. As those

76. For a description of the materials presented in a slide show by Women against Violence in Pornography and Media, see Teresa Hommel, "Images of Women in Pornography and Media," 8 *New York University Review of Law and Social Change* 202 (1978–79). See also MacKinnon, "Pornography," p. 18; Gershel, "Evaluating a Proposed Civil Rights Approach," p. 56.

77. See, e.g., Jane Root, *Pictures of Women: Sexuality* 43–48 (1984), especially p. 45 (illustrations of "The Look" from pornography and commercial advertising).

78. See Steven Marcus, *The Other Victorians: A Study of Sexuality and Pornography in Mid–Nineteenth Century England* 270–79 (1966); "The Place of Pornography," p. 33 (statement by Midge Decter).

79. See Root, *Pictures of Women*, p. 43.

80. See id., pp. 46–47; Hommel, "Images of Women," p. 205; MacKinnon, "Not a Moral Issue," p. 344.

81. See, e.g., Lynn, " 'Civil Rights' Ordinances," pp. 72–73; Brief Amici Curiae of Feminist Anti-Censorship Task Force, in American Booksellers' Ass'n. v. Hudnut, 771 F.2d 323 (7th Cir. 1985), pp. 3, 20–22; Weir and Casey, "Subverting Power," p. 76.

critics stress more emphatically, regulation is underinclusive because so much more than pornography in the culture contributes to, or helps construct, the system of male domination.[82]

People who observe this overinclusiveness and underinclusiveness usually treat the observation as in itself a criticism of the arguments for regulation.[83] The observation, however, is a criticism only if arguments must rest on instrumental rationality. Overinclusiveness and underinclusiveness may be characteristics, not the basis for criticism, of arguments that appeal to our noncognitive deliberative capacities. We can see these characteristics by examining the underlying structure of the analysis of pornography's argument. That structure involves what might be called essentialism, the taking as exhaustive one or a few facets of a complex phenomenon, or metonymy, the treating of a part of a phenomenon as if it were the whole.

The underinclusiveness of the antipornography arguments is one example of metonymy, in that the evil to be attacked is the subordination of women, of which pornography is only a part.[84] "The Look" characterizes much commercial advertising as well as much pornography.[85] Definitional ambiguity is another example, in that the causal connection between pornography and violence is established by referring to a particular subset of all pornography.

The essentialism of the antipornography arguments may be more interesting. Essentialism denies that pornography's images are ambiguous.[86] Yet there are ways in which the world depicted in pornography is, and is

82. This point would not hold if pornography were defined as that which contributes to the subordination of women.

83. In general, it is difficult to treat the critics' observations about overinclusiveness and underinclusiveness as recommendations to rewrite the legislative proposals. Most of the critics want no regulation of pornography at all, although they may divide on whether pornography is something that we regrettably have to tolerate or whether it has enough positive value to be defensible in itself. But see David Bryden, "Between Two Constitutions: Feminism and Pornography," 2 *Constitutional Commentary* 147 (1985).

84. In making this observation I do not intend to take a position on the relative causal importance of pornography as compared with other things in the society that contribute to the subordination of women. Further, as stated in note 82, this point would not hold if pornography were defined as that which contributes to the subordination of women.

85. For a description of the techniques used in commercial advertising consistent with this account of pornography, see Judith Williamson, *Decoding Advertisements: Ideology and Meaning in Advertising* (1978).

86. This is at least one sense in which pornography is constitutive of a way of understanding the world. See MacKinnon, "Pornography," pp. 18–19. For discussions of the ambiguities in pornography's depictions of sexuality, see Ellis, "I'm Black and Blue," pp. 111–13; Lynn, "'Civil Rights' Ordinances," pp. 81–82. For criticism of the antipornography argument on the ground of its essentialism, see Ellis, "I'm Black and Blue," pp. 113–14 (using the term); Duggan, Hunter, and Vance, "False Promises," pp. 140–41; Sara

known by the viewer to be, nonexistent. The women who are universally available in pornography cannot readily be found outside its pages, and the women outside its pages are not in fact universally available. Still, like much utopian literature, pornography might impel its readers to attempt to bring the real world into line with the imagined one; that is the reason that pornography is causally connected to violence against women. Utopian literature has an underside, though: it can promote a resigned acceptance of the world as it is, given the apparent impossibility of transforming it into the world as it is imagined. Resignation can be produced as well by the prominent depictions of heterosexual activities in some pornography. The male viewer sees a male participant engaging in sexual activities with women whom the viewer wants to possess. The male participant is like the viewer in some ways, being of the same gender, but is unlike him in others, in that the viewer can only fantasize himself as having the gendered attributes of the man he is watching. Again, the fantasy may lead to action, but contrary to the essentialist claim, it may also lead to resignation.[87]

Essentialism also denies the ambiguities of irony and detachment.[88] The infamous "meat grinder" cover of *Hustler* is one example. There, intending to comment on the argument that pornography treats women like pieces of meat, *Hustler's* publisher showed a woman's body being ground up in a meat grinder.[89] Essentialism rules out, or defines as improper, the intended ironic comment.[90] It makes other kinds of detachment impossible too. "The Look" and other depictions of women in pornography invite viewers to appropriate the women they show, yet the pictures are

---

Diamond, "Pornography: Image and Reality," in *Women against Censorship* 43–44 (using term *essence*).

87. See Marcus, *Other Victorians*, pp. 273–74 (anxiety pervades pornography); Diamond, "Image and Reality," p. 45; Ellis, "I'm Black and Blue," pp. 115 (discussing "unevenness" of system depicted in pornography). Cf. Root, *Pictures of Women*, p. 66 (hopelessness communicated to women by images of sexuality in women's magazines).

88. For discussions of the tension between sexual pleasure and sexual danger, see *Pleasure and Danger: Exploring Female Sexuality* (Carole Vance ed. 1984). The political context out of which this volume emerged is described in Ellis, "I'm Black and Blue." Other discussions of the ambiguities of pornography are Pally, "Ban Sexism"; Ann Snitow, "Retrenchment versus Reformation: The Politics of the Antipornography Movement," in *Women against Censorship*, pp. 115–16. Fullinwider, "Feminism and Pornography," describes pornography as a "special-interest genre," in which the focus on the sexual features of life does not mean that the viewer fails to understand that life, and women, have other dimensions as well.

89. See "Is This the Real Message of Pornography?" *Harper's*, Nov. 1984, p. 35.

90. On the definition of detachment and irony as impermissible, see text accompanying note 94 (on silencing).

known by the viewer to be posed and artificial.[91] The photographs in pornography objectify their subjects, something that all photographs do.[92] The essentialist claim is that viewers of pornography cannot simultaneously consume it and understand its artificiality.

Obviously, that is not an epistemological claim.[93] We have been examining the antipornography arguments that seek to explain how pornography causes women's subordination. As causal arguments they are nonstandard. They may be more important as arguments supporting the fourth, definitional claim about pornography and subordination. As rhe-

91. For discussions of artifice in pornography, see Ellis, "I'm Black and Blue," p. 106; Myrna Kostash, "Second Thoughts," in *Women against Censorship*, pp. 35–36; Lynn, " 'Civil Rights' Ordinances," p. 101. Contra MacKinnon, "Pornography," p. 19 (pornography depicts "real women to whom, in most cases, something real is being done"). One example of self-consciousness about the artifice involved in pornography is the regular provision in *Penthouse* of information regarding the cameras used in their displays.

92. See Weir and Casey, "Subverting Power," pp. 144–45; Gregg Blachford, "Looking at Pornography: Erotica and the Socialist Morality," in *Pink Triangles: Radical Perspectives on Gay Liberation* 67–69 (Pam Mitchell ed. 1980) (objectification of sexuality sometimes appropriate). On photography as representation, see generally Erving Goffman, *Gender Advertisements* (1976); Bryden, "Between Two Constitutions," p. 147 (quoting Susan Sontag on photography turning people into objects). See also Susanne Kappeler, *The Pornography of Representation* (1986). Contra "The Place of Pornography," p. 37 (statement by Susan Brownmiller that "a photograph makes people think that what they are seeing is the truth"). One version of the antipornography argument might be that pornography explicitly denies the existence of an active subject whereas other representations implicitly affirm it.

An example of the role of representation in pornography is the feminist attack on the film *Snuff*, which continued even after it became widely known that the film did not show the actual murder and dismemberment of a woman, although it did depict such acts. See John Leonard, " 'Snuff,' Built on Rumor, Lacking Credit," *New York Times*, Mar. 10, 1976, p. 41. In some circumstances pornography is distinguishable from art photography primarily by its use of color, as compared with the artificial black and white of nonpornography. See, e.g., Cynthia McAdams, *Rising Goddess* (1983). In this connection it may be worth noting again that each issue of *Penthouse* contains a description of the photographic equipment used in making the pictures, which tend to employ such artistic devices as filters. *Hustler*, in contrast, is completely hard-edged in its photographic style.

93. That viewers can appreciate the artificiality of pornography is suggested by the discussions of "production values" in reviews of pornographic movies.

An alternative interpretation of pornography, focusing on what I have called the definitional harm that pornography does, is offered by Ronald Meister, "Vigilante Action against Pornography: The Symbolic Destruction of Symbols," 12 *Social Text* 3, 6 (Fall 1985), which defines obscenity as "treating something real as if it were a symbol in order to degrade it in reality." This definition takes account of both the underlying reality that is depicted and the artificiality in its presentation. Meister understands that this definition, unlike those of pornography, has no necessary connection to sexuality. To the extent, however, that Meister's definition implicates a relatively specific intent to degrade, it may not describe much pornography; if the intent to degrade is omitted from the definition, the definitional linkage between reality and artifice in pornography is substantially weakened.

torical strategies, essentialism, metonymy, and definitional ambiguity make standard types of cognitive arguments impossible. The opponent of regulation is likely to be driven wild by these rhetorical strategies, finding that the ground is unfairly shifted under his or her feet. Or, perhaps better, the opponent is likely to be driven into silence. That is, the definitional approach that pornography is subordination, and does not cause it, disempowers opponents of regulation in just the way that pornography disempowers women. Pornography disempowers women by discrediting them so that men will ignore or devalue their objections to pornography, among other things.[94] The definitional approach disempowers opponents because their denial that pornography is harmful confirms the definitional approach.[95]

The antipornography arguments under discussion are powerful because of their rhetorical strategies. They are constructed to appeal to our (or to women's) noncognitive deliberative capacities and to discredit counterarguments that appeal to cognitive capacities. It may be significant that several important figures in the development of these arguments are poets and literary critics.[96]

Thus, according to the feminist antipornography arguments examined here, pornography is an argument for male domination of women that works by means of its appeal to men's noncognitive deliberative capacities.[97] The feminist antipornography arguments establish this point by means of their appeal to noncognitive deliberate capacities.

94. See generally MacKinnon, "Pornography"; Note, "Feminism, Pornography, and Law," p. 522; Note, "Anti-Pornography Laws and First Amendment Values," 98 *Harvard Law Review* 460, 475–76 (1984).

95. See Ellis, "I'm Black and Blue," p. 108. In this way the definitional approach attempts to capitalize on one general function of dominant ideologies, which is to devalue the rationality of their competitors. See Tushnet, "Book Review," 1984 *Wisonsin Law Review* 129.

96. Major works in the field are Susan Griffin, *Pornography and Silence: Culture's Revenge against Nature* (1981), and Andrea Dworkin, *Pornography: Men Possessing Women* (1979). After some consideration I decided not to cite these works for specific points despite the books' importance in the development of the feminist antipornography argument. Their arguments are sufficiently complex and allusive that, although it would not violate the general rules about citation to cite them for specific points, doing so would unduly minimize the power of the arguments they make. See Joan Cocks, "Wordless Emotions: Some Critical Reflections on Radical Feminism, 13 *Politics and Society* 27, 51 n. 3 (1984) ("The respective power, . . . and originality of style of Dworkin . . . and Susan Griffin are inseparable from the substance of their works"). Among the contributors to another important collection, *Take Back the Night*, are Marge Piercy, Alice Walker, Audre Lorde, and Adrienne Rich.

97. For a feminist critique of the construction of the distinction between reason and emotion in some feminist works, see Cocks, "Wordless Emotion." If the appeal to noncognitive deliberative capacities is effective, men may find it instrumentally rational to exercise

Some feminists have argued in addition that the Constitution permits governments to regulate the production and distribution of pornography more extensively than many people think. Yet it is an interesting characteristic of the constitutional argument that it would allow regulation of pornography because pornography appeals to noncognitive deliberative capacities, precisely those capacities to which the antipornography argument appeals. That is, the constitutional argument treats instrumental rationality as a favored mode of discourse, whereas the feminist antipornography argument rests on the view that instrumental rationality is not a favored mode of discourse. This does not vitiate the feminist arguments; it merely adds weight to the point of this chapter, that the law of free expression favors one of many possible ways of coming to understand the world.

The feminist argument against pornography seems to create a strong prima facie case *against* the constitutionality of regulating it. That argument is that pornography is itself an argument, appealing to noncognitive capacities, for a particular arrangement of power in society. Because politics involves the distribution of power, it looks like pornography is a political argument.[98] Further, feminists have insisted that one cannot exempt sexuality or "personal matters" from the domain of the political because, in a celebrated phrase, the personal is the political.[99] Political arguments are usually thought of as the kind of thing that deserves the highest degree of protection under the first amendment.[100]

---

the power that pornography tells them they have. The key to this process, however, is the first, noncognitive step.

98. See MacKinnon, "Not a Moral Issue," p. 345 (pornography "distributes power").

99. The phrase is quoted in Brief Amici Curiae, American Booksellers' Ass'n., p. 28.

100. Again, the prohibition on coercing women to participate in the production of pornography, see note 64, would appear to raise no special problems and may already be illegal. If so, the first amendment does not bar government from applying general rules of law to "the press." See, e.g., Associated Press v. National Labor Relations Board, 301 U.S. 103 (1937). There might be some question about regulating the press in a distinctive way. At least such regulation will receive a high degree of scrutiny. See Minneapolis Star v. Minnesota Commissioner of Revenue, 460 U.S. 575 (1983). If the pornography industry receives the protections of the first amendment that "the press" receives, it might be unconstitutional for legislation to apply distinctive standards for determining when coercion exists in the production of pornography. Thus, the "labor law" aspects of regulation require us to examine the same issue that the other aspects of regulation do, that is, whether pornography receives a high, moderate, or low amount of protection under the first amendment.

Note that I am not interested in discussing whether coercion should be defined to include coercion by market forces. Contra Lynn, " 'Civil Rights' Ordinances," p. 100; Duggan, Hunter, and Vance, "False Promises," pp. 147–48.

That understanding of the first amendment, however, it not the Supreme Court's understanding of it.[101] As Frederick Schauer has argued, the prevailing view on the Court treats the first amendment as rather like a complex legal code.[102] According to the Court, not all verbal utterances deserve the same degree of protection. For example, although as we have seen the Court now believes that commercial speech is covered by the first amendment, commercial speech can be regulated in ways that political speech could not. States may ban certain types of face-to-face commercial solicitation because it might be coercive, although they could not ban door-to-door political solicitation for the same reason;[103] they can prohibit misleading advertisements for commercial products but not for politicians.[104] Thus, "speech" has to be broken down into a set of smaller categories, and the fact that one category of speech gets the highest degree of protection does not imply that every other category is protected in the same way. Indeed, Schauer has argued, the obvious social need to regulate some verbal utterances, such as solicitations to commit murder, makes it essential to recognize that not all categories of speech receive the same degree of protection; otherwise the social need to regulate some speech without having to show a very close connection between the speech and some imminent danger would produce a system in which all speech, including ordinary political speech, received not very much protection at all.[105]

The Court has not clearly identified the principles that guide its construction of categories of speech, but some principles can be discerned in the pattern of the Court's decisions. The first principle governs all the rest,

101. The general structure of first amendment doctrine has been discussed in Chapters 2 and 3. For present purposes it is enough to note that the Court has divided speech into at least two categories. The state may regulate "low-value" speech to avoid social harms that it reasonably believes are causally related to the speech. It may regulate "high-value" speech to avoid social harms only if the speech is rather clearly a cause of the harms. Further, it may not distinguish among types of speech because of the viewpoints expressed in the speech; that is, it may not permit one type of speech within a category while prohibiting another if the prohibition is based on disapproval of the viewpoint expressed in the prohibited speech. For a summary in the context of the pornography debate, see Geoffrey Stone, "Comment: Anti-Pornography Legislation as Viewpoint-Discrimination," 9 *Harvard Journal of Law and Public Policy* 461 (1986).

102. Frederick Schauer, "Codifying the First Amendment: New York v. Ferber," 1982 *Supreme Court Review* 285.

103. See Ohralik v. Ohio State Bar Ass'n., 436 U.S. 447 (1978).

104. See Friedman v. Rogers, 440 U.S. 1 (1979), in which the Court upheld state's prohibition on the use of trade names by opticians on the ground that it might be misleading.

105. For a brief but comprehensive discussion of the incompatibility between the anti-pornography arguments and the current treatment of "high-value" speech, see Stone, "Anti-Pornography Legislation."

although as we will see it produces a serious analytic problem: we are to determine the degree of protection that a category of speech gets by considering paradigmatic examples of speech in that category, not by considering unusual or merely possible examples. Thus, suppose that some category is given a high degree of protection because most people who use that sort of speech are predominantly motivated by a concern for the public good, while another category receives less protection because most of its users are motivated by private interest. This may describe the Court's view of political and commercial speech respectively.[106] If the paradigmatic speaker's purpose is political, it will not matter that some political activists see politics simply as a way to make a living, nor would it matter that some advertising copywriters think that advancing the cause of capitalism is their mission in life.

Within this framework four additional principles help define the categories of speech.[107] First, the more the paradigmatic example of a category deals with topics traditionally regarded as political, the greater is the protection that the category receives.[108] Thus political speech is more protected than commercial speech even though, as the Court put it, people's interest in price information might be "keener by far" than their interest in the relative merits of various proposals for tax reform. Similarly, it is harder for politicians to recover damages from those who libel them than it is for private citizens, and libels about public matters are less regulated than libels about private ones.[109]

Second, a category of speech will receive greater protection if its paradigmatic examples appeal to cognitive rather than to noncognitive capacities.[110] For example, the Court has said that "fighting words" receive little protection on the theory that such words, when uttered at the times they

106. As to political speech a more precise formulation might be "private interest mediated by public institutions" and as to commercial speech something like "direct private interest." The point should be clear.

107. This catalog is drawn from Cass Sunstein, "Pornography and the First Amendment," 1986 *Duke Law Journal* 589.

108. This way of analyzing the problem obscures the difficulties that it presents for the protection of scientific speech, which is not political in the usual sense. For general discussions, see Steven Goldberg, "The Constitutional Status of American Science," 1979 *University of Illinois Law Forum* 1, 2–16; John Robertson, "The Scientist's Right to Research: A Constitutional Analysis," 51 *Southern California Law Review* 1203 (1978). If scientific speech receives the usual first amendment protection, as it seems likely that it should, it does so because scientific speech is the paradigm of cognitive speech.

109. See Dun & Bradstreet v. Greenmoss Builders, 472 U.S. 749 (1985) (private matters); Gertz v. Robert Welch, Inc., 418 U.S. 323 (1974) (private citizen).

110. See Note, "Anti-Pornography Laws," pp. 471–72.

tend to be uttered, act as mere triggers to violent action in response, bypassing virtually all of the listener's cognitive processes.[111]

Third, speakers who intend to communicate ideas or ideologies are more protected than those who communicate ideas as a side effect of their more fundamental efforts. The lesser protection given to commercial speech, despite its relation to the ideology of consumerism, illustrates how this principle operates.

Finally, free speech law is motivated in part by a concern that governments tend to suppress speech that attacks the status quo.[112] Yet almost any speech causes harms other than mere subversion of the existing order, harms that some people will seek to avoid by prohibiting the speech that causes them.[113] The fourth principle seeks to identify categories of speech where we suspect that governments invoke such ordinary harms to justify suppression of speech when they really just want to preserve the status quo. If the reasons for regulating a category of speech do not seem to be masks for these impermissible purposes, the category may be more extensively regulated.[114] Sedition statutes lie at one extreme. Governments justify their efforts to suppress speech that criticizes the existing order on the ground that such criticism may lead to disorder and violence. But even though the fear of civil disturbance is not fanciful, even though, that is, this reason identifies a real social harm other than simple change in the social order, sedition statutes must meet a more stringent test because too often they suppress speech merely because it criticizes government. Child pornography statutes lie at the other extreme. They are designed to reduce child abuse—the sexual abuse of the children who take part in its production.[115] That reason seems so unrelated to the mere desire to preserve the status quo that child pornography statutes are obviously constitutional.

111. Chaplinsky v. New Hampshire, 315 U.S. 568 (1942).

112. See Blasi, "Checking Value in First Amendment Theory."

113. For example, it could reasonably be thought that seditious speech leads to rioting. On the theory criticized in the text, a legislature might prohibit seditious speech in order to avert the harm of rioting. Perhaps the only regulation of speech as to which there are no identifiable harms, under ordinary assumptions, would be a prohibition of blasphemy. Even there the state might be concerned about the breakdown of respect for the views of others.

114. The Supreme Court overlooked this problem in City of Renton v. Playtime Theatres, Inc., 475 U.S. 41 (1986), in which it focused entirely on harms not on whether the invocation of harms was a surrogate for a desire to suppress speech. It is somewhat striking that the Court also refused to inquire into the actual motivation for restricting the areas in which "adult theaters" could locate. This refusal may, however, reflect an institutional incapacity rather than a matter of principle. See Lawrence Sager, "Fair Measure: The Status of Underenforced Constitutional Norms," 91 *Harvard Law Review* 1212 (1978). But see Washington v. Davis, 429 U.S. 229 (1976); Hunter v. Underwood, 471 U.S. 222 (1985) (both making motive dispositive in equal protection cases).

115. New York v. Ferber, 458 U.S. 747 (1982).

Under this scheme pornography receives the most modest protection. The paradigmatic example of pornography deals with matters far removed from the traditional concepts of politics, and its implicit arguments are noncognitive. The producers of the paradigmatic example of pornography certainly do not intend to influence political decisions, and the state's purpose is to reduce harms to women, not to suppress a point of view. Under these circumstances regulation is justified if a legislature can rationally conclude that regulation reduces the harms with which it is concerned. The evidence about pornography and subordination satisfies that modest demand.[116]

The Court's framework for analyzing categories of speech is, however, analytically unsatisfying. First, whenever a constitutional test requires the Court to combine several independent factors, it is likely to be manipulated so that the Court can uphold statutes it likes and strike down those it dislikes by varying the emphasis placed on each factor depending on the Court's views about the policy wisdom of the statutes. This is particularly true when some of the factors deal with matters of degree, like the "political" and "cognitive" factors here.

In addition, a multifactor approach involving paradigmatic examples has no resources to avoid a proliferation of categories. We understand that someone who defaces an American flag to protest the invasion of Cambodia in 1970 is intending to make, and is making, a political statement by noncognitive means.[117] Price advertising is nonpolitical cognitive speech; most advertisements for tobacco products are nonpolitical and noncognitive; the tobacco industry's advertisements that counter anti-smoking arguments are cognitive and probably political. It is easy to generate additional categories. For example, *Playboy* has a cognitive

116. See Note, "Anti-Pornography Laws." Although I am not entirely certain about my understanding of her argument on this point, I take this to be the meaning of MacKinnon's statement that "the fact that pornography . . . furthers the idea of the sexual inferiority of women, which is a political idea, doesn't make the pornography itself into a political idea. One can express the idea a practice embodies. That does not make that practice into an idea. Segregation expresses the idea of the inferiority of the group to another on the basis of race. That does not make segregation an idea." MacKinnon, "Pornography," p. 65. The initial difficulty with this formulation is that pornography appears to be an expressive practice in a way that segregation is not. MacKinnon's point may be that pornography, although it may be an expressive practice, is not very much so. That point then fits into the framework developed in the text.

Given the understanding of the first amendment described in the text, the criticisms made in Lynn, " 'Civil Rights' Ordinances," pp. 92–96, of the evidentiary weaknesses of the case in favor of regulation have little bearing on the analysis of the constitutionality of anti-pornography regulation, although of course they are relevant to policy discussions of such regulations.

117. Spence v. Washington, 418 U.S. 405 (1974).

philosophy that is intended to be political; *Hustler* has a less cognitive but equally intentional philosophy; the depictions of women in *Hustler* are indistinguishable from those in other pornographic publications whose producers are less conscious of their political aspects. The Court's analytic approach almost invites us to treat each of these publications as falling into a separate category. We may think at the start that the relevant category is "pornography" and that *Playboy* and *Hustler* fall into that category even though they are not precisely the same as the paradigmatic examples of pornography. Yet the Court's approach suggests that we ought to distinguish between two categories, one including "pornography" and the other including "*Playboy*-type pornography," because the paradigmatic examples of each category are different. The Court gives us no guidance on what to do about the creation of new categories of speech.

Further, the Court's factors are themselves problematic. The speaker's purpose seems to be relevant, yet we know from the commercial speech cases that the Constitution provides some protection because of listener interests.[118] Suppose some communication has a powerful, cognitive, but unintended effect on political beliefs. Nothing in the Court's scheme tells us whether that communication should be given high, moderate, or low protection in light of its impact on listener interests.[119] The feminist argument is that pornography has powerful noncognitive effects, sometimes intended and sometimes not, on beliefs about the proper distribution of power between men and women. If pornography is to receive low protection, it would seem that we must disregard the listener "interests" here. Doing so seems to make the cognitive factor dispositive and the speaker's purpose factor irrelevant.

Similarly problematic is the implicit judgment that material that appeals to cognitive capacities deserves greater protection than material that appeals to noncognitive ones. The discussion of the campaign finance problem demonstrated that even at the heart of politics conventionally defined, we cannot readily separate the noncognitive from the cognitive elements of political rhetoric.

The Court's scheme asks us to try to separate those elements because cognitive appeals are somehow better than noncognitive ones. As we have seen, that judgment appears to rest on the more conservative elements in the republican tradition. The distinction between politics conventionally defined and politics more generously conceived is even more obviously

118. See also Kleindienst v. Mandel, 408 U.S. 753 (1972).

119. We might limit the inquiry by thinking about the category into which the communication falls, at which point the problem of proliferation of categories arises. See text accompanying note 117.

status quo oriented. The feminist argument in support of the constitutionality of regulating pornography might require that pornography be of low value because it is noncognitive and nonpolitical in conventional terms. Yet it is an important aspect of feminist thought that conventional definitions of politics and cognition suppress the female voice. The constitutional defense of antipornography legislation might thus reproduce the oppression that the legislation is designed to overcome.

This conclusion could be avoided by developing a different constitutional justification for the legislation. That justification is apparent from the definitional approach to pornography, but it is quite unconventional. In this view the criterion for constitutionality is simply whether the action at issue serves the interests of women.[120] Antipornography legislation is constitutional, it might be said, because it does. To address this contention we would have to examine the likely impact of antipornography legislation on women's interests. Feminists are divided on that question.[121] Some feminists believe that, in a political world in which women's interests are regularly subordinated to men's, it is unlikely that the pornography that would be suppressed would be the pornography that harms women; they have suggested that lesbian and heterosexual erotica produced by women are at least as likely to be suppressed as "true" pornography.[122] This concern actually can be fit into the Court's analytic framework. These feminists believe that antipornography regulation is said to be intended to avoid harms to women but is actually a surrogate for their continued oppression.[123]

120. See, e.g., MacKinnon, "Pornography," p. 21 ("If a woman is subjected, why should it matter that the work has other value?"). Gary Peller, "The Metaphysics of American Law," 73 *California Law Review* 1152, 1180–81 (1985), calls approaches like this "partial discourses of liberation."

121. See, e.g., Pally, "Ban Sexism"; Brief Amici Curiae, American Booksellers' Ass'n.; "The Place of Pornography," at p. 33 (statement by Erica Jong). For a discussion of the intrafeminist controversies, see Ilene Philipson, "Beyond the Virgin and the Whore," nos. 75–76 *Socialist Review* 129 (May–Aug. 1984); Kathleen Lahey, "The Canadian Charter of Rights and Pornography: Toward a Theory of Actual Gender Equality," 20 *New England Law Review* 649, 649–51, 665–72 (1984–85).

122. See, e.g., Brief Amici Curiae, American Booksellers' Ass'n., p. 14. But see Pam Mitchell, "Lesbians and Gay Men: Hetero Sexualities, Common Cause," in *Pink Triangles*, pp. 54–55 (lesbian erotica sometimes suppresses physicality of sexual encounters). An exchange on this issue is *Coming to Power: Writings and Graphics on Lesbian S/M* (Samois ed. 1982); *Against Sado-Masochism: A Radical Feminist Analysis* (Robin Linden et al. eds. 1982).

123. See Brief Amici Curiae, American Booksellers' Ass'n., pp. 38–41 (proposals reinforce sexist stereotypes); Judith Walkowitz, "The Politics of Prostitution," in *Women: Sex and Sexuality* 145 (Catherine Stimpson and Ethel Person eds. 1980); Judith Walkowitz, "Male Vice and Female Virtue: Feminism and the Politics of Prostitution in Nineteenth Century Britain," in *Powers of Desire* 419 (Ann Snitow, Christine Stansell, and Sharon

Conclusion

The problems of campaign finance, commercial speech, and pornography share two characteristics. The analysis of each problem reveals the important role played in constitutional law of cognitive processes and instrumental rationality and reveals the questions we might raise about the assertion that those processes should receive priority. In addition, efforts to regulate each type of speech are designed to reform the very system of rationality that produced both the speech and the regulatory urges. Under such circumstances we might reasonably be skeptical about the possibility that the reforms will succeed.

Sometimes, though, political systems produce what have been called nonreformist reforms.[124] Such reforms are not far out of line with the ordinary legislative product of an unreformed political system, so political activists can realistically place them on the political agenda. Nonreformist reforms have one of two possible dynamic effects. Their enactment might set in train a larger transformation of the political system; successful campaign finance legislation might be an example. Alternatively, the effort to secure such reforms might mobilize people to seek additional reforms, even if the particular effort fails or if it produces legislation that is itself not really a reform.[125] Distinguishing among reactionary backpedaling, mere reforms, and nonreformist reforms is of course no minor matter.

Thompson eds. 1983); Bryden, "Between Two Constitutions," p. 174; Note, "Feminism, Pornography, and Law," pp. 532–33. For analyses of analogous campaigns in Great Britain from a similarly skeptical point of view, see Martin Barker, *A Haunt of Fears: The Strange History of the British Horror Comics Campaign* (1984); *The Video Nasties: Freedom and Censorship in the Media* (Martin Barker ed. 1984). These books contain useful discussions of the ambiguities and ironies in horror comics and films. See also Susan Star, "Swastikas: The Street and the University," in *Against Sado-Masochism*, pp. 131–35 (on limits of ability to transform discourse; made in opposition to theories attempting to justify sadomasochism as a form of uncoerced sexuality but applicable to efforts to regulate pornography as well).

124. See Erik Wright, *Classes* 290 (1985) ("nonreformist reforms . . . within the existing society . . . transform the conditions of subsequent struggle and potentially expand the very horizon of historical possibilities").

125. See Note, "Feminism, Pornography, and Law," pp. 499, 533–34.

Conclusion

THE basic argument of this book is fundamentally simple: the liberal tradition makes constitutional theory both necessary and impossible. It is necessary because it provides the restraints that the liberal tradition requires us to place on those in power, legislators and judges as well. It is impossible because no available approach to constitutional law can effectively restrain both legislators and judges: If we restrain the judges we leave legislators unconstrained; if we restrain the legislators we let the judges do what they want.

It is possible to reject the proposition that constitutional theory is necessary and impossible, and people usually do so by denying the impossibility of constitutional theory.[1] They insist that the words of the Constitution are clear enough, when read as the framers understood them, to support a modest textualism or originalism. Or they think that there is enough consensus on what is morally valuable to justify a restrained reliance on moral philosophy. The difficulty with these positions is the sociological one: either the judges are not representative enough to generate a normatively compelling understanding of plain meaning, history, or consensus or the shared understandings, values, and the like are so obviously historically contingent that we cannot explain why anyone, legislator or judge, should have the final say on constitutional questions. Whenever someone invokes these moderate theoretical positions, we can be sure that he or she is about to explain why the values of a particular elite ought to be imposed on people who are not part of the elite.

---

1. Some present-day conservatives deny the necessity of judicial review by supporting an unconstrained majoritarianism. The position rejects the fundamental assumptions of the liberal tradition and, if experience is any guide, is politically shortsighted: Someday legislatures may again be controlled by forces the conservatives fear, and they will then want the courts to obstruct those majorities. See Chapter 4 (appendix).

Books on constitutional theory usually conclude with an alternative synthesis to the critique they offer of competing theories. This book cannot end like that. True, some elements of a republican conception can be identified. As Chapter 4 suggested, its primary concern would be the maintenance of a constitutional politics among the citizenry. Such a politics must first be created. I have repeatedly stressed that, in the republican tradition, substantial equality in wealth was a predicate for a constitutional politics, and Chapter 7 concluded with some thoughts about how decentralization might promote a more republican society. The social conditions under which republicanism can thrive—broadly distributed property holdings, a relatively narrow gap between the better and the less well off, and the like—are themselves preconditions for the realization of republicanism. This makes it extremely difficult to design a political course that would help bring about a republican society.

We must remember, however, a point made in Chapters 3 and 7. In considering political programs like decentralization, we should not imagine that they will be adopted tomorrow. If they are adopted it will be the result of long and difficult periods of political organizing, during and as a result of which the boundaries of the possible will change, though not always for the better. The program of revitalizing federalism might be a bad idea overall. Under current political circumstances a program favoring decentralization might end up with a system in which political authority is decentralized while economic power remains tightly controlled. That outcome would make things even worse than they are now.[2] Or decentralization might be a nonreformist reform. Deciding which it is requires a sort of political analysis that cannot be offered in this kind of book. The discussion at the end of Chapter 9 indicates the complexity of the political analysis that would be needed to support such proposals.

We can, however, approach the question of an alternative synthesis indirectly. Every chapter of this book plays existing theories and doctrines off against an implicit inchoate vision of a society as commonwealth, inhabited by citizens who seek to promote the common good rather than individual interests. One approach would bring that vision to the foreground. So, for example, the chapter on representation-reinforcing review would offer a definition of citizenship consistent with the idea of a commonwealth. The chapter on moral philosophy would discuss the social preconditions for ethical knowledge. We could return to a theme stated in the Introduction and consider how to revitalize those aspects of a federal system that were at least in part the embodiment of the republican

2. For a discussion of the political dimensions of efforts to increase democratic participation, see Hanna Pitkin and Sara Shumer, "On Participation," 2:4 *democracy* 43 (1982).

tradition. Revitalizing a federalism of the sort the framers designed requires us to rethink the concept of property as the foundation of a citizen's independence and would probably lead us to conclude that a revitalized federalism demands expansion of "new property" entitlements, development of the idea that the government must be the employer of last resort, creation of tenure in "private" employment, and the like.[3]

A revitalized federalism would insist on, indeed even expand, the framers' commitment to decentralization.[4] But decentralized institutions need not be defined by geographic boundaries and would certainly not be defined by the boundaries of the present states.[5] We might instead take as our models of decentralized institutions the various intentional communities in the United States. Those communities operate on a principle of consensus/unanimity in decision making. In a republican community the process of reaching agreement differs from the process of majority rule that characterizes our present political system. A proposal is made and any objections open the issue up to reconsideration on both sides. The discussion of mutual forbearance in Chapter 8 provides one model: the proponents can attempt to explain why they desire the project so strongly as to make it appropriate for objectors to go along, however reluctantly; the objectors can attempt to explain why they would be hurt if the project went through, so as to make it appropriate for proponents to defer, however reluctantly. Objectors can threaten to leave, and proponents can threaten to expel, but both would understand that their joint project—the

3. See Chapter 7. There have been many works recently that propose political and economic changes broadly consistent with the suggestions sketched here. See, e.g., Barber, *Strong Democracy*; Cohen and Rogers, *On Democracy*; Jane Mansbridge, *Beyond Adversary Democracy* (1980), for suggestions in the political domain; Arthur Jacobson, "Democratic Participation and the Legal Structure of the Economy of Firms," 50 *Social Research* 803 (1983); Comment, "Industrial Democracy and the Managerial Employee Exception to the National Labor Relations Act," 133 *University of Pennsylvania Law Review* 441, 457 n. 118 (1985) (citing sources), for suggestions in the economic domain. I have refrained from relying directly on these works because analysis of the specific proposals requires a sort of expertise that I lack.

4. For discussions of recent developments in federalism that suggest arguments along the lines pursued here, see Carol Lee, "The Federal Courts and the Status of Municipalities: A Conceptual Challenge," 62 *Boston University Law Review* 1 (1982); Frug, "The City as a Legal Concept"; Gelfand, "The Burger Court and the New Federalism."

5. Two provocative and mutually reinforcing articles on National League of Cities v. Usery, 426 U.S. 833 (1976), overruled, Garcia v. San Antonio Metropolitan Transit Auth., 469 U.S. 528 (1985), were flawed by their effort to identify the values of federalism with the existing geographic boundaries of state and local governments. See Laurence Tribe, "Unravelling National League of Cities: The New Federalism and Affirmative Rights to Essential Government Services," 90 *Harvard Law Review* 1065 (1977); Frank Michelman, "States' Rights and States' Roles: Permutations of 'Sovereignty' in National League of Cities v. Usery," 86 *Yale Law Journal* 1165 (1977).

community—would be impaired by migration or expulsion. In this view proponents of and objectors to specific projects are strongly committed to the community as a whole and are likely to work things out. Further, as the framers understood, the smaller the community the more likely that face-to-face interactions will lead each member to understand the foibles and the contributions of the others, making it more likely than in larger groups that consensus can be reached.[6]

One objection to the use of consensus in decentralized intentional communities is commonly made.[7] The process of reaching consensus may be extended and painful, diverting time and effort from other projects that community members would like to try.[8] The process of reaching consensus in a revitalized federal system might be less difficult. The framers' understanding of face-to-face communication foreshadowed the idea, developed in Chapter 9, that we may have and develop noncognitive deliberative capacities for resolving conflict. That is, perhaps consensus often seems difficult to reach precisely because of the predominant role that instrumental rationality has come to play in constituting our society, as the last three chapters have discussed. Face-to-face interactions may provide a model for an alternative way of resolving conflict.

We must note several points about this approach. First, the republican ideal that it invokes is not external to our Constitution and our traditions. The ideal builds on our real experiences with friends, in families, at churches, in neighborhoods. Those experiences are complex, but along with moments of fear, anger, and alienation they contain moments of warmth, love, and connectedness. The approach sketched here would make those moments the ones on which we should build our political life.

6. See generally Joseph Carens, *Equality, Moral Incentives, and the Market* (1981), reviewed by J. Donald Moon, "Book Review," 94 *Ethics* 146 (1983).

7. Another objection to intentional communities is that they reproduce power relations found elsewhere in the society. See, e.g., Mansbridge, *Beyond Adversary Democracy*, pp. 97–114. This is undoubtedly true, but so long as the discussion is confined to a reconstituted society, the point seems to lose some of its bite. A third is that decentralization may preclude the implementation of socially valuable projects that require large-scale coordination. There is some reason to believe that this concern is overdrawn. Some studies suggest that the present amount of centralization is as much the result of efforts to enhance the power of managers as it is of efforts to achieve efficient levels of output. See, e.g., Stephen Marglin, "What Do Bosses Do?: The Origins and Functions of Hierarchy in Capitalist Production," 6 *Review of Radical Political Economy* 60 (1974); Katherine Stone, "The Origin of Job Structures in the Steel Industry," 6 *Review of Radical Political Economy* 113 (1974). In addition, coordination among decentralized communities may be difficult, but it is not impossible. The same process of consensus building within a community can operate between communities, at least if their differences on matters of principle are not so severe as to overwhelm their desire to carry out the joint project.

8. See Michael Walzer, *Obligations* 229–38 (1970).

Second, a movement interested in securing nonreformist reforms should use whatever forms of political action that can help. Sometimes this will mean using the courts as a forum for political advance. For reasons of their own judges may decide that some holding, which its proponents believe will propel reform, is constitutionally appropriate. The proponents should have no interest in the courts' justifications for their decisions; they will find the issues discussed in this book irrelevant to their concerns. Again, deciding when the courts are a useful forum requires an explicit political analysis.[9]

Finally, it is not clear that the commonwealth would have a Constitution or constitutional theories of the sort we have examined. The Constitution and constitutional theory are solutions to problems specific to one of our traditions. A republican constitutional theory would be a form of civic education, part of the dialogue among citizens that creates a public. It would not, however, be directed at judges; it would thereby displace the concerns about power expressed in the discussion of antiformalist theories in Chapter 4. The commonwealth might be organized pursuant to a written document that speaks of institutions and rights. The document would not be a set of legal rules that were said to determine anything. It would contain a bunch of rules of thumb that experience had proven to be useful. Their utility in any new circumstances would be open to challenge, and nothing about the fact that they were written down would affect decisions to follow them under new circumstances.[10]

This approach to an alternative synthesis would make the commonwealth idea explicit, but it would be followed by another. The republican tradition emphasizes experiences of love and connectedness that the liberal tradition places in the background; it places in the background experiences of threat, anger, and autonomy that the liberal tradition

9. For a discussion of the limits of litigation strategies which is informed by the analysis in this book, see Mark Tushnet, "Political Aspects of the Changing Meaning of Equality in Constitutional Law," 74 *Journal of American History* (1987).

10. Recent philosophical works that seem to me broadly consistent with the approach taken here include Bellah et al., *Habits of the Heart*; Bernstein, *Beyond Objectivity and Relativism*; Sandel, *Liberalism and Limits of Justice*; MacIntyre, *After Virtue*; Thomas Spragens, *The Irony of Liberal Reason* (1981); William Galston, *Justice and the Human Good* (1980); Sheldon Wolin, "What Revolutionary Action Means Today," 2:4 *democracy* 17 (1982); Stephen Toulmin, "Regaining the Ethics of Discretion: The Tyranny of Principles," 11:6 *Hastings Center Reports* 31 (Dec. 1981). These authors, however, plainly disagree among themselves on issues that they believe are important, and, as with the suggestions made by political scientists for political changes, see note 2, I find myself without the expertise to adjudicate the disagreements; I have therefore confined to this footnote the observation that these perspectives seem to me to resemble my own. For an application of some of them to constitutional theory, see Milton Regan, "Community and Justice in Constitutional Theory," 1985 *Wisconsin Law Review* 1073.

emphasizes. The second approach would reconstruct constitutionalism as a critique of the republican tradition. Human experience consists of connectedness and autonomy, love and hate, toleration of others and anger at their differences from an ever-changing "us." Neither the liberal tradition nor the republican one can accommodate the aspects of experience that the other takes as central. Critique is all there is.

Index of Cases

General Index